MW01518641

Advanced BSP Programming

SAP PRESS is issued by
Bernhard Hochlehnert, SAP AG

SAP PRESS is a joint initiative of SAP and Galileo Press. The know-how offered by SAP specialists combined with the expertise of the publishing house Galileo Press offers the reader expert books in the field. SAP PRESS features first-hand information and expert advice, and provides useful skills for professional decision-making.

SAP PRESS offers a variety of books on technical and business related topics for the SAP user. For further information, please visit our website: *www.sap-press.com*.

Horst Keller
The Official ABAP Reference
2-volume set with 3 CDs
2nd Ed. 2005, 1216 pp., ISBN 1-59229-039-6

Horst Keller
The ABAP Quick Reference
Instant access to keywords, additions, syntax diagrams and more
2005, 231 pp., ISBN 1-59229-057-4

Ulli Hoffmann
Web Dynpro for ABAP
2006, approx. 450 pp., ISBN 1-59229-078-7

Harald Röser
Workshop SAP Controls
SAP PRESS Essentials 10
2006, approx. 160 pp., ISBN 1-59229-073-6

Brian McKellar, Thomas Jung

Advanced BSP Programming

SAP PRESS

First Edition 2006

SAP PRESS is an imprint of Galileo Press,
Fort Lee (NJ), Bonn (Germany)

Editor Florian Zimniak
Copy Editor John Parker, UCG, Inc., Boston, MA
Cover Design Silke Braun
Printed in Germany

ISBN 1-59229-049-3

Contents

Introduction

The history of BSP began in the late 1990s. Back then, the SAP Internet Transaction Server (ITS) and the SAP Workplace—SAP's first attempt at a portal—depended heavily on the use of external Web servers. These solutions neither leveraged the inherent strengths of the ABAP technology nor re-used current developers' skill sets.

Therein lay the greatest technical challenge to SAP as Web-based technologies became essential to all businesses. Companies began to realize that E-business was still just business and therefore expected their ERP solutions to transition easily into this brave new world.

Starting with Release 6.10, SAP began a major overhaul of its ABAP technology stack. The company broke the traditional Basis layer away from the applications that ran on it and renamed this new technology layer *Web Application Server* (Web AS). But this name change was far more than a marketing move. With this release, SAP had begun to build native Web server technology into the ABAP Kernel. No longer would SAP technology be dependent upon external Web servers or programming languages. ABAP itself was now HTTP-enabled!

Naturally, ABAP was extended with a new Web development environment, called *Business Server Pages* (BSP). Like all other ABAP programming tools, BSP is integrated into the ABAP Workbench (SE80) and fully supports the Transport Management System (TMS). And, given its recent birth, BSP also fully embraces the new ABAP object-oriented technology.

Target Audience

The target audience for this book is anyone who is currently an ABAP developer or who is interested in becoming an ABAP developer. BSP is another tool in the developer's tool box, one that adds value to any ABAP development team.

It does not matter if you have never done BSP development, are a novice BSP developer, or have several years of BSP development under your belt; there should be something for everyone in this book. We attempted to make this the definitive work on the subject of BSP, revealing behind-the-scenes aspects and discussing features in a new way.

This book is not based solely on the underlying technology. Several years of experience building real-world BSP applications at a customer site were also used in writing this book. Therefore, you will find solutions and sample source code to help you overcome common development hurdles. Toward that goal, you will find all the example source code presented in this book on the accompanying CD.

On What Releases Can You Use BSP?

BSP has been shipped as an integrated part of the ABAP technology stack since Web AS Release 6.10. Release 6.10 contains the functionality to create basic BSP pages with flow logic.

With Web AS Release 6.20, SAP introduced major enhancements to the BSP technology: Model View Controller and BSP Extension Elements. With Release 6.20, Service Pack 34, a new HTML rendering engine, and a complete new BSP Extension library, PHTMLB, were added. Because of these additional enhancements to BSP, customer development should really only be done on Web AS 6.20 with SP34 or higher.

SAP continued to enhance BSP with SAP NetWeaver '04 (Web AS 6.40) and SAP NetWeaver '04S (Web AS 7.0); however, nearly every feature of BSP is in sync between the major releases. This means that even if you are on an older Web AS 6.20, you still reap the benefits of new developments within the NetWeaver releases. Although you will rarely find in this book that a feature is limited to a specific release, we will point this out when it occurs.

With the coverage for BSP within the latest technology releases of ABAP, you will find BSP present in the equivalent releases of the SAP application components as well. This means, for instance, that R/3 Enterprise (with or without Extension Set 1.10 and 2.00) and mySAP ERP 2005 (also known as Enterprise Core Component 5.00 or ECC 5.00) both contain the technology necessary to create BSP applications.

BSP vs. Web Dynpro ABAP

In the past year, much of the attention within the SAP world has focused on SAP's next generation technology: Web Dynpro. As this book goes to print, Web Dynpro for ABAP is scheduled for general availability in spring of 2006.

In truth, Web Dynpro contains many of the enhancements that BSP developers have always wanted. Enhancements like built-in value-help and select options will become standard in Web Dynpro, but must be added by the customer into the BSP environment. Do not worry, however: The task of adding many of these enhancements to BSP is the subject of the last one-third of this book.

All this begs the question: If Web Dynpro ABAP (WDA) is so great, why continue to use BSP (or for that matter why write a book about it?). There are several architectural differences between BSP and WDA. WDA may have some more advanced features compared to BSP, but it is a far more restrictive framework. First of all, WDA is stateful only. BSP supports both stateful and stateless programming models. Stateless programming is essential to high-performance Internet-facing applications.

WDA is also designed to be future-proof, obscuring the specific client's rendering technology. As a consequence, the tool does not allow low-level access to include your own custom HTML, JavaScript, or other controls. WDA targets the browser today, but tomorrow it might well be running within a smart client using entirely different technologies (such as XML and native UI controls). To keep this technology switch possible, the rendering logic is completely hidden from the developer, presenting only an abstract UI layer with abstract controls. On the other hand, BSP has no such restrictions. BSP is strictly centered on browser-based deployment and therefore allows an extreme level of custom rendering. This makes BSP a perfect platform for applications that require pixel-perfect layout or specialized UI elements.

The other aspect to consider is that Web Dynpro ABAP will not be available until NetWeaver '04S. Therefore, you must upgrade your existing system to be able to use these new development tools. BSP, on the other hand, has been available for several years and is included in the vast majority of supported SAP product releases. For several more years, BSP may be your only choice for Web development using the ABAP language.

Acknowledgements

First, we would like to thank the SAP Developer Network (SDN) content team, particularly Mark Finnern and Craig Cmehil, for not only providing a great service in the form of SDN, but also making sure that BSP has its comfortable little home there.

This book itself has deep roots within SDN. In fact, it is doubtful that it would exist at all if were not for SDN. Several sections of the book have their roots as SDN weblogs. The two authors of this book (who to this day have never met in person or even spoken on the phone) would likely never have crossed paths were it not for the virtual community that is SDN.

For their support, guidance and suggestions, Thomas would like to thank coworkers and friends: Chris Cassidy, Sam Mason, Lynn Scheu, and Sandy Smith. A special thanks goes to Steffen Knoeller, who behind the scenes has influenced many chapters in this book, without even knowing it!

Brian would wish to thank the complete team that made BSP happen. There is Albert Becker, who showed a team can work across many groups, and who taught the lesson late one night that VPs still know how to debug ABAP code. There are the ICM colleagues, Oliver Luik and Bernhard Braun, who measured performance in CPU cycles and give a new appreciation for "blazing fast." Not to be forgotten are their partners in crime, the ICF colleagues: Masoud Aghadavoodi, Christoph Hofmann, and Daniel Walz, who has helped many hours so that we could write our first Web-based logon application. Then there are the men in black, the security group: Wolfgang Janzen and Martin Rex. The last import group required to start the project was the ABAP Language Group: Andreas Blumenthal, who fights like a lion for anything with ABAP stamped on it and who did a lot for BSP (even although it was not called ABAP Server Pages!); Holger Janz, who taught me the elegance of ABAP programming; Jürgen Lehmann and Peter Januschke, who taught me the complexities of compiler writing in ABAP and that it is actually quiet easy; Klaus Ziegler and Kay Mueller-Silva, who integrated JavaScript, Ulrich Elsaesser, who always used a short pencil for the pre-compiler; and the x-team, Karsten Bohlmann (XSLT) and Rupert Hieble (XML).

In building BSP itself, the Workbench needed minor tweaking, plus some hard development by: Sigrun Wintzheimer, Michael Wenz, Margarethe Czarnecki, Andreas Herrmann, and, of course, Jürgen Remmel. The runtime was done by our small group: Rüdiger Kretschmer, who had the idea (and together with a colleague wrote the first ABAP book, and always knows the answers to everything or knows someone that knows); Björn Goerke who hacked the runtime years ago; Regina Breuer who did MVC; Jutta Bindewald, and Arndt Rosenthal.

And then there is Steffen Knoeller, who shared my office for years and taught me HTML. Quality management was done by Michael Lottbrein, who rolled the first sneak preview out the door, Judith Rabetge, and Rainer Liebisch. Heidi von Geisau and Tina Haug wrote all documentation. Our first support steps were handled by Dongyan Zhao. Not to be forgotten is our extended support troop: Artem Gratchev, Vitaly Romanko, Yulia Kuznetsova, Dmitry Vladimirov, and Andrey Alimov. They not only taught me two words in Russian, but they also showed each and every time that the trickiest problems are theirs to solve! Finally, a good product required a few good salesmen: Axel Kurka (who passed away unexpectedly and before his time; we will remember him fondly) and Dirk Feeken, who came up with the BSP name over lunch!

Brian can only say: It is still a great team!

For his guidance and patience, we wish to thank our publisher from Galileo Press, Florian Zimniak. Although we broke every rule and deadline he gave us, he stuck with us till the end. We also thank John Parker of SAP PRESS America for his editorial skills and for also putting up with our rule-breaking nature.

Finally we must thank our families who put up with us through this experience. Without the support of our wives, Shari and Anja, we would never have pulled it through.

1 What is BSP?

This chapter gives an overview of BSP, showing both the design and runtime aspects. Infrastructure such as the MIME repository, debugging and logging are touched on, to show BSP as a complete Web-authoring environment.

Whenever one is asked "What is BSP?", the best answer is usually "a plain white sheet of paper, ready to be drawn on." At the most abstract level, BSP provides both a complete development environment in which Web pages can be written and the runtime to serve these pages on request to a browser. BSP does not place any constrains on what can be rendered with a BSP page.

However, at a technical level, BSP can be split into a number of different components, all of which are closely integrated. This chapter provides an overview of the major components, which together can be called BSP. In all cases, an abstract view will be given to help you better visualize how each component works within the Web AS.

1.1 Internet Communication Manager

The Internet Communication Manager (ICM) is responsible for handling all aspects of the HTTP communications between all browsers and the Web AS. The ICM is completely implemented inside the Web AS kernel, and always runs as a separate process, to be able to handle the high overhead involved in establishing and managing TCP/IP connections. Figure 1.1 provides a graphical overview.

When the user enters a URL in the browser that points to the Web AS, the browser will first open a TCP/IP connection to the Web AS. The ICM will accept the incoming TCP/IP connection and then will wait until the complete HTTP request has been received from the browser before dispatching it to the next layer for processing. After processing within the ABAP stack, an HTTP response is available for transmission to the browser. The HTTP requests and responses are transferred between the ICM (running in a separate process) and the ABAP stack using shared memory pipes.

The ICM rarely, if ever, examines the incoming HTTP request. Not even authentication information is extracted from the HTTP request. All of this processing is done within the ABAP stack.

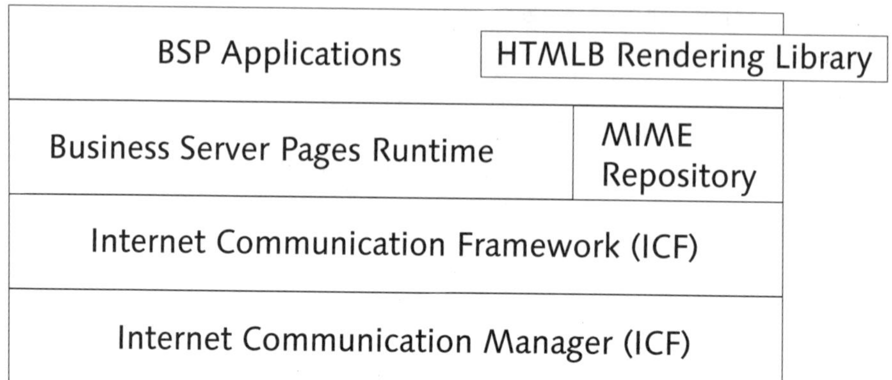

Figure 1.1 Block Diagram of BSP and Other Relevant Components

Whereas the ICM runs as one process for all HTTP requests, within ABAP different sessions are executed in their own "processes." The most important decision that ICM must make is into which session a HTTP request is placed. Either it can be an existing session, or the ICM can open a new session for the specific HTTP request. Whether the session is switched to stateful, to also handle future requests for the same application, is decided by the upper layers within the ABAP stack, which are also responsible for setting a session identifier in the HTTP response. Session identification is done by ICM, but the application at the upper level carries the responsibility for associating a session with a specific browser instance. This can be done either by setting a cookie that contains the session ID, or to encode the session ID into the URL.

To improve performance, the ICM is capable of opening many connections in parallel. In addition, the browser normally uses at least two connections for loading Web pages from the server. For some requests, loading images for example, it is not critical whether the requests are processed in parallel in different ABAP sessions. However, once multiple HTTP requests are received for the same session, as happens when a complete frameset is loaded, the ICM will queue the HTTP requests that all must be processed in the same session. It is not deterministic in which sequence requests are processed. However, it is guaranteed that the requests will be serialized for each session and that only one request will be processed at any time within a specific ABAP session.

The last important aspect of the ICM layer is that it supports a cache, into which frequently requested resources can be placed. The decision to cache a specific HTTP response is done by the upper layers. Once the flags are set, ICM will associate the URL from the HTTP request with the results from the HTTP response. This information is placed into the cache. All subsequent HTTP requests for the same URL are answered directly from the cache and do not even enter the ABAP stack. This infrastructure is frequently used to cache all non-volatile objects usually associated with a Web page, for example cascading style sheet files, JavaScript files, and images.

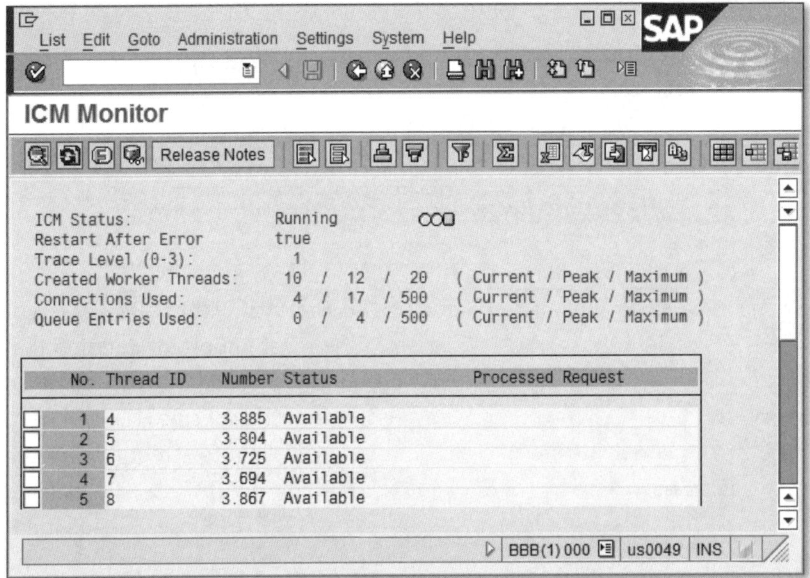

Figure 1.2 Transaction SMICM

The operation of ICM is controlled via transaction SMICM (see Figure 1.2). This transaction gives a complete overview of all facets of ICM. For developers, the following aspects are particularly interesting:

- Overview of available ports and the associated protocols (HTTP/HTTPS).
- Activating HTTP tracing and reviewing the trace file.
- An overview of the HTTP log, which shows all HTTP requests for the specific Web AS server. This is also off interest to review for unusual HTTP traffic, or to see unexpected HTTP requests (for example a broken link resulting in a "Not Found" message each time).
- An overview of the ICM cache and the possibility to clear the server cache.

This high-level overview of the ICM has only highlighted those aspects that are important for a BSP developer. In essence, ICM accepts HTTP requests, places them into the ABAP stack (the correct session) and will return a HTTP response afterwards. The question now is: What happens within the ABAP stack?

1.2 Internet Communication Framework

The Internet Communication Framework (ICF) handles access control, authentication, and dispatching of incoming HTTP requests. In addition, the ICF starts and controls the debugging of HTTP requests. The operations of the ICF layer is controlled by transaction SICF (see Figure 1.3).

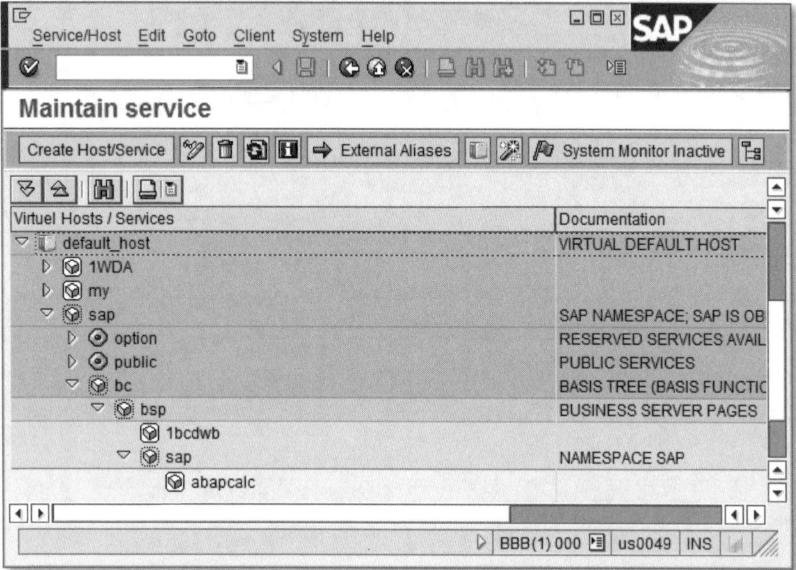

Figure 1.3 Transaction SICF

As a basis for its work, the ICF maintains a tree of URL segments, which looks very similar to a directory structure on disk. For each incoming HTTP request, the requested URL is split into segments. Each segment is then matched against a node in the tree. In effect, the segments are used to navigate the tree.

The first check done by ICF is to ensure that all nodes traversed are active. SAP only ships the complete ICF tree in an inactive state, and customers are advised to activate only those parts of the tree that will be used productively. This is just a first line of defence for enabling only required ICF nodes. All inactive nodes will cause a HTTP answer of "Not Active" to the browser, preventing the specific HTTP handler from even being started. If the incoming URL can not be matched with a tree traversal, ICF will answer with "Not Found."

After a valid path has been followed through the ICF tree, an authentication step is performed. Authentication information is either read from the incoming request, or can be configured for a specific ICF node. If no authentication information is available, the HTTP request is answered with "Unauthorized," in order to trigger the browser to bring up a small popup asking for the user's name and password.

After the authentication step is completed successfully, all handlers that were found traversing the tree are processed in sequence, starting at the handlers for the root node and moving down to the handlers for the leaf node. Each handler is started and given the HTTP request to process. Should the handler not process the HTTP request, the request is passed to the next handler. For BSP, the HTTP handler is installed on the BSP root node along the path `/sap/bc/bsp`. ICF handlers are discussed in detail in Chapter 3.

1.3 BSP Development Environment

A BSP application is essentially a collection of BSP pages (or controllers). The application itself is only a logical object for collecting the pages, and setting some global attributes. There is no true functionality tied to the BSP application, with the exception of an application class that is made available to all BSP pages.

The BSP development environment is completely integrated into the ABAP Workbench (transaction SE80). In the navigation tree, all BSP pages, controllers, views, and MIME objects are displayed. On the right side, it is possible to edit the BSP pages (see Figure 1.4).

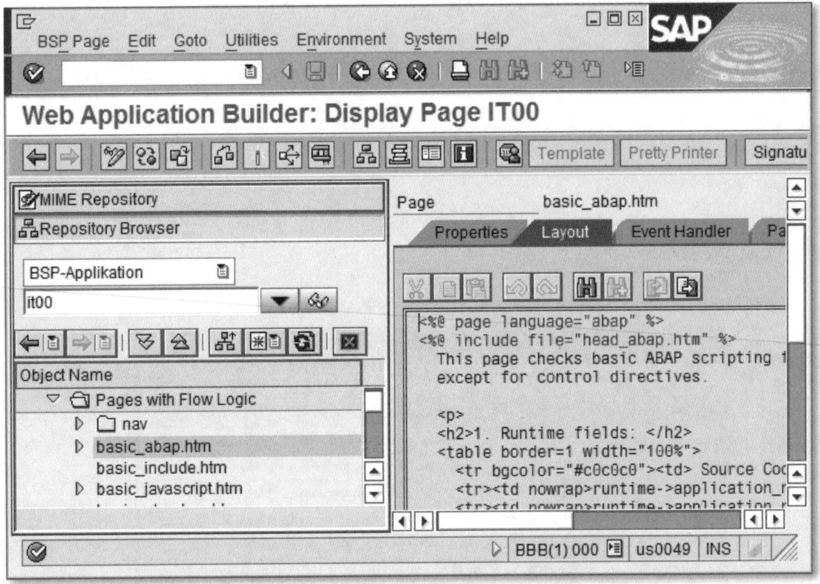

Figure 1.4 BSP Development Environment

The first important aspect of the BSP development environment is the support of all development-related activities, such as creating new BSP applications, editing, and deleting. The second important aspect is that the BSP development environment also manages the integration into the transport system. BSP applications are effectively development objects, and they have the same integration into SE80 do normal ABAP classes.

The other major responsibility of the BSP development environment is to trigger the BSP compiler when requested.

1.4 HTMLB Rendering Family

Although the BSP approach itself is a "clean sheet of paper" for the developer's own creativity, BSP does provide a complete rendering library, called HTMLB (HTML for Business). With this library, it is possible to use high-level programming constructs to achieve an excellent rendering, much faster than can be done by hand. For example, using one control such as `<htmlb:tableView>` is sufficient to render out a table in HTML that supports paging (see Figure 1.5).

The HTMLB library initially supported nearly all typical controls that are required for a feature rich Web user interface. Later, the HTMLB library was extended with two additional libraries: XHTMLB (Extended HTMLB) and PHTMLB (Pattern HTMLB). These two libraries contain more complex controls that are useful for improving the user interface.

The HTMLB family of libraries are discussed in detail in Chapters 9 and 10.

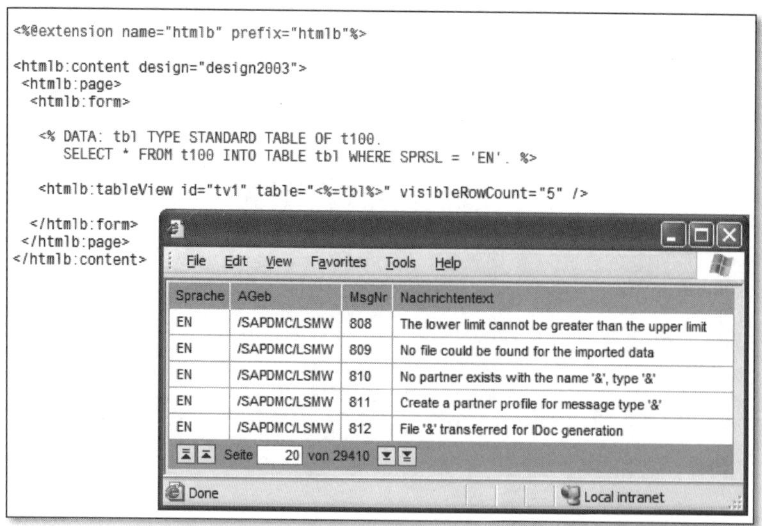

Figure 1.5 Example Program Using HTMLB Library

1.5 BSP Compiler

BSP pages are written as normal text. However, if you were to process these dynamically in any form, you would never be able to achieve an acceptable performance. Therefore, BSP pages are "compiled" into normal ABAP classes, which can be executed at runtime. The actual generation and compilation of the BSP pages is done the very first time that a BSP page is requested. As the first step, a small part of Workbench code will retrieve the BSP layout from the database, and request that the BSP compiler transform the layout into ABAP code within one method of a class. The ABAP compiler is used to compile the class, and store a load for it. Thereafter, the BSP runtime can work with the class. On subsequent requests, the same ABAP class will be used.

It is worthwhile to learn a little more about what the BSP compiler does. Let us assume a small BSP application with the following code, which is a mixture of HTML and ABAP coding.

```
<html><body><form>
  <% DATA: tbl TYPE STANDARD TABLE OF t100,
           row LIKE LINE OF tbl.
     SELECT * FROM t100 INTO TABLE tbl WHERE SPRSL = 'EN'. %>
   <table border=1>
   <% LOOP AT tbl INTO row. %>
     <tr><td><%=row-SPRSL%><td><%=row-TEXT%></tr>
   <% ENDLOOP. %>
   </table>
</form></body></html>
```

For each BSP page, a separate class is generated, usually with a very complex name consisting mainly of numbers. The BSP development environment will store the mapping of URLs of pages onto the generated class name. The class will have one `layout` method that is generated by the BSP compiler. Note that this code below has been extremely simplified, so as to retain the character of the transformation without having too much complexity here.

```
METHOD layout.
  print( '<html><body><form>' ).
  DATA: tbl TYPE STANDARD TABLE OF t100,
        row LIKE LINE OF tbl.
  SELECT * FROM t100 INTO TABLE tbl WHERE SPRSL = 'EN'.
  print( '<table border=1>' ).
  LOOP AT tbl INTO row.
    print( '<tr><td>' ).
```

```
    print( row-SPRSL ).
    print( '<td>' ).
    print( row-TEXT ).
    print( '</tr>' ).
  ENDLOOP.
  print( '</table></form></body></html>' ).
ENDMETHOD.
```

Similarly, all event handlers of BSP pages are placed into separate methods on the same class. Page attributes become class attributes. With this model, the BSP runtime will have one class that contains all relevant functionality of a BSP page.

Handling of rendering libraries, such as the HTMLB library, is very similar. Let us look at the one line that rendered the table.

```
<htmlb:tableView id="tv1" visibleRowCount="5" table="<%=tbl%>">
</htmlb:tableView>
```

This BSP code will be transformed by the BSP compiler into the following ABAP statements:

```
DATA: _tag123 TYPE REF TO cl_htmlb_tableview.
CREATE OBJECT _tag123.
_tag123->id = 'tv1'.
_tag123->visibleRowCount = '5'.
GET REFERENCE OF tbl INTO _tag123->table.
_tag123->BEGIN( ).
_tag123->END( ).
```

The BSP compiler has a mapping table to determine how specific controls are mapped onto classes. Code is generated in order to have a reference available to instantiate the class, set the attributes correctly, and then call the class to render the corresponding HTML.

1.6 BSP Runtime

Given the already excellent infrastructure of the HTTP framework, the BSP runtime is simply hooked into the framework with one HTTP handler class. It is this class that receives the incoming requests, installs an error handler, and then does the main processing required for the BSP page.

The main processing of the BSP runtime is actually a very lightweight layer. Its main function is to map the incoming URL onto the generated class that represents the BSP page. The class is instantiated, and then the corresponding methods are called to do event handling. Finally, the `layout` method is called to write the answer for the browser.

1.7 BSP Debugger

A debugger is a must in a good development environment, and BSP it is no different. Breakpoints can be set from within the BSP development environment (see Figure 1.6). When the BSP page is executed, the processing of the BSP page will be stopped within the debugger at the breakpoint. Note that this requires the developer to have an open SAP GUI session with the application server.

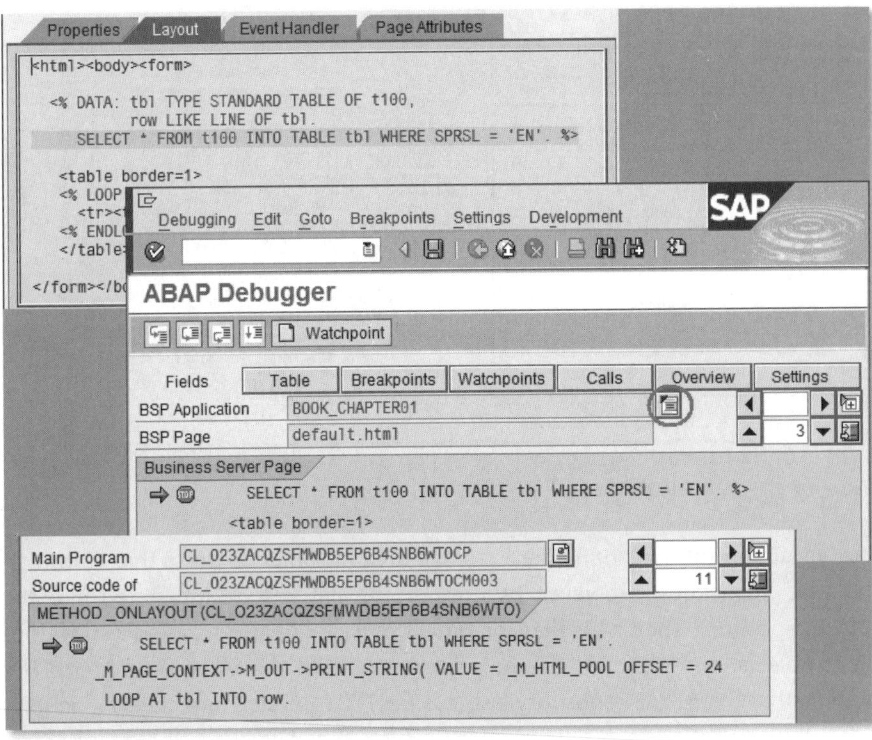

Figure 1.6 BSP Debugger: Setting a Breakpoint, Source View, and Code View

When looking at Figure 1.6, we see first the BSP debugger in a source-view mode. The BSP source is displayed as it was entered by the developer, and it is possible to step through the page at source level. Notice also the display of the BSP application and page names. Next to the application name is a button with which the display view can be toggled between source and generated code. When the view is toggled, the generated name of the BSP class also is visible, and the real generated ABAP source code is displayed.

1.8 MIME Repository

Web applications consists not only of HTML pages, but also require a diverse collection of other resources to enable a rich user interface. Typically, CSS files, JavaScript source, and images are used within an application. For this the storage of these objects, the BSP MIME repository is available (see Figure 1.7).

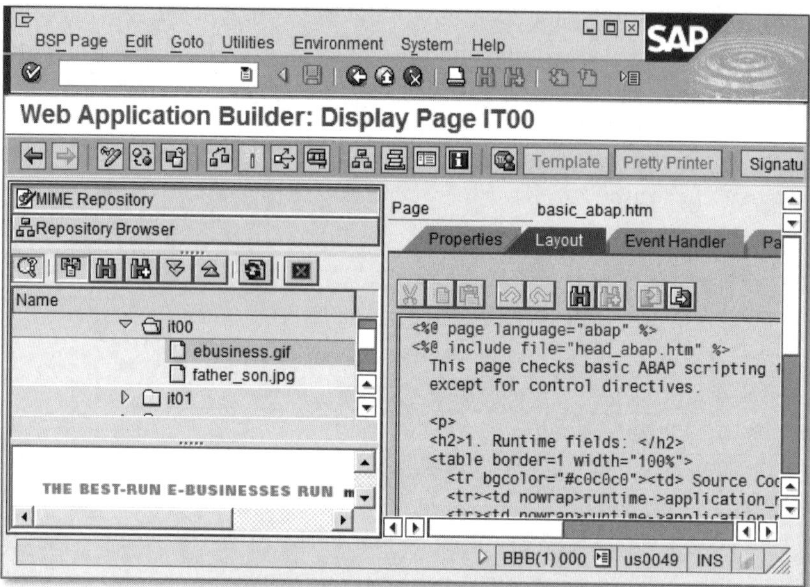

Figure 1.7 BSP MIME Repository

The MIME repository is primarily a storage area for binary objects that belong to the Web application. However, two important features are integrated into the MIME repository. The first is that the binary objects are also handled as development objects, and therefore are fully integrated into the transport system. The other is that the MIME repository also has a HTTP interface (effectively a handler class plugged into the ICF tree), with which requests from the browser for resources can be handled.

1.9 Summary

As this chapter has shown, BSP is actually the sum of many parts to create one complete development environment. This environment includes both the design-time integration into the usual tools as expected by ABAP developers, and the runtime aspects that are needed to truly develop Web applications. Especially important for Web applications is the availability of high-level rendering libraries and a repository for the additional binary objects required.

2 HTTP and HTML

Often, developers will make good progress by using the BSP rendering libraries without looking at the basics of HTTP and HTML. However, once the going gets tough, it is this fundamental understanding of HTTP and HTML that an advanced programmer need to complete the work or troubleshoot a problem.

In this chapter, we will examine HTTP (Hypertext Transfer Protocol) and HTML (Hypertext Markup Language), and the relationship between the two. We only concentrate on those aspects we know from practical experience to be important. This chapter is not to be a final reference; its goal is to lay the foundation. For the interested reader, we recommend using RFC2616 as a search keyword in your favorite search engine.

HTTP is the protocol used between the browser and the server. HTTP is strictly a request-response protocol, whereby the client (usually the browser) will send an HTTP request to the server and wait for the HTTP response from the server. It is not possible for the server to initiate a transfer to the browser; it is only possible for the server to answer an HTTP request with a response.

Typically, a single HTTP request is transmitted over one connection, and then the first received HTTP response is matched to this outstanding request. Although HTTP now allows streaming—whereby a browser can transmit a number of requests on one connection and match received responses in sequence to the transmitted requests—this is not commonly in use in any current browsers. However, what is standard is that the browser opens parallel connections (usually two) to have more than one HTTP request outstanding: one per connection. For the Web AS, this could imply that the same browser has a number of requests outstanding that must be processed in the same Web AS session. To prevent race and deadlock conditions, the HTTP requests will be queued in the ICM, and only processed in serial within one session.

HTML is a text-based markup language that tells the browser what should be rendered on screen and how it should look. HTML is the payload of an HTTP response; effectively, it is the answer from the server. It is important to point out that HTML is not sent from the browser to the server in the HTTP request, but only in the HTTP response from the server to the browser.

2.1 Viewing the HTTP Traffic

In the browser, one sees only the HTML that is returned each time from the server as mark-up. The underlying HTTP protocol is not visible. To see this traffic, the typical technique would be to use an HTTP proxy. This is an approach whereby a program will install itself between the browser and the server, allowing it trace the HTTP traffic. The use of a proxy between the browser and the server has the disadvantage that it is not possible to trace secure HTTP (HTTPS) data that is encrypted end-to-end.

Over time, HTTP-tracing tools have become available that plug directly into the browser. This allows the tool to also trace HTTP traffic, and in some cases even to show information about the cache behavior of the browser. For this chapter, we will use one such a tool, HttpWatch[1], to trace HTTP traffic and show how HTTP works. Any other tool that can trace both HTTP and HTTPS data and can show both the HTTP headers and bodies can be used alternatively.

See Figure 2.1 for an example of such a tool used to trace a website. We see in the first window an overview of all HTTP requests/response cycles. It is important that the tool matches the HTTP request to the correct HTTP response (keep in mind the existence of parallel HTTP requests outstanding). What this tool shows, in addition, is a summary of the requests (useful to see errors at a glance), the roundtrip time (useful to analyze performance), and the type of response (HTML versus images) returned by the server.

2.2 Structure of HTTP

As a first step, let us build a small BSP application with which we can show the basic behavior of HTTP. All that this program does is render out a button to the browser, using the current system time as the text for the button (see Figure 2.2).

```
<html>
  <body>
    <form>
      <input type="submit" value="<%=sy-uzeit%>">
    </form>
  </body>
</html>
```

1 HttpWatch is a tool that is available from Simtec Limited (*www.simtec.ltd.uk*), and of which we bought a copy. As such, it will be used within this chapter to illustrate all aspects of HTTP tracing. There are many other tools available that also can be used to trace HTTP traffic. Our selection of this program just reflects the fact that it is widely in use within our environment, and that we are very familiar with it.

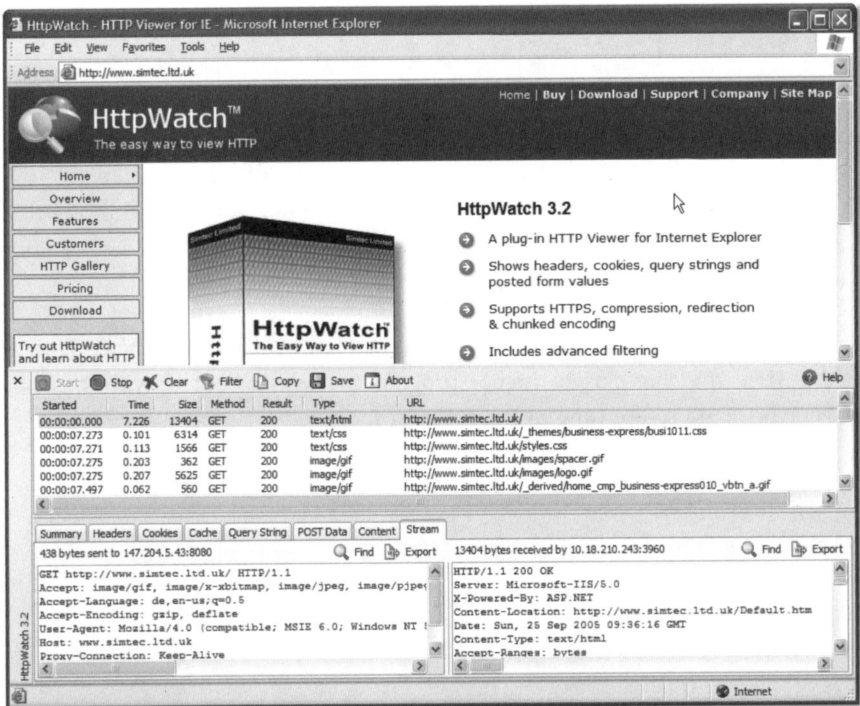

Figure 2.1 Example of an HTTP Plugin Tool

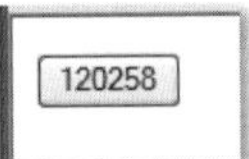

Figure 2.2 Example BSP Application to Show Time on a Button

Assuming that the button has now been pressed a few times, we press it once more, and look at the HTTP traffic. The first important aspect highlighted immediately is the asymmetric nature of HTTP and HTML. When the user presses the button, we see that an HTTP request is send to the server. In this example, the HTTP request has only headers and no payload. With later examples, we will see HTTP requests that have a body.

```
GET /sap(bD1X==)/bc/bsp/sap/chapter02/example1.htm HTTP/1.1
Accept: image/gif, image/x-xbitmap, image/jpeg, image/pjpeg,
        application/vnd.ms-excel,
        application/vnd.ms-powerpoint, application/msword,
        */*
Referer: http://us4049.wdf.sap.corp:1080/sap(bD1X==)/
         bc/bsp/sap/chapter02/example1.htm
```

```
Accept-Language: de,en-us;q=0.5
Accept-Encoding: gzip, deflate
User-Agent: Mozilla/4.0 (MSIE 6.0; Windows NT 5.1)
Host: us4049.wdf.sap.corp:1080
Connection: Keep-Alive
Cookie: sap-appcontext=c2F...UVA
Authorization: Basic VGhhbmtzIGZvciBidXlpbmcgYm9vayE=
```

Listing 2.1 HTTP Request

The server will answer with an HTTP response that contains HTML as body. Notice that the HTML matches closely the BSP program that was executed, with the print sequence resolved to the time of the actual response.

```
HTTP/1.1 200 OK
Content-Type: text/html; charset=iso-8859-1
Content-Length: 111
Expires: 0
Pragma: no-cache
Cache-Control: no-cache
Server: SAP Web Application Server (1.0;640)

<html>
  <body>
    <form>
      <input type="submit" value="120256">
    </form>
  </body>
</html>
```

Listing 2.2 HTTP Response

The HTTP request and HTTP response always have this format:

- The status line, terminated with one carriage-return/linefeed (CRLF).
- Any number of HTTP headers separated by CRLF.
- An empty line (effectively only a CRLF) that separates the headers from the body.
- The bodies of the HTTP request and response. For the HTTP request, the body is only send with a POST request and will usually be of the form `name=value` pairs, separated by &-characters (see Section 2.4). For the HTTP response, the body is typically either HTML or an image (binary object).

HTTP header lines are always terminated by a CRLF, never in the middle of the line. The above listing has header lines over more than one text line, but only due to technical limitations of a printed page. For all following examples, we will shorten or remove headers that are not important, so that the HTTP headers are more correct in print.

In addition, the HTTP specification recommends, but does not enforce, capitalization of HTTP header names. Within a Web AS system, we will find these always only lowercase because of an optimization done in the kernel. For this book, the headers will be capitalized again, to match more closely the real nature of the HTTP protocol.

2.2.1 The HTTP Request Status Line

The first token in the request line is the called *method*, where we will usually only see `GET` and `POST` requests. Although other methods are defined (example `OPTIONS`, `PUT`, etc.), they are not typically used for browser to server communication and won't be further discussed here. The difference between the two methods will be described in Section 2.4.

After the method, separated by a space character, is the URL for which we are fetching the data. Notice that only the absolute path is used when the browser is connecting directly the server. If the browser is connecting via a proxy, then the absolute URL (protocol, host, and absolute path) will be given.

The last token on the line is the HTTP version. Only two versions, HTTP/1.0 and HTTP/1.1, are standardized and widely in use. For us, at a practical level, the biggest difference is that HTTP/1.1 also supports the possibility of having the response compressed before transfer.

2.2.2 HTTP Request Headers

All HTTP headers are of the form `Name: value CRLF`. As we will see when we examine the HTTP response as well, there are some headers that are common to both request and response, whereas some headers are only used in one or the other. A number of different headers are specified, and we will concentrate on those that we commonly see and use. A few additional headers will be discussed in later sections.

- **`Accept`**
  This header lists all the MIME types that the browser can accept in the HTTP response. In this example, we see `image/gif` and `image/jpeg` listed to show that GIF and JPEG images are welcome. The last entry in the list `*/*`, shows that the browser will also accept any type of document. The reason for listing

specific MIME types followed by the wildcard, is to inform the server that the browser prefer answers in the more specific format if available; otherwise the server should just send whatever is possible. For the rest of the chapter, we will shorten this header in the listings to just `*/*`.

- **`Accept-Encoding`**
  This header is only available since HTTP/1.1 and indicates to the server that the browser is willing to accept a compressed HTTP response. It is important to remember that this does not force the server to compress the answer. It only indicates the browser's capabilities to also decompress specific types of HTTP responses.

- **`Accept-Language`**
  This header lists the languages that the user has defined within the browser. This field is also by default used to determine the logon language if no other is set. The `q=0.5` is a quality indicator, that signals to the server `de` as first preference (`q=1.0`), followed by `en` (50 % value). This string allows the server to better match preferences against its capabilities.

- **`Authorization`**
  This header lists the user credentials, in this case the user name and password is encoded as value. The topic of authentication is discussed in detail in Chapter 5 and not further considered here, nor listed.

- **`Connection`**
  Also a header new in HTTP/1.1, this informs the server not to close the underlying TCP connection. The connection is left open for a few seconds extra, allowing the browser to reuse the same TCP connection for the next request. This HTTP header is not listed again for all other examples in this chapter.

- **`Cookie`**
  This header sends a browser cookie to the server. The specific `sap-appcontext` cookie is one that is used by the BSP runtime. Cookies are discussed in detail in Section 2.6. For clarity, we will also not list this specific BSP cookie for these examples.

- **`Host`**
  This very important header contains the name of the application server that the browser is connected to (including the port number). It is exactly the string as entered in the URL, and does not have to match the true server name. For example, when a proxy is used, this header contains the server name as the browser sees it, even although the proxy can forward the request to another server for answering.

- **`Referer`**
  This header contains the name of the HTTP request that triggered this new request. Note that the header was misspelled (instead of "referrer") in the original specification, and has kept this spelling. This header is useful only in limited troubleshooting scenarios to find HTML pages triggering bad links to resources, and is not further listed in this chapter.
- **`User-Agent`**
  This header tells the server what type of browser is used. This is important when rendering HTML, as not all HTML constructs are supported by all browsers. The exact format of the string is not standardized, making it difficult to easily parse the string. There are many websites that list the strings in all variations and match these to different browser versions. For a Web AS, the kernel already provides routines to parse the string correct (see Section 2.3).

2.2.3 HTTP Header/Body Separator

An empty line (only a CRLF) is used to terminate the HTTP headers, and to start the HTTP optional body.

2.2.4 HTTP Request Body

Although not shown in the above example, the HTTP request also can have a body when it is a POST request and will be signaled by a `Content-Length` header. The body, if available, will normally be of the form `name=value` pairs, separated by `&`-characters. This will be described in more detail in Section 2.3.

2.2.5 The HTTP Response Status Line

The first token in the HTTP response status line is the protocol version. This will usually match the protocol version from the request, although it is possible for the server to "switch down" to a lower protocol in the response.

This is followed by the HTTP return code, which is the most important bit of information from this line. Last, a short textual description is given of the return code. This phrase is intended for human readers and does not necessarily have to be in English or stated exactly as in the specification.

Although many different HTTP return codes are specified, only a few—listed in the table below—are in everyday use and should be known to any advanced programmer.

Return Code and Phrase	Explanation
200 OK	The HTTP request was correctly processed and the HTTP response contains the answer.
302 Moved Temporarily	The requested URL is not available, and the browser is redirected to another URL for the answer. See Section 2.7.
304 Not Modified	The browser already has an object in its cache and then queried the server for a new version. With the 304 answer, the server states that the browser's copy is still up to date, and no content is transferred again. See Section 2.8.
401 Unauthorized	The browser sends an HTTP request with user credentials. The server rejects the request. Authentication is discussed in detail in Chapter 4.
403 Forbidden	The server has found the requested object, but does not have permission to answer the HTTP request. This scenario usually indicates that the ICF node is not active.
404 Not Found	In this case, the requested object was not found, and therefore the server answers with 404.
500 Internal Server Error	Any severe error. Usually an exception was raised at the server that caused a short dump to be written (see transaction ST22). Thereafter, the ABAP session is destroyed.

Table 2.1 HTTP Return Codes

2.2.6 HTTP Response Headers

The HTTP headers for the response are structured the same as that of the header. Often the same headers are used in both the request and the response. Again, we will examine those headers we see often.

- **`Content-Length`**
  This is the transfer length of the HTTP response body. Specifically, if the HTTP response is compressed (`Content-Encoding: gzip`), the length will be that of the compressed content that is transferred, and not the real length.
- **`Content-Type`**
  Describes what type of content the server has placed in the HTTP response. For normal HTML pages, this is typically `text/html`, followed by the character set in which the HTML was written. Note that each type of resource will have a different content-type. For example `image/gif` for GIF images, `text/css` for CSS files or `application/x-javascript` for JavaScript resources.
- **`Server`**
  This is a string that is similar to the `User-Agent` from the browser. This tells the HTTP client what server and version is active. For our purpose, this is only of interest to confirm that we are really interacting with a Web AS.

The headers Cache-Control, Pragma, and Expires all control caching of the HTTP response. Caching is a very complex functionality that was changed extensively between HTTP/1.0 and HTTP/1.1. Often, there are still older versions of proxies that do not interpret these fields correctly. Therefore, a complete series of headers are always set to conform to both protocol versions of caching. For us, it is only important to know that pages are either cached or not cached. The BSP runtime always assumes that a BSP page is dynamically generated, and therefore cannot be cached (these defaults can be overwritten on the properties tab of the page). For our discussion, except when necessary, only the Cache-Control header will be shown.

2.2.7 HTTP Response Body

The HTTP response body can be any data stream. Typically, it is either HTML or a resource that was requested for the page.

2.3 Server Objects for HTTP Request and Response

We have now seen that HTTP is characterized by a request and a corresponding response. We now will see how one can access these from within a BSP application. Let us create a small example, where we ourselves read data from the incoming request and write the outgoing response completely. The application has an input field of which all entered text is rendered on a button. Figure 2.3 shows the application in the browser.

```
<%
   DATA: btntxt TYPE string.
   btntxt = request->get_form_field( 'btntxt' ).

   DATA: html TYPE string.
   CONCATENATE
          `<html><body><form>`
            `<input type=text name="btntxt" value="">`
            `<input type="submit" value="` btntxt `">`
          `</form></body></html>`
    INTO html.

    response->set_cdata( html ).
%>
```

When looking at the source code, we see that a variable request is used without having been declared at all. This is a variable made available in all BSP pages, of type IF_HTTP_REQUEST, and is the ABAP representation of the HTTP request. Similarly, there is also a response variable of type IF_HTTP_RESPONSE available.

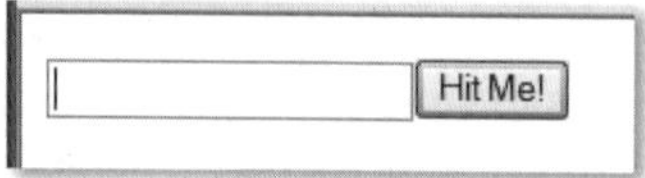

Figure 2.3 Example BSP Application to Show the HTTP Request/Response Objects

When looking at the two HTTP interfaces, we will find many methods that seem to make no immediate sense, for example SET_HEADER_FIELD on the request interface. An HTTP request is received at the server, and thus it seems as though we should be more interested in getting the header fields. However, keep in mind that the Web AS itself can play "browser" and make an outgoing connection to another Web service. In this case, the setter methods are justified.

Let us look briefly at the functionality provided by the interfaces, concentrating only on those methods that are useful in the Web AS' traditional role as HTTP server. Only those methods in everyday use will be listed. Interested readers should check the online documentation for a complete overview.

On the IF_HTTP_REQUEST interface, we have:

- Some methods that allow us to read the status line: GET_METHOD and GET_VERSION.
- A method that will give us the exact type and version of browser in use: GET_USER_AGENT. The integer constants for browser types are defined in the IHTTP type pool.
- Methods that allow us to read header fields GET_HEADER_FIELD(S).
- We have briefly touched on the fact that in the HTTP request, data is transferred in the form name=value pairs, called form fields (see Section 2.4). There are a few methods to deliver this data in a "ready to use" format: GET_FORM_FIELD(S).
- In Section 2.5.3, we will learn how to perform a file upload where we use the methods: NUM_MULTIPARTS and GET_MULTIPART.
- Cookies will be discussed in detail in Section 2.6. Cookies are in effect small bits of data transferred in one HTTP header, and these methods will allow us to read the cookies as semantic entities: GET_COOKIE(S).

On the IF_HTTP_RESPONSE interface, we have similarly interesting methods:

- A method to set the HTTP response correctly on the status line: SET_STATUS.

- Methods for special headers, such as content-type (SET_CONTENT_TYPE), or special situations, such as handling an HTTP redirect (REDIRECT), discussed later in Section 2.7.
- Methods to set the header fields of the response: SET_HEADER_FIELD(S).
- Again methods to set cookies, which are just logical objects mapped onto header fields: SET_COOKIE and DELETE_COOKIE_AT_CLIENT.
- The HTTP response is effectively a data stream that is either HTML (character data), or binary objects (normal data). For writing data, methods are available to either completely set the body of the response (SET_(C)DATA), or to append data onto the response (APPEND_(C)DATA).

When we review the test application again, we can see that only two calls were used to complete the simple Web page. The first, request->get_form_field, is used to retrieve the data of the input field from the incoming HTTP request. This complete HTML is then constructed and written using response->set_cdata. Although not shown, the BSP runtime also, at a minimum, calls response->set_header_field to set the content-type of text/html and response->set_status with a value of 200 OK to show to the browser that the response is correct.

With this understanding of the principles of an HTTP request/response cycle, and how the objects can be manipulated within BSP, it is possible to look at more detailed aspects.

2.4 HTML Forms and Data Handling

A HTML document starts with an <html> tag, then can have an <header/> sequence, a <body/> sequence, and ends with the </html> tag. Within the body, the next-most important element is the <form> sequence. An HTML document can have more than one form, but forms must be placed one after another. They cannot be nested.

Each form is exactly the transfer unit for submitting an HTTP request to the server. Only those fields within the form are actually submitted. Thus, one would typically use different forms for different parts of the screen, so as to transmit only relevant data back to the server for the specific query.

Each <form> tag has a method attribute that can be set to either the value GET (default) or POST. With the GET method, all form fields are appended onto the URL, using the ?-character as separator between the URL and the form fields and the &-character as separator between the individual name=value pairs. As the data is sent as part of the URL, the amount of data is limited by the maximum length of a URL, usually 2,048 bytes.

For the POST method, all data is sent in the body of the HTTP request. There is no (theoretical) limit to the amount of data that can be sent. The data volume is only constrained by the memory limits of the browser.

To look at this difference in more detail, let us construct a small program that uses both form methods.

```
<html><body>

    <form method="GET">
      <input type="text" name="klm" value="456">
      <input type="text" name="klm" value="789">
      <input type="text" name="xyz" value="bsp">
      <input type="submit" value="GET!">
    </form>

    <form method="POST">
      <input type="text" name="klm" value="456">
      <input type="text" name="klm" value="789">
      <input type="text" name="xyz" value="bsp">
      <input type="submit" value="POST!">
    </form>

    <%
        DATA: ffs  TYPE tihttpnvp,
              ff   TYPE  ihttpnvp.
        request->get_form_fields( CHANGING fields = ffs ).
    %>
    <table border="1">
    <% LOOP AT ffs INTO ff. %>
       <tr><td><%=ff-name%></td><td><%=ff-value%></td></tr>
    <% ENDLOOP. %>
    </table>

</body></html>
```

This example program has two identical forms. The only difference is in the method attribute. Note that the forms must be placed after one another. Thereafter, additional code is added to show the behavior of form fields in the different cases. The results of the application can be seen in Figure 2.4.

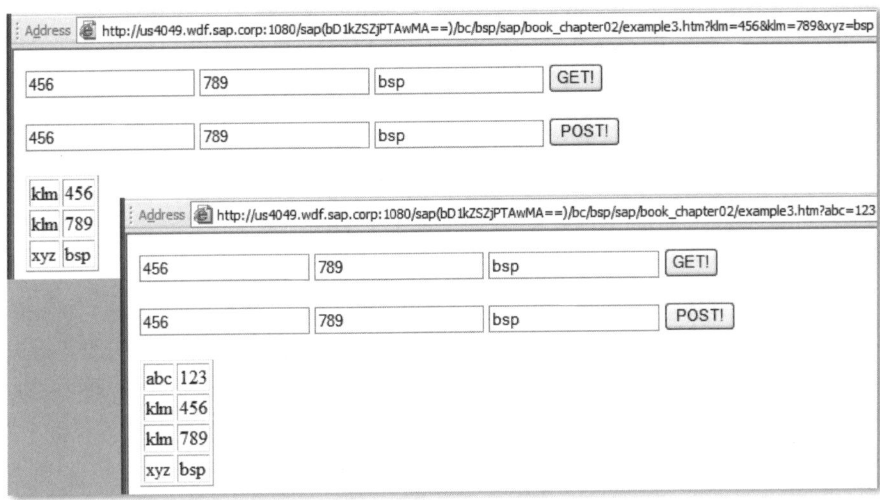

Figure 2.4 Example BSP Application to Show the Form GET and POST

For the first test, we start the application with an additional parameter in the URL (`.../chapter02/example3.htm?abc=123`), and then press the **GET!** button. Let us first examine the HTTP request.

```
GET /sap(bD1X==)/bc/bsp/sap/
     chapter02/example3.htm?klm=456&klm=789&xyz=bsp HTTP/1.1
Accept: */*
Accept-Language: de,en-us;q=0.5
Accept-Encoding: gzip, deflate
User-Agent: Mozilla/4.0 (MSIE 6.0; Windows NT 5.1)
Host: us4049.wdf.sap.corp:1080
```

In the source, the `<form>` tag had the attribute `method=GET`. This results in a `GET` HTTP request (see first token in status line). The next important aspect is that data from the form is carried as `name=value` parameters within the URL, separated from the URL with the `?`-character and from one another with the `&`-character. Duplicate names are allowed (see `klm` twice in URL). The `GET` request has no body, and therefore no `Content-Length` header is set.

The other interesting aspect is that initially the application was started with the sequence `?abc=123` in the URL. We see in the trace and also in Figure 2.4 that this URL with its parameters has been completely replaced with the new `GET` URL.

The request is processed by the BSP application, and a new HTTP response is written. The first part of the response is just static HTML code, and exactly the same as listed on the BSP page.

```
HTTP/1.1 200 OK
Content-Type: text/html; charset=iso-8859-1
Content-Length: 696
Cache-Control: no-cache
Server: SAP Web Application Server (1.0;640)

<html>
  ...
    <table border="1">
       <tr><td>klm</td><td>456</td></tr>
       <tr><td>klm</td><td>789</td></tr>
       <tr><td>xyz</td><td>bsp</td></tr>
    </table>
  </body>
</html>
```

Pay close attention to the small bit of source code that we had on the BSP page to dump out all the form fields that was received by the BSP application. We see in the HTTP response above, and also in Figure 2.4, that exactly three fields were found, matching the three fields that were in the form, and transferred as URL parameters to the server.

We start the BSP application new, again with the URL parameter abc=123, and then press the **POST!** button.

```
POST /sap(bD1X==)/bc/bsp/sap/
                    chapter02/example3.htm?abc=123 HTTP/1.1
Accept: */*
Accept-Language: de,en-us;q=0.5
Content-Type: application/x-www-form-urlencoded
Accept-Encoding: gzip, deflate
User-Agent: Mozilla/4.0 (MSIE 6.0; Windows NT 5.1)
Host: us4049.wdf.sap.corp:1080
Content-Length: 23

klm=456&klm=789&xyz=bsp
```

The first difference is the POST method in the HTTP request status line. Next, note that the URL in the status line, to which the HTTP request is posted, is exactly the same as that with which the application was started. Our URL parameter abc=123 is still part of the URL that is also transmitted to the server.

Because of the POST request, all data from the form is now transported within the body of the HTTP request, again separated by &-characters. Notice the use of the empty line to terminate the list of HTTP headers, and to start the body of the HTTP request. The server must be informed about the length of the body (Content-Length header) and the type of the body (Content-Type). The Content-Type usually has the value x-www-form-urlencoded to indicate name/value pairs separated by &-characters. In Section 2.5.3 we see how this header field changes when a file is uploaded.

The HTTP response and the output shown in Figure 2.4 are now similar to that of the GET request, except that the table now shows four entries.

```
HTTP/1.1 200 OK
Content-Type: text/html; charset=iso-8859-1
Content-Length: 742
Cache-Control: no-cache
server: SAP Web Application Server (1.0;640)

<html>
  ...
    <table border="1">
      <tr><td>abc</td><td>123</td></tr>
      <tr><td>klm</td><td>456</td></tr>
      <tr><td>klm</td><td>789</td></tr>
      <tr><td>xyz</td><td>bsp</td></tr>
    </table>
  </body>
</html>
```

The table was rendered based on the values that the get_form_fields method returned. This method collects all data from both the URL, which the POST did not change, and from the body of the HTTP request. This helps the programmer by removing the need to worry about parsing different parts of the HTTP request for similar data.

However, the method can cause major problems if duplicate names exist in both the URL data and in the body. We know that duplicate names are valid and that the request object will just return all of them. This could result in the application using the wrong value. For this reason, we recommend that you always set the action attribute in the <form> tag as well with the URL of the target page.

We also recommend using a POST rather than a GET, as the data capabilities of the GET request is limited by the maximum length of an URL, typically 2KB.

2.5 Mapping of HTML onto HTTP Requests

Until now, we have only used simple input fields to show the basic structure of HTTP. Let us now look in more detail how different HTML controls will transfer their information back to the server. This is not an exhaustive list, but will concentrate on the basics that any Web programmer should know.

2.5.1 Input Fields

To examine the behavior of input fields, we will first quickly build a small test program that used different types of input fields, with the results shown in Figure 2.5.

```
<html><body>
 <form method="POST">
  <input type="text"   name="abc"          value="123">
  <input type="text"   name="klm" id="abc" value="456">
  <input type="text"              id="xyz" value="789">
  <input type="text"   name="dis" value="disabled" disabled>
  <input type="text"   name="ro"  value="readonly" readonly>
  <input type="hidden" name="hid" value="hidden">
  <input type="submit" name="btn" value="Hit Me!">
  </form>
</body></html>
```

Figure 2.5 Example BSP Application to Show the Behavior of Input Fields

The program first uses three input fields that have either names, IDs, or both set. This is followed by a disabled and a read-only input field (notice in Figure 2.5 the difference in visualization). Finally, an input field of `type=hidden` is used. This is the typical way that data in the form of `name=value` pairs are persisted in the browser, to be returned later. One sees that the hidden input field is not visualized by the browser.

Let us look at the HTTP request to see what happens when the button is pressed. The HTTP response will not be examined, as it just statically renders out the same HTML page again.

```
POST /sap(bD1X==)/bc/bsp/sap/chapter02/example4.htm HTTP/1.1
Accept: */*
Accept-Language: de,en-us;q=0.5
```

```
Content-Type: application/x-www-form-urlencoded
Accept-Encoding: gzip, deflate
User-Agent: Mozilla/4.0 (MSIE 6.0; Windows NT 5.1)
Host: us4049.wdf.sap.corp:1080
Content-Length: 52

abc=123&klm=456&ro=readonly&hid=hidden&btn=Hit+Me%21
```

The first input field is transferred as we expected with `abc=123`. For the second input field, both the `name` and an `id` attributes are set, but the data is transferred with the name value of `klm=456`. The third input field (with the `value=789` attribute) has only its `id` attribute set, and we see immediately that this data is *not* in the HTTP request. This already demonstrates the first important aspect of HTML controls and their mapping onto HTTP requests. The HTML controls can have both `id` and `name` attributes, where the `id` attribute is only of interest within the rendered HTML code. The `name` attribute is significant for the HTTP request. Only named data is actually transferred to the server.

This naming aspect will play a big role in programs based on Model-View-Controller. The `id` attribute matches what the programmer used in the HTML, and allows manipulation of the HTML with JavaScript based on this known `id` value. The `name` attribute will be set to match exactly the position of the data within the model. This allows the server to update the model with incoming data from the HTTP request. See this simple example:

```
<input type="text" id="age" name="model.childAge" value="1">
```

The next two input fields were flagged `disabled` and `readonly` respectively. This influences the way that the browser will visualize the two input fields. (For the interested reader: Disabled input fields appear dimmed, do not respond to user input, and cannot be focused. With read-only, the input field can be focused but still cannot be changed.) It is worth noting that a disabled input field is *not* transferred back to the server, and we can not see any data `dis=disabled` in the HTTP request.

The hidden input field is transferred back to the server within the HTTP request without further semantics being attached to them. This is the technique that state information can be "stored" within the HTTP request/response cycle, allowing stateless programming, but still having the necessary data available to process the next incoming HTTP request. For example, assume that we must also have a key available to update the user's data. We could write:

```
<input type="hidden" name="user_key" value="D027140">
```

The last interesting aspect is the onscreen button that is achieved with the input=submit sequence. As this is again an input field, and named, it is also transferred back to the server. The value, btn=Hit+Me%21, has been encoded to match the Content-Type header. In the encoding, spaces are replaced with +-characters, and some characters are replaced with a %-character and their two byte hex code (%21=!).

In summary, we can say that all named and not disabled input fields within the <form> will be returned to the server.

2.5.2 Checkboxes, Radio Buttons and Dropdown List Boxes

Following the same approach as above, we first quickly develop a small test program with which we can show the behavior of checkboxes, radio buttons, and dropdown list boxes. The rendered page can be seen in Figure 2.6.

```
<html><body>
 <form method="POST">
  <input type="checkbox" name="chk1" value="123" checked>123
  <input type="checkbox" name="chk2" value="456">456
  <input type="radio"    name="rad1" value="123" checked>123
  <input type="radio"    name="rad1" value="456">456
  <input type="radio"    name="rad1" value="789">789
  <select name="sel1">
    <option value="123" selected>123
    <option value="456">456
    <option value="789">789
  </select>
  <input type="submit"   name="btn"  value="Hit Me!">
 </form>
</body></html>
```

☑123 ☐456 ◉123 ○456 ○789 123 ▾ Hit Me!

Figure 2.6 Example BSP Application to Show the Behavior of other Basic Controls

Again, only the HTTP request is examined. The HTTP response will be the same static page rendered again.

```
POST /sap(bD1X==)/bc/bsp/sap/chapter02/example5.htm HTTP/1.1
Accept: */*
Accept-Language: de,en-us;q=0.5
```

```
Content-Type: application/x-www-form-urlencoded
Accept-Encoding: gzip, deflate
User-Agent: Mozilla/4.0 (MSIE 6.0; Windows NT 5.1)
Host: us4049.wdf.sap.corp:1080
Content-Length: 38

chk1=123&rad1=123&sel1=123&btn=Hit+Me%21
```

The first part of the application shows two checkboxes, one having its checked attribute set. The rendering is expected, but in the HTTP request we see only the data for the checkbox that is actually checked (chk1=123). In the HTTP request, we do not see any reference to the unchecked checkbox chk2. This conforms to the idea that the check will enable the transfer of the value back to the server. A request->get_form_field method call on an unchecked checkbox will find no value in the incoming HTTP request and will return an empty string, effectively signaling no value.

Radio buttons are actually a group of buttons, where all buttons with the group are given the same name (name=rad1). Only one of the buttons can be selected at any time (have its checked attribute set), and exactly this named value will be returned to the server (rad1=123).

Dropdown list boxes, using the <select> tag in HTML, have a similar construct. Each dropdown list box has a number of <option> tags, one of which can be selected. This value is then returned to the server for the name of the <select> tag (sel1=123).

In summary, the named and not-disabled aspects still hold. In addition, only checked checkboxes are transferred. For radio buttons and dropdown list boxes, the selected value is returned against the name of the control.

2.5.3 File Upload and Download

The last type of input that we wish to quickly examine is type=file. This is the basic, and only, HTML building block for handling a file upload to the server.

```
<html><body>
  <form method="POST">
    <input type="text" name="fld1" value="abc">
    <input type="file" name="fil1">
    <input type="submit" value="Failure!">
  </form>
  <form method="POST" enctype="multipart/form-data">
```

```
    <input type="text" name="fld1" value="abc">
    <input type="file" name="fil1">
    <input type="submit" value="Hit Me!">
  </form>
</body></html>

<%
DATA: entity          TYPE ref to if_http_entity,
      name            TYPE string,
      content         TYPE xstring,
      content_type    TYPE string,
      idx             TYPE i VALUE 1.

WHILE idx <= request->num_multiparts( ).
 entity = request->get_multipart( idx ).
 name = entity->get_header_field( '~content_filename' ).
 IF name IS NOT INITIAL.
  content_type = entity->get_header_field( 'Content-Type' ).
  content      = entity->get_data( ).
  response->set_data( content ).
  response->set_header_field( name  = 'Content-Type'
                              value = content_type ).
  EXIT.
 ENDIF.
 idx = idx + 1.
ENDWHILE.
%>
```

The example program is slightly more complex, as there is a small complication that one should know about when programming a file upload. First, the BSP application shows a `<form>` tag as used previously in all other examples, followed by a modified `<form>` tag with the additional `enctype` attribute (transfer encoding type). The last part of the application looks into the incoming request and fishes out the file. This will be discussed after examining the HTTP requests.

The result of the application is depicted in Figure 2.7, showing the application, and—in the success case—the downloaded image.

> **Note** Often developers will ask for a technique to change the "Browse..." string displayed by the HTML control. This is not possible, because the string is set by the browser and the language used is determined from the client language.

It cannot be influenced by the server. The other request one often sees is to programmatically set the filename for uploading. This is not possible because, for security reasons, a user must explicitly select a file that will be transmitted to the server. The browser does not allow the server to snag files without the user's active participation.

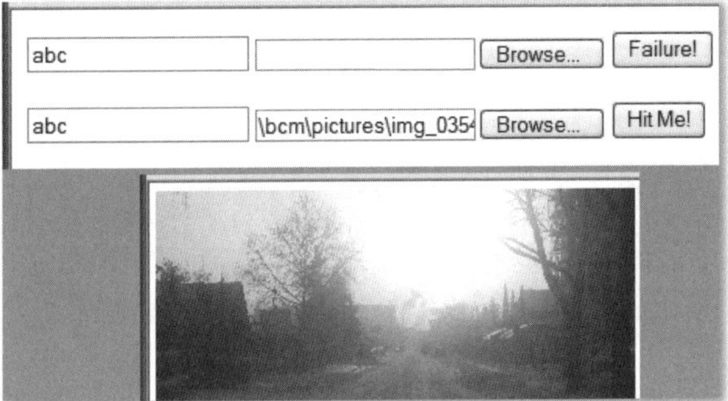

Figure 2.7 Example BSP Application to Show the Behavior of a File Upload

Let us examine first the request for the **Failure!** case. Here, a normal form is used to `POST` the data to the server.

```
POST /sap(bD1X==)/bc/bsp/sap/chapter02/example6.htm HTTP/1.1
Accept: */*
Accept-Language: de,en-us;q=0.5
Content-Type: application/x-www-form-urlencoded
Accept-Encoding: gzip, deflate
User-Agent: Mozilla/4.0 (MSIE 6.0; Windows NT 5.1)
Host: us4049.wdf.sap.corp:1080
Content-Length: 46

fld1=abc&fil1=%5Cbcm%5Cpictures%5Cimg_0354.jpg
```

We see that data for the input field (`fld1=abc`) is transferred. However, the file upload sequence also behaves exactly like an input field, sending the name (`fil1=%5Cbcm%5Cpictures%5Cimg_0354.jpg`) of the selected file only. Notice the URL encoding that replaces the `\`-character with `%5C`.

The reason for the failure is that the specification requires that a file upload must be done with a multi-part `POST` request. This is one HTML programming mistake that is seen quite often. The second `<form>` tag does have this additional `enctype` attribute set to `multipart/form-data`. Let is look at the new HTTP request.

```
POST /sap(bD1X==)/bc/bsp/sap/chapter02/example6.htm HTTP/1.1
Accept: */*
Accept-Language: de,en-us;q=0.5
Content-Type: multipart/form-data; boundary=---7d53433beca
Accept-Encoding: gzip, deflate
User-Agent: Mozilla/4.0 (MSIE 6.0; Windows NT 5.1)
Host: us4049.wdf.sap.corp:1080
Content-Length: 563726

---7d53433beca
Content-Disposition: form-data; name="fld1"

abc
---7d53433beca
Content-Disposition: form-data; name="fil1";
                      filename="\bcm\pictures\img_0354.jpg"
Content-Type: image/pjpeg

...binary data of image...
```

The first difference between this and past examples is that the `Content-Type` header was changed to a new value of a `multipart`, plus the additional information that the different bits of data are now separated by the boundary string `---7d53433beca`. This boundary string is a random-generated string, relatively long (in this example shortened to fit one book page), that indicates the start of each field that is submitted to the server.

Within the body, we actually now have sub-bodies, submitted one per field. Each sub-body is again a sequence of HTTP headers, an empty line, and then the value string. This shows the large overhead of a `multipart` submit, and why it should only be used when uploading files.

For the input field, the first part has only the HTTP header `Content-Disposition`, listing the name of the field. The value is transferred within the body of the part.

In the next part, we see the file to be uploaded. The `Content-Disposition` header now also lists the (local) filename that is uploaded and the `Content-Type` of the file, determined at the client. The body contains the binary data of the image.

Note that each part does not have a separate `Content-Length` HTTP header. The length is set for the complete HTTP request, and the boundary string is used to split the request into different parts.

The important aspect of multi-part requests is that each form field is listed in a separate part, and that all files uploaded in the same HTTP request are also listed in parts. To read the form fields (for example the value of fld1 above), do we have to now parse the HTTP request body ourselves? Luckily no; the same methods request->get_form_field(s) also work with multi-part requests, and will return the same values as when the data is transferred in a GET or a normal POST. These methods shield us on the server from the complexity of reading the form fields in all the different cases.

However, uploaded files are not considered to be form fields and cannot be retrieved as such. They are handled as separate parts of the request. Let us look at a small extract of the text program in more detail.

```
WHILE idx <= request->num_multiparts( ).
 DATA: entity TYPE ref to if_http_entity,
 entity = request->get_multipart( idx ).
 name = entity->get_header_field( '~content_filename' ).
 IF name IS NOT INITIAL.
  content_type = entity->get_header_field( 'Content-Type' ).
  content      = entity->get_data( ).
  length       = XSTRLEN( content ).
  ...
 ENDIF.
 idx = idx + 1.
ENDWHILE.
```

First, the number of parts is determined. Included in this list are all parts, not only those that are uploaded files. For each part, we get a reference onto that part and then can again query the header fields. We saw before that both parts had a Content-Disposition header. This header is already parsed into its different attributes within the request object. We can identify file uploads by the fact that the filename attribute is also specified, made available with the pseudo header ~content_filename. Once a file name is found, we extract the content type and the actual content from this specific part. The actual file size can be computed with the ABAP operation XSTRLEN.

With the extracted information, the minimum requirement to echo the file back to the browser consists of the response->set_data call and the response->set_header_field to set the Content-Type header. The remaining requirements are met by default values set by the HTTP response object.

```
HTTP/1.1 200 OK
Content-Type: image/pjpeg; charset=iso-8859-1
```

```
Content-Length: 563426
Cache-Control: no-cache
Server: SAP Web Application Server (1.0;640)

...binary data of image...
```

The HTTP response, although it is our first binary response, amounts to business as usual. Figure 2.7 also shows the uploaded image displayed in the browser.

2.6 Cookies

A cookie is a small bit of information that the server sends to the browser to "remember" until the next HTTP request. This is a very convenient way for a server, especially in stateless cases, to store application-relevant data for each user and to have the relevant data returned with the next incoming request. There are strict limits to the size of each cookie (usually a maximum 4KB) and the number of cookies allowed per server (a maximum of 20).

There is controversy whether cookies are good or bad, but we do not wish to become too deeply involved in the debate here. In principle, cookies are good, but can be misused to follow a user's travels through the Internet. If this is a concern for you, then we highly recommended you use your favorite search engine to read up a little on cookies and the possibility for misuse. As "the good guys," we will concentrate on a number of valid uses of cookies.

A cookie can be sent to the browser with the `Set-Cookie` HTTP header within the HTTP response. The basic form of the cookie is the `name=value` data. In addition, a number of attributes can be set. An interesting aspect of cookies names and values is that they may not include semicolon, comma, or white-space characters, as these are used as separators within the cookie attributes. This is especially important for the value string and also for the path string. These must not contain any of the separator characters.

```
Set-Cookie: NAME=VALUE; expires=DATE; domain=DOMAIN_NAME;
                                        path=PATH; secure
```

The `name` can be any user-assigned name and the `value` effectively can be any string, as long as it does not contain any of the excluded characters. The optional expiry `date` controls the timeframe for which the browser will store and use the cookie. If timeframe is not specified, the browser will store the cookie only until the end of the browser session.

The optional `domain` can be used to indicate that the cookie is not only valid for this specific web server ("default if not set"), but also must be sent to other computers with the same tail-matched domain. For example, if one is setting domain to `sap.com`, then the cookie will be sent with any HTTP request to a Web server within SAP.

The `path` attribute limits the cookie to specific URLs on the server. A value of / would indicate that the cookie is valid for all URLs on the server, whereas `/sap/bc/bsp` would limit the cookie so that it could be be sent only to BSP applications.

The optional `secure` flag limits the browser to sending the cookie only over HTTPS connections.

For our further investigation of cookies, we again have a small test program, with the output shown in Figure 2.8.

```
<%
   DATA: cookie TYPE string.
   request->get_cookie( EXPORTING name  = 'myCookie'
                        IMPORTING value = cookie ).
%>
<html>
  <body>
    <form method="POST">
      Cookie: <%= cookie %>
      <input type="submit" value="Hit Me!">
    </form>
  </body>
</html>
<%
   response->set_cookie( name    = 'myCookie'
                         path    = runtime->runtime_url
                         value   = '123' ).
   response->set_cookie( name    = 'myCookie'
                         path    = runtime->page_url
                         value   = '456' ).
   response->set_cookie( name    = 'myCookie'
                         path    = '/'
                         value   = '789' ).
%>
```

For this example, we are going to turn around the viewing perspective and start by examining the HTTP response. Initially, when the application is started, it will find no cookies with the data it requires, and a cookie will be set.

Figure 2.8 Example BSP Application to Show the Behavior of Cookies

It is very important to remember that cookies are *set* from the server to the browser, and the correct call is **response->set**_cookie. It is also possible to call the get_cookie method on the HTTP request, but this only makes sense in cases where the server is functioning as client to another server.

In the example application, we will set three cookies, all with the same name but different values and on different paths. This action can now be easily seen in the HTTP response. Pay particular attention to the different paths used for the different cookies.

```
HTTP/1.1 200 OK
Set-Cookie: myCookie=123; path=/sap(bD1X==)/bc/bsp
Set-Cookie: myCookie=456;
          path=/sap(bD1X==)/bc/bsp/sap/chapter02/example7.htm
Set-Cookie: myCookie=789; path=/
Content-Type: text/html; charset=iso-8859-1
Content-Length: 147
Cache-Control: no-cache
Server: SAP Web Application Server (1.0;640)

<html>...</html>
```

With the above HTTP response, the browser now receives three new cookies. If the cookie jar is full, older cookies are discarded, and the new cookies are stored. As no expires attribute is set, the cookies will only be stored until the end of the browser session.

When the user presses the button again, the browser knows the target server and the URL for which the HTTP request will be generated. In the cookie jar on the browser, all cookies are gathered that match this specification. In this example, we set three different cookies, but in all cases the paths we used did match the URL of the current running application. Let us look at the POST request.

```
POST /sap(bD1X==)/bc/bsp/sap/chapter02/example7.htm HTTP/1.1
Accept: */*
Accept-Language: de,en-us;q=0.5
Content-Type: application/x-www-form-urlencoded
Accept-Encoding: gzip, deflate
User-Agent: Mozilla/4.0 (MSIE 6.0; Windows NT 5.1)
```

```
Host: us4049.wdf.sap.corp:1080
Content-Length: 0
Cookie: myCookie=456; myCookie=123; myCookie=789
```

We see a new Cookie header with the HTTP request, containing three name=value pairs matching our three myCookie value sets. However, even though our application set the cookies in the sequence 123, 456, and 789, they returned in a different sequence with 456 first. The reason is that cookies are sorted by the strongest path. The cookie with a path that matches the most characters against the URL is placed first in the list. In addition, only the cookie values are returned to the server. No path, domain or expires attributes are set on the Cookie header.

Within the test application, a cookie can be read with the **request->get_** cookie method. This method can also export the other attributes, but we saw already that they exist nowhere within the HTTP request. This method can only return these extra attributes in cases where the server is functioning as client and to read the actual set cookie.

We see in Figure 2.8 that the get_cookie method returned only the first name-matched cookie, and the value will be rendered out into the HTTP response.

```
<html>
  ...
      Cookie: 456
  ...
</html>
```

It is not possible to delete cookies at a client. A cookie can be set to a new value only if it has effectively expired. The browser then will place the newly set cookie into the cookie jar, find that it is stale, and discard it. As the setting of dates in a correct HTTP format is complex (you have to know that January 1st, 1980 was a Tuesday, for example), the response object also supports a method delete_cookie_at_client.

```
response->delete_cookie_at_client( name = 'myCookie'
                                   path = '/' ).
```

This method then will set the correct HTTP header.

```
Set-Cookie: myCookie=0;
            expires=Tue, 01-Jan-1980 00:00:01 GMT; path=/
```

In summary, remember that cookies are set on the HTTP response and later retrieved with a get call on the incoming HTTP request.

2.7 HTTP Redirects

An HTTP redirect is typically used on a website after reorganization, so that HTTP requests for old bookmarks will be forwarded automatically to the correct page. The other use is for simple website navigation. After the server has evaluated the incoming HTTP request, it can decide to have the user view a different page. This is also achieved with a redirect.

At a technical level, the browser has already sent an HTTP request to the server, and the server has no choice but to answer with an HTTP response. As the server does not have the valid data, but knows where it can be obtained, the server will answer with an HTTP return code of `302 Moved Temporarily` and also supply the new destination. The browser will automatically, without the user's intervention, start a new HTTP request to the new destination.

As a first step, we will build a small test program with one input field for a new target URL. If the input field is filed, we go to the new website. For this example, we do not do any error checking. However, in any real-world website, it is important to first validate that the URL does not contain any form of code that will allow a cross-site scripting attack. This topic is unfortunately beyond the scope of this book. The results of the application can be seen in Figure 2.9.

```
<html>
  <body>
    <form method="POST">
      Redirect:
      <input type="text" name="redirect">
      <input type="submit" value="Hit Me!">
    </form>
  </body>
</html>
<%
   DATA: redirect TYPE string.
   redirect = request->get_form_field( 'redirect' ).
   IF redirect IS NOT INITIAL.
     response->redirect( redirect ).
   ENDIF.
%>
```

The first part of the BSP application is just a simple layout to collect the new target URL. The second part looks for the availability of such a new redirect URL, and if entered, will use the `response->redirect` method to instruct the browser to go to the new Web page.

Figure 2.9 Example BSP Application to Show the Behavior of Redirects

For this application, as it has only one input field, the `POST` request will have only the body: `redirect=http%3A%2F%2Fwww.sap-press.com`. Notice the effect of the URL encoding on the incoming data, with the `:`-character replaced with `%3A` and the /-character with `%2F`. We are interested in the HTTP response that the server gives to the browser.

```
HTTP/1.1 302 Moved Temporarily
Content-Type: text/html; charset=iso-8859-1
Content-Length: 0
Cache-Control: no-cache
Location: http://www.sap-press.com
Server: SAP Web Application Server (1.0;640)
```

In the HTTP response, note first the return code in the status line. The value of `302` indicates to the browser that the answer it seeks is to be found by following another URL. The second difference is the `Location` HTTP header that specifies the new target URL. The browser will start a new HTTP sequence with the specified URL.

```
GET http://www.sap-press.com/ HTTP/1.1
Accept: */*
Accept-Language: de,en-us;q=0.5
Proxy-Connection: Keep-Alive
Accept-Encoding: gzip, deflate
User-Agent: Mozilla/4.0 (MSIE 6.0; Windows NT 5.1)
Host: www.sap-press.com
```

One subtle point in this HTTP request is the status line that now contains the absolute URL (protocol, host, and absolute path) as this request is sent by the browser to a proxy to complete the request.

2.8 Handling of HTML Resources in HTTP

Until now, we have concentrated mostly on HTML and the relevant HTTP conditions. Let us look also at the way resources are loaded. We will write quickly a small application that just shows an icon and a button to trigger server round trips. The result is shown in Figure 2.10.

```
<html><body><form method="POST">
   <img src="<%=CL_BSP_MIMES=>SAP_ICON( id='ICON_OKAY' )%>">
   <input type="submit" value="Hit Me!">
</form></body></html>
```

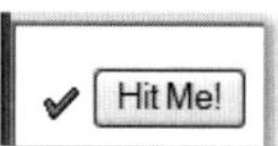

Figure 2.10 Example BSP Application to Show the Behavior of Resource Caching

Let us concentrate on the loading of the image itself. Once the HTML page is loaded, the browser starts a second GET HTTP request to fetch the image for display, a process similar to all requests we have seen before. However, let us look at the HTTP response received.

```
HTTP/1.1 200 OK
Content-Type: image/gif
Content-Length: 191
Last-Modified: Fri, 13 Aug 2004 12:17:27 GMT
Cache-Control: max-age=604800
Server: SAP Web Application Server (1.0;640)
Date: Sun, 25 Sep 2005 12:32:49 GMT
Expires: Sun, 02 Oct 2005 13:23:22 GMT

GIF89a ...
```

We see that a number of new headers are available. The Cache-Control header with the value max-age=604800 (seconds) informs the browser that the returned data can be cached for seven days without further problems. Some of the other HTTP headers (Last-Modified, Date and Expires) are set in addition to convey the same message for older HTTP/1.0 based proxies that might be encountered enroute. Thus, the browser now has an image in cache that is valid for the next seven days. Figure 2.11 shows a summary of the HTTP traffic.

× Start Stop Clear Filter Copy Save About

Started	Time	S...	Met...	Re...	Type	URL
00:00:00.000	0.073	363	GET	200	text/html...	http://us4049.wdf.sap.corp:1080/sap(bD1kZSZjPTAwMA==)/bc/bsp/sap...
00:00:00.112	0.003	513	GET	200	image/gif	http://us4049.wdf.sap.corp:1080/sap/public/bc/icons/s_B_OKAY.gif
00:00:05.254	0.048	363	POST	200	text/html...	http://us4049.wdf.sap.corp:1080/sap(bD1kZSZjPTAwMA==)/bc/bsp/sap...

Figure 2.11 The First Time a Resource is Loaded

After we have played around with this complex application, we close the browser and take a break. Later in the afternoon, we start the application again. Figure 2.12 shows what happens at the HTTP level. The first GET HTTP request loads the application. The HTML page contains the reference to an image for displaying. The browser looks into its cache, finds an image matching the requested URL that is still valid for at least six days and a few hours, and uses the image. This behavior is shown to us by our HTTP trace tool with the (Cache) indicator for the result of the HTTP request.

Start Stop Clear Filter Copy Save About

Started	Time	S...	Met...	Result	Type	URL
00:00:00.000	0.073	570	GET	200	text/html...	http://us4049.wdf.sap.corp:1080/sap(bD1kZSZjPTAwMA==)/bc/bsp/sap...
00:00:00.091	0.003	0	GET	(Cache)	image/gif	http://us4049.wdf.sap.corp:1080/sap/public/bc/icons/s_B_OKAY.gif
00:00:05.570	0.071	363	POST	200	text/html...	http://us4049.wdf.sap.corp:1080/sap(bD1kZSZjPTAwMA==)/bc/bsp/sap...

Figure 2.12 Resource is Loaded from Browser Cache

As this application bores us a little, we take a longer break from the content of this chapter and return eight days later to test the application once more. Looking at the results from our HTTP trace tool (Figure 2.13), we see that the server decided to send a new GET HTTP request to load the image (the copy it had has now expired) and was answered with an HTTP return code of 304.

Start Stop Clear Filter Copy Save About

Started	Time	S...	Met...	Result	Type	URL
00:00:00.000	0.078	570	GET	200	text/html...	http://us4049.wdf.sap.corp:1080/sap(bD1kZSZjPTAwMA==)/bc/bsp/sap...
00:00:00.093	0.004	252	GET	304	image/gif	http://us4049.wdf.sap.corp:1080/sap/public/bc/icons/s_B_OKAY.gif
00:00:08.057	0.059	363	POST	200	text/html...	http://us4049.wdf.sap.corp:1080/sap(bD1kZSZjPTAwMA==)/bc/bsp/sap...

Figure 2.13 Resource is Verified with the Server to be Valid

It is interesting to examine the GET HTTP request first.

```
GET /sap/public/bc/icons/s_B_OKAY.gif HTTP/1.1
Accept: */*
Accept-Language: de,en-us;q=0.5
Accept-Encoding: gzip, deflate
If-Modified-Since: Fri, 13 Aug 2004 12:17:27 GMT
User-Agent: Mozilla/4.0 (MSIE 6.0; Windows NT 5.1)
Host: us4049.wdf.sap.corp:1080
```

We see a relatively standard HTTP request, but with one new HTTP header: If-Modified-Since. This informs the server that the browser already has the object matching this URL and that the copy the browser has was last changed on Friday, August 13, 2004. This date matches the date from the Last-Modified header that was set when the resource was initially loaded.

The server looks at the If-Modified-Since header and compares this date against the last modified date of the actual resource. As the date matches exactly, the server answers with return code 302. Because the browser already has the correct resource, the Content-Length is set to zero, and the resource is not transmitted again. With this, the browser again has the resource for a valid period of seven days before it will check once more.

```
HTTP/1.1 304 Not Modified
Content-Type: image/gif
Content-Length: 0
Date: Sun, 25 Sep 2005 12:47:03 GMT
Last-Modified: Fri, 13 Aug 2004 12:17:27 GMT
Server: SAP Web Application Server/7.10
Cache-Control: max-age=604800
```

As images are usually cached in the server at the ICM level as well (in the kernel before the ABAP stack), these HTTP requests can be answered very quickly and do not place much load on the server.

2.9 Troubleshooting Examples

Knowing how HTTP works and having a good HTTP trace tool at hand, we are able to troubleshoot many different types of situations without even looking at the source code. In this section we will look at a few problems that we often encounter.

2.9.1 Missing Resource

The "little red X" is seen often (see Figure 2.14). It is very annoying, but actually very simple to at least isolate to specific URLs.

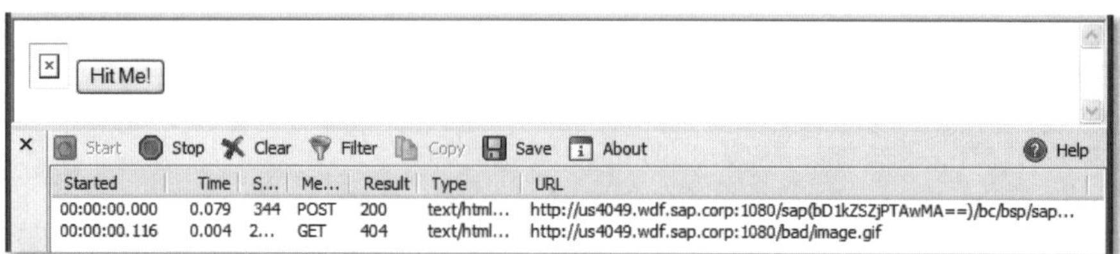

Figure 2.14 Troubleshooting a Missing Resource

Looking at the HTTP trace, we see that an HTTP request is first answered with a return code of 200, and the content type is set to text/html. This is an HTML page that contains a reference to an image. The next HTTP request attempts to load the image itself, and is answered with an HTTP return code of 404 (not found).

The 404 shows immediately that this is the HTTP request that was not loaded correctly. There are typically two problems that can account for this situation. The first is that the URL itself is not correct. In this case, use the Referer HTTP header from this request to see what HTML page contains the bogus link (always one higher up in the HTTP trace), and start there to investigate further. The other alternative is that the URL is correct, and the server has a problem answering the request for the resource. Paste this requested URL directly into the browser and debug the server side to resolve the issue.

2.9.2 Non-Secure Warnings

The warning message "page contains non-secure items" always causes calls for help. This warning message usually indicates that the website is been accessed via an https:// protocol, and that now one of the resources on the page is been requested via the http:// protocol. Let us look at the HTTP trace in Figure 2.15.

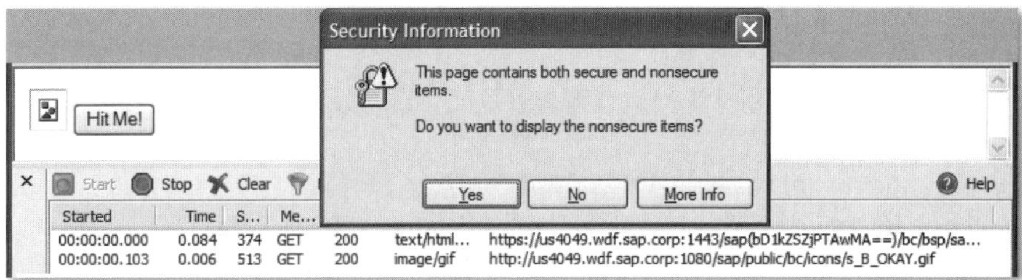

Figure 2.15 Troubleshooting Non-Secure Warnings

We can see that the last HTML page (type text/html) is loaded with https:// protocol. However, the next HTTP request (with a response of type image/gif) was with http:// protocol. This is the reason for the warning. Using the Referer HTTP header of the image, it is possible to easily cross reference it to the HTML page that requested this image and that contains the URL with the wrong protocol.

The other reason that we often see for this warning is that <iframe> tags are used on page with the src attribute set. This is a typical technique in HTML for later triggering the <iframe> loading dynamically.

2.9.3 Relative URLs That Become Invalid

The next example is from an application that worked for a long time. Then one day, the same application was not started under its usual URL, but via a short alias. Figure 2.16 shows the "little red X" and the corresponding HTTP trace.

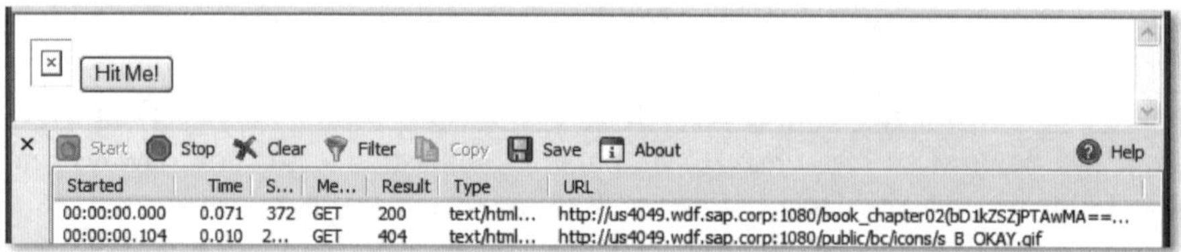

Figure 2.16 Troubleshooting Invalid URLs

We see already from the first HTTP request that it is not our usual /sap/bc/bsp path, but a much shorter alias. The next HTTP request for an image is now answered with an HTTP return code of 404, and a quick examination shows that the URL is wrong (the /sap segment is not specified). From this, we know that the URL is invalid. Let us look at the last response received for the HTML page.

```
HTTP/1.1 200 OK
Content-Type: text/html; charset=iso-8859-1
Content-Length: 186
Cache-Control: no-cache
Server: SAP Web Application Server (1.0;640)

<html><body><form method="POST">
   <img src="../../../../public/bc/icons/s_B_OKAY.gif">
   <input type="submit" value="Hit Me!">
</form></body></html>
```

We see in the HTTP response that the HTML page is requesting a relative URL ../../../../public/.... This URL on its own looks to be perfectly acceptable. However, from the HTTP trace we know that the URL of the requested HTML page is /book_chapter02(...)/exampleNN.html. Given this absolute URL, plus the relative URL specified, we now can see why the browser constructed the new URL /public/.... Effectively, the relative path stripped all tokens from the original URL until none were left. All other /.. sequences to specify the parent node are ignored, and then the browser starts again with the first token /public from the relative path to build the new URL.

In HTML pages, we recommend using absolute paths to public resources. If relative paths are used, then it should only be in the relative-as-child relationship, and not over the parent (/..) path.

2.9.4 Estimating Performance

In this section, we want to highlight other uses of an HTTP trace tool. Often, we are interested in having some performance numbers for a website. An HTTP trace can already help to get a rough estimate of a Web application's performance.

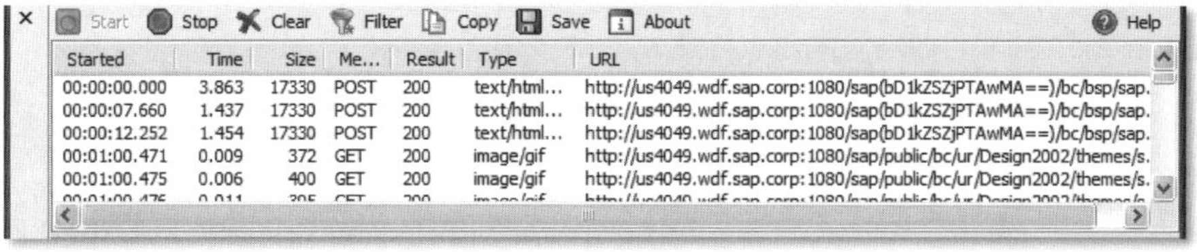

Start Stop Clear Filter Copy Save About Help

Started	Time	Size	Me...	Result	Type	URL
00:00:00.000	3.863	17330	POST	200	text/html...	http://us4049.wdf.sap.corp:1080/sap(bD1kZSZjPTAwMA==)/bc/bsp/sap.
00:00:07.660	1.437	17330	POST	200	text/html...	http://us4049.wdf.sap.corp:1080/sap(bD1kZSZjPTAwMA==)/bc/bsp/sap.
00:00:12.252	1.454	17330	POST	200	text/html...	http://us4049.wdf.sap.corp:1080/sap(bD1kZSZjPTAwMA==)/bc/bsp/sap.
00:01:00.471	0.009	372	GET	200	image/gif	http://us4049.wdf.sap.corp:1080/sap/public/bc/ur/Design2002/themes/s.
00:01:00.475	0.006	400	GET	200	image/gif	http://us4049.wdf.sap.corp:1080/sap/public/bc/ur/Design2002/themes/s.

Figure 2.17 Troubleshooting Performance of HTTP Requests

In Figure 2.17, we can see the number of requests, the size in bytes that each request retrieves from the server, the resources that are loaded, and whether in subsequent testing these resources are cached or continuously reloaded. For example, the same HTML page was loaded three times, and in all three cases 17,330 bytes were loaded. However, the first request took 3.8 seconds to complete, while each of the other two requests took only 1.4 seconds. As the pages rendered the same (sized) HTML output, it looks as though initialization of the page on the first request took a long time. These measurements are round-trip latencies, and reflect the time to transfer data to the server, process the data, and respond to the server.

3 HTTP Handler

Understanding the underlying structure of the ICF tree and its inner implementation through handler classes is a powerful addition to any BSP developer's toolbox. Handler classes are especially useful because they allow for direct access and complete control over the HTTP request and response objects.

3.1 URL Handling in the ICF Tree

A Web server is like a large shopping center where thousands of incoming customers are all asking for specific shops. In the case of the Web server, we have thousands of incoming requests, all asking to be processed. The problem is how to dispatch each HTTP request to the correct handler.

This is the work of the Internet Communication Framework (ICF). The ICF takes the URL from the HTTP request and splits it into tokens. The tokens are used to route the HTTP request through a tree of services.

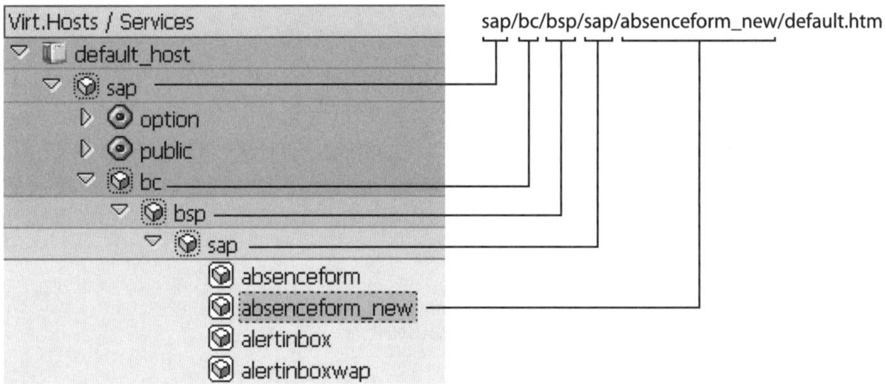

Figure 3.1 URL to ICF Tree Mapping

Each node within the ICF tree can be configured to contain zero or more HTTP handlers. The handlers are processed in sequence, until one handler signals that it has processed the request completely. After that, the HTTP response is returned to the browser. The sequence of processing is primarily from the root node down, and then secondarily in sequence for each node. You effectively process all handlers for the specific node (one can use the expression that the handlers are chained), and then go to the next deeper node. A node does not require a handler. If no handler is found on a specific node, the next deeper node is checked.

For example, in Figure 3.1, the nodes `sap` and `bc` have no handlers. The node `bsp` contains the BSP runtime handler. It will look at the incoming HTTP request and process it completely. Because the BSP runtime indicates to the ICF that the request has been fully processed, no further searching is done through lower levels of the ICF tree.

The important concept to grasp is that ICF uses the tokens one by one to navigate deeper into the handler tree until one handler signals that the HTTP request has been processed. The rest of the URL is then not considered at all. The feature also can be used to embed data into the URL as part of the URL segments. It is simply a question of what the receiving handler will do with the rest of the URL, which is considered to be effectively data (one string) passed to the handler.

Note The usual problem of one global namespace, and how to segment it, also applies to the ICF tree and in effect to the domain of all possible URLs. Here, the agreement that is enforced is that all SAP development take place within the `/sap` sub-tree. At the next level, the `bc` node represents SAP basis development. Similarly, it is expected that customers will do their development under a `/customer` namespace.

3.2 URL Mapping

For each handler, it is important to know what part of the URL was used to find the handler and to have the rest of the URL available to make its own decision on what actions it wishes to take. ICF makes this information available in special header fields. These header fields are added to the incoming request by ICF, and are not actually part of the original request.

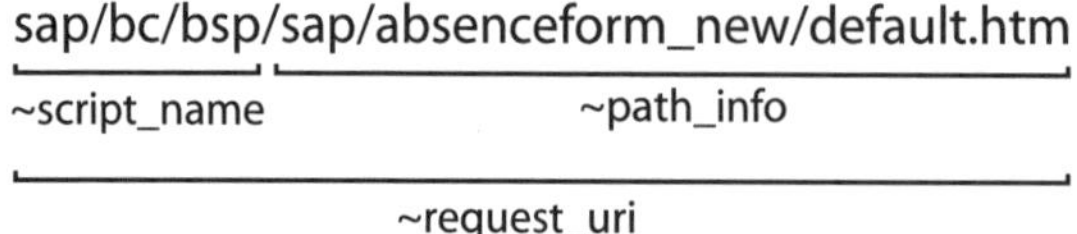

Figure 3.2 URL Separation into Request Headers

The three most interesting fields are:

- `~request_uri`: This is the complete URL requested from the browser.
- `~script_name`: This is the first part of the URL that was used to navigate through the ICF tree until this specific handler was found.
- `~path_info`: The rest of the URL that has not yet been used to resolve a handler. The handler uses it to decide what action to take.

In Section 3.4, the other fields will be discussed in detail with a small example.

3.3 Sample Handler for Reading Images

An HTTP handler is a normal ABAP class that implements the interface IF_HTTP_EXTENSION with one method HANDLE_REQUEST. Once the ICF has found a node that contains a handler, the class is instantiated and called to process the request. As an input parameter, this method gets a server object, which is effectively a wrapper object containing the HTTP request and response objects.

This information should already be sufficient for us to create a first simple HTTP handler. We will use the following test case: We have many pictures already stored in a database, and we want to make them accessible in the browser. In our BSP pages, we would like to have a symbolic way to reference these pictures. What we would like to write, is something like:

```
<%@page language="abap"%>
<html>
   <body>
      <image src="/my/images/ICON_ARROW_LEFT">
      <image src="/my/images/ICON_ARROW_RIGHT">
   </body>
</html>
```

The results we would expect to see in the browser are displayed in Figure 3.3.

Figure 3.3 Example Results

For the actual HTTP handler, we start this example by creating the class YCL_IMAGE_HANDLER and specifying that it implements the interface IF_HTTP_EXTENSION. For the HANDLE_REQUEST method, we will start with some very simple placeholder coding to test that we have all the pieces in order.

```
METHOD if_http_extension~handle_request.
  if_http_extension~flow_rc = if_http_extension=>co_flow_ok.
  server->response->set_status( code = 200 reason = 'OK' ).
  server->response->set_cdata(
                  '<html><body>Hello World!</body></html>' ).
ENDMETHOD.
```

The flow-return code informs the ICF that we have finished processing the request and have written a complete response. For this simple example we do not set any of the content specific headers and rely on the default behavior of ICM. This is not recommended for actual production programs. The only value that we set explicitly is the HTTP return code (value `200` implies it is OK for HTTP traffic). The last line is the classic *Hello World!* for Web servers.

We now have a handler class that will respond with valid HTML coding when called. We now must decide where we wish to place this handler in the ICF tree. The handler is not a BSP application and therefore should not be placed under `/sap/bc/bsp`. We have seen that our images are loaded from a path `/my/images`. Thus, we must effectively create these two nodes within the ICF tree and can theoretically put our new handler on any of the two nodes. However, we might later want to install other handlers below the `/my/` path, so let us put our handler on the next node.

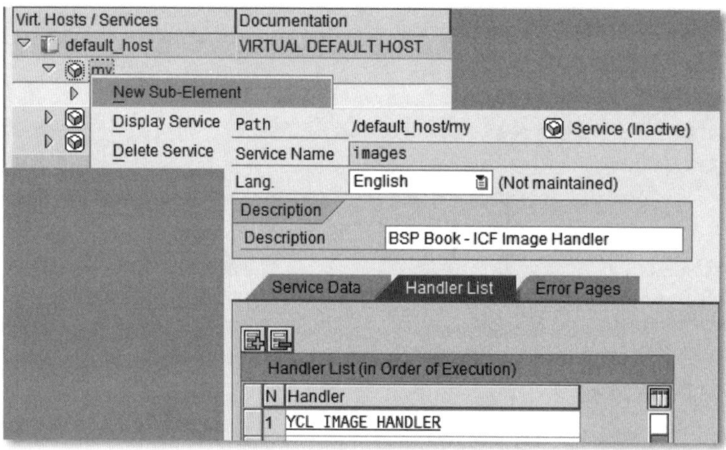

Figure 3.4 Creation of New Handler Class Node

With this, we have defined a new HTTP handler. We activate the node and use the context menu to start a test for this node. In our output we should see our simple *Hello World!* placeholder.

We can see from Figure 3.5 that our handler works for all types of URLs that start with `/my/images`. The `~script_name` part of the URL is used to find the handler. The rest of the URL, `~path_info`, is ignored by the handler at this time.

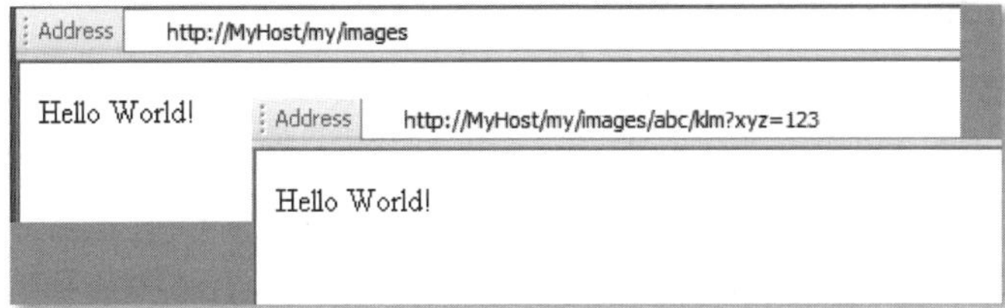

Figure 3.5 Handler Initial Output

3.3.1 URL Syntax

There are two ways that URLs can be defined. We could use the rest of the URL to contain additional information we need. For example, we could expect `/my/images/NAME` where `NAME` is the image we will display. The other option is to apply parameters to the URL to define the image required. In this case, our URL would be `/my/images?name=NAME`. Both techniques are similar, but the first is more elegant and slightly shorter.

You remember from our initial code that we placed the images directly on our BSP page. This required us to know exactly where in the ICF tree this handler is installed. However, this is not very flexible for future changes and opens the possibility of typing mistakes. What we really want is a method that can generate the correct URLs for us. Should we later decide to change anything in our system setup (using for example an external image server), we only need to update the URL generator once.

We will add a new static public method `URL( )` to the class, with `name` as the import parameter, and `url` as the return parameter. Both are type STRING. The complete source code is:

```
METHOD url.
   CONCATENATE '/my/images/' name INTO url.
ENDMETHOD.
```

You might be tempted to consider appending `.gif` onto the URL to help the browser determine what type of image it is loading. However, this is not required. The browser will use the `Content-Type` header from the loaded images to determine the image type.

With our new URL generator, use of our images can now be done with less possibility of typing mistakes with this sequence:

```
<image src="<%=YCL_IMAGE_HANDLER=>URL(
                                   'ICON_ARROW_LEFT' )%>">
```

3.3.2 Handler Coding

We are now ready to write the core logic of the handler itself, most of which resides in the single method HANDLE_REQUEST. The HANDLE_REQUEST method can be broken into four distinctive parts, each with fewer than ten lines of code!

We start by informing ICF that this handler has finished processing the HTTP request. Due to the use of the URL( ) static method to build our URLs, we expect that most HTTP requests will be correct. If any errors occur, we just raise an exception.

```
METHOD if_http_extension~handle_request.
  if_http_extension~flow_rc = if_http_extension=>co_flow_ok.
```

Next, we must determine the required image. The ~path_info header field contains the part of the string that has not yet been used by ICF. Keep in mind that the beginning of the URL was used to find this node in the ICF. The string is determined and manipulated slightly: uppercase conversion, strip leading /-character, etc.

To avoid hard-coding the name of the ~path_info header field, we use instead the interface IF_HTTP_HEADER_FIELDS_SAP. We actually have two interfaces IF_HTTP_HEADER_FIELDS_SAP and IF_HTTP_HEADER_FIELDS to cover all the possible header field names via public constants.

```
* Determine image name from ~path_info (= image_name)
  DATA: name TYPE string.
  name = server->request->get_header_field(
       name = if_http_header_fields_sap=>path_info ).
  TRANSLATE name TO UPPER CASE.
  IF STRLEN( name ) >= 1 AND name(1) = '/'.
     SHIFT name LEFT.
  ENDIF.
```

Up to now, all code has used relatively common handling of HTTP requests. A little application logic is now required to determine the graphics interchange format (GIF) image and load it. Starting this block of code, we have the name of the image as input and expect an XSTRING containing the GIF image as output. The exact storage mode and location are not relevant to our discussion here.

Error handling is done with the usual ABAP exceptions. The ICF has an exception handler installed, and will correctly render out an error message should we encounter any problems loading the image content.

```
* Application logic
  DATA: content TYPE xstring.
  content = me->load( name ).
  IF XSTRLEN( content ) IS INITIAL.
     RAISE EXCEPTION TYPE cx_http_ext_exception
           EXPORTING msg = 'Invalid URL!'.
  ENDIF.
```

The last part of the handler is the HTTP response-handling. First, we set the HTTP return code to 200. This is the defined code to indicate that the HTTP request was processed correctly (see Chapter 2). HTTP status code descriptions can be found in the global interface IF_HTTP_STATUS. The Content-Type header is set to indicate that this is a GIF image.

```
* Set up HTTP response
  server->response->set_status( code = 200 reason = 'OK' ).
  server->response->set_header_field(
    name = if_http_header_fields=>content_type
    value = 'image/gif' ).
  server->response->server_cache_expire_rel(
    expires_rel = 86000 ).
  server->response->set_header_field(
    name = if_http_header_fields=>cache_control
    value = 'max-age=86000' ).
  server->response->set_data( content ).
ENDMETHOD.
```

Notice that the Content-Length header is not set. It will automatically be set when the HTTP response is streamed to ICM. In addition, some older kernel versions present a minor problem. If the Content-Length is set and the HTTP response is gzip encoded, then the Content-Length is not reset. This causes the browser to wait indefinitely on the rest of the input.

The HTTP response is flagged so that both the browser and the server will cache it. Caching the image also in the ICM improves performance when the next user requests the same image.

The final statement places the content into the HTTP response. Notice that there are methods for handling both XSTRINGs, set_data and append_data, as well as STRINGs, set_cdata and append_cdata.

The handler is finished, so let us try our test program.

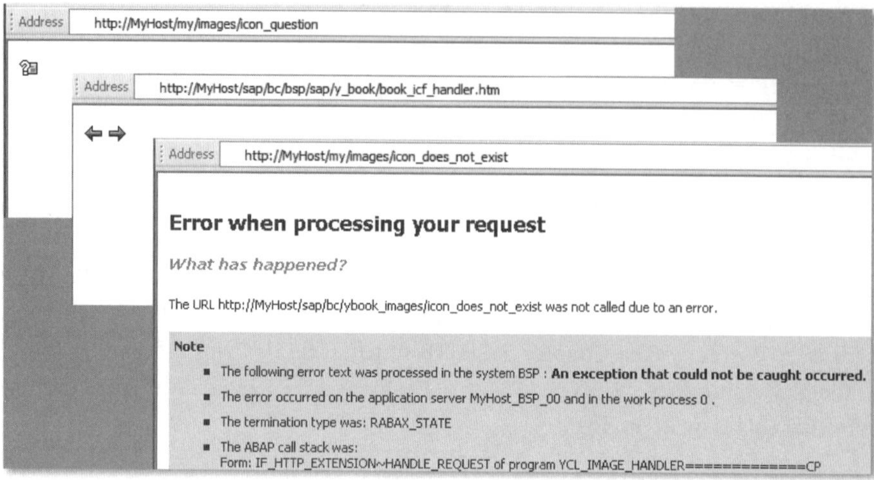

Figure 3.6 Handler Final Output

For our first test, we enter a URL to a new image in the browser directly, and see that the new image is displayed as well. Notice that this URL contains no `.gif` extension. Nevertheless, the browser knows that it is an image due to the `Content-Type` header. For our final test, we enter an illegal URL. Remember the check for this plus the `raise exception` sequence. The ICF returns an error page for the caught exception.

3.4 Alias Handling

As we have seen, the exact URL has an important meaning for mapping onto the handler list. However, a deep hierarchy of nodes in ICF leads to lengthy URLs which reduce the usability of your application. Luckily, there is an alias technique that can be used to reduce the length of the URL while still maintaining the service hierarchy.

This alias type is created as a normal ICF node from within transaction SICF by selecting **Reference to an Existing Service**. It has no associated handler class, but just points to another place in the ICF tree where the URL resolving is continued.

ICF also supports the concept of external aliases. These are treated as local configurations, whereby string comparisons are made against the incoming URLs and are matched against external aliases, which again point back into the ICF tree. The difference is that, while normal aliases are considered development objects that are also transported through the landscape, external aliases are simply local configuration data.

As HTTP handler writers, we are very dependent on the URL form and structure to decide what the actual request is. However, developers and system administrators have a different aesthetic sense and can create URLs that have no relationship to those we are used to.

Let us look at a small example. In the first step, we write a small handler class that will just echo back to us all the different header fields set by the ICF framework (all start with '~'). The complete source code is only a few lines long.

```
METHOD if_http_extension~handle_request.
  if_http_extension~flow_rc = if_http_extension=>co_flow_ok.

  DATA: hfs  TYPE tihttpnvp,
        hf   TYPE  ihttpnvp,
        html TYPE string.

  server->request->get_header_fields(CHANGING fields = hfs).

  html = '<html><body><table>'.
  LOOP AT hfs INTO hf WHERE name CS '~'.
    CONCATENATE html
      '<tr><td>' hf-name '</td><td>' hf-value '</td></tr>
    INTO html.
  ENDLOOP.
  CONCATENATE html '</table></body></html>' INTO html.

  server->response->set_status( code = 200 reason = 'OK' ).
  server->response->set_header_field(
         name  = if_http_header_fields=>content_type
         value = 'text/html' ).
  server->response->set_cdata( html ).
ENDMETHOD.
```

This handler is placed into the ICF tree on the path /my/echo. We then add a new node abc without a handler below /my/echo. With the URL /my/echo/abc in the browser, the ICF framework will also match the abc from the URL against the node in the tree, and test that this node is active before starting the handler. Should a customer not wish to have service abc active, it can simply be deactivated, and ICF will correctly answer the incoming HTTP request. Now, with a path /my/echo/xyz, ICF will match only the first two segments, find them active, and start the handler.

This is why BSP adds a node to the ICF tree for each BSP application. At runtime, BSP verifies that the specific application actually started does have a node in the ICF tree. With this approach, only one handler is installed in the ICF tree, but all applications are shown, with each application capable of being deactivated (this is the default case when shipped).

Given the nodes along the path `/my/echo/abc` in the ICF tree, we create an additional alias in the ICF tree `/sap/public/123` that points directly onto our path `/my/echo/abc`.

With this ICF configuration, one possibility is to call our handler with the path `/my/echo/abc/klm/xyz`. The handler will be found after processing the nodes `/my/echo`, leaving the sequence `/abc/klm/xyz` as `~path_info`.

Let us look more closely at our alternative ICF path. In this case, it is possible to call the handler with the URL `/sap/public/123/klm/xyz`. Keep in mind that we specifically created the alias with a name that is more meaningful to us . In this case, the ICF runtime will use `/sap/public/123` to find the alias for `/my/echo/abc`, where the handler is also found. The remainder of the URL for the `~path_info` is only `/klm/xyz`. The `/abc` segment was never in the URL and never visible at any time. Should our echo handler have required three segments in the URL, the `~path_info` would definitely have made it fail. See Figure 3.7 for the output from the handler in two different cases.

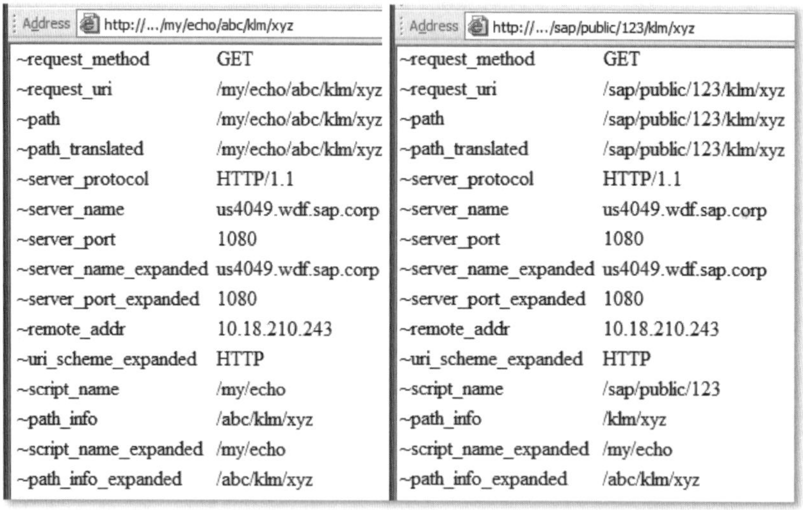

Address http://.../my/echo/abc/klm/xyz

~request_method	GET
~request_uri	/my/echo/abc/klm/xyz
~path	/my/echo/abc/klm/xyz
~path_translated	/my/echo/abc/klm/xyz
~server_protocol	HTTP/1.1
~server_name	us4049.wdf.sap.corp
~server_port	1080
~server_name_expanded	us4049.wdf.sap.corp
~server_port_expanded	1080
~remote_addr	10.18.210.243
~uri_scheme_expanded	HTTP
~script_name	/my/echo
~path_info	/abc/klm/xyz
~script_name_expanded	/my/echo
~path_info_expanded	/abc/klm/xyz

Address http://.../sap/public/123/klm/xyz

~request_method	GET
~request_uri	/sap/public/123/klm/xyz
~path	/sap/public/123/klm/xyz
~path_translated	/sap/public/123/klm/xyz
~server_protocol	HTTP/1.1
~server_name	us4049.wdf.sap.corp
~server_port	1080
~server_name_expanded	us4049.wdf.sap.corp
~server_port_expanded	1080
~remote_addr	10.18.210.243
~uri_scheme_expanded	HTTP
~script_name	/sap/public/123
~path_info	/klm/xyz
~script_name_expanded	/my/echo
~path_info_expanded	/abc/klm/xyz

Figure 3.7 Handler Output for two URL Tests

From this example, we see that the use of `~script_name` and `~path_info` could in specific cases lead to the wrong result. These fields reflect the data from the

URL that the user enters into the browser and the path that was logically traversed to relate the URL to a handler. They do not reflect the true path within the ICF tree, which is what developers work against. For this, we must look at the fields `~script_name_expanded` and `~path_info_expanded`, which again has the correct values.

The other '~' fields are used from time to time; but not at the same critical level as these specific two fields.

3.5 Handler Example—Table Query

Although BSP is the focus of this book, we hope this small excursion into HTTP handler programming has been very useful. With only 20–40 lines of code, a new service can be plugged into the HTTP framework.

With such an HTTP handler, you are completely in control of the HTTP request and response, and can better control the exact rendering. For specific scenarios, the services of the BSP runtime are not required, so you can use this alternative technique of rendering directly.

In our last example, we returned the binary content of image. We also saw how we could render HTML directly in the previous example. But we could just as easily return XML. We now have the ability to build small data interfaces with the handler approach.

To explain this ability, we will take the first example and modify it. Instead of passing in the name of an image on the URL, we will pass the name of a database table instead. We will then query the records from this table, convert the results from an ABAP internal table to a binary XML stream, and then return this XML stream with the HTTP response.

We will even take this example one step further. Not only will the table name be passed on the URL, but we will support `WHERE` conditions for our table query to be passed as URL parameters. Therefore the following URL would generate the output in Figure 3.8.

```
http://<host>/my/book_query/sflight?carrid=AA&connid=0064
```

One word of warning: This is a very powerful handler that should not be installed in a system unless the necessary precautions are taken. At a minimum, the code *must* be extended to include an authorization check. Also, *never* run this code on any public node. The handler effect provides direct database access. It is similar to a hex editor. It is hardly ever required, but it is the only tool for this particular job.

Address http://MyHost/my/book_query/sflight?carrid=AA&connid=0064


```
<?xml version="1.0" encoding="utf-8" ?>
- <asx:abap xmlns:asx="http://www.sap.com/abapxml" version="1.0">
  - <asx:values>
    - <ITAB>
      - <SFLIGHT>
          <MANDT>088</MANDT>
          <CARRID>AA</CARRID>
          <CONNID>0064</CONNID>
          <FLDATE>2004-11-19</FLDATE>
          <PRICE>422.94</PRICE>
          <CURRENCY>USD</CURRENCY>
          <PLANETYPE>A310-300</PLANETYPE>
          <SEATSMAX>280</SEATSMAX>
          <SEATSOCC>267</SEATSOCC>
          <PAYMENTSUM>130358.67</PAYMENTSUM>
          <SEATSMAX_B>22</SEATSMAX_B>
          <SEATSOCC_B>21</SEATSOCC_B>
          <SEATSMAX_F>10</SEATSMAX_F>
          <SEATSOCC_F>9</SEATSOCC_F>
        </SFLIGHT>
      - <SFLIGHT>
          <MANDT>088</MANDT>
          <CARRID>AA</CARRID>
          <CONNID>0064</CONNID>
          <FLDATE>2004-12-17</FLDATE>
```


Figure 3.8 Table Query Handler Output

3.5.1 Table Query Handler Implementation

We begin our process much the same way as our first example. We still pull the table name out of the URL just like we extracted the image name earlier. Thereafter, we collect all URL parameters for our WHERE condition.

```
* Determine table name from URL ~path_info (= Table Name)
  data: name type string.
  name = server->request->get_header_field(
      name = if_http_header_fields_sap=>path_info ).
  translate name to upper case.
  if strlen( name ) >= 1 and name(1) = '/'.
    shift name left.
  endif.
  server->request->get_form_fields(
                              CHANGING fields = m_parameters ).
```

All we need now is the call to the application-specific logic and then the buidling of the HTTP response that we had in the original example. The only difference now is that, because we are retrieving dynamic data instead of static image content, we do not activate the server and client caching of the response.

```
* Application logic
  DATA: content TYPE xstring.
  content = me->load( name ).
  IF XSTRLEN( content ) IS INITIAL.
    RAISE EXCEPTION TYPE cx_http_ext_exception
          EXPORTING msg = 'Invalid URL!'.

  ENDIF.
  server->response->set_data( content ).
```

This time, however, let us take a closer look at the application logic. We will start the application logic by dynamically creating an internal table that matches the database table we are going to select from.

```
DATA: itab TYPE REF TO data.
FIELD-SYMBOLS: <tab> TYPE table.
CREATE DATA itab TYPE TABLE OF (i_name).
ASSIGN itab->* TO <tab>.
```

Next, we will take the parameters that we have pulled out of the URL and use them to build the database query.

```
FIELD-SYMBOLS: <wa_parameter> TYPE t_parameter.
DATA cond_syntax TYPE string.
LOOP AT m_parameters ASSIGNING <wa_parameter>.
  CONCATENATE cond_syntax <wa_parameter>-name
              ` = '` <wa_parameter>-value `'`
         INTO cond_syntax.
  IF sy-tabix = sy-tfill.
  ELSE.
    CONCATENATE cond_syntax ` and ` INTO cond_syntax.
  ENDIF.
ENDLOOP.
IF cond_syntax IS INITIAL.
  SELECT * FROM (i_name) INTO TABLE <tab>.
ELSE.
  SELECT * FROM (i_name) INTO TABLE <tab>
   WHERE (cond_syntax).
ENDIF.
```

Now that we have our data in an internal table, we just need to convert it to XML.

```
DATA: g_ixml TYPE REF TO if_ixml,
      g_stream_factory TYPE REF TO if_ixml_stream_factory,
```

```
      g_encoding TYPE REF TO if_ixml_encoding.
CONSTANTS encoding TYPE string VALUE 'UTF-8'.
DATA: resstream TYPE REF TO if_ixml_ostream,
      ressize TYPE i VALUE 0.
****Create an instance of the Ixml Processor
g_ixml = cl_ixml=>create( ).
****Create the Stream Factory
g_stream_factory = g_ixml->create_stream_factory( ).
****Create an Endcoding and Byte Order
g_encoding = g_ixml->create_encoding(
  character_set = encoding   byte_order = 0 ).
****Create the output stream with a pointer to our binary
resstream = g_stream_factory->create_ostream_xstring(
  r_content ).
****Set the Encoding into a stream
  resstream->set_encoding( encoding = g_encoding ).
****Call Transformation using the simple XSLT id_indent
  CALL TRANSFORMATION id_indent
    SOURCE     itab = <tab>   RESULT XML resstream.
```

The returned XML content works well if you want to use this handler for some sort of data interface, but the XML output is not particularly human- readable. This is a problem with a simple solution. We can add some logic that will further convert our XML stream into HTML using XSLT.

We do not want to have to create a whole new handler class for just this one slight branch in our logic. Instead we will just create another ICF service but use the same handler class for it.

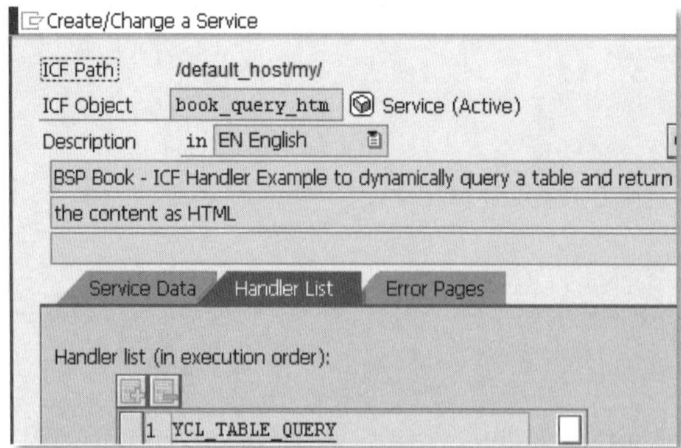

Figure 3.9 Second ICF Service Linked to the Same Handler Class

In the coding of our handler class, we can now check for the unique portion of our URL and branch our logic accordingly.

```
IF i_server->request->get_header_field(
   name = if_http_header_fields_sap=>request_uri )
   CS 'book_query_htm'.
    DATA: xsource TYPE xstring.
    xsource = r_content.
    CLEAR r_content.
    CALL TRANSFORMATION xmlgroup
       SOURCE XML xsource
       RESULT XML r_content.
ENDIF.
```

For this example, we have used an SAP's XSLT program called `XMLGROUP` for conversion from XML to HTML.

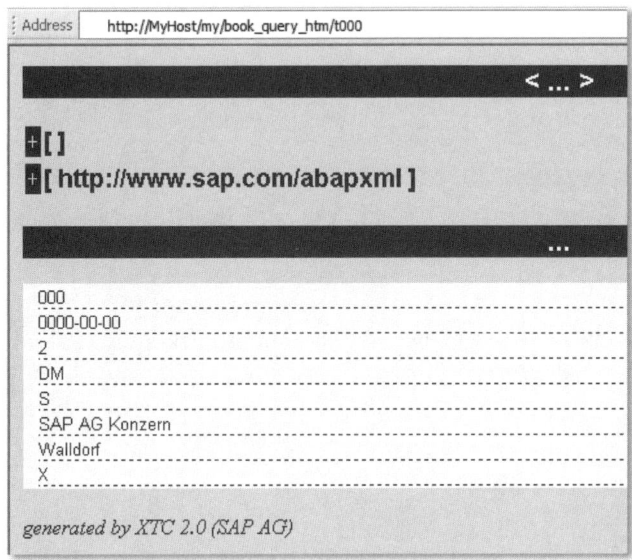

Figure 3.10 Table Query Handler Output—HTML

4 URLs in BSP

The URL is a versatile part of any Web application. It is the entry point, transaction code, and command-line interface equivalents all rolled together. In this chapter, we will look at certain unique aspects of the URL, such as URL mangling and Fully Qualified Domain Names, in the context of BSP.

4.1 URL Mangling

4.1.1 What is URL Mangling?

When accessing a website, the URL of the page usually is shown exactly as entered. However, once a URL is entered for BSP applications, it has a nasty habit of changing itself quickly.

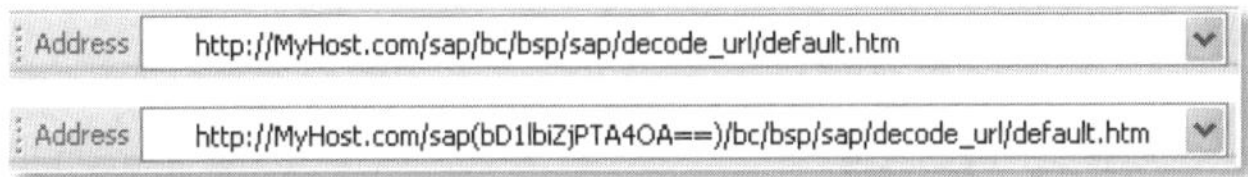

Figure 4.1 BSP URL Before and After a Change by BSP Runtime

This process is called URL mangling, and it is worth looking at it in more detail.

The first question is always *what is hidden inside the URL*. Usually, the current logon client and language are written into the URL. However, additional onfiguration information is stored inside the URL from time to time. Typical examples are the theme in use, portal start-up information and, in extreme cases, a session ID.

SAP provides a small BSP application called `decode_url/default.htm` to decode the mangling.

Figure 4.2 decode_url—a BSP Application that Decodes the URL Mangling

The second question is: *Why* did SAP introduce this mangling? During Web AS 6.10 development, a theme concept was devised whereby specific objects in the MIME repository can be overwritten into different themes. For each BSP application, a cookie is set with all relevant information. However, this cookie is set exactly to the matching URL of the BSP application and is not sent by the browser when the MIME repository is accessed (`/sap/something_else/...`).

The logic behind this concept is that you could have more than one active BSP application at the same time, and each application must convey its own configuration information over different stateless HTTP GET requests to the MIME repository. As the same MIME repository URL is accessed, it is not possible to set different cookies in different windows of the browser, locked onto the same path. The only reliable solution was to encode information into the URL.

Encoding information into the URL has proved to be very useful in some cases, but in others has made life difficult. Currently, this coding is so deeply engrained into the BSP runtime that for Web AS 6.20 and 6.40 it is impossible to reverse the situation. We must accept that URL mangling is a fact of life and that it cannot be switched off or prevented.

4.1.2 How is URL Mangling Done?

For the first request into the server, the BSP runtime sees that the URL is not in mangled form. In this case, an HTTP redirect is done, with the mangled URL as the new location. In the new URL, all relevant configuration information is encoded.

A small HTTP trace, with all irrelevant headers deleted, shows this process:

```
GET /sap/bc/bsp/sap/it00/default.htm HTTP/1.1
User-Agent: Mozilla/4.0 (compatible; MSIE 6.0)
Host: MyHost.com:80

HTTP/1.1 302 Moved temporarily
Content-Length: 25
Location: /sap(bD1lbiZjPTAwMA==)/bc/bsp/sap/it00/default.htm
Content-Type: text/html

GET /sap(bD1lbiZjPTAwMA==)/bc/bsp/sap/it00/default.htm HTTP/1.1
User-Agent: Mozilla/4.0 (compatible; MSIE 6.0)
Host: MyHost.com:80

HTTP/1.1 200 OK
Content-Length: 336
Content-Type: text/html

...content...
```

We see that the first request is received without URL mangling. The server answers with a redirect—HTTP return code 302—and supplies the new URL. On the next HTTP request, the browser accesses the server with the new, mangled URL.

4.1.3 Attempting to Hide the URL Mangling

The nature of the BSP framework makes it impossible to disable the URL mangling. However, you can *hide* the mangling. Consider the following HTML code snippet:

```
<frameset>
 <frame src="http://<host>/sap/bc/bsp/sap/it00/default.htm">
</frameset>
```

Effectively, this loads a frameset into the browser, which loads the application into a frame. Inside the browser, we now have a stable URL (in this example loaded from local disk of the client machine) and the mangled URL is hidden inside the <frame>.

Figure 4. 3 shows the results of this action in the browser. We can see that the loaded URL has not changed and we see the original URL only via the properties page.

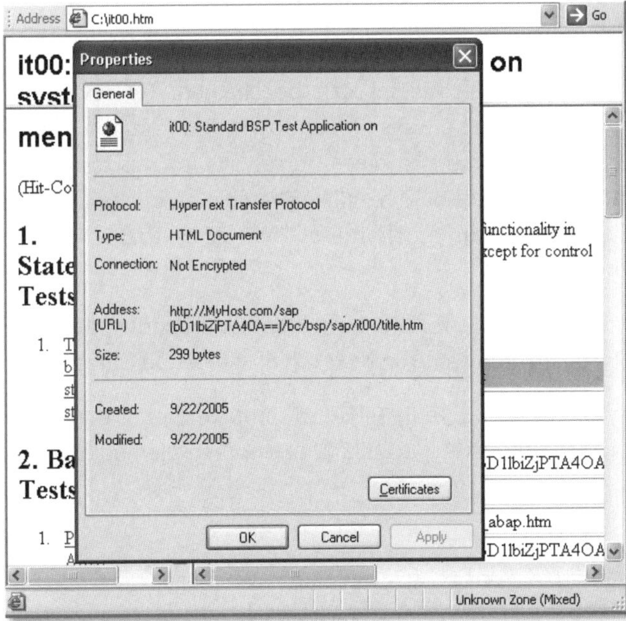

Figure 4.3 Hiding the URL Mangling Using a Frameset

However, it is difficult to distribute such a file to all users. We must insert this frameset directly before the application is loaded.

Let us look briefly at the process that is followed when an application is started. The URL from the incoming HTTP request is matched segment-for- segment against the ICF tree. On each node of the tree, you can specify a handler class for the URL. For the BSP node, we have already defined one handler that will be executed for all BSP applications. Figure 4.4 shows the BSP handler within the ICF tree.

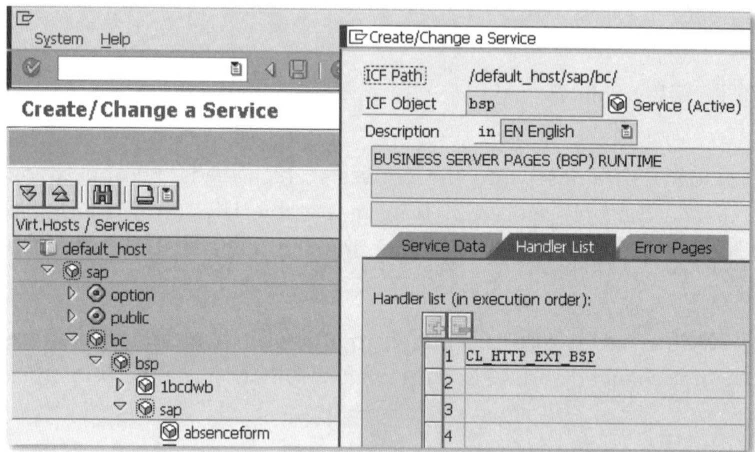

Figure 4.4 Standard BSP Handler Class

As we learned in Chapter 3, handler classes can be chained. However, the sequence for processing handler classes always moves downward from the root of the ICF tree. This means that if we want to place ourselves into this chain, we would require a new handler before the BSP handler. The new handler will intercept the initial request and write out the frameset first. After that, the next request is processed as usual.

First, you must write a small handler class. All that the handler class must do is signal that it has finished processing and that the next handler must be called.

Create a new class `YCL_BSP_EX_HIDE_URL_MANGLING` implementing the interface `IF_HTTP_EXTENSION`. For the `HANDLE_REQUEST` method, implement the following code:

```
if_http_extension~flow_rc =
                      if_http_extension=>co_flow_ok_others_mand.
```

Save and activate.

Now that we have our HTTP request handler completed, let us insert this into the ICF tree. But beware: For this example we are making a modification to an ICF node that is a transportable change. Only try this in a development system!

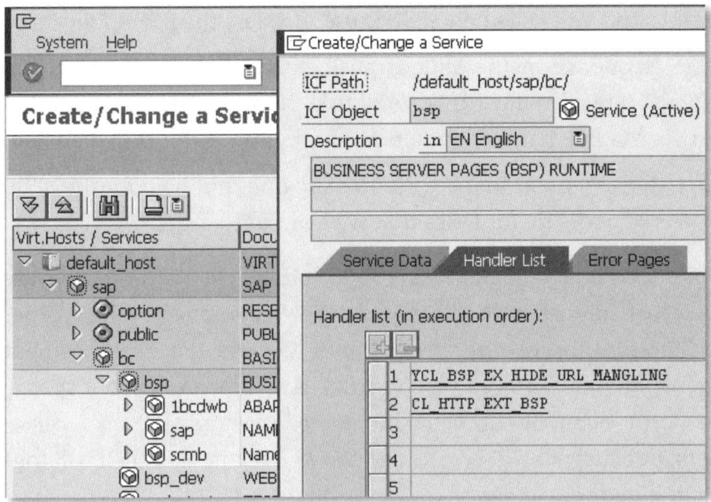

Figure 4.5 New BSP Handler Assignment

Test with any BSP application. Each time, the new handler will be called before the BSP handler is called.

The most difficult aspect now is ensuring that this new handler class will recognize the first request instead of all other requests. A number of techniques exist, but none are 100 % perfect.

- Assume that all the BSP applications are stateful. The first HTTP request will open a session; all other HTTP requests will run into an existing session. However, stateless applications and their support is an absolute must for scalable Internet applications.
- Use the "Referer:" HTTP header field to see whether the new incoming HTTP request is from our running BSP application. This would mean that it is not a first request. This is a very promising approach, but still will not be 100 % reliable. There exist HTTP proxies and firewall technologies that excel in stripping these header fields.
- Use a cookie that is set on the first incoming HTTP request. On all subsequent requests, the browser sends this additional cookie. It fails when a new browser window is opened, as the cookie also applies for the new window. However, typical experience shows that new windows are usually popup windows, where the toolbars are hidden.

- Use a special start URL. Usually the BSP application is started with /namespace/application/page.ext as part of the URL. Consider distributing bookmarks where the page is not specified. The default start page is usually specified for a BSP application and can be queried on the first request to rebuild a new URL. This will fail when SE80 is used to start the BSP application.
- Consider the "()"-sequence in the URL as an indicator that the redirect has already happened. Here, you must be careful to exclude MIME resources that are also loaded via the BSP handler and do not always have the URL mangled.
- Add an extra signature segment to the URL. This still does not help for the SE80 test cases, but works perfectly for URLs that we send out.

None of the above techniques guarantees 100% success. In the end, you are forced to use a set of heuristics to distinguish the first request versus other requests reliably. For the purpose of this example, we use the extra-segment approach to demonstrate how this can be done. Let us assume that all our special URLs are of the form /sap/bc/bsp/~/namespace/application/page.ext. Just before emailing out such an URL, we added the /~/ segment, which will trigger our handler and hide the mangling.

```
METHOD if_http_extension~handle_request.

* Get URL to check for signature, possible for <frame>
  DATA: url TYPE string.
  url = server->request->get_header_field(
              if_http_header_fields_sap=>request_uri ).
  IF url NS '/~/'.
    if_http_extension~flow_rc =
                 if_http_extension=>co_flow_ok_others_mand.
    RETURN.
  ENDIF.

* Build HTML string for frameset
  DATA: html TYPE string.
  REPLACE '/~/' IN url WITH '/'.
  CONCATENATE `<html><frameset><frame src="` url
             `"></frameset></html>`
        INTO html.

* Set response
  server->response->set_cdata( data = html ).
  server->response->set_status( code = 200 reason = 'OK' ).
```

```
  server->response->set_header_field(
          name    = if_http_header_fields=>content_type
          value   = 'text/html' ).

* This handler finished processing request
  if_http_extension~flow_rc = if_http_extension=>co_flow_ok.

ENDMETHOD.
```

However, we need to keep in mind a few negative aspects of this solution:

- One additional round trip is required to first install the loader frame. In a LAN, this adds about 10–15ms to the time it takes for the application to be displayed.
- The additional round trip also implies the one-off cost of about 500 extra bytes (keep the HTTP headers of the request and response in mind). For each additional round trip, the extra cookie is transported.
- For each incoming request, the new ICF handler is triggered first before the BSP handler is called. This implies a small code overhead per request.
- A repair transport to the ICF node is required to insert the additional handler. This node still has SAP as the owner, and it does not fall into the customer's domain.

All of the above are minor overhead concerns compared to the latency added by the BSP runtime; they are listed here for technical precision. This approach is not an ideal solution, especially because using such a handler before the BSP handler requires a system modification. Even so, this investigation has been very instructive, both for understanding URL mangling and for exploring further the use of ICF handlers.

4.2 Fully Qualified Domain Names

One of the most common errors that new BSP developers encounter is what we call the *Fully Qualified Domain Name check* (FQDN).

In essence, FQDN requires that the host name be specified with a complete domain name when addressing the server. For example `http://MyHost.sap.com/sap/bc/bsp/sap/it00` instead of `http://MyHost/sap/bc/bsp/sap/it00`.

Usually, only the host name in the URL is required for the browser to determine the IP address to use. You can use a ping tool to verify this with any of your SAP servers.

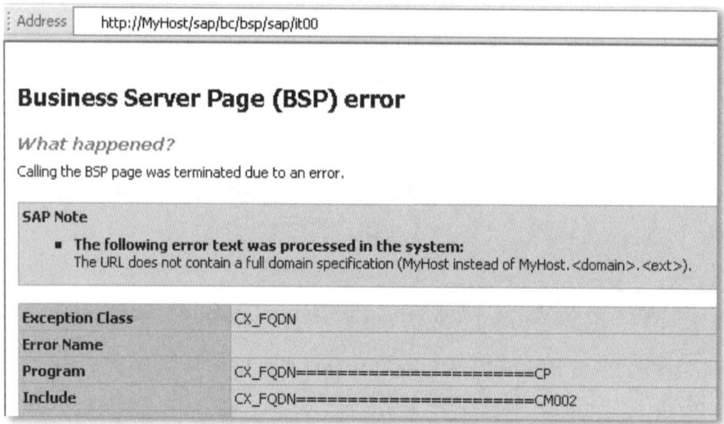

Figure 4.6 Fully Qualified Domain Name Error

In the first instance, the host-name part of the URL exists only so the browser can find a route to the Web server. Once on the Web server, the rest of the path starting at the first / is used to resolve the specific page to view. So why would BSP require a FQDN and other Web services would not?

4.2.1 Motivation for FQDN

The first important fact to understand is that the host name in the URL is effectively a routing string, which tells the browser how to reach the target. A typical situation is that a host might have an intranet name (example `ls0028.wdf.sap.corp`) that is totally different from the Internet name (example `bsp.sap.com`). This means that the FQDN is determined by the browser's position relative to the Web AS it is connecting to. The name entered in the URL is important for the SAP Web AS, as this tells us the route that was followed to the server.

This host name is always placed into the HTTP header (header field `Host:`). Information is available on the server concerning what the browser thinks the correct name is.

There are three reasons why the browser must access the Web Application Server (Web AS) with a fully qualified domain name:

- It is important for the use of the HTTPS protocol. Secure Sockets Layer (SSL) requires that the server and browser names match the names in the certificates.
- When setting cookies for a specific domain, it is important to know the domain the browser requires for the cookie, so that the cookie will always be returned

to the server. A typical example is the SSO2 cookie used for Single Sign-On (SSO) over multiple servers.

- For JavaScript calls to work over different frames (from different hosts in the same domain), each frame must relax its document domain. Typically, the host name is stripped, and the domain is set to the FQDN. For this to work, the browser must already know the FQDN for the document that it is retrieving. This information cannot be set from the server and must be correct from the beginning of the request. This concept of domain relaxation is especially important for BSP/portal integration.

Especially for the domain-relaxation aspect, the BSP runtime cannot know beforehand if the domain-relevant aspects will influence the application. If FQDN is not enforced, the door is open for many other types of more difficult-to-diagnose problems.

The above obstacles also prevent the acceptance of an IP address as host name, even although the browser can handle it correctly. In such cases, it is again impossible to set domain wide cookies correctly or to participate in cross-frame communications with a portal page.

4.2.2 ICM Configuration

Usually, FQDN and its use constitute a browser-related problem. The URL is entered at the browser and should be correct.

However, there are cases where a URL is created at the server. One typical example occurs when a BSP application is tested in the Development Workbench—SE80. A browser window is opened with the URL to test. In this case, of course, the URL must also be a FQDN.

By default, the ICM picks up the correct name and domain for the server from a domain name server (DNS). However, there are some cases where this does not work accurately. For these, ICM supports a profile parameter, `icm/host_name_full`. SAP recommends you configure this parameter. This is the host name that will be used to build fully qualified URLs.

4.2.3 Browser Requirements

In addition to the checks that the BSP runtime will enforce for FQDN, there are certain similar browser specifications that you should be aware of. These specifications effect BSP when cookies, SSOS, HTTPS, or portal integration come into play.

The browser has certain criteria that must be met before it will transmit a cookie back to the server. These criteria differ between Microsoft and Netscape. Both browsers require a domain specification. Netscape allows domains with the extension "com," "edu," "net," "org," "gov," "mil," or "int" to pass with only one additional domain component. For any other extension, the URL must contain at least two additional domain parts.

For example, *http://www.sap.com* is fine, whereas *http://www.sap.de* would not pass. You would need a URL like *http://www.bsp.sap.de* to pass the Netscape test.

Microsoft is less strict with its check. Internet Explorer allows domains with only one additional component, as long as that component has three or more characters in it. Therefore *http://www.sap.de* would now be fine, but *http://www.co.uk* would not.

To further complicate matters, Internet Explorer 6.0 or 5.5 with Security Patch MS01–055 will also reject domain names that contain an underscore.

4.3 Namespace Mapping

SAP decided that each BSP application must have its own node inside the ICF tree. This allows the ICF to also support additional functionality and configuration options for the individual BSP applications. Typically, you can activate or deactivate a specific BSP application via its corresponding ICF node. It is also possible to configure user-logon information for the specific BSP application in its ICF node.

However, the biggest motivation is that of security. With these sub-nodes checked and enforced by the BSP runtime to be available, the ICF runtime will actually have checked that all the nodes for the application are active, before starting the BSP runtime. This way, a higher level of security is reached by disabling all nodes for BSP applications that are not required. Nodes are, by default, shipped in a disabled state.

The usual problem of one global namespace, and how to segment it, also applies to the ICF tree and effectively applies to the domain of all possible URLs. Here, the enforced agreement is that all SAP development will be within the `/sap` subtree. At the next level, the `bc` node represents SAP NetWeaver development. Similarly, it is expected that customers will also do their own development under a `/customer` namespace.

SAP recommends that customers do register and create unique namespaces for their own development. This can be done on the Service Marketplace (*http://service.sap.com/namespaces*). However, for BSP development, customers can also follow the traditional Z & Y reserved object name range within the SAP namespace. Therefore the following situations are possible.

Scope	BSP Application	ICF Tree
SAP	`abc`	`/sap/bc/bsp/sap/abc`
CUSTOMER	`zabc`	`/sap/bc/bsp/sap/zabc`
CUSTOMER with registered namespace	`/company/abc`	`/sap/bc/bsp/company/abc`

Table 4.1 Namespace Patterns for BSP Development

For this exercise, we will simulate the use of a namespace by *borrowing* one of the SAP delivered namespaces. We will start by specifying the ABAP Workbench Generated Object namespace as we create our BSP application.

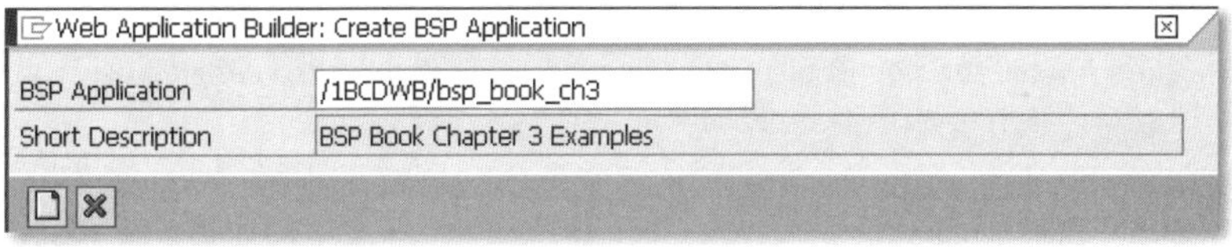

Figure 4.7 BSP Application Creation Within a Namespace

Now, when we navigate to transaction SICF and view the ICF tree, we should see a new path that has been generated to hold the objects within our namespace.

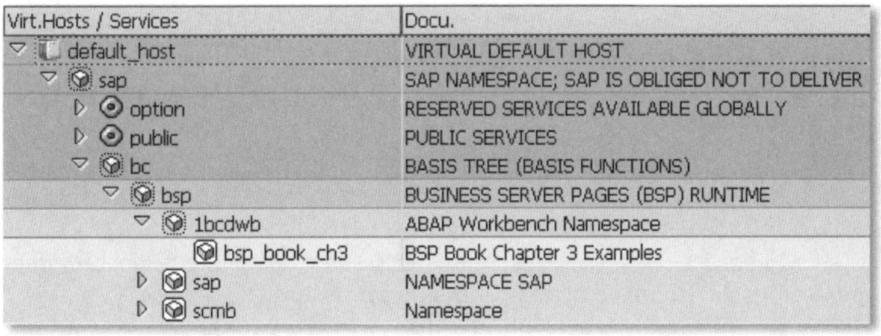

Figure 4.8 Namespace Entry in the ICF Tree

4.4 URL Parameters

Several specially named forms fields can be set as URL parameters. These can be used to set and control important system variables, such as the logon language and client. You might see them added to a standard BSP URL such as the following: `/sap/bc/bsp/sap/it00?sap-client=001&sap-language=DE` to start the BSP application `IT00` in client 001 in German.

URL Parameter	Description
sap-accessibility	Activation/deactivation of the accessibility flag for the HTMLB libraries. Activation of this option will cause additional tags and descriptions to be written into the rendered output in order to support screen readers for the visually impaired. Please note: This flag only expresses the wish for accessibility support. The application itself must contain the additional rendering logic to handle this case. If the HTMLB libraries are used, accessibility is handled correctly for the relevant rendered HTML.
sap-client	Sets the logon client. If specified, this parameter overrides the default client.
sap-htmlb-design	Allows you to set the HTMLB Design (see Chapter 9 for more details). This is the same as setting the attribute `design` of the element `<htmlb:content>`. Valid values are CLASSIC, 2002, or 2003. This parameter will only switch between designs that the application states it support, and cannot be used to force an application onto a design it was not tested with.
sap-language	Sets the logon language. The language value must be specified via the ISO language key.
sap-password	It is possible to logon to a BSP application by supplying the user name and password as URL parameters. However, be careful if you enter the password directly in the URL, as it will most likely be stored in your browser's history in clear text.
sap-rtl	This parameter activates/deactivates the flag for right-to-left rendering in the HTMLB libraries. This option is used to support proper rendering in languages such as Arabic. Please note: as with accessibility, this flag has only a meaning for the HTMLB rendering library. If you have hand-coded HTML on the page, you have to test this flag and add your own additional support.
sap-sessioncmd	This parameter sends actions to the session manager: `open`—starts a new session. `close` or `logoff`—ends the current application and redirects the browser to the URL supplied by the parameter sap-exiturl. `cancel`—is similar to close, but already handled by ICM. `usr_abort` and `usr_close`—is used by the portal to control BSP sessions.
sap-contextid	This is where the BSP runtime stores its session cookie. The session cookie groups requests into one common session for a stateful application. Can also be used as URL parameter, but not as form field inside the body of a `POST`.
sap-syscmd	The only value supported is `nocookie`. This tells the BSP runtime to mangle the session ID into the URL, and not use a cookie for handling the session id. This is especially required when the same stateful application must be run multiple times in situations where session `ids` in cookies would have resulted in all applications mapping onto the same session.

Table 4.2 URL Parameters

URL Parameter	Description
sap-theme	This is the same value that can be set from the **BSP application • Properties** tab. This is the older concept of theme for MIMEs that is deprecated and not be used anymore.
sap-themeRoot	This sets the themeRoot for the HTMLB libraries Design (see Chapter 9 and Chapter 17 for more details). This is the same as setting the attribute themeRoot of the element <htmlb:content>.
sap-trace	This allows you to trigger the activation of a developer runtime trace for the current application.
sap-user	It is possible to logon to a BSP application by supplying the user name and password as URL parameters.

Table 4.2 URL Parameters (cont.)

4.5 URL Escaping

We have already seen how special URL parameters are used to control system settings such as the logon language. However you also can use URL parameters to pass data from page to page or to initialize a value at the start of an application.

URLs have to be parsed by the browser and the server to process their separate sections of data. Characters such as /, ?, and & have special meanings when trying to process the information on the URL. What happens when the data that you want to pass along through a parameter also contains one of these special characters?

In such a situation the process of escaping comes into play. Escaping simply means that you replace the offending character with an escape sequence. This is similar process within HTML itself to include reserved or special characters.

Let us take for example the following fictional URL: http://www.sap.com?exit=http://sdn.sap.com. We have a parameter called exit with a value of `http://sdn.sap.com`. We know that we will need to encode this parameter as we add it to the URL. The results would be: `http://www.sap.com?exit=http%3a%2f%2fsdn%2esap%2ecom`, where `%3a` is the encoding for `:`, `%2f` for ' and `%2e` for `.`. Be careful that only the values are encoded; do not encode the full URL.

Luckily, we do not have to perform this conversion on our own. SAP offers a static method of class CL_HTTP_UTILITY called ESCAPE_URL.

```
DATA: url TYPE string.
url = cl_http_utility=>escape_url( `http://sdn.sap.com/` ).
CONCATENATE `reload.htm?exit=` url INTO url.
```

But there is an even simpler solution if you are going to be building a URL that links to another BSP application. In this case, you can use the static method of class CL_BSP_RUNTIME called CONSTRUCT_BSP_URL. This method has an importing parameter, IN_PARAMETER, which allows you pass in all your name/value pairs. This method then is responsible for assembling the complete URL, including the URL escaping.

5 Authentication

Authentication is very much like the game "Knock-Knock/Who's there?" that we played as children. Each HTTP request has to play this game before being processed. Although the question "Who's there" is simple, the answer can be complex. Let us explore this situation.

In Chapter 1, we showed the basic block diagram with the HTTP framework. The Internet Communication Manager (ICM) will accept HTTP requests from any browser, and then will pass them to the Internet Communication Framework (ICF) layer for processing. However, before any processing can start, the incoming HTTP request has to be connected to a known ABAP user. This is the authentication step, and each incoming HTTP request is effectively subjected to it.

Authentication plays no immediate role in normal BSP development. Being prompted for a name and password at startup is an everyday experience that, all users have long accepted. However, if suddenly, in the middle of the session, the user is prompted again for authentication, the support desk soon faces confused questioning. The "Why authentication again?" question can only be answered if one understands what form of authentication allowed all previous HTTP requests to be processed, and why that method fails now. And for *this* question, one has to address the potential complexity of all different forms of authentication.

Knowing how authentication works also allows one to understand the difference between authentication and session management (discussed in the next chapter). Every once in a while, we see the following problem: "One user has successfully logged off from the server and leaves the browser running. Now, the next user sitting at this terminal is treated as the previous user. Why is he not prompted for his password?" Effectively, the logoff sequence just closes the session on the server; it does not make the browser forget the credentials[1] that it has available. On the next HTTP request to the server, the same credentials (from the previous user) are transmitted with the request, allowing the server to process the new HTTP request by starting the BSP application in a new session. Thus, understanding authentication also helps us to see ways of removing the credentials from the browser (although this turns out to be impossible in many cases).

1 Credentials imply any form of user authentication information used between the browser and the server, and are not limited to the typically used name-and-password approach.

5.1 Basic Authentication

Basic authentication is the most common and familiar authentication form.

Let us start a browser for the first time and request a URL from the server. For this testing, any BSP application will do. The browser first sends the HTTP request to the server, attempting to see if the server will answer the request as is.

```
GET /sap/bc/bsp/sap/it00/default.htm HTTP/1.1
Accept: */*
Accept-Language: en-us,de;q=0.5
User-Agent: Mozilla/4.0 (MSIE 6.0; Windows NT 5.1)
Host: us4449.wdf.sap.corp:1080
```

The server receives the HTTP request, and a new ABAP session is opened to process the request. As a first step, authentication information is required to assign an ABAP user to the session. No authentication information is available in the request. The server therefore refuses to process the HTTP request and answers the browser that the user is not authorized for the request.

```
HTTP/1.1 401 Unauthorized
Content-Type: text/html; charset=iso-8859-1
Content-Length: 2041
SAP-System: BBO
SAP-Client: 000
WWW-Authenticate: Basic realm="SAP Web App Server [BBO]"
Server: SAP Web Application Server (1.0;710)

<html>
  <head><title>Logon Error Message</title></head>
  <body><h1>Logon failed</h1>...
```

There are a number of very interesting aspects in this HTTP response. The first is the HTTP return code of `401`. This is standard defined HTTP return code for authentication failures. The browser must now obtain the user's credentials and supply them to the server.

The server also sets two headers: `SAP-System` and `SAP-Client`. The system header is the one against which the authentication failed and useful for troubleshooting. The client header displays the client that will be used for the authentication. As no client was specified in the URL, the default system client, in our case `000`, will be used.

The most interesting header is `WWW-Authenticate` header. The first token informs the browser that only basic authentication is accepted. The other, more complex digest authentication is not supported. The next token, the realm, is a string that defines a specific part of the server's URL space and allows the browser to associate different sets of credentials with different URLs on the server. With the realm, it is possible for the server to require different name and password sets, depending on which URL is accessed. The browser would then store the user-supplied data with the realm as key. Should the server challenge the browser later with exactly the same realm, the same credentials are used. This way, the server can group URLs and require the browser to prompt the user for different authentication data depending on the URL requested. For the SAP Web Application Server, only one realm is supported, and it always contains the name of the server as well.

The last interesting aspect is that the HTTP response actually has a body that contains an error message. However, this HTML code is *not* shown immediately (see Figure 5.1).

Figure 5.1 Basic Authentication Prompt

Once the browser receives a `401` HTTP response, it is faced with the problem that it requires a user name and password. For this, a standard browser dialog is displayed that prompts the user to enter a name and password. Notice that the realm is also displayed in the popup. Often, when the server does not accept the authentication, it is worthwhile to double-check this string. In cases where different Web AS systems run on the same physical computer, but use different HTTP ports, this string is the best indicator that the HTTP request, and thus the attempted authentication, has been addressed to the wrong Web AS server (effectively to the wrong HTTP port).

It is impossible in the popup dialog to set the client for which the authentication is required. The dialog is provided by the browser, and cannot be influenced by the server. If the logon is required against a specific client, then this must be set beforehand with the URL parameter `sap-client`. If it was not set, the default configured SAP client is used together with this authentication information (refer to `SAP-Client` header field that was set by the server).

Impossible in the dialog is also to request that the logon be in a specific language. By default, the configured language from the browser is used (see the `Accept-Language` header), or the requested language can be explicitly set with the URL parameter `sap-language`, using two character ISO codes as values.

Should the user decide not to supply authentication information, but to cancel the browser dialog, then the error HTML page sent with the `401` HTTP response is displayed (see Figure 5.2).

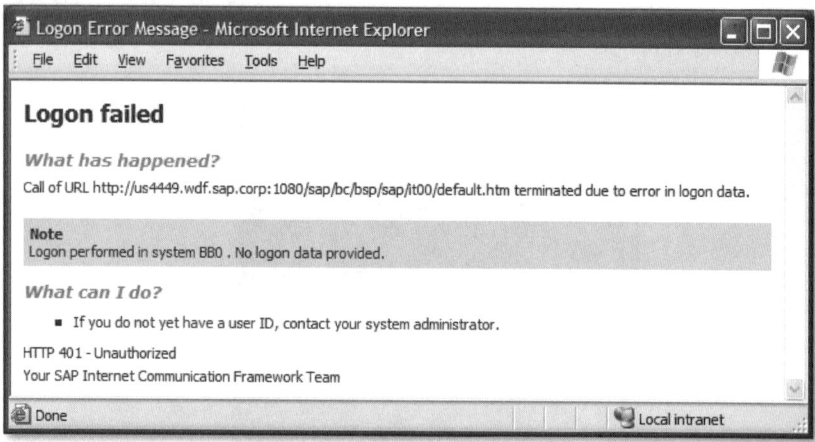

Figure 5.2 Cancelled Basic Authentication

Let us enter our name and password and see what the browser does then.

```
GET /sap/bc/bsp/sap/it00/default.htm HTTP/1.1
Accept: */*
Accept-Language: en-us,de;q=0.5
User-Agent: Mozilla/4.0 (MSIE 6.0; Windows NT 5.1)
Host: us4449.wdf.sap.corp:1080
Authorization: Basic VGhhbmtzIGZvciBidXlpbmcgYm9vayE=
```

The only difference we see from the first request is the addition `Authorization` header. The first token again indicates that basic authentication is used, and the next token is the authentication data. The user name and password are stored in one string "username:password" and then base64 encoded. It is not encrypted, and even our children would require less than three minutes to find a base64 decoder in the Internet and read our passwords. So, always be careful when sending out HTTP traces to the help desk for analysis. In general, you should carefully consider whether to use basic authentication and probably should do so over HTTPS networks or use switched Ethernet in order to protect passwords from network snooping.

```
HTTP/1.1 302 Moved temporarily
Content-Type: text/html; charset=iso-8859-1
Content-Length: 25
Location: /sap(bD1k==)/bc/bsp/sap/it00/default.htm
Server: SAP Web Application Server (1.0;710)

BSP URL requires rewrite.
```

As the HTTP request now contains acceptable credentials, the BSP runtime is started to process the incoming HTTP request. As an HTTP response, the URL mangling (see Chapter 4) is started with a `302` HTTP response to cause the browser to redirect to a new URL (see the `Location` header).

We would expect that from the next URL, the browser will now always set the `Authentication` header, allowing the server to process each HTTP request. Let us look at the next HTTP request/response cycle.

```
GET /sap(bD1k==)/bc/bsp/sap/it00/default.htm HTTP/1.1
Accept: */*
Accept-Language: en-us,de;q=0.5
User-Agent: Mozilla/4.0 (MSIE 6.0; Windows NT 5.1)
Host: us4449.wdf.sap.corp:1080

HTTP/1.1 401 Unauthorized
WWW-Authenticate: Basic realm="SAP Web App Server [BB0]"
...
```

We see that the new BSP-mangled URL is requested from the server, but without any authentication information. The server therefore again sends a `401` HTTP response. The reason for this is that the URL has changed from `/sap/...` to `/sap(bD1k==)/...`. For the browser, this is a different part of the URL namespace, and it will always attempt to first get a response *without* any authentication information. As the HTTP request was answered with an authentication request that contains exactly the same realm for which the browser already has our user name and password, it does *not* again display the popup prompting for data.

The browser just takes note that the URL namespace `/sap(bD1k==)/...` also requires the same authentication information. It will resend the HTTP request immediately, but this time with the Authorization header set.

```
GET /sap(bD1k==)/bc/bsp/sap/it00/default.htm HTTP/1.1
Accept: */*
Accept-Language: en-us,de;q=0.5
User-Agent: Mozilla/4.0 (MSIE 6.0; Windows NT 5.1)
Host: us4449.wdf.sap.corp:1080
Authorization: Basic VGhhbmtzIGZvciBidXlpbmcgYm9vayE=
```

From now on, the basic authentication data will "stick," and it will be transmitted with each HTTP request for the BSP application.

It's worth noting that basic authentication supports only a name and password. But how does the server know to which client the credentials belong? If no information is set or available, as in the traces above, it is assumed that the credentials are for a default-configured client. However, if the basic authentication was done for another client by setting the URL parameter `sap-client`, then this information also must be known. The ICF layer handles this with the `sap-usercontext` cookie. If either the client or language is changed to be different than the default values, the cookie will be set and used in conjunction with the basic authentication information.

```
Set-Cookie: sap-usercontext=sap-client=003; path=/
```

Note that the basic authentication information is tied to a specific system (via the realm string) and client (via the `sap-usercontext` cookie). This information can only be set once for the browser, and it is not possible to have two sets of data for the same Web AS system. This constraint also means that it is not possible to run two BSP applications in different clients from the same browser.

5.2 Single Sign-On

Single Sign-On (SSO) within the browser environment usually refers to the use of a HTTP cookie to store the user's identity. The process is relatively simple. If the browser is started anew, no credentials are available when the user requests an URL from the server. In this situation, no SSO2 cookie is available either, and thus SSO cookies are not a technique that can be used for the first round of authentication. Another form of authentication is required, such as the basic authentication described above.

Once the user has been authenticated, and if the server is so configured, it will set a SSO cookie (called `MYSAPSSO2`) that is typically valid for the complete domain.

The server can also be configured to set the cookie to be returned only to the specific server. Now, on all subsequent HTTP requests, the browser will send the cookie with the HTTP request. The targeted server then can use the information within the cookie as credentials to authenticate the user.

Let us look at a HTTP trace of this process first. In the first round, the URL is requested as we saw in the previous section without any form of authentication, and the server replies with a 401 HTTP response. The HTTP trace is exactly as it was before and is not shown again. The browser will display the popup window prompting the user for name and password. On the next request the Authorization header will be set.

```
GET /sap/bc/bsp/sap/it00/default.htm HTTP/1.1
...
Authorization: Basic VGhhbmtzIGZvciBidXlpbmcgYm9vayE=


HTTP/1.1 302 Moved temporarily
Set-Cookie: MYSAPSSO2=AjExM...+615...kOv5d; path=/;
                                      domain=wdf.sap.corp
Content-Type: text/html; charset=iso-8859-1
Content-Length: 25
Location: /sap(bD1k==)/bc/bsp/sap/it00/default.htm
Server: SAP Web Application Server (1.0;710)

BSP URL requires rewrite.
```

The HTTP response from the server contains the answer from the BSP runtime and an additional Set-Cookie header. The server has verified the credentials supplied from the basic authentication, and now sets a MYSAPSSO2 cookie. Notice that the cookie is set with the root path and for the complete domain. Effectively, for each new HTTP request to any server within this domain, the cookie will be added.

The cookie itself is roughly 625 characters and now shown completely in the HTTP trace. Just keep in mind from Chapter 2 that cookies are set only once to the browser, but always returned for each and every HTTP request where the server domain and path match. This means that all following HTTP requests will have the additional payload of the 625 characters. This is the price paid for the functionality provided by SSO.

The next HTTP request has the MYSAPSSO2 cookie set, and is answered with a 200 HTTP response and the correct HTML for the application.

```
GET /sap(bD1k==)/bc/bsp/sap/it00/default.htm HTTP/1.1
Accept: */*
Accept-Language: en-us,de;q=0.5
User-Agent: Mozilla/4.0 (MSIE 6.0; Windows NT 5.1)
Host: us4449.wdf.sap.corp:1080
Cookie: MYSAPSSO2=AjExM...+615...k0v5d


HTTP/1.1 200 OK
Content-Type: text/html; charset=iso-8859-1
Content-Length: 334
Server: SAP Web Application Server (1.0;710)

<html>...
```

Notice that this HTTP request does not contain the Authentication header. As discussed in the previous section, the URL change for the browser (because of mangling) implies a new URL namespace, and the browser will never send the basic authentication until challenged for it (by a 401 HTTP response with matching realm). In this case, the MYSAPSSO2 cookie has now assumed the role of providing a different set of credentials for each HTTP request.

Looking at the last HTTP request, one quickly concludes that, at the end of the BSP application, the browser can be instructed to stop running in the name of a user by deleting the MYSAPSSO2 cookie. Theoretically, then, there are no credentials in the browser, and the next user will be prompted to supply his or her user name and password. However, the basic authentication is still slumbering in the background. Once the cookie is deleted, the next request will have no credentials and the server will answer with a 401 HTTP response, causing the browser to just retry again with the Authentication header set. This proves that to really understand authentication one has to understand each and every type of authentication that could be active and also understand what type of authentication allowed each HTTP request to be processed.

Using SSO cookies against the same server is one technique for easily handling credentials over the lifetime of the browsing session, although at a corresponding payload price for each HTTP request. The more interesting facet of SSO cookies is the SSO principle. The first server did all the work to authenticate the user. The SSO cookie is send to all other servers and also accepted without further ado. This is effectively a single sign-on over all systems!

To understand how this works, we have to look at an abstract level at exactly what a SSO cookie is. For our discussion, the important aspect for is that it contains our SAP user name. This is effectively the user name (`sy-uname`) of the logged-on system. What the cookie does *not* contain are any client settings (as this can be different per system), nor language, email addresses, etc. The server will extract the name from the cookie, take also the additional information about the correct client to use (either default client or from cookie), and verify that the user name is valid for the system. Note that the SSO cookie forces the user name to be constant over all systems.

How does the server protect itself against a fake cookie? This is achieved by signing the user name in the cookie with the server's own digital certificate. This also explains why the cookie is so large! Any receiving server will first look into the cookie to see which server issued the cookie. It then looks in its store of digital certificates to see if it has the public part of the issuing server's certificate. Using this, it will verify that the data is actually correct. The principle of SSO cookies is that servers must have a trusted relationship with one another. This is achieved by configuring each server with the certificates of the other servers it may trust (see transaction STRUST).

5.3 Digital Certificates

Within the Web context, digital certificates always refer to X.509 certificates. A X.509 certificate binds a public key to a distinguished name that is issued by a certificate authority. The security aspects of X.509 certificates, although very interesting, are not the focus of this book. We primarily need to understand that a certificate is so constructed (digitally signed by a certificate authority) that the receiving web server can again validate the distinguish name. The distinguished name itself is usually of the form `C=<country> O=<company> CN=<certificate name>` and can include other attributes that uniquely name a person. There are standard procedures whereby a company can obtain and issue such certificates to each employee.

The first step is to import the certificate into the browser (see Figure 5.3). With this, the browser now has our identity in a digital format that can be verified again by the server.

The next step is to update the Web AS server be able to map the distinguished name onto a user name. This mapping can be configured with transaction SM30, in the table `USREXTID` (see Figure 5.4). The external ID is the distinguished name from the X.509 certificate and must be entered exactly the same into the table, including the preservation of case and spaces.

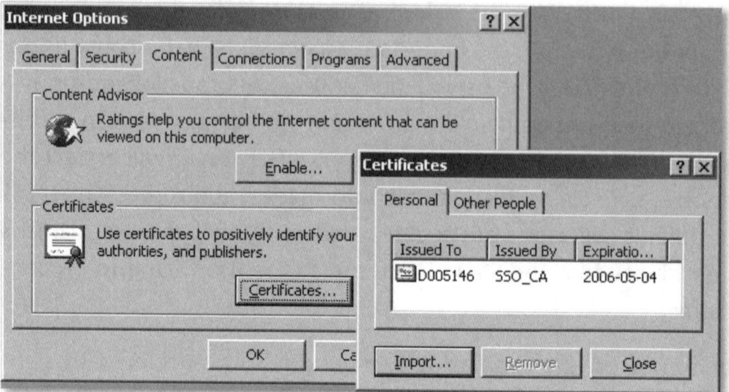

Figure 5.3 Import of Digital Certificate

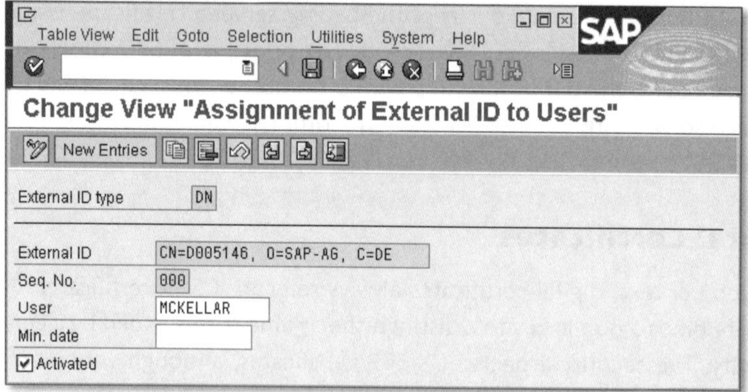

Figure 5.4 Mapping of Certificate Distinguished Name to User Name

Although it is slightly tedious to complete this process for one user, it is shown here to highlight the basic principle of integrating certificates and using them to identify users. In large corporations, this configuration usually is done centrally as part of the user management for the Web AS system.

The question now is how to get the browser to send the certificate to the server. This answer turns out be very simple. The moment the protocol is switched from HTTP to HTTPS, the certificate is automatically sent as part of the encryption layer used to secure the HTTPS connection. No further work is required.

Let us make a very simple BSP application: <html><%=sy-uname%></html>. The first time, we execute the application with an http:// URL, and thereafter with an https:// URL. See Figure 5.5. It is important that each protocol requires its own port number. If the default port numbers are configured, :80 for HTTP and :443 for HTTPS, we need not specify port numbers.

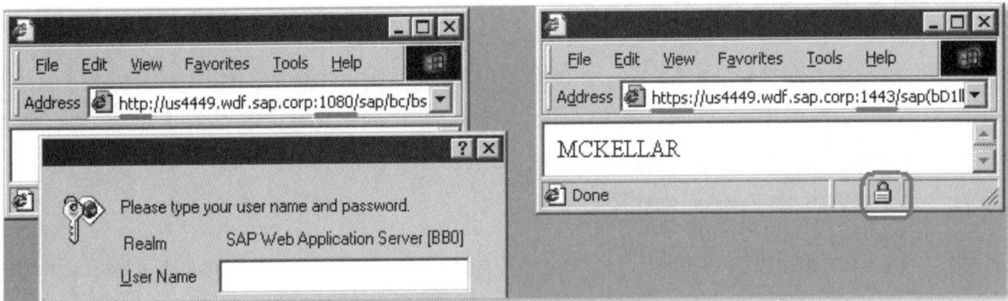

Figure 5.5 Access Same BSP Application with HTTP and HTTPS

With the HTTP request, the server finds no available authentication information, and answers with the expected 401 HTTP response. With the HTTPS request, the server answers immediately with the response from the BSP application. Notice the small lock symbol to show that a secure connection is active.

This "automatic authentication" aspect also helps typical logon applications. The connection is switched to HTTPS mode to transfer securely the user name and password. However, at that moment the browser supplies a certificate. This allows the server to identify the user, set a SSO cookie, and then switch back to HTTP. With two HTTP round trips and no user interaction, the authentication was completed. However, this only works together with a SSO cookie. Otherwise, the return back to HTTP leaves us again without credentials.

For BSP pages, it is possible to set a checkbox that states whether these pages must be run in secure mode. Once the checkbox is set, the BSP runtime will automatically switch the connection into secure mode if the page is accessed. This function was designed for shopping scenarios, where only the checkout phase (with credit card numbers, etc) must be secure. One could be tempted to expect the checkbox to also help get the certificate authentication working without user interaction by forcing HTTPS. However, authentication is handled and completed at ICF layer, long before the BSP runtime is started. Any answer from the BSP runtime implies also that authentication has been completed.

If one should look at the HTTPS traffic itself, there is nothing special to see. The certificate handling is done at the encryption layer below the HTTP traffic, and the HTTP traffic itself is effectively the same as described in the next section on anonymous services. We have incoming HTTP requests that are immediately answered without any visible trace of authentication information.

5.4 Anonymous Services

Sometimes we need Web AS be able to run Web applications in the way a normal Web server would, without any form of authentication checks. However, the ABAP session itself must run within the context of a specific user. It is not possible to have anonymous ABAP services.

The technique for achieving this is to configure a specific node, or sub-tree, within the ICF tree (see transaction SICF) to store the authentication information that must be used for all URLs that are matched through the specific node. When the server sees an incoming HTTP request that contains no authentication information, it checks whether one of the ICF nodes has a user name and password stored. If it does, these credentials are used to open the ABAP session and process the HTTP request. We highly recommend that you first read the documentation so as to be aware of all aspects of anonymous nodes. This allows unchecked access to the specific application.

We recommend creating a `/myCompany/public` path, similar to `/sap/public` that is the only anonymous access granted to the system. Only this `public` node gets assigned a user name and password. Then use internal ICF links within this public path to specific BSP applications that must be run anonymously (see Figure 5.6). This way, one can see immediately which BSP applications can be accessed without any form of authentication.

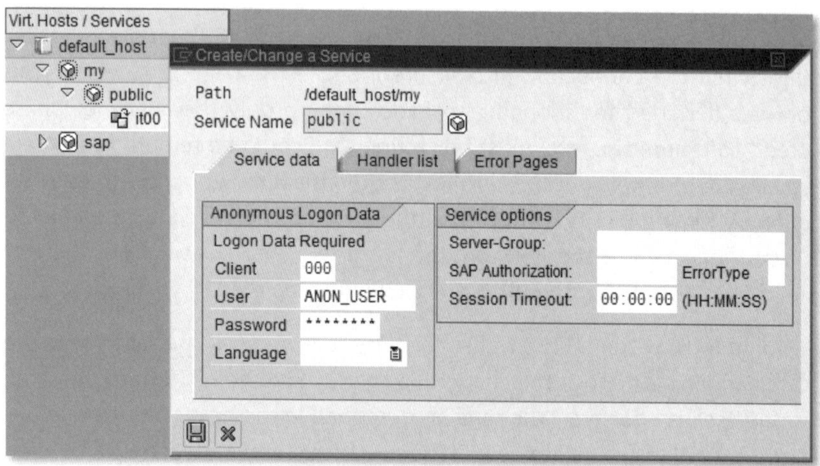

Figure 5.6 Configuring an Anonymous Service in Transaction SICF

Let us link BSP application `IT00` under a newly created public path, and look at the HTTP trace of the application.

```
GET /my/public/it00/default.htm HTTP/1.1
Accept: */*
Accept-Language: en-us,de;q=0.5
User-Agent: Mozilla/4.0 (MSIE 6.0; Windows NT 5.1)
Host: us4449.wdf.sap.corp:1080

HTTP/1.1 302 Moved temporarily
Location: /my(bD1k==)/public/it00/default.htm
...


GET /my(bD1k==)/public/it00/default.htm HTTP/1.1
Accept: */*
Accept-Language: en-us,de;q=0.5
User-Agent: Mozilla/4.0 (MSIE 6.0; Windows NT 5.1)
Host: us4449.wdf.sap.corp:1080

HTTP/1.1 200 OK
Content-Type: text/html; charset=iso-8859-1
...
```

The HTTP trace shows no form of authentication information. Not even `MYSAPSSO2` cookies are set for anonymous access. In principle, the application behaves like a normal Internet website.

5.5 Form-Based Authentication

Form-based authentication is achieved by setting two form fields: `sap-user` and `sap-password`. The other two form fields that can be considered to be set are `sap-language` and `sap-client`. From Chapter 2 we know already that form fields can be transported either as part of the URL or within the body of a HTTP `POST` request.

The simplest technique is via URL parameters: `http://.../default.htm?sap-user=username&sap-password=password`. We definitely do *not* recommend this technique, as the browser will store all URLs—now including authentication information—in the browsing history. But it is a fast and convenient technique to test some forms of authentication problems and definitely worthwhile to understand.

```
GET /sap/bc/bsp/sap/it00/default.htm
        ?sap-user=username&sap-password=password HTTP/1.1
Accept: */*
```

```
Accept-Language: en-us,de;q=0.5
User-Agent: Mozilla/4.0 (MSIE 6.0; Windows NT 5.1)
Host: us4449.wdf.sap.corp:1080


HTTP/1.1 302 Moved temporarily
Content-Type: text/html; charset=iso-8859-1
Content-Length: 25
Location: /sap(bD1k==)/bc/bsp/sap/it00/default.htm
                 ?sap-user=username&sap-password=++++++++
Server: SAP Web Application Server (1.0;710)

BSP URL requires rewrite.
```

The HTTP request contains the correct form fields and is answered immediately with a `200` HTTP response. Pay attention to the `Location` header. We see that the `sap-password` form field has been overwritten by security rules. And this makes itself noticeable in the next HTTP request/response cycle.

```
GET /sap(bD1k==)/bc/bsp/sap/it00/default.htm
        ?sap-user=username&sap-password=++++++++ HTTP/1.1
Accept: */*
Accept-Language: en-us,de;q=0.5
User-Agent: Mozilla/4.0 (MSIE 6.0; Windows NT 5.1)
Host: us4449.wdf.sap.corp:1080


HTTP/1.1 401 Unauthorized
...
```

This means that form-based logon cannot work without another form of saving the credentials after the first HTTP roundtrip. One technique could be the activation of SSO. Then, the very first request that still had the valid user name and password would be authenticated, the `MYSAPSSO2` cookie would be set, and all subsequence HTTP requests would use SSO for credentials.

```
HTTP/1.1 302 Moved temporarily
Set-Cookie: MYSAPSSO2=AjExM...
```

5.6 Implementing a Simple Logon Application

Now that we have grasped the basics of form-based authentication, let us quickly look at how one can use it for a very simple logon application. Let us assume that we wish to start the BSP application IT00 using form based logon. As a first step, the user must call some form of URL that will at least render the form to enter authentication data, without itself requiring credentials. We create a small HTTP handler (discussed in Chapter 3), or an alias to a different BSP application under some path, for example the `/my/public/start_it00`.

The HTML displays two input fields to enable the user to enter his user name and password. It is very important that the names of the input fields be correctly set to match exactly the corresponding `sap-user` and `sap-password` fields required for form-based authentication. The form `action` attribute is set to start the application when the form is submitted.

```
<html><body>
  <form method="POST"
        action="/sap/bc/bsp/sap/it00/default.htm">
  <table>
    <tr>
      <td>User:</td>
      <td><input type="text"     name="sap-user"></td>
    </tr><tr>
     <td>Password:</td>
     <td><input type="password" name="sap-password"></td>
    </tr><tr>
     <td><input type="submit" value="Logon!"></td>
    </tr>
  </table>
  </form>
</body></html>
```

With this HTML available via an anonymous URL, it is now possible to start our minimal logon application without any authentication, and render out the real logon screen. See Figure 5.7.

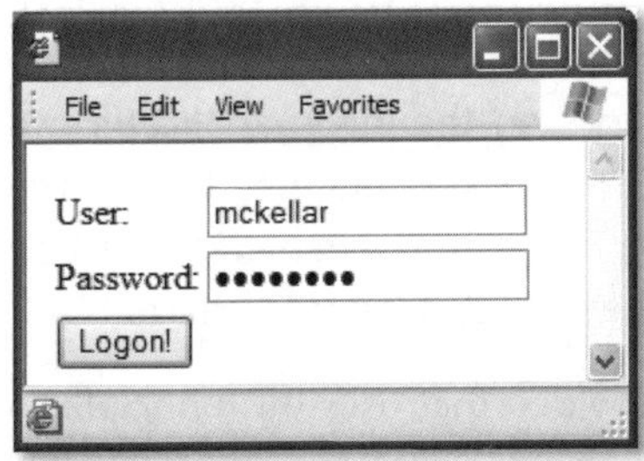

Figure 5.7 Minimal Form-Based Logon

The BSP application is started via the public path /my/public/start_it00. The first HTTP round trip just renders out the HTML of our minimal form- based logon application. The user now enters his user name and password and presses the button to start the application.

```
POST /sap/bc/bsp/sap/it00/default.htm HTTP/1.1
Accept: */*
Accept-Language: en-us,de;q=0.5
Content-Type: application/x-www-form-urlencoded
User-Agent: Mozilla/4.0 (MSIE 6.0; Windows NT 5.1)
Host: us4449.wdf.sap.corp:1080
Content-Length: 39

sap-user=username&sap-password=password
```

```
HTTP/1.1 200 OK
Set-Cookie: MYSAPSSO2=AjExMD...
Content-Type: text/html; charset=iso-8859-1
Content-Length: 334
server: SAP Web Application Server (1.0;710)

<html>...
```

The POST is submitted directly against the application URL, and sap-user and sap-password form fields are set in the HTTP body. Given the valid credentials, the BSP application is stared immediately. Within the HTTP response, the MYSAPSSO2 cookie is set, enabling authentication for all subsequent HTTP requests.

This example is very simple and only useful for showing the principle that is used to write logon applications. A real logon application must also handle all different types of problems around user logon, for example users who are locked, users who are forced to change their password, and those users who wish to change their passwords. Also, the BSP runtime does not support applications that are started with a POST, forcing some additional work on the logon application to handle the first POST itself to acquire the MYSAPSSO2 ticket, and then to start the application with a GET HTTP request. All application startup parameters must be saved during the logon application and reset when the application is started.

In Release 6.20, a BSP application SYSTEM is provided that uses this principle to build a complete logon application. This is replaced in 6.40 with a much better logon application that is tightly integrated into the ICF layer, and the old SYSTEM application will not be supported from 6.40 upwards in the future. Chapter 17 describes the new ICF logon application in detail.

5.7 De-Authentication

Unfortunately, this is the thorniest section to write, as there is actually very little that can be said on this topic. Once the browser has stored a fixed set of credentials, it is difficult if not impossible to remove these.

The typical scenario that triggers the question on de-authentication is that of a shared computer somewhere on the factory floor. One person has finished working and presses the logoff button. The next finds the browser open, and starts to work, running suddenly in the name of the previous co-worker. The reason for this is that the logoff sequence terminates the server session, but does not remove any credentials from the browser.

Probably the safest solution to this problem is to close the browser at the end of each session. From JavaScript, this can be achieved with a `top.close()` sequence. If it is a browser window previously opened with JavaScript, this sequence works without further prompting. However, if the user opened the browser window, a confirmation prompt is first shown by the browser, and this must be confirmed. Many usability experts object to software that just closes the browser window. Whether this practice matches your scenario is a decision that you must make yourself.

Basic authentication is widely used, and nearly impossible to remove from the browser. The only technique that we are aware of works only for Microsoft Internet Explorer 6.0 SP1+. You can call the `execCommand` method on the document, passing in `ClearAuthenticationCache` as the command parameter. This flushes all credentials in the cache, so that no basic authentication headers are sent. Here a very small test program that closes the session on logoff (discussed in detail in Chapter 6) and then clears the browser's authentication cache.

```
<html><form>
  <% DATA: counter TYPE string.
     counter = request->get_form_field( 'counter' ) + 1. %>
  <input type="submit" name="counter" value="<%=counter%>" >
  <input type="submit" name="logoff"  value="Logoff" >

  <% IF request->get_form_field('logoff') IS NOT INITIAL. %>
    <% runtime->keep_context = 0. %>
    <script>
      document.execCommand( 'ClearAuthenticationCache' );
```

```
      document.URL = '/sap/bc/bsp/sap/myApp/startPage.htm';
    </script>
  <% ENDIF. %>
</form><html>
```

Remember that this technique only works for Internet Explorers 6 SP1 onwards. One should only consider it in a corporate network where the browser installations can be centrally managed. No equivalent techniques that work for other browsers are known to the authors at the time of writing.

With SSO, the situation is complicated for a different reason. As SSO is handled with the MYSAPSSO2 cookie, de-authentication can theoretically be achieved by deleting the cookie with a response->delete_cookie_at_client or with JavaScript operations on the document.cookie.Computing the correct domain string to use can be tricky, because this depends on profile settings. However, SAP considers the SSO concept to be also "sticky" once set. In theory, one does not know who sets the MYSAPSSO2 cookie, and deleting it could cause other software components, for example an SAP Enterprise Portal, to suddenly fail.

With certificates, the handling is completely under the browser's control, and there is not much to do. Elegant solutions using certificates with a card reader are available on the market, but very seldom used because of their cost. The use of smart card readers has the benefit that when the user leaves the computer, his credentials leave with him.

For anonymous access through the corresponding /public path in the ICF tree, nothing more can be done. The browser never required any authentication information, and thus none is available for deleting.

Unfortunately, there is no easy answer to this question. Probably the best approach that also works over all browsers is to consider the closing of the window. When the logoff sequence is started, redirect to a final page that contains a good description on security (to scare everyone), and then place a window-close button on the page (<button onclick="top.close();">Close Window</button>). This gives the user at least a much better feeling that the application was closed correctly, and did not just die on him or her.

6 Session Management

Using stateful BSP applications provides a programming model that should feel very familiar to those experienced in traditional ABAP dynpro programming. However, it also introduces new challenges in properly managing the state. In this chapter, we will look at a number of these challenges and possible solutions to them.

Typically, Web pages are designed to be stateless, meaning that the server will process an incoming request from a browser and then completely forget about that browser. In such scenarios, all possible state information required must be stored with the browser. The server stores no state information. This model allows one server to handle many clients and even may allow different requests from the same client to be handled by different servers each time, governed by a load-balancing algorithm.

However, for more complex business applications, where more information is involved or where database locks are required until an application is completed, a stateful approach is required. This implies that the ABAP session is not destroyed after the HTTP response has been processed but rather left in memory. All subsequent HTTP requests will not start new sessions but will all be processed within the same session. This session is exactly the same as a session opened with SAP GUI.

The only difference between these sessions is that SAP GUI sessions are managed over TCP/IP connections that are not closed until the end of the session. Should the server suddenly see that a TCP/IP connection is closed, it knows that the SAP GUI was closed prematurely and can clean up the session. For HTTP, no such permanent TCP/IP connection is used, and the server does not know whether the browser has been closed suddenly.

Open sessions can be seen in transaction SM04. In Figure 6.1, notice that the HTTP sessions have a different "type" than the SAP GUI sessions, allowing one to separate them easily. It is also possible to close session from this transaction.

6.1 Session Identification

We saw in Chapter 1 that the session selection is done by the Internet Communication Manager (ICM). For all intents and purposes, once an incoming HTTP request is placed into the ABAP stack, it is already in the correct user session where it must be processed.

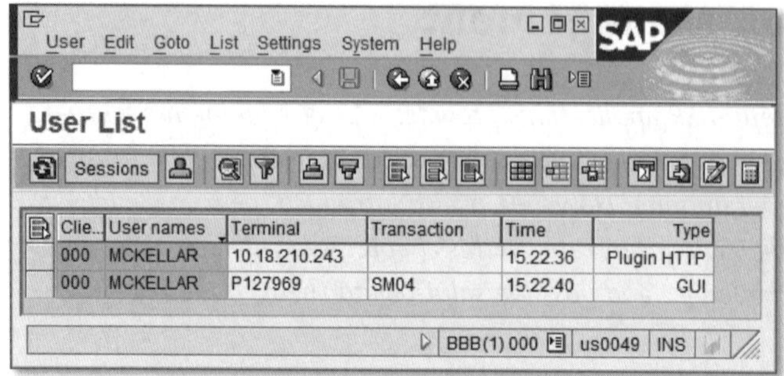

Figure 6.1 SAP GUI and HTTP Sessions in Transaction SM04

A session ID is required for session identification. This is a relatively complex string containing random elements that uniquely identifies the session. The exact format is not important and not really known outside of the ICM layer. The session ID will nearly always be identified as `sap-contextid` with the HTTP request.

The ICM layer will look at a number of different places within the incoming HTTP request to find the session ID and map the HTTP request into the correct session.

The first three places are all variations on having the session ID stored as part of the URL. Session `ID` can be mangled into the URL, it can be part of the URL itself (using a `;`-character as separator), or it can be a form field attached onto the URL.

```
POST /sap.../main.htm?sap-contextid=sid-NEW HTTP/1.1
POST /sap.../main.htm;sap-contextid=sid-NEW HTTP/1.1
POST /sap(s=sid-NEW)/.../main.htm HTTP/1.1
```

Although the first two entries look nearly the same, they are very different in subtle ways. In the first case, the session ID is transferred as a form field, and can be part of any number of form fields in the URL. In this case, the Web application must take care to each time add this extra form field to any URL. In the second case, the session ID is actually part of the URL, effectively the last segment of the URL is `main.htm;sap-contextid=sid-NEW`. For the browser, the `;`-character sequence in the URL has no further meaning. If an URL generator is used, this approach can correctly attach the session ID onto each URL generator, and the form fields are left for the use of the application. The one problem is that a relative navigation (for example to a new URL `../page2.htm`), will drop the session ID with the last segment from the URL.

In the last form, the session ID is mangled into the URL, where it does not interfere with form fields and is immune to relative URLs. As it is mangled onto the first segment, the session ID will also exist in all URLs used for the application. It sure looks ugly though!

SAP does not support having the session ID stored as form field within the body of a POST request.

The biggest negative aspects of having a session ID within an URL is that resources (images, etc) loaded with a session ID will be cached with the session ID part of the URL, and will thus only be valid for the specific session. A new start of the application will cause the resources to be reloaded. The best workaround is to load resources with an URL that contains no session ID. This will cause the loading to be done in a new stateless session.

The last possibility is to transfer the session ID as a cookie within the HTTP request. This has the benefit that the browser will always send the cookie with all HTTP requests that match the cookie path.

```
POST /sap... HTTP/1.1
Cookie: sap-contextid=sid-NEW;
```

The downside is that the application must set the path correctly, so that the cookie will only be transported for the specific application. Also, it is not possible to run a second session with the same URL, as the sessions will then share the same cookie, with the second session then overwriting the session ID of the first session.

In all the above examples, the session was only shown as sid-NEW. The sid is representative of the session ID itself, of which the format is neither known nor important. However, the session ID also has a sub-comment -NEW or -ATT attached to it. The sequence -NEW is an indicator to the ICM layer to place the incoming HTTP request into an existing session or to create a new session if the old session is not found. This ensures that the HTTP request will be processed. With -ATT, if the session does not exist any more, the ICM layer will display a session-timeout message, and the HTTP request will never be processed within the ABAP layer.

The BSP runtime uses only two formats for storing the session IDs. The first is to set a cookie with the -NEW sequence directly on the path of the application. The makes the handling of URLs and navigation with the application very easy, but does have the two disadvantages mentioned before: Only one instance of a specific BSP application can be executed at any time, and the application is given no notice of this fact in case of a session timeout and restart.

The second format used by the BSP runtime is to mangle the session ID into the URL. This can be requested only on the very first startup request (before any URL mangling has been completed) with the URL parameter sap-syscmd=nocookie. In this case the -ATT subcommand is used, so that on a timeout, the application is not restarted. The reason for the difference in subcommand is that once the session ID is in the URL, it will stay there all the time. If a new `POST` was to open a new session, the old session ID itself in the URL is still stored in the browser, and the newly assigned session ID is not stored. Each subsequent request from the stale URL will open a new session. Thus, the `-ATT` mode is used, so that—once a timeout happens—processing is stopped, and the application must be restarted.

The advantage of this approach is that it is now easy to run any number of instances of the same BSP application, as each will store its own session ID mangled in the URL, and the BSP applications will not overwrite the session `ids` of one another. One disadvantage is that the URL length is dramatically increased, and this payload price is also paid twice in each HTTP request, once mangled in the URL and the second time in the `Referer` header field.

6.2 Session Timeout

Due to the "disconnected" model of HTTP, it is never known whether the user is actually still browsing our specific application or has already moved to another website. To protect critical resources, inactive sessions are cleaned up by ICM after a configured idle time has been exceeded.

The maximum idle time is configured in the system profile with the parameter `rdisp/plugin_auto_logout`; 30 minutes by default. The profile parameter also can be changed (until next system restart) using transaction RZ11.

HTTP is a strict request/response protocol, where the browser will always send a HTTP request, and the server can only answer at that time with a HTTP response. It is not possible for the server to send any HTTP traffic to the browser at other times. Therefore, when a timeout condition is detected, the server has no way to inform the browser of the situation. The session will just be terminated.

Within the browser, no update will appear. When the user returns at a later stage, he will still find the browser indicating a normal running Web application. Only on the next action that triggers a server roundtrip will the lost session be noticed.

The maximum idle time is used for the complete application server. It is not possible to have idle sessions that are longer than this time. You can set the idle time for specific applications within transaction SICF to be shorter than this time. If a longer idle time is required, then the profile of a specific application server has to be updated and those applications only executed against this one application server.

6.2.1 Catching and Handling a Session Timeout

Normally, when a session is cleared because of a timeout situation, a rollback is done, all locks are released, and the session is cleared. This is sufficient for nearly all types of applications.

However, let us assume your application also acquires resources that must be released on timeout. For our small example, we use a counter merely to reserve something until the transaction is completed. The reservation counter is stored in memory, and all those objects reserved cannot be taken into consideration by other users.

```
<%@extension name="htmlb" prefix="htmlb"%>
<%
   DATA: reserveCounter TYPE string.
   IMPORT reserveCounter = reserveCounter
          FROM SHARED MEMORY indx(qq) ID 'reserveCounter'.
   reserveCounter = reserveCounter + 1.
%>
<htmlb:content design="design2003"><htmlb:page><htmlb:form>
  <htmlb:button text    = "<%=reserveCounter%>"
                onClick = "myClickHandler" />
</htmlb:form></htmlb:page></htmlb:content>
<%
   EXPORT reserveCounter = reserveCounter
          TO SHARED MEMORY indx(qq) ID 'reserveCounter'.
%>
```

If the application runs into a timeout, we certainly would like to clear this reservation counter, so that the reserved objects will be available for other users.

The ICF layer does provide an ABAP event when the session is cleared. It is a simple step to hook this event and clear the counter in shared memory. For the example, we will use the application class of the BSP application. This application class can implement an optional interface IF_BSP_APPLICATION_EVENTS, which will cause the BSP runtime to then call the application at different time points. We define a new class that implements the event interface.

In the application class, we define a new method on_timeout that is an event handler for the timeout event available on the IF_HTTP_SERVER interface (see Figure 6.2).

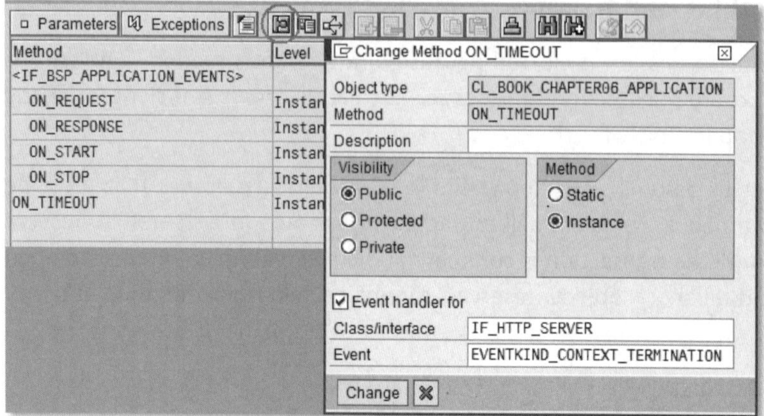

Figure 6.2 Defining Method As Event Handler

Two methods merit our interest. The first is the `on_start` method that is called by the BSP runtime when the application is started. Here we just register our timeout handler against the server instance.

```
METHOD if_bsp_application_events~on_start.
   DATA: reserveCounter TYPE string VALUE '0'.
   EXPORT reserveCounter = reserveCounter
          TO SHARED MEMORY indx(qq) ID 'reserveCounter'.
   SET HANDLER me->on_timeout FOR runtime->server.
ENDMETHOD.
```

The second method to implement is the actual timeout handler itself. Here we just reset our reservation counter.

```
METHOD on_timeout.
   DATA: reserveCounter TYPE string VALUE '0'.
   EXPORT reserveCounter = reserveCounter
          TO SHARED MEMORY indx(qq) ID 'reserveCounter'.
ENDMETHOD.
```

This simple hook allows us to clean up in critical cases where more than database locks are held.

6.2.2 Session Timeout in Browser

As we have discussed before, a session timeout in the server happens while no HTTP request is being processed. Thus, it is not possible for the server to write an update to the browser. The user who now returns to his or her desk will still find an application that gives no indication of the timeout.

One simple hack after we suspect a server timeout has happened is to clear the browser screen.

```
<script>
  var T = (30+3) /*min*/ * 60 /*sec*/ * 1000 /*millisecs*/;
  window.setTimeout("document.URL = 'about:blank';", T);
</script>
```

As long as the user interacts with the application, each page loaded will return the previous running times and set itself a new timer. The timer is set to be the configured idle time plus three minutes. Note that the JavaScript function requires the values in milliseconds. Should the user now leave the program unattended for 33 minutes, the screen will be blanked, so that on return the application that was terminated at the server will not be displayed in the browser.

6.3 Confusion with Processing Timeout

Note also the length of time that one HTTP request will be processed before it is aborted. This time can be seen in transaction SMICM (see Figure 6.3). It is a value that defined per service (open HTTP port) and that controls the time that one HTTP request can be processed by the ABAP stack. It can be configured within the system profile as part of the `icm/server_port` parameter.

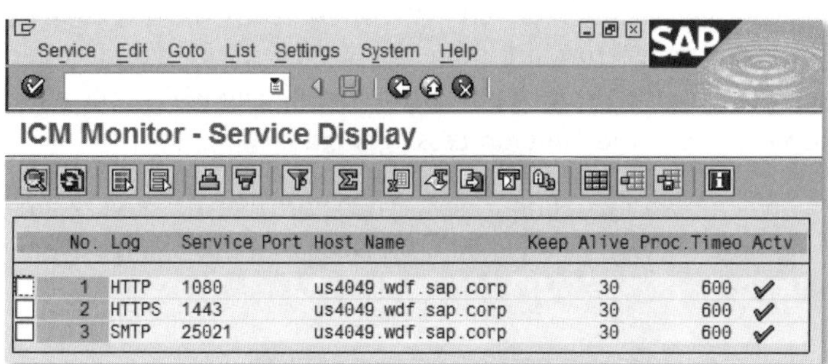

Figure 6.3 Processing Timeout in Transaction SMICM

When the HTTP request takes too much time within the ABAP stack, the ICM layer will terminate the ABAP session and write back an error message to the browser (see Figure 6.4).

Notice in Figure 6.4 that the time shown by the HTTP trace tool is a little over 604 seconds, just marginally longer than the configured 600 seconds for this specific port. The "Connection timed out" message reflects the fact that the "connection" between the ICM layer and the ABAP stack has timed out; the message does not have anything to do with the idle timeout.

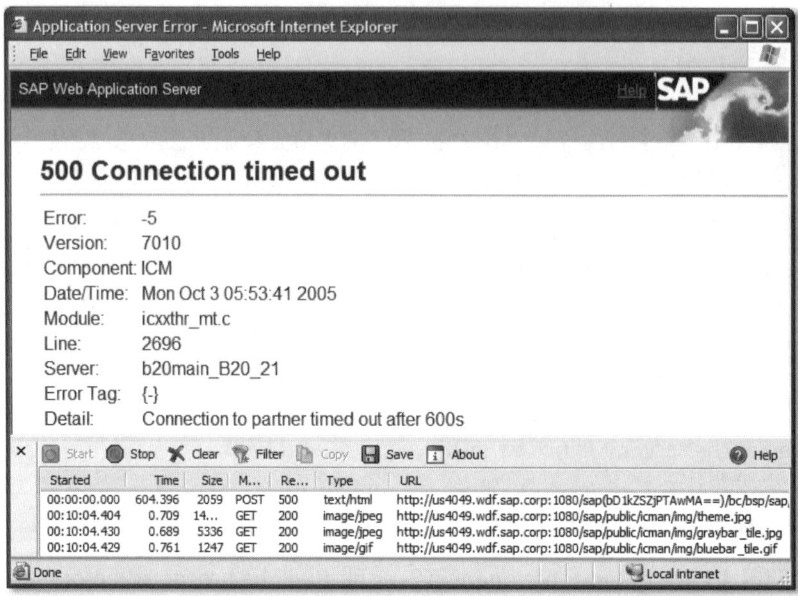

Figure 6.4 Processing Timeout as Seen in Browser

For production systems, the processing time usually is set relatively short so that no runaway HTTP request can block work processes for a long time. The latter situation could be a nightmare on HTTP connections, where such long-running requests are very easy to trigger from a browser. However, the downside of an optimal configuration is that it is also not possible to debug any BSP application. The debugger is also subject to the same processing limits.

The workaround is to temporarily define a new HTTP port that has a very long maximum processing time allowed (see Figure 6.5). Note that this change is only available until a restart.

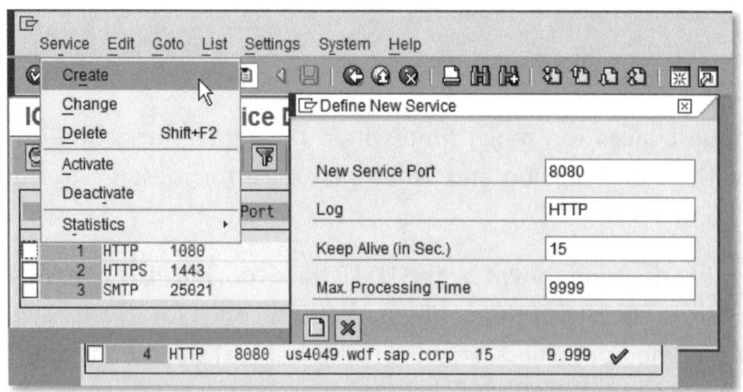

Figure 6.5 Defining a New Port with Long Processing Timeout Value

In the last step, just change the start URL of the application within the browser to use the new port, in our example `:8080`.

For readers especially interested in the subject: The keep-alive time sets the time in seconds that the ICM layer will keep an idle TCP connection open, waiting for a new request from the browser, before closing it. Reusing TCP connections helps improve the total latency of HTTP requests, as no additional roundtrips are required to first set up the TCP connection. However, the server is limited in the number of open TCP connections it can maintain at any one time. Therefore, unused connections are closed after a few seconds idle time. This relates well to the HTML model, whereby one HTML page and then all of its referenced resources are loaded in one burst.

6.4 Catching and Handling a Restart after Timeout

We saw earlier that the BSP runtime will use by default session `ids` that instruct the ICM layer just to call the application in a new session if the old one timed out (the `-NEW` subcommand). We also saw that at the moment the timeout happens it is not possible for the server to update the browser. Thus, should the user now return to the application and trigger any event, the application will be restarted in a clean environment.

What happens next is really up to the application. Perhaps the application is relatively simple and had all information in the incoming HTTP request, so that the lost session was not noticed. This behavior would normally have indicated an application model more suited to stateless mode. What more normally happens, though, is that the application suddenly runs into a situation that was not foreseen, and it generates a logical error. All of this causes unnecessary calls to the support desk.

It would better if the application actually caught such a session restart, and then restarted the application anew.

This solution actually turns out to be quite simple. A BSP application class, when implementing the interface `IF_BSP_APPLICATION_EVENTS`, will have its method `on_request` called for each incoming request.

The first task is to filter out the first `on_request` method that starts the application. This is done with a class attribute (type `abap_bool`) that is just toggled after the first time.

The question now is whether this an initial start of the application or a restart of the application. In the case of a restart, we would like to show the user a small error page and start the application from the beginning.

We need something that tells us if the HTTP request we are receiving is for a restart. The best way is to check if the incoming HTTP request contains any form fields with htmlb in the name, as this indicates a previously rendered HTML page with HTMLB library of elements (assuming they are used).

Another good form field to check for is onInputProcessing. This is a very special field that indicates to the BSP runtime that an event requires processing from the HTTP request, and it will also be set by the HTMLB library.

We use the same small example that was started before (see Section 6.2.1). The on_request method is implemented to contain our restart guard, and if required, to navigate to a restart page.

```
METHOD if_bsp_application_events~on_request.
* Class Attribute: first_time TYPE abap_bool VALUE abap_true
  IF first_time = abap_true.
    first_time = abap_false.
    IF request->get_form_field( 'onInputProcessing' )
                                        IS NOT INITIAL.
      navigation->exit( 'restart.htm' ).
      RETURN.
    ENDIF.
  ENDIF.
ENDMETHOD.
```

The restart page now just shows a small error message, and has a button to start the application anew.

```
<%@extension name="htmlb" prefix="htmlb"%>
<htmlb:content design="design2003"><htmlb:page><htmlb:form>
   <htmlb:textView text    = "Session has timed out!"
                   design = "EMPHASIZED" />
   <htmlb:button   text    = "Restart"
           onClientClick = "document.URL = 'main.htm';" />
</htmlb:form></htmlb:page></htmlb:content>
```

The document.URL sequence will set the reference for the HTML page to a new value, triggering the browser to load the new page.

If you want to test the timeout situation, it is easy to simulate it without having to actually wait for a timeout. In transaction SM04 you can see all connected users whether the connection is from the SAP GUI or from the browser. You can double-click on an entry in this list and then end the session with a menu option. This will have the same result as if the ICM had cancelled the session because of a timeout. Just be sure to choose the correct session and not to accidentally kick yourself out of the system.

6.5 Session Management from the Browser

Until now, we have only looked at the aspect of a server-triggered session timeout. What happens if the user navigates outside of our application or shuts down his or her browser? The server state remains, consuming valuable resources and also maintains locks that prevent other users from working. These lost sessions will only be cleaned up by the ICM after the maximum idle timer has expired, which is a very course-grained protection.

We need a technique for also closing the server session once the browser "closes" its concept of the session. This can happen because the user decides to navigate to a different website, or to just close his browser.

The first problem is to hook into the browser to detect these conditions. One technique is to use the `onunload` event of each page. This is a JavaScript event that will call our code if the current page is unloaded because the user decided to navigate to another page. However, each time that our page is also submitted to the server because of a user event, the page is also effectively unloaded and reloaded. Here, we do not want to trigger the session to be closed prematurely.

The solution is to use a HTML `<frameset>`. This loads a very small document into the browser, which itself will then load the actual application. As the application is now in one `<frame>`, its roundtrips are not significant.

```
<html>
  <script language="JavaScript">
    function appUnload() {...}
  </script>
  <frameset name="guard" rows="*,0"
                                onUnLoad="appUnload();">
    <frame src="main.htm">
  </frameset>
</html>
```

When looking at the source skeleton above, we see that we have a defined a JavaScript function `appUnload` that is tied to the `onUnLoad` event of the `<frameset>`. Should the user now navigate to any other website, the frameset will be unloaded by the browser, triggering our function. The `<frame>` itself will load the main page of the application, and the user will not even be aware of the guard we placed into position.

However, the browser close is a very special situation. Some browsers will also fire this event when the browser is closed (our experience shows that Microsoft Internet Explorer does it), whereas other browsers, for example older versions of Netscape, will not fire the event.

With the hook in place, it is necessary to inform the server to close the current session. In this JavaScript code, there is no information available about the next URL to which the browser will navigate. Any algorithm of the form: "first go to server and close session, then redirect to next URL" will fail. Any solution using the current `document.URL` to first force our session to close will either fail or cause many user complaints, because the targeted URL of the user then will not be navigated to. Essentially, it must be possible to trigger a HTTP request to server that is not part of the current document.

The initial methods we used had a `window.open` to load the session termination URL into a small window. However, this causes user irritation because the popup window flashes onto screen, to be closed moments later, and is relatively slow.

This approach works reasonably well under most situations. But it does have some minor problems. To most end users, popup windows that fire without their triggering an action are as unwelcome as spam. The situation has become so serious that we have popup blockers being built into just about every Internet browser that will prevent the window from opening at all, thus breaking session management completely.

The alternative solution that we found to work very well is to load an image. This will trigger a server roundtrip and can be done without setting the `document.URL` new.

```
function appUnload()
{
   var img=new Image;
   img.src = ...;
   var stop = (new Date()).getTime() + 1000 /*millisecs*/;
   while((new Date()).getTime() < stop)
      for(e in document.all) tmp=e.innerHTML;
}
```

The one problem with attempting to load an image at this moment is that after the `appUnload` function has completed, the browser will terminate all outstanding HTTP requests, thus stopping the image request before it has even had time to reach the server. JavaScript has no technique for easily putting a function to sleep. We use a busy loop that will keep the function active for one second, so that the image has time to be loaded. It is actually not important that the image be completely loaded, just that the request will reach the server and terminate the session.

For the image to load, we use a special 1x1 URL. The BSP runtime has a performance improvement that will always reply with a `1x1.gif` for an incoming URL of the format `.../1x1.gif`. To create such an URL, we just take the current document URL and add the sequence below. This URL will then be intercepted by the BSP runtime and answered immediately.

```
img.src = document.URL + "/1x1.gif"
        + "?sap-contextid=<%= cl_http_utility=>escape_
url( runtime->session_id )%>"
        + "&sap-sessioncmd=CANCEL";
```

Now that we have the image to load, we need to add the session ID so that the ICM layer will know to which session we are referring.

The last step is to actually get the session terminated. Here we use the fact that the ICM layer supports an URL parameter `sap-sessioncmd=CANCEL` that will terminate the session for which the URL is received. The URL then is processed in a new session. This is acceptable, as in the new session, still stateless, the BSP runtime will answer the request for the GIF image.

The benefit of this brute-force approach is that by using `document.URL`, the session ID either stored in a cookie on the application path or mangled inside the URL is actually already available. We add the session ID onto the URL again just to ensure that the session is really killed.

We place this coding onto a `default.htm` page within the application and always start it with this page. This will install the guard first, and then start the application. If the user now navigates away, the session will still be closed (see Figure 6.6).

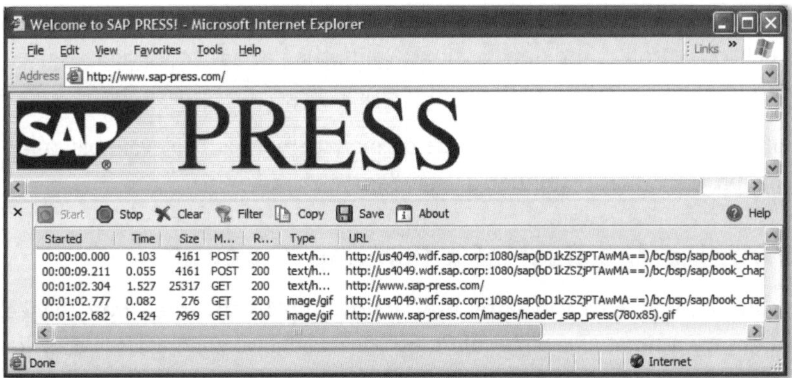

Figure 6.6 HTTP Trace of the Termination URL

When we look closely at the HTTP trace, we see that it looks as though the new URL is first loaded before the termination URL. This is mostly an artifact of the HTTP trace tool. A final check in transaction SM04 shows no HTTP sessions for our user.

If we look back at Section 6.4, we also had a restart page that was used to show a small message to the user and then to replace the URL of the page with the new start URL. The problem is now that our `default.htm` page is guarding the session, and the application is running within a child `<frame>`. Should the restart mechanism be used within this context, it will reload the application with `document.URL`, which will then effectively load a new `default.htm` within the old `<frame>` as guard. A number of small changes are required to the client JavaScript code used for restarting.

```
<script language="JavaScript">
function restart()
{
   parent.document.getElementById("guard").onunload = null;
   parent.document.URL = 'default.htm';
}
</script>
<htmlb:button   text   = "Restart"
        onClientClick = "restart();" />
```

The `restart.htm` page will be called at a time that the old session has already expired, or was closed by someone. As a result, the guard page is protecting a session that does not exist anymore. The first line of code we now have will unhook the `onUnLoad` event handler, so that it cannot continue to fire. Notice the use of `parent.document` to reference the `<frameset>` where the guard page is and not the document of the restart page itself.

The next small step is to now load the `default.htm` page so that a new guard page is installed to protect the new session. Again, the `parent.document` is used so that the old page can be unloaded and the new page can replace it.

A more complex example for handling session management is also available in the BSP application ITSM that is shipped as standard.

6.6 Warning the User of a Pending Timeout

You are bound sometime to encounter users who complain that they were logged off the system for a timeout even while they were actively working. It is easy for a user to get distracted with a phone call or work in another window. Or, perhaps the user has been typing for some time into a text box and simply has not done anything to trigger a server event.

An elegant solution would be to warn users shortly before the timeout and give them an opportunity to preserve their sessions and reset the timeout timer. The session timeout still has a valuable purpose to protect your system's precious memory resources, so you do not want to disable it all together.

As we already have the extra `<frameset>` installed to protect the session against navigation steps to other websites, let us extend this to include our warning code. All of the following code will be added onto the `default.htm` page.

```
<%
   DATA: timeout TYPE i.
   IF runtime->server->session_timeout IS INITIAL.
     DATA: name  TYPE pfeparname,
           value TYPE pfepvalue.
     name = 'rdisp/plugin_auto_logout'.
     CALL 'C_SAPGPARAM' ID 'NAME'  FIELD name
                        ID 'VALUE' FIELD value.
     timeout = value.
   ELSE.
     timeout = runtime->server->session_timeout+0(2)  * 3600
             + runtime->server->session_timeout+2(2)  * 60
             + runtime->server->session_timeout+4(2).
   ENDIF.
   timeout = timeout - 60.    " one minute warning
   timeout = timeout * 1000. " milliseconds for JavaScript
%>
```

The first step is to quickly determine the current timeout value. By default, the session timeout value is controlled by the profile parameter `rdisp/plugin_auto_logout`, set in seconds. However, it is also possible to configure a shorter value with a specific node within transaction SICF, that will then be available on the `server` object in the format `HHMMSS`. From the computed timeout value, we deduct 60 seconds as warning time (see Figure 6.7, below).

As a next step, we need the actual warning code.

```
var timer_id = 0;
function warning()
{
  var prompt;
```

```
  prompt = (new Date()).toLocaleString()
         + '\r\n'
         + 'Session will timeout in 1 minute, '
         + 'would you like to renew it?';
  if(confirm(prompt))
  {
    var img=new Image;
    img.src = document.URL+"/1x1.gif?sap-contextid=<%= cl_http_
utility=>escape_url( runtime->session_id )%>&sap-
unique="+((new Date()).getTime());
    timer_id = window.setTimeout('warning()',<%=timeout%>);
  }
}
```

The function just uses a simple JavaScript `confirm()` call to place the prompt on screen. Upon confirmation, the same `1x1.gif` hack is used as before to quickly update the session-inactivity timer. The only problem is that the server will instruct the browser to cache the image after the first roundtrip. Therefore, we add a unique number (timestamp in milliseconds) onto the URL, to ensure that the URL really will be loaded from the Web server and not from a cache.

The last part of the code is just to install our timer that will trigger on a session timeout and to restart it with each new page loaded.

```
function pageLoaded()
{
   window.clearTimeout(timer_id);
   timer_id = window.setTimeout('warning()',<%=timeout%>);
}

<frameset ... onLoad="pageLoaded();">
```

This code updates the `<frameset>` to also trigger a call each time that a new page is loaded. This is elegant, as the trigger code is not required on each page but rather installed centrally in the guard page. For each new page loaded, the old timer is stopped, and a new timer is started.

This current coding does have one slight disadvantage. The JavaScript `confirm()` method cannot be interrupted again with a timeout. Thus, the prompt will stay on screen until the user returned (this is the reason for the added timestamp!). A more complex solution would involve using a `window.open()` and `window.focus()` to load the prompt text into a separate window.

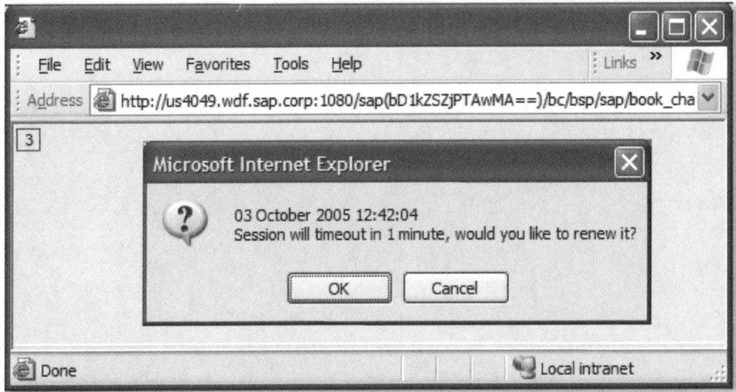

Figure 6.7 Warning on Session Timeout Pending

In addition, a timer is then installed in order to close the prompt window after a minute and just redirect the application to a termination page. In such a more complex example, care must be taken that the newly opened window does not in anyway trigger a request into the existing session, as this will reset the idle timer, giving the session a new lease on life.

WARNING Given the state of the art described above, a developer can become very quickly tempted to skip the `confirm()` sequence completely, and just tickle the session automatically. However, this will definitely keep sessions open, resources pinned down, and locks set, even though users are not in the office, possibly for the whole day. This is definitely not recommended.

6.7 Summary

Although it might seem that only one technique for session management is required, it is more likely that all are required in parallel. The `<frameset>` is required to guard against user navigation that leaves a dangling session. The restart protection is required for cases where the backend session suddenly gets terminated without our knowledge (for example from transaction SM04). The event handler to catch a server timeout is only critical in cases where resources are held, other than database locks that are freed automatically. The warning message is probably not critical from a technical point of view, but does help to reduce calls to the support desk.

7 Using BSP Applications in SAP GUI

Running BSP applications in the SAP GUI might seem strange at first, but there are times when it is required. This chapter shows how to do this and—even more important—the pitfalls to avoid.

The question naturally arises: "Why run a BSP at all in the SAP GUI"? Here we have a brand new Internet application, and yet we wish to tie it to the old world of ABAP dynpro programming. The answer is that dynpro programming is still the technique used most frequently for developing SAP programs, and often it is the best solution for a specific task.

Often, one wishes to develop a new add-on for an existing application in such a way that both the old application and the add-on are available via browser. For this, BSP applications are one alternative. They can run stand-alone in a browser, and one just needs to deal with the SAP GUI integration.

Other reasons for running the BSP application in the SAP GUI is to integrate new types of browser-based applets or to achieve specific rendering effects. For example, there are a number of Java applets available for BSP that also come with libraries to use these applets in a BSP application. When they are required in SAP GUI, the simplest approach is to just use them as usual in a BSP application, and integrate the complete BSP application.

Effectively, BSP applications within SAP GUI provide a slow migration path, whereby new features can be developed with Web technology, and thereby also used in stand-alone fashion, but at the same time be integrated into existing applications.

The ABAP dynpro has an HTML Viewer control that can be used to show HTML within a dynpro. It is in essence a wrapper control around an Internet Explorer browser. This control can be used by placing a custom control on the dynpro and using the class `cl_gui_html_viewer` to instantiate and configure the browser. See transaction DWDM for a number of example programs.

7.1 Using a BSP Application in a Dynpro

Let us start by quickly developing a small BSP application that we can use. Although the test program might at first look strange and useless, the next section will show the method in our madness. All that the following section of code does is list the number of ABAP sessions that we have open and provide two buttons.

The first increments a side-side counter, and the second opens a new window where the same application will continue running.

The BSP application is set as stateful, and one page is added with a page attribute `counter type string`. Having the counter attached to the page, rather than being stored as a hidden input field within the HTML rendering, shows that session is stateful, and that each time we return to the server it will be possible to update the same counter in the same session.

```
<%@extension name="htmlb" prefix="htmlb"%>
<htmlb:content  design = "design2003"
      controlRendering = "browser">
  <htmlb:page>
    <htmlb:form>
      <% counter = 1 + counter. %>
      <htmlb:button      id = "btn1"
                       text = "<%= counter %>"
                    onClick = "increaseCounter" />
       
      <htmlb:button    text = "New Window"
              onClientClick = "window.open(document.URL);" />
      <br><br>
      <%
        DATA: userlist TYPE TABLE OF UINFO,
              user     LIKE LINE OF userlist.
        CALL FUNCTION 'TH_USER_LIST'
          TABLES      LIST = userlist.
        DELETE userlist WHERE BNAME <> sy-uname.
      %>
      <htmlb:tableView  id = "tv1"
                     table = "<%= userlist %>" />
    </htmlb:form>
  </htmlb:page>
</htmlb:content>
```

Once the BSP application is finished, it can be activated and tested quickly. The next step is for the dynpro to host the BSP application. For this we write a new report and start Dynpro 100, which contains a custom control as the only screen element. Most of the code sample comes directly from the examples of the HTML Viewer control and the relevant documentation.

The only BSP specific part is the URL generation, shown in the code below. This is achieved using the `cl_bsp_runtime=>construct_bsp_url` method with the name and page of our test application. Figure 7.1 shows the BSP test application, both running both in the SAP GUI and also running stand-alone directly in the browser.

```
REPORT book_chapter07_example1.

DATA: html_viewer    TYPE REF TO cl_gui_html_viewer,
      html_container TYPE REF TO cl_gui_custom_container,
      fcode          LIKE sy-ucomm.

SET SCREEN 100.

MODULE status_0100 OUTPUT.
  SET PF-STATUS 'TESTHTM1'.
  SET TITLEBAR '001'.
  IF html_viewer IS INITIAL.

    CREATE OBJECT html_container
                  EXPORTING container_name = 'HTML'.
    CREATE OBJECT html_viewer
                  EXPORTING parent = html_container.

    DATA: url TYPE string, urlc(2048) TYPE c.
    cl_bsp_runtime=>construct_bsp_url(
          EXPORTING in_application = 'book_chapter07'
                    in_page        = 'example1.htm'
          IMPORTING out_abs_url    = url ).
    urlc = url. " type conversion STRING to C
    html_viewer->show_url( url = urlc ).
  ENDIF.
ENDMODULE.

MODULE user_command_0100 INPUT.
  IF fcode = 'BACK'.
    html_viewer->free( ).    FREE html_viewer.
    html_container->free( ). FREE html_container.
    LEAVE PROGRAM.
  ENDIF.
  CALL METHOD cl_gui_cfw=>dispatch.
  CLEAR fcode.
ENDMODULE.
```

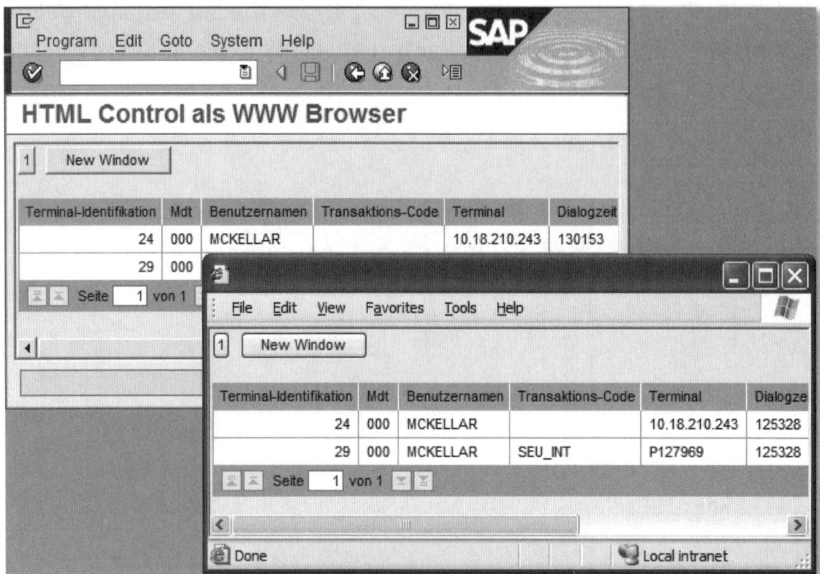

Figure 7.1 The Same Application in SAP GUI and in the Browser

7.2 Pitfalls when Using BSP Applications with SAP GUI

As we have seen from the coding above, placing a BSP application on a dynpro amounts to a few lines of code and works out of the box. However, there are a number of pitfalls in this scenario, which will be addressed in this section, along with solutions to solve them.

7.2.1 Communication Path

Probably the most difficult problem to anticipate involves the different communication paths that are used. This problem usually only arises in complex production landscapes, at a moment when we did not expect it.

The SAP GUI uses the DIAG protocol (effectively, binary data in TCP/IP) for communicating with the server. The browser uses HTTP (also a TCP/IP connection, usually text). As long as the client can reach the server with a direct TCP/IP connection, you will experience no problems. However, once a complex landscape is in use, the SAP GUI could begin communicating with the server via a SAP router.

Typically, this happens in scenarios where satellite offices are connected to the data center via the wide-area networks managed by the SAP router. In this case, only DIAG data streams can be transferred via the SAP router. When a dynpro appears that contains a HTML Viewer control, the container browser will attempt to set a HTTP connection back to the server. For this to work in practice, an additional HTTP route must be available.

One possible solution is to route the HTTP traffic out into the Internet and then back over the corporate firewall to the server. There is no need for the two data streams to follow the same communication path. However, in such a case, care should be taken to use—at a minimum—encrypted HTTPS connections.

7.2.2 The Second Authentication

When the BSP application is started within the SAP GUI, a second authentication is required (see Figure 7.2). Effectively, the SAP GUI already knows the credentials of the user. However, the embedded browser is a completely different entity that is started anew and is not aware of the credentials. This second authentication is very annoying!

Figure 7.2 Second Authentication Requested

The SAP GUI team built an unorthodox solution to the problem. User credentials usually are transferred via a Single Sign-On (SSO) cookie. However, it is not possible to set a cookie into the browser instance that is started by the SAP GUI.

What *was* possible was to set a special header field. The problem is that the newly set header field is only used in the next HTTP request for which it has been set. Thereafter, the information is again lost. To make the information sticky, a cookie is really needed, and the browser will only accept cookies that are received from the server.

Thus, when the browser is first started with the request to navigate to a specific URL, the request is changed by the SAP GUI to navigate to the very special destination /sap/public/myssocntl. In addition, two header fields are set. The first is the SSO data with a very short timestamp. The second aszheader is the real target URL. The handler on the server for the destination /sap/public/myssocntl will retrieve and validate the SSO header. Once accepted, a real SSO cookie is set. Thereafter, a HTTP redirect is made to the original URL requested. No second authentication is required with this approach, as the server can now retrieve the user credentials from every HTTP request just by looking at the SSO cookie.

This described behavior is not the default, and must be explicitly requested by the code that hosts the HTML Viewer. (See also SAP Note 612670, "SSO for local BSP calls using SAP GUI HTML Control.") To accomplish this, after creating the HTML-viewer control in our report, we add the additional method call enable_sapsso. This one method call alone activates the complete SSO mechanism, and a second authentication is not required.

```
CREATE OBJECT html_viewer EXPORTING parent = html_container.
html_viewer->enable_sapsso ( enabled = 'x' ).
```

A note of caution: This method requires that SSO be configured correctly for the server by the system administrator, and the path /sap/public/myssocntl within ICF must be active.

7.2.3 The Second Session

When we examine the source code of our test BSP application closely, we see that it lists the number of sessions that are open for our specific user. However, when looking closely at Figure 7.1, we can see that there are two sessions open!

The first is the SAP GUI session. The second session is opened by the BSP application. It is impossible to run the BSP application within the SAP GUI session. There are a number of implications that the developer must consider.

One is that of scalability. Once a (stateful) BSP application is used with a typical SAP GUI application, each end user will immediately require two sessions on the server to complete the transaction. This factor-of-two increase in sessions must be taken into consideration when the sizing of the application servers is done.

The next problem is that of data handling. If the same data is to be manipulated by both the SAP GUI and the BSP application, then some form of shared data space should be used. This can be done via database tables, shared memory, or from NetWeaver releases with ABAP shared objects. One additional alternative is to use SAPEVENTS between the SAP GUI and the browser (discussed in Section 7.3).

The biggest problem that must be handled is that of session management. When the dynpro is closed, the HTML Viewer control will also be unloaded. It is important at this moment to also terminate the BSP session.

The previous chapter already discussed session management in detail. All we need to do now is to add the additional few lines of code to build a session, terminate URL, load it into the browser, and wait a moment to give the browser time to transmit the URL to the server and have the BSP session terminated.

```
IF fcode = 'BACK'.

  html_viewer->get_current_url( IMPORTING url = urlc ).
  cl_gui_cfw=>flush( ).
  CONCATENATE urlc '/' sy-uzeit '/1x1?sap-sessioncmd=cancel'
         INTO urlc.
  html_viewer->show_url( url = urlc ).
  cl_gui_cfw=>flush( ).
  WAIT UP TO 1 SECONDS.

  html_viewer->free( ).      FREE html_viewer.
  html_container->free( ).   FREE html_container.
  ...
ENDIF.
```

The additional `flush( )` calls are required by the fact that calls to the HTML viewer control (such as retrieving the current URL) are queued and only executed on the next roundtrip. This call ensures that the data is retrieved immediately.

7.2.4 Window Open Behavior

In the BSP application example, there is also a button to open a new window using the typical JavaScript sequence `window.open()`. From the previous chapter on session management, we know that the new browser window will have the same browser instance on the client, and thus share the same set of cookies with the old window. As the session ID is stored in a cookie, all requests from the new window will be processed in the same session. This is the expected behavior, and it can be important, for example when F4-help windows are used.

Figure 7.3 shows this expected behavior. With the BSP application started in the browser, the first button was pressed five times, and then the new window was requested. On each round trip to the server, the counter is incremented, and we see in the new window the expected value six.

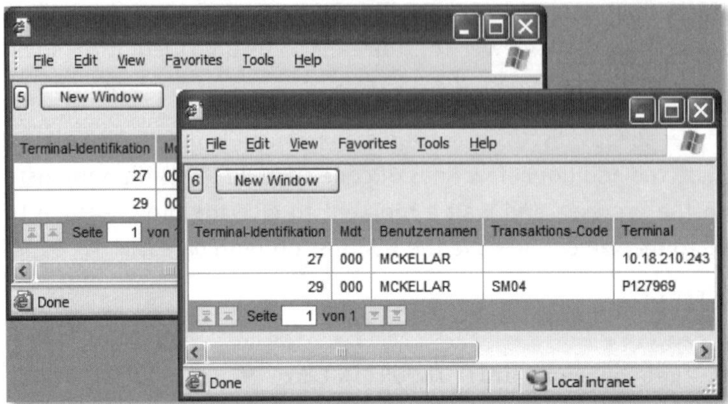

Figure 7.3 Expected Behavior of an Open Window Sequence

The same steps are repeated (see Figure 7.4), with the exception that the BSP application is now started in the SAP GUI. After five button presses, the new window is opened. Instead of the counter now showing the value six as we expected, the counter is showing again the value one.

This behaviour is also highlighted by the fact that the newly opened browser window now lists three sessions for our user, instead of the expected two.

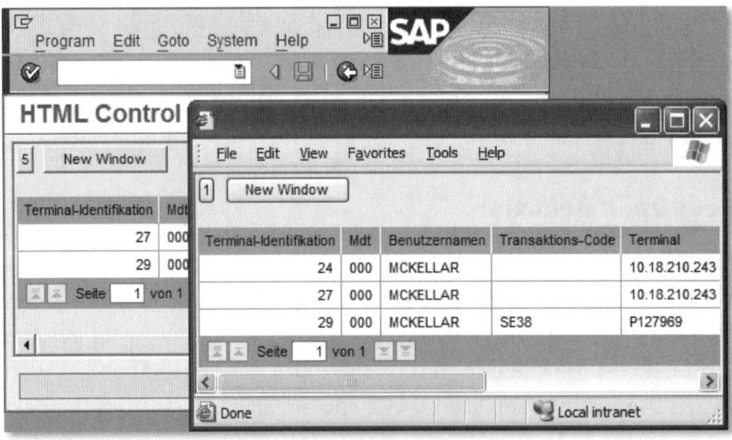

Figure 7.4 Real Behavior of an Open Window Sequence

The reason for this change is that within the HTML Viewer control, the `window.open()` sequence will give a new window with a new browser instance, which of course starts with an empty cookie jar. The HTTP request to fill the new window reaches the server without a session cookie, a new session is opened, and a new session cookie is set.

This behavior of the HTML Viewer can break application logic that depends on having different windows working against the same session; typically this would happen in F4 help systems. The best solution to this problem is to request that the BSP runtime not use cookies to identify sessions, but rather mangle the session identification into the URL. This is done by adding the URL parameter `sap-syscmd=nocookie`.

```
cl_bsp_runtime=>construct_bsp_url(
     EXPORTING in_application = 'book_chapter07'
                in_page       = 'example1.htm'
     IMPORTING out_abs_url    = url ).
CONCATENATE url '?sap-syscmd=nocookie' INTO url.
urlc = url. " type conversion STRING to C
```

Now a window-open sequence (using a relative URL) will use an URL that has a session identifier mangled into the URL, causing the request to land in the same session.

7.2.5 Effects of SAP's New Visual Design

When looking at Figure 7.1, we see that the buttons are rendered differently, depending on whether the BSP application is running with an external browser or within the SAP GUI hosted browser. These differences are especially noticeable in the rendering of buttons, dropdown list boxes and checkboxes.

The reason for this different rendering of the same BSP page is the combination of two aspects. The first is that the browser renders many user interface elements using the native Window controls. However, once the browser is used with SAP GUI, the complete control rendering is intercepted by the SAP GUI, so that it can render the requested controls in SAP's new visual design. This causes all controls to be rendered similarly to those of the SAP GUI, once the BSP page is executed within the HTML Viewer.

The solution to have the same visual rendering over all browser windows is to change the HTML rendering so that native window controls are not triggered by the browser. For the HTMLB family of rendering libraries (discussed in detail in Chapter 9), this can be achieved by setting the `controlRendering` attribute from `browser` to `SAP`.

```
<%@extension name="htmlb" prefix="htmlb"%>
<htmlb:content  design = "design2003"
      controlRendering = "SAP">
```

Figure 7.5 shows that with this code change, the buttons are now rendered the same in both the SAP GUI and in the browser.

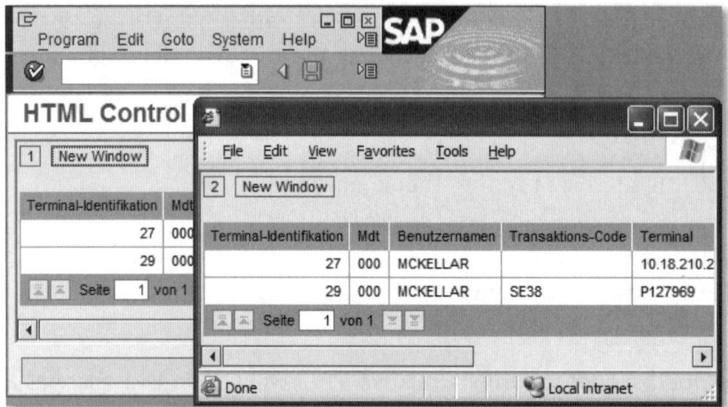

Figure 7.5 Effect of Setting controlRendering="SAP"

7.2.6 Loading HTML Pages Directly

Often, using a BSP application within the SAP GUI amounts to using a solution that is much bigger than the problem. A typical example would be to host a Java applet on an HTML page. Having a separate BSP application, implies a second development object, and possibly a second session at runtime. In such cases, it would be nice to just load the HTML directly into the HTML Viewer.

Another situation where this feature would also be very helpful is a "Loading..." page that gives the user immediate feedback that the BSP application is starting. This is usually important in cases where the BSP application must still be activated and started.

The HTML Viewer does support such a direct HTML load feature. The HTML is just concatenated into a string and loaded. Instead of calling the `show_url( )` method directly, we write a small HTML page that will display the text message and then auto-submit the form to the start the actual BSP application.

```
DATA: html TYPE string.
DATA: source TYPE TABLE OF char255.
CONSTANTS: crlf TYPE string VALUE
                                    cl_abap_char_utilities=>cr_lf.
CONCATENATE
         `<html>`
   crlf  `<body onload="document.all['frm'].submit();">`
   crlf   `<form id="frm" method="GET" action="` url `">`
```

```
   crlf    `<table border="0" width="100%" height="100%">`
   crlf     `<tr>`
   crlf      `<td align="CENTER" valign="MIDDLE"> `
   crlf       ` Loading...`
   crlf      `</td>`
   crlf     `</tr>`
   crlf    `</table>`
   crlf   `</form>`
   crlf  `</body>`
   crlf `</html>`
INTO html.

"SPLIT html AT crlf INTO TABLE source.
CALL FUNCTION 'SCMS_STRING_TO_FTEXT'
      EXPORTING text      = html
      TABLES    ftext_tab = source.
html_viewer->load_data( IMPORTING assigned_url = urlc
                        CHANGING  data_table   = source ).
html_viewer->show_url( url = urlc ).
```

In this example, the most significant call is the `load_data( )`, which will place the HTML into that data container for transfer to the SAP GUI, and return a new pseudo URL that can then be used for the `show_url( )` call. The new improved version of our application is shown in Figure 7.6.

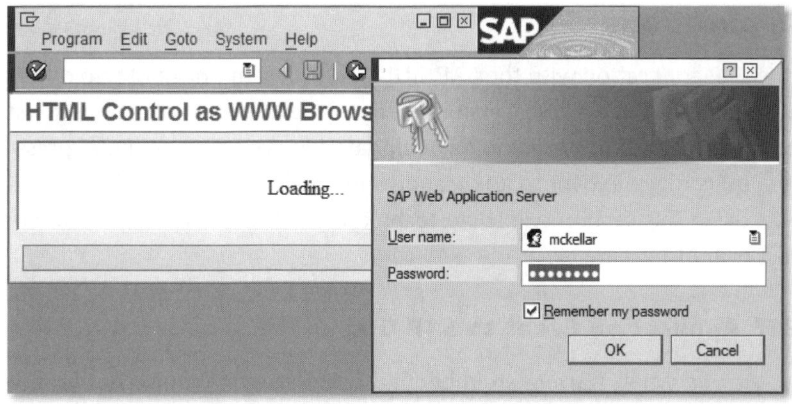

Figure 7.6 Use of a Small Loader Page

Is it really improved? It is true that the user sees immediately the "Loading..." text in the HTML Viewer, but suddenly the second authentication problem is back! The problem is that with this technique no initial URL is available that will be send to the server with the SSO information. The data is effectively made immediately available, and then subsequent HTTP requests do not have a SSO cookie available to transport the user credentials.

There are also a few other pitfalls that must be considered when loading HTML directly. For one, the HTML is transferred to the SAP GUI by the data container as a table of 255-character lines. It is important that the nicely formatted HTML code be repacked as 255-character lines. A simple split on the end of line sequences will result in each 255-character line being filled with spaces, thereby increasing the download size dramatically.

Should the HTML become too large (either because of space-filling or actual HTML coding), it will not be downloaded in time to the SAP GUI. Then the `show_url( )` method will then reference HTML that has not yet available (or only partially available), causing rendering errors in the SAP GUI. This constraint limits this feature to small HTML pages (a few kilobytes) with the recommendation to also "pack" into each line as much HTML as possible.

The positive benefit of such a technique of also removing the second BSP session has the downside that now the complete HTML generation must also be done in the SAP GUI update cycle. For large HTML pages, this additional HTML generation and downloading will affect the SAP GUI responsiveness. Having a separate BSP application brings the benefit that the HTML generation is done in a separate session and does not affect SAP GUI at all.

7.3 Interaction between SAP GUI and BSP Applications

Running the BSP application with the SAP GUI is actually a marriage of two different applications, running in two sessions. Often, these two applications must exchange small pieces of information or be updated in sync. For example, pressing the save button in the dynpro application should also cause the BSP application save its data. This section will show techniques to fire events in both directions or just to transfer data.

7.3.1 BSP Application Event to SAP GUI

The HTML Viewer, when starting an imbedded browser control, also hooks into the browser control to handle some forms of navigation. The most interesting of these are pseudo URLs of the form `SAPEVENT:...` (instead of the typical `http:...` or `ftp:...` forms). Once such an URL is triggered, the browser will delegate the fetching of the "URL" to the HTML Viewer control.

So the solution comes down to using any form of HTML that will cause the browser to load an URL of the form SAPEVENT:. SAP Note 191908, titled "Collective Note: HTML Viewer Control," describes this technique, and also describes the constraints when using it.

For our BSP application, we will add a new button that when pressed must inform the SAP GUI (effectively, the dynpro code) what the current counter value is. For this, we add one new button to the code that will call our JavaScript function postCounter() to do the hard work.

```
<htmlb:button       text = "Post Counter"
           onClientClick = "postCounter();" />
```

For the actual data transfer, we just use a normal form, as we would do for submitting data to a server. The form will just have one input field to transfer the data. The postCounter() method sets the input field correctly and submits the form.

```
<form id="sapForm" name="sapForm" method="POST"
                          action="SAPEVENT:POST_COUNTER">
   <input name="counter" type="hidden">
</form>

<script>
   function postCounter()
   {
     document.all["counter"].value =
                          document.all["btn1"].innerText;
     document.forms["sapForm"].submit();
   }
</script>
```

The only unusual aspect about this HTML code is the form action that does not point to an URL on the server, but is the special SAPEVENT: URL. The rest of the string is just an action name that has an application-specific meaning.

Two minor HTML aspects must be kept in mind. In HTML, forms cannot be nested but must be placed below one another in the HTML. Just place the above code towards the end of the page, outside the <htmlb:form> used. Also, when submitting a form, a response usually is received from the server that is then rendered again by the browser. This would replace our BSP application with something else. However, this is not so for SAPEVENT:-based forms. They do not return any form of response from the server.

With these minimal changes of one new form and a button to submit it, it is possible to fire an event with data from the BSP application directly to the SAP GUI. The next step is to catch and process the event.

As we will require in the next steps features from the HTML Viewer that are only accessible in protected methods, we will just create a new class that inherits from the cl_gui_html_viewer class.

```
CLASS cl_my_html_viewer DEFINITION
                        INHERITING FROM cl_gui_html_viewer.
PUBLIC SECTION.
   METHODS: constructor
              IMPORTING parent TYPE REF TO CL_GUI_CONTAINER.
   METHODS: on_sapevent
              FOR EVENT sapevent OF cl_gui_html_viewer
              IMPORTING action postdata.
ENDCLASS.
```

The most interesting part of this code is the on_sapevent method, which is declared as an event handler for the sapevent event. This ABAP event will be fired in the server when the HTML Viewer receives a SAPEVENT: within the SAP GUI.

The constructor method will inform the HTML Viewer that we are interested in this event and then set our on_sapevent method as handler for this event.

```
METHOD constructor.
   super->constructor( parent = parent ).
   DATA: event_tab TYPE cntl_simple_events,
         event     TYPE cntl_simple_event.
   event-appl_event = 'X'.
   event-eventid    = me->m_id_sapevent.
   APPEND event TO event_tab.
   me->set_registered_events( events = event_tab ).
   SET HANDLER me->on_sapevent FOR me.
ENDMETHOD.
```

When the on_sapevent method is called (because the button had been pressed in the browser), it will have two parameters (see signature of this method in the class definition above). The first is the action string that is the value that was used in the SAPEVENT: URL (everything after the colon character). The other parameter is postdata, which is just a table of strings of the form name=value that reflects the form fields submitted in the browser. All that our coding does is to read the value of the counter and to display it with a MESSAGE statement.

```
METHOD on_sapevent.
  IF action CS 'COUNTER'.
    DATA: counter TYPE string.
    READ TABLE postdata INDEX 1 INTO counter.
    SPLIT counter AT '=' INTO counter counter.
    MESSAGE counter TYPE 'I'.
  ENDIF.
ENDMETHOD.
```

As a last step, the only change to the report itself is to change the `html_viewer` object to be an instance of this newly created class. The rest of the report was not changed.

```
DATA: html_viewer TYPE REF TO cl_my_html_viewer.
```

See Figure 7.7 for the results. Pressing the button in the browser displays a message within the SAP GUI with the correct current value from the button.

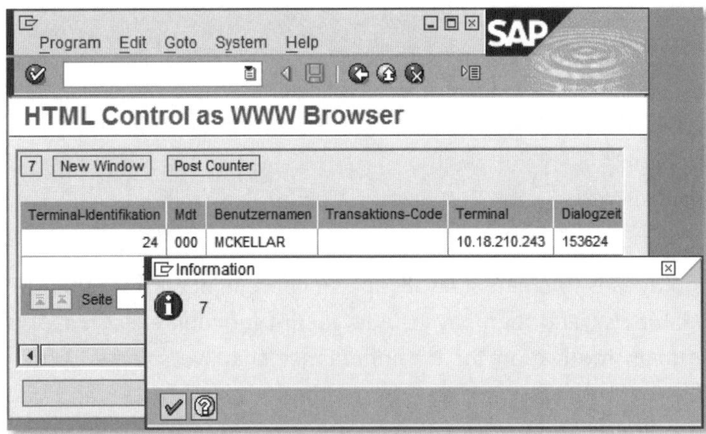

Figure 7.7 Interaction with SAP GUI

7.3.2 SAP GUI Event to BSP Application

For the reverse route, we add a new method `get_counter` to our class and wire the method call to a button on the dynpro. Now, when the button is pressed, we call the `get_counter` method and expect that it will show exactly the same message as previously.

We know already how to cause the browser send events and data to the SAP GUI. So the problem amounts to injecting some code into the BSP application that will fill and submit such a special `SAPEVENT` form. Let us first look at the complete source code.

```
METHOD get_counter.
  DATA: js    TYPE STANDARD TABLE OF CHAR255,
        line TYPE STRING.
  APPEND:
  `function _getCounter() {`                              TO js,
  ` var _value = document.all["btn1"].innerText;`        TO js,
  ` var _frm = document.createElement('form');`          TO js,
  ` _frm.setAttribute('id',      '_sapForm');`           TO js,
  ` _frm.setAttribute('name',    '_sapForm');`           TO js,
  ` _frm.setAttribute('method', 'POST');`                TO js,
  ` _frm.setAttribute('action','SAPEVENT:COUNTER');`     TO js,
  ` var _if = document.createElement('input');`         TO js,
  ` _if.setAttribute('name',   '_counter');`             TO js,
  ` _if.setAttribute('type',   'hidden');`               TO js,
  ` _if.setAttribute('value', _value);`                  TO js,
  ` _frm.appendChild(_if);`                              TO js,
  ` document.body.appendChild(_frm);`                    TO js,
  ` document.forms["_sapForm"].submit();`                TO js,
  `}`                                                     TO js,
  `window.setTimeout("_getCounter();", 200 /*ms*/);`     TO js.
  me->set_script( script = js[] ).
  me->execute_script( ).
ENDMETHOD.
```

All that this method does is to create a JavaScript function, inject it from the SAP GUI into the HTML Viewer, and then have the JavaScript function executed. This approach was the main motivation for the inheritance that we selected previously. The `set_script` and `execute_script` methods are protected and can only be used from a derived class.

The JavaScript function itself will just use dynamic HTML (DHTML) to create a new form, attach a new input field with the correct value to the form, and then attach the form to the document. As a last step, the form is submitted, which will again trigger the `on_sapevent` method in our class.

An important aspect of this script is that the execution of the injected method is delayed by 200ms. This value was empirically determined, and is required because of the distributed nature of solution. The ABAP code itself runs in the server, but the actual JavaScript injection and handling are done in the SAP GUI. The delay gives the SAP GUI time to complete its round trip before the browser fires a new event again. When the programmed button is triggered on the dynpro, we will see exactly the same results as in Figure 7.7.

7.4 Starting a New Browser Outside the SAP GUI

The last section of this chapter describes a technique that can be used to start a new separate browser window. Although not exactly part of the topic in executing a BSP application within the SAP GUI, the solution is tied very closely to the HTML Viewer.

There are a number of techniques, all encapsulated in functions, that allow the SAP GUI to start an external browser to the server. However, they all require that the user must perform a second authentication. Again, it would be better if the browser could be started with a call that will also transfer the user credentials from the SAP GUI to the browser. For this, there exists a method called `show_url_in_browser`. However, this method has many constraints which makes it usable only in very special cases.

To enhance this functionality, a new method—`detach_url_browser`—was added. This method is very new. It will only be available with a new SAP service pack and also with the installation of a new SAP GUI. See SAP Note 864528 (Detach URL in Browser) for the exact dates and releases.

The more pertinent question is: How can we program one technique that will start a BSP application in a browser window, and in the most optimal case not require a second authentication? In the cases where the new functionality is not available, the browser should just perform the second authentication routine (as it always done up to now).

The solution amounts to placing a dynamic call to the new method, and, if it fails, just to use an older function as fallback.

```
REPORT book_chapter07_example4.

DATA: url TYPE string, urlc(2048) TYPE c.
cl_bsp_runtime=>construct_bsp_url(
    EXPORTING in_application = 'book_chapter07'
              in_page        = 'example1.htm'
    IMPORTING out_abs_url    = url ).
urlc = url. " type conversion STRING to C

TRY.
  DATA: viewer          TYPE REF TO cl_gui_html_viewer.
  DATA: empty_container TYPE REF TO cl_gui_container.
  CREATE OBJECT viewer  EXPORTING parent = empty_container.
  CALL METHOD viewer->enable_sapsso
      EXPORTING  enabled = 'X'
```

```
      EXCEPTIONS OTHERS  = 1.
  CALL METHOD viewer->('DETACH_URL_IN_BROWSER')
      EXPORTING url = urlc.
  cl_gui_cfw=>flush( ).
CATCH cx_root.
  CALL FUNCTION 'CALL_BROWSER' EXPORTING url = urlc.
ENDTRY.
```

Notice the use of the dynamic-call method. If this code executes on an older SAP release, the call will fail, and the catch code will call the old function.

8 Performance Measurements

In these days of gigahertz and gigabytes, one can be tempted not to worry about performance. However, the performance of an application is critical to its scalability. The chapter will look at different ways to gauge the application performance.

We usually recognize performance problems by observing that "the application is slow." But this should only be the starting point for a thorough inspection in which we take the application apart and to look at the different components. The frequently heard comment that "BSP is slow" shows that the developer did not do his or her homework, or was not sure how to do it. Let us dive deep into the performance-measurement topic and demonstrate tools that help get an accurate number for everything moving on a Web page.

A good place to start is the user's perception of performance: A button is pressed, and the answer is rendered moments later. This is the only real latency that users care about. At a technical level, there are a number of components that play a role in the complete delay the user experiences.

For the user, time crawls by in seconds. However, for each component, time flies by, and each component usually requires only a small slice of one second. So, for our measurements we will always work in milliseconds.

The first temporal component is the time that the browser requires to submit a form, effectively the time from the pressing of the button until the HTTP request is dispatched. For typical HTMLB-based applications (discussed in Chapters 9 and 10), this time is insignificant. However, we have seen frameworks that hook into the submit sequence, and their additional JavaScript code added a few hundred milliseconds. For our applications, we will not consider this, but do keep the factor in mind if you are hooked into the submit sequence.

The next component is the transfer time for the HTTP request to the server. Usually, HTTP requests are small and do not contribute much to the total latency. However, when Single Sign-On (SSO) is active, the `MYSAPSSO2` cookie alone is already a few hundred bytes, and then the HTTP request becomes an aspect worth considering.

Once the HTTP request reaches the server, the work really starts, and the complete server processing time is added onto the total latency. This is usually the first large number to measure.

Thereafter, the HTTP response is returned to the browser. As this is HTML code for the complete screen rendering, it can easily be 100KB or more. If GZIP compression is switched on, the data transfer volume is low, but the transfer time is now replaced by the compression and decompression time.

The last big component is the HTML-rendering time. For complex screens, for example using tables and tabstrips, this time can also be a few hundred milliseconds.

In the next sections, we will look at a number of approaches to get a handle on the performance of each component of the latency.

8.1 Test Applications

Naturally, we are interested in the performance of our own test application. However, just having one final performance number without knowing the effects of the different components, makes it harder to understand the significance of that number.

The best technique for understanding the effects of the different components is to start a full measurement, but with only a simple "Hello World!" application. This already provides a baseline number for the network latency to the server and back, plus the time required to pass through the complete BSP runtime and have one BSP page executed. This provides an absolute minimum number and reflects accurately the total BSP overhead. Such a test page is shipped within the BSP application `IT03`, page `text0KB.htm`.

As a next step, we want to see the effects of network-transfer time and "memory bandwidth" of the application server (the speed at which data can be passed through all layers). These numbers can later be compared to the actual page size of our application page to determine the pure transfer time. Again, `IT03` has a number of test pages to help. These pages are all named `text`**<N>**`KB.htm`, where **<N>** can be one of 1, 2, 4, 8, 16, 32, or 64. This allows us to measure the effects of, for example, pages that are 32KB in size. In such a case, we are measuring the time to get the data into an ABAP buffer, transferred to the Internet Communication Manager (ICM) layer (in kernel), streamed out onto the network and transferred from the server to the browser.

Similarly, our application can have images of different sizes. These are usually cached in the server and also at the browser. The fact that these images must be loaded has its costs. To measure this effect, use the images `image`**<N>**`KB.gif`, again from `IT03` and with the same range for **<N>**. Because these images are loaded into the ICM cache on the first request, we have a load test as a measurement of the ICM-cache and network-transfer times. Usually, the ICM cache involves just one memory transfer, which is insignificant compared to the network component, so that we can use this test to get a good estimate of the true network-transfer cost.

The other application worth looking at is `IT05`, starting at page `main.do`. This is effectively a mock-up of a complex screen from a real application. When measuring with this application, we are not only looking at the network component and the BSP runtime, but also adding the HTMLB family of rendering libraries. Unfortunately, these libraries do add some overhead, and their total overhead is proportional to the number of controls used and their complexity. For serious performance measurements, having such a mock-up of a representative screen with its measurement number available helps to quantify the total cost of the BSP runtime plus the rendering libraries. When this number is later compared to the overall time of the real application, the difference will give a very good indicator of true application runtime.

A final aspect to consider is that of page activation and URL mangling. When a BSP page is new in the system, no temporary class is available to process it. On the first request, such a class is created, loaded into the ABAP program buffer and can only then be executed. On subsequent requests, the class representing the page can always be executed directly from the program buffer. For this reason, we always measure a number of times, so that the system is in a "warm" state. Similarly on the first request, the BSP runtime will mangle the URL (see Chapter 4), causing an additional roundtrip. Only start measurements after the URL has been mangled.

8.2 Quick Sizing with HTTP Trace Tool

The simplest technique for getting a good overview of an application's behavior is to execute it while using a HTTP trace tool. This gives a very good overview of the pages and the additional resources (style-sheet pages, JavaScript code and images) that the pages load. The tool will also show which resources are correctly cached. More important, though, will be numbers that the trace tool shows. This presents a complete measurement of the network and server times. With these numbers alone, a developer already has a very good overview of an application's performance. This is the minimum testing that should be done!

Looking at Figure 8.1, we see first a number of load sequences for the `text32KB.htm` page. The first request took 377ms, whereas all other requests for this page took about 80ms. This shows that the first time the page is requested, it has first to be activated and loaded into the ABAP program buffer. For our performance measurements, the lower numbers from the warm system is used, as this reflects the normal operating state of the system. The slow numbers will only be experienced once by the first user accessing the page.

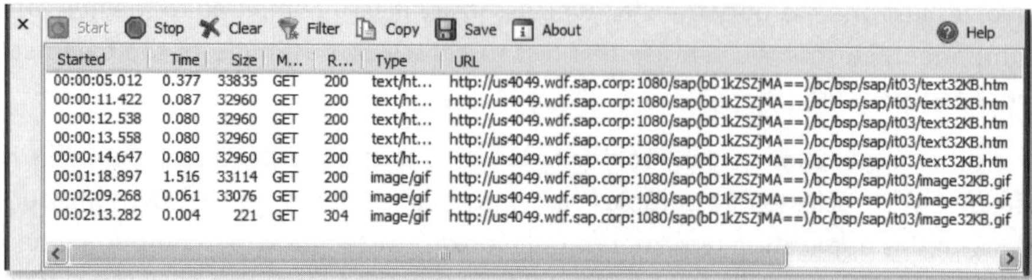

Started	Time	Size	M...	R...	Type	URL
00:00:05.012	0.377	33835	GET	200	text/ht...	http://us4049.wdf.sap.corp:1080/sap(bD1kZSZjMA==)/bc/bsp/sap/it03/text32KB.htm
00:00:11.422	0.087	32960	GET	200	text/ht...	http://us4049.wdf.sap.corp:1080/sap(bD1kZSZjMA==)/bc/bsp/sap/it03/text32KB.htm
00:00:12.538	0.080	32960	GET	200	text/ht...	http://us4049.wdf.sap.corp:1080/sap(bD1kZSZjMA==)/bc/bsp/sap/it03/text32KB.htm
00:00:13.558	0.080	32960	GET	200	text/ht...	http://us4049.wdf.sap.corp:1080/sap(bD1kZSZjMA==)/bc/bsp/sap/it03/text32KB.htm
00:00:14.647	0.080	32960	GET	200	text/ht...	http://us4049.wdf.sap.corp:1080/sap(bD1kZSZjMA==)/bc/bsp/sap/it03/text32KB.htm
00:01:18.897	1.516	33114	GET	200	image/gif	http://us4049.wdf.sap.corp:1080/sap(bD1kZSZjMA==)/bc/bsp/sap/it03/image32KB.gif
00:02:09.268	0.061	33076	GET	200	image/gif	http://us4049.wdf.sap.corp:1080/sap(bD1kZSZjMA==)/bc/bsp/sap/it03/image32KB.gif
00:02:13.282	0.004	221	GET	304	image/gif	http://us4049.wdf.sap.corp:1080/sap(bD1kZSZjMA==)/bc/bsp/sap/it03/image32KB.gif

Figure 8.1 HTTP Trace Tool Analysis

The next numbers show the same behavior for loading an image. On the first request, the image must be retrieved from the MIME repository and then written into the ICM cache before transmission. The total time of 1,515ms is again only experienced once by the first user. All other users will find the request already in the ICM cache, from where the image will be streamed out again, giving us a speedy 61ms for the image. As a last test, we looked at the time for a cache check, when the browser just needs to confirm that its image is still valid. As the image is not transferred again, only the `Not Modified` message (HTTP return code 304), we see the complete roundtrip completed in 4ms!

With a good HTTP trace tool, it is already possible to get an accurate answer to the question on the application's behavior.

8.3 Network Latency

The simplest technique for measuring strictly the network transfer time is to use the `ping` tool. This is an application that will send out a small test request to the server (by default 32 bytes), and the server will simply echo the data back. This is done at the operating-system level and thus does not contain much server overhead. The time is dominated by the network time.

Using a small request of 32 bytes produces only network latency, without the influence of the network bandwidth. Effectively, a slow dial-up line will test comparably to a fast DSL line, as the requests are small and the time is dominated by the overhead to traverse the physical distance.

To test a more realistic scenario, set the request size to the expected size of our HTTP traffic using the `-l` parameter for `ping` command. However, this command is symmetric, in that it sends and then receives the same data volume. In HTTP, the request is normally small, whereas the response is large and contains the complete answer from the server. For example, for our `text32KB.htm` test from Section 8.2, we see am HTTP request size of 1,302 bytes (size is influenced by SSO cookie that is active) and an HTTP response size of 32,960 bytes (includes HTTP headers). Thus, we must test these two cases individually.

Also, the numbers from `ping` reflects both the sending and receiving of the same data. But, in the HTTP traffic, the HTTP request is only sent, and the HTTP response only received. So, in each case divide the number by two.

```
Command Prompt

C:\>ping -w 1000 us4049.wdf.sap.corp
Reply from 10.21.82.172: bytes=32 time<1ms TTL=251
Reply from 10.21.82.172: bytes=32 time<1ms TTL=251
Reply from 10.21.82.172: bytes=32 time<1ms TTL=251

C:\>ping -l 1302 -w 1000 us4049.wdf.sap.corp
Reply from 10.21.82.172: bytes=1302 time=1ms TTL=251
Reply from 10.21.82.172: bytes=1302 time=1ms TTL=251
Reply from 10.21.82.172: bytes=1302 time=1ms TTL=251

C:\>ping -l 32960 -w 2000 us4049.wdf.sap.corp
Reply from 10.21.82.172: bytes=32960 time=6ms TTL=251
Reply from 10.21.82.172: bytes=32960 time=6ms TTL=251
Reply from 10.21.82.172: bytes=32960 time=6ms TTL=251
```

Figure 8.2 Ping Command Used to Determine Network-Transfer Speed

Looking at Figure 8.2, we can see that the simple ping to our server takes less than 1ms. But it carries effectively no data. Using more realistic numbers from our test scenario, we have roughly 0.5ms for the upstream data representing the HTTP request, and 3ms for the down stream data representing the HTTP response.

Accepting measurement inaccuracies, we can say that a 32KB HTTP request/response cycle should consume roughly 4ms. This is still slightly less than the 6ms we measured with an image download from cache. Keep in mind that the image download amounts to the small HTTP request, and a 32KB HTTP response. The difference between the two numbers is of a technical nature: In effect, the HTTP traffic is transferred within a TCP connection, where a slow-start algorithm with a sliding window prevents the complete use of available bandwidth, but slowly scales up the data transmission. The `ping` command sends it data without TCP. It only matters that the two numbers must be in the same ball park and must confirm our estimates of network-transfer time.

8.4 Server Processing Time

The simplest technique for estimating the complete server processing time is to measure it with two `GET RUN TIME` calls, bracketing the page.

```
<% DATA: server_start TYPE i.
   GET RUN TIME FIELD server_start.
```

```
%>

<%@extension name="htmlb" prefix="htmlb"%>
<htmlb:content design="design2003"><htmlb:page><htmlb:form>
   <htmlb:button text    = " Hello World!"
                 onClick = "myClickHandler" />
</htmlb:form></htmlb:page></htmlb:content>

<%
  DATA: server_end TYPE i,
        run_time   TYPE string.
  GET RUN TIME FIELD server_end.
  server_end = ( server_end - server_start ) / 1000.
  run_time   = server_end.
  CONDENSE run_time.
%>
<script>
  window.status = "Server=" + "<%=run_time%>" + "ms";
</script>
```

At the beginning of the page, the first time point is stored. At the end of the page, a new time point is taken and the difference calculated in milliseconds. As a last step, the time is written in the browser into the status line (see Figure 8.3). This measures only the time spent within the application coding. It does not include the BSP runtime overhead.

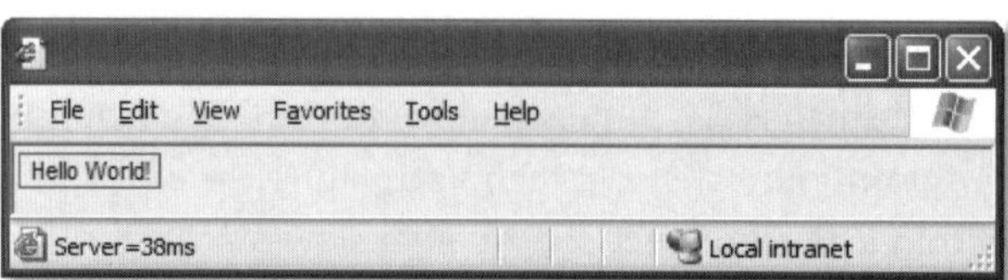

Figure 8.3 Example of Server Runtime Measurement

A better technique to measure the actual processing time of the server is to use statistical records. These are very small timestamps written by the Internet Communication Framework (ICF) layer. These reflect the complete ABAP runtime, leaving only an insignificant time from the ICM layer unmeasured.

Statistical records are by default not enabled for HTTP. They either can be enabled with the profile parameter `rdisp/no_statistic` or with the ABAP program `RSSTATISTIC` (from transaction SE38). After statistical records have been enabled, execute the BSP application.

Use transaction STAD to view the statistical records. Set the time filter around the time of the tests and limit output to that of program SAPMHTTP. (The program SAPMHTTP is the very first basic activation step where HTTP calls are placed into the ABAP stack.)

When the program is started, a list of statistical records according to the filter criteria is shown (see Figure 8.4). Already one can see that the first hit takes much longer than the following hits on the same page. For the first run, the ABAP load for the BSP page has to be fetched from the database and loaded into the program execution buffer. This hit includes a large database overhead. All subsequent hits on the same test page have no database overhead.

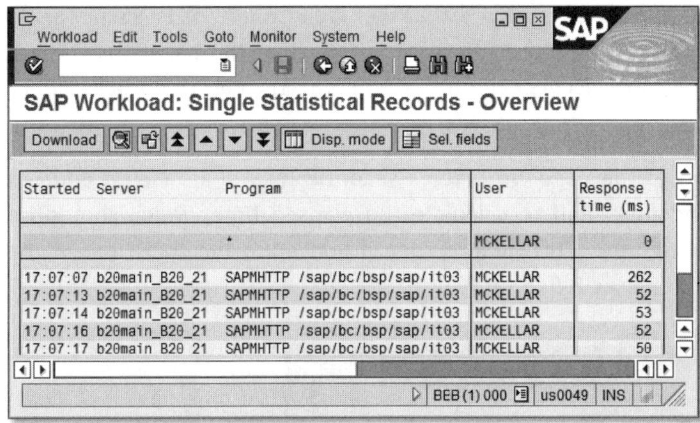

Figure 8.4 Output from Statistical records

Looking at these records, we see that after the first page, all other pages have a server component of roughly 52ms. This is in line with our measurements of HTTP roundtrip latency of 80ms for the same page.

The statistical records reflect the complete ABAP runtime, but do not include the ICM time (kernel part). This additional time, plus the network time of roughly 6ms, will explain a difference of a few milliseconds between the statistical records (ABAP runtime) and the HTTP roundtrip latency. The remaining time difference must be attributed to inaccuracies in the entire process.

8.5 Browser Rendering Time

Investigating the browser rendering time is slightly more difficult. For us, the browser is a closed box, and we do not know much about what is happening from the moment the HTTP response is received until the bitmap is actually placed onto screen. The only easy technique we have is to use JavaScript coding.

```
<script>
  var render_start = new Date();
</script>
...
<script>
  var render_end  = new Date();
  var render_time = render_end.getTime() -
                                          render_start.getTime();
  window.status =        "Server=" + "<%=run_time%>" + "ms"
                 + "  RenderTime=" + render_time     + "ms";
</script>
```

Looking at the above program, we see that we added a line of JavaScript code right at the beginning of the page to mark the time that the page was started. Although this script block occurs even before the `<html>` tag, the browser does accept it.

Directly at the end of the page we place a second block of JavaScript code to again mark the end time, and to calculate the elapsed time, which should be roughly the rendering time. This value is then displayed in the status bar of the browser as shown in Figure 8.5.

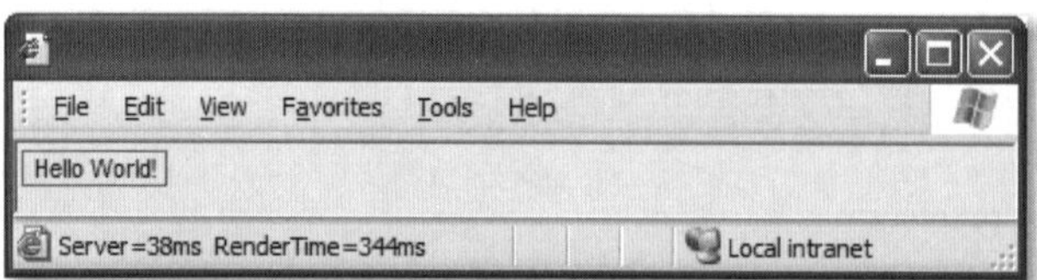

Figure 8.5 Example of Browser-Rendering Measurement

Although these are the last statements on the page that does not necessarily mean that the browser is finished. It is typical for browsers to first build parts of the HTML page into a bitmap, which is only displayed after it has finished HTML rendering. But still, this measurement is already a good indicator of the rendering time required for the page.

Given these performance-measurement ideas, one could consider to place the coding into a BSP element (see Chapter 9) for easy use on all pages. Then the BSP element can turn the measurements on only when required. For BSP, such an example is available in the `benchmark` library and shown in use in BSP application `IT05`.

8.6 Determining Hotspots

After a first round of performance measurements, the next logical question is: can we improve that performance? This question can only be answered if we know what the application in question is doing.

For this piece of the puzzle, we will use runtime analyses to get a detailed picture of an application's runtime behavior. The runtime analysis of a BSP application is activated from transaction SICF. Just select from the **Edit** menu the entry **Runtime Analysis**. Thereafter, execute the test BSP application.

The data collected by the runtime analyses can be seen using transaction SE30. Simply select **Other File...** for the specific user, then double-click on any of the URLs listed (see Figure 8.6).

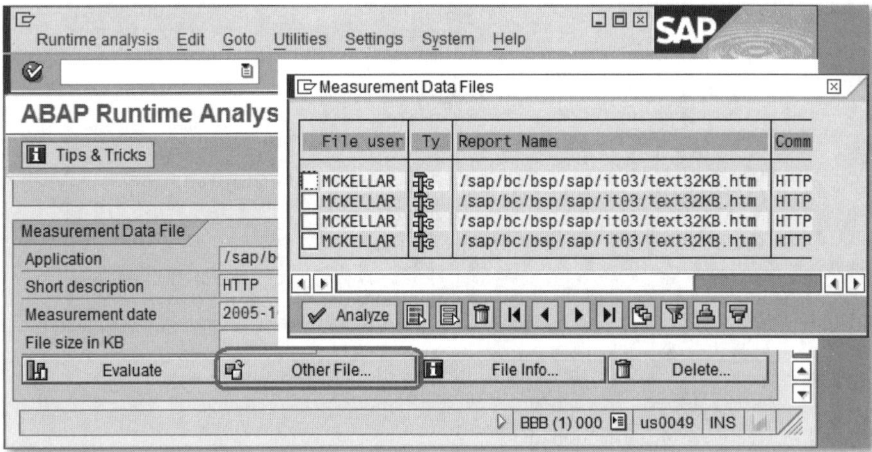

Figure 8.6 Selecting One Request from SE30 for Runtime Analysis

Let us look briefly at the type of information that can be learned from transaction SE30. The true value of this tool can only be learned from practical work and as such we will not dive into low-level detail, but we recommend that each developer invest some time with the tool to see its potential (see Figure 8.7).

The first notable aspect is the **Hit List**. This shows all methods and functions called, and their gross and net times. To get an overview of which methods have the longest runtimes, sort on the net times.

Database access is usually the more expensive part of an application, and the **Database Hit List** provides detailed information about database tables that were accessed.

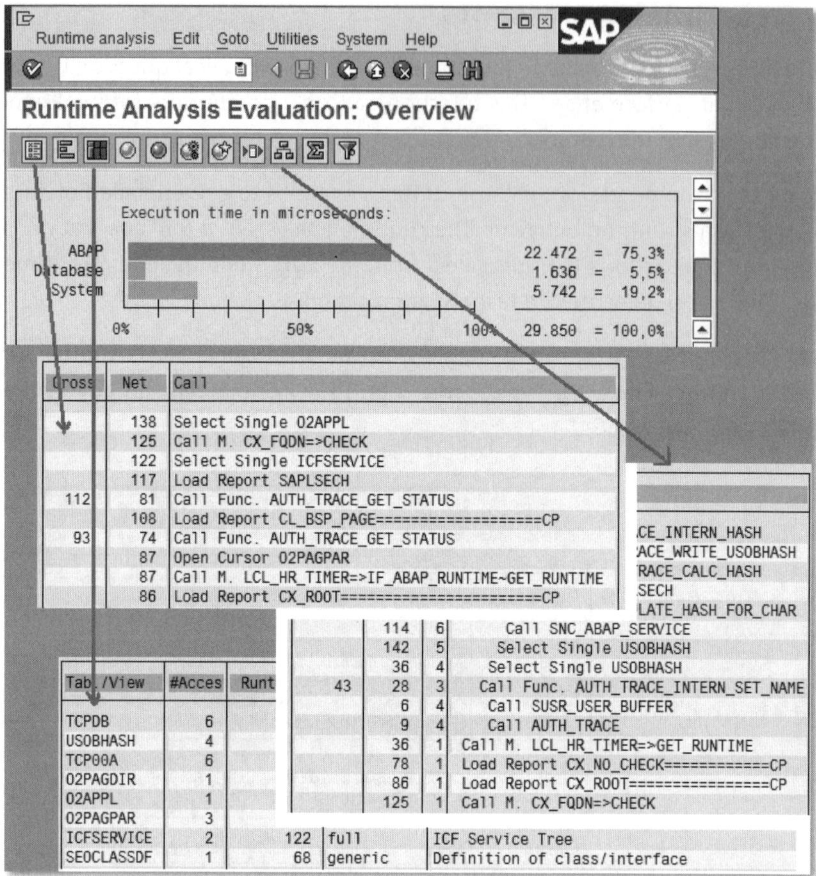

Figure 8.7 Overview of Transaction SE30

The **Call Hierarchy** shows the calling sequence of the application. This can be a daunting display for complex applications, but does help to correlate the dynamic behavior of the application to the more static code one sees in the editor. This is especially helpful in understanding paths taken through the code, and to answer the "who-called-this-method" type of questions.

It is always possible to use forward navigation (double-clicking) to get more detailed information about any specific sequence that is displayed. Use the blue **Display Source Code** button at any point to jump directly to the relevant source code.

For the application `IT03`, there is no application-relevant logic. The results are dominated with ICF layer and BSP runtime aspects. Experience has shown that in larger applications the application code itself, and also the rendering from the HTMLB libraries, usually dominates the performance.

8.7 Load Testing

Performance measurement (How fast does it go?) is the inverse of the question of scaling (How large must the box be?). We have now already looked at approaches to calculate the performance times for simple "Hello World!" pages, for larger sized pages, and images. However, at the end of the day, one has to measure all pages from one application.

There are many programs available for stress testing Web applications. In principle, any program can be used. We will use the Web Application Stress Tool from Microsoft[1]. It is quick to install and contains all the necessary features required for good stress testing.

The stress tool permits a record mode, whereby we just browse through a website while the stress tool itself records all the URLs that we accessed, including all resources loaded by the browser. We use this feature to quickly load our `text32KB.htm` and `image32KB.gif` pages (see Figure 8.8).

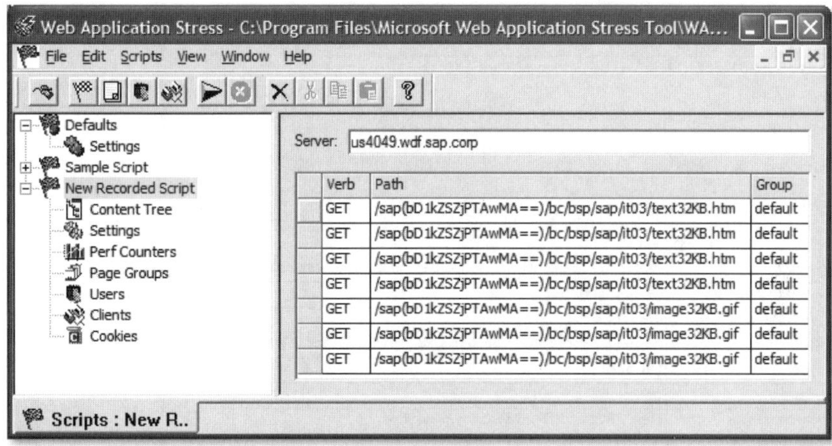

Figure 8.8 Web Application Stress Tool: Recorded Session

A comment on the stress tool: In recording mode, the server field is not set correctly and must be later quickly corrected.

One of the factors to consider is that of URL mangling. When conducting performance measurements, the goal is to run the same test many times to generate a real load on the server. However, most test programs are structured so that each test is run individually, the results are recorded, and then the test is started anew.

---

1 The program can be downloaded from Microsoft's website, *http://www.microsoft.com*. Recommended is to search for "Web Application Stress Tool," as the exact location on the website changes from time to time.

This dictates that specific actions experienced only once by a user are measured continuously by the test. URL mangling is one such action. Thus, to measure the real performance, and not the start-up time of the redirects to mangle each URL, we use only mangled URLs in our tests.

A similar one-time cost is that of authentication. The very first HTTP request will be rejected by the server, requesting that authentication information first be supplied. Once the browser has the authentication information from the user, this data will also be set, and does not play any additional role. The Web stress tool works similarly. It will also send an HTTP request without authentication, and only after the authentication challenge will it send its available authentication data. In this case, two roundtrips for each test are measured, once for the authentication challenge and once for the real work.

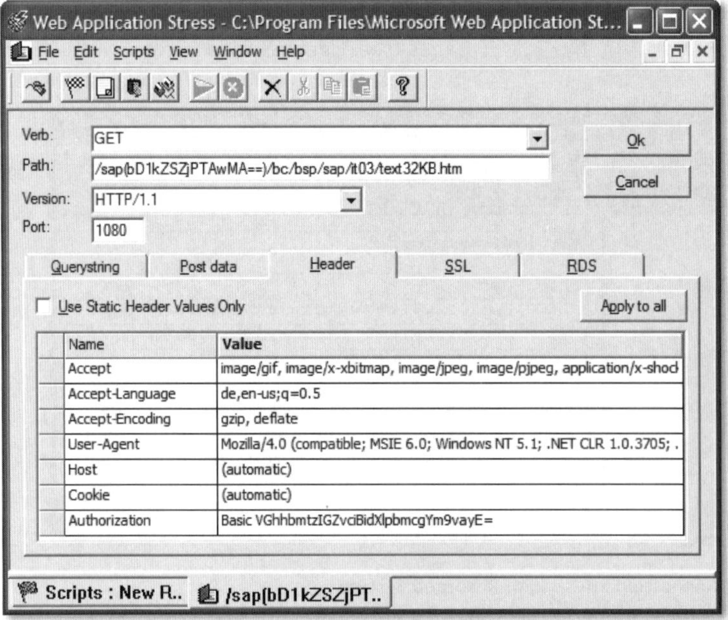

Figure 8.9 Web Application Stress Tool: Setting Authentication

To suppress this additional roundtrip, we add from the beginning authentication data to all requests. In Figure 8.9 we can see that we manually added the Authorization header (we saved the string while the recording was done). Thereafter, we pressed the **Apply to All** button so that this header is set on all recorded requests.

With this, we are ready to configure the actual stress test (see Figure 8.10).

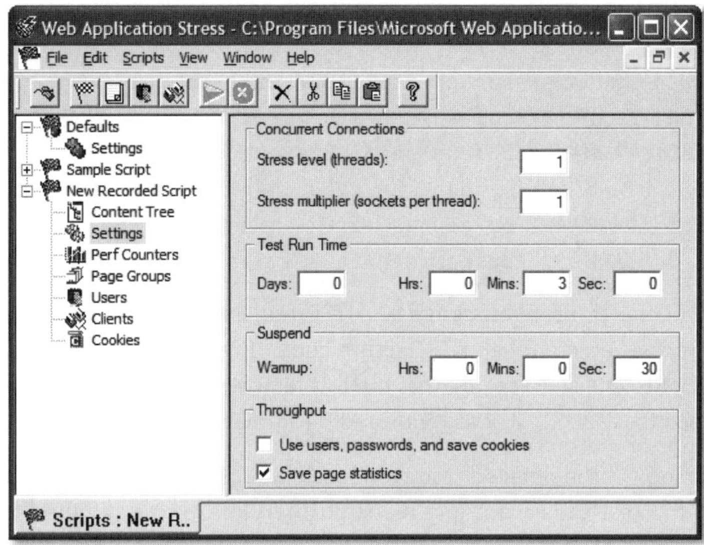

Figure 8.10 Web Application Stress Tool: Configuring Test Run

For the test, we don't wish to simulate many browsers. If we did so, we would get effects of all HTTP requests competing for resources, with the result that, once the server comes under heavy load, more time would be spent with queue management than with real processing. For our test runs, we are interested in the maximum load that the server can handle for one browser. This gives us the average processing time per request. From this, we can compute an upper maximum per time unit. Thus, we configure to exactly one the number of threads to use.

We also know that the first request always has a higher overhead to ensure that the matching temporary class for the BSP page is generated and loaded into the program buffer. Similarly, the first request for an image requires additional overhead to load the image and place it into the ICM cache. These start-up times are very expensive and can influences the average times (specifically on short runs). Therefore, we configure a short warm-up time.

For this test run, three minutes is sufficient to provide an example and to see that everything is working correctly. For serious stress testing, one can consider running the test over 24 hours.

After a test run, we should first look at an overview of the results, just to confirm that the test ran successfully.

Code	Description	Count
200	OK	3780

```
Page                                                      Hits
GET /sap(bD1kZSZjPTAwMA==)/bc/bsp/sap/it03/text32KB.htm   540
GET /sap(bD1kZSZjPTAwMA==)/bc/bsp/sap/it03/text32KB.htm   540
GET /sap(bD1kZSZjPTAwMA==)/bc/bsp/sap/it03/text32KB.htm   540
GET /sap(bD1kZSZjPTAwMA==)/bc/bsp/sap/it03/text32KB.htm   540
GET /sap(bD1kZSZjPTAwMA==)/bc/bsp/sap/it03/image32KB.gif  540
GET /sap(bD1kZSZjPTAwMA==)/bc/bsp/sap/it03/image32KB.gif  540
GET /sap(bD1kZSZjPTAwMA==)/bc/bsp/sap/it03/image32KB.gif  540
```

We can see that in the three minutes 3,780 HTTP requests were sent to the server, and all were answered with an HTTP return code of `200 OK`. This is always the very first number to check, to ensure that the test ran correctly. The rest of the overview just shows that each URL was requested 540 times.

The next step is to look at the detailed results for each request. As we did not use different URLs in the test series, but just repeated the same URL a number of times, let us look at one of each.

```
                                   text32KB.htm        image32KB.gif
Hit Count:                                  540                  540

Time to First Byte (in milliseconds)
Average:                                  68.26                 2.33
Min:                                      44.02                 1.93
25th Percentile:                          68.93                 2.41
50th Percentile:                          70.98                 2.67
75th Percentile:                          73.04                 2.95
Max:                                      77.82                 8.44

Time to Last Byte (in milliseconds)
Average:                                  72.99                 7.16
Min:                                      47.88                 5.42
25th Percentile:                          73.30                 6.11
50th Percentile:                          75.40                 6.45
75th Percentile:                          77.33                 8.09
Max:                                      84.67                25.12

Downloaded Content Length (in bytes)
Min:                                      32772                32799
25th Percentile:                          32772                32799
50th Percentile:                          32772                32799
75th Percentile:                          32772                32799
Max:                                      32772                32799
```

When testing in an ideal environment, one would expect that all data is transferred in one packet from the server to the browser. However, at low levels, data is split into small packets for transmission (typically 1,500 bytes over Ethernet). In addition, we have the slow-start algorithm in TCP that slowly increases the use of available bandwidth to determine a network saturation point. This has motivated the developers of the stress tool to give both the "Time to First Byte" received (TTFB) and "Time to Last Byte" (TTLB) received. We know that the ICM will only send complete HTTP responses, and not stream out answers incrementally as they are generated. Thus, the difference between these two numbers shows the network latency. Especially in wide-area networks, these numbers will be far apart. Typically, for our tests, we use the TTLB, as this is really the time that data transfer is finished.

The other interesting aspect is the difference between the average and 50th percentile values. Only a few out-risers in the measured data can dramatically influence the average value, specifically over a short test time. Because of this, we usually use the 50th percentile values as the reference value.

Looking at the data, we see that the server took roughly 75.40ms for a `text32KB.htm` page and took 6.45ms for an `image32KB.gif` page over 540 hits. As both pages were roughly the same size, we can see the 6ms to be about the complete network component, and place the server-processing time for the `text32KB.htm` page at 69ms (75 – 6).

From these numbers, one can now calculate rough estimates of how many hits per minute are possible. As only one browser was active, the server also used only one processor, and it was ideal whenever the data was in transit. So one can multiply the hit rate with the available processors, and then use the same stress tool to generate load to slowly bring the server to saturation. The approach would be to increase the number of threads around the point where we calculated the upper limits to be, while at all times the HTTP return codes must still be `200 OK`. Also, the 25th, 50th, and 75th percentile numbers must still be relatively close to one another. The presence of numbers spread far out indicates many requests had to be queued until processing was completed.

8.8 SQL Traces

BSP applications are to all intents and purposes just normal ABAP classes that are loaded by the BSP runtime and called to render HTML output. For this reason, all the tools that are used for analysis of normal ABAP programs can also be used for BSP applications. One such important tool is SQL traces, used to see the behavior of the BSP application in terms of database usage.

```
<%@extension name="htmlb" prefix="htmlb"%>
<%
   DATA: counter TYPE string.
   cl_bsp_server_side_cookie=>get_server_cookie(...).
   counter = counter + 1.
%>
<htmlb:content design="design2003"><htmlb:page><htmlb:form>
    <htmlb:button text    = "<%=counter%>"
                  onClick = "myClickHandler" />
</htmlb:form></htmlb:page></htmlb:content>
<%
   cl_bsp_server_side_cookie=>set_server_cookie(...).
%>
```

The above test program shows a button that contains a counter, incremented for each roundtrip. The value of the counter is stored in a server-side cookie, which will cause updates on the database.

SQL traces are activated from transaction SE80 using the menu path **System**, **Utilities** and **Performance Trace**. Here the SQL tracing can be activated. The application can then be started and executed as usual. Afterwards, the tracing can be disabled again, and reviewed (see Figure 8.11).

Duration	Obj. name	Op.	Statement
967	SSCOOKIE	OPEN	SELECT WHERE "MANDT" = '000' AND "RELID" = 'BP' AND "NAME" = 'counter'
103	SSCOOKIE	FETCH	
61	SSCOOKIE	CLOSE	
609	SSCOOKIE	EXECSTM	UPDATE SET "EXPIRYD" = 20051010 , "EXPIRYT" = 082354 , "CLUSTR" = 53 ,
369	SSCOOKIE	EXECSTM	DELETE WHERE "MANDT" = '000' AND "RELID" = 'BP' AND "NAME" = 'counter'
2.049		EXECSTA	COMMIT WORK

Figure 8.11 Extract from SQL Trace of a BSP Application

Although this section showed only SQL traces, deemed to very important, many other standard ABAP traces that can be used together with BSP applications. This is because BSP applications are relatively standard ABAP classes at runtime.

9 BSP Extensions

BSP Extensions present what is perhaps the most powerful aspect of BSP programming. This technology makes it possible to encapsulate large and complicated sections of user-interface coding, thereby creating simple reusable components.

9.1 Extension Overview

BSP application development gives you the freedom to create and use whatever browser presentation technology that you want. This means that you can code your own HTML, JavaScript, style sheets, and even include calls to ActiveX controls or Java applets if you wish.

However, combining all these raw elements together to create consistent user-interface (UI) components can become quite a chore. Take, for example, the common business requirement for displaying tabular data. A simple HTML table is hardly appropriate for most business applications. Users need the ability to sort and filter their data. Column presentation needs to be clear and have explicit column headers. Users often have huge amounts of data that they need to present. Scrolling through a large HTML table quickly becomes impractical.

In order to meet the needs of the modern business-application user, you would need a presentation that looks something like the one shown in Figure 9.1.

	test Datepi...	Advanced Link1 *	Advanced...	test Currency	Lang...	CHECKED	DDLB	P	Popup
	12/15/2004	TableViewItera...	TableViewIterato	422.94 USD	FR	☐		777.99	0017
	01/12/2005	TableViewItera...	TableViewIterato	422.94 USD	IT	☐		456,456.70-	0017
	02/09/2005	TableViewItera...	TableViewIterato	422.94 USD	PL	☐		89.99	0017
		TableViewItera	TableViewIterato	422.94 USD	RU	☑	ICON_SYSTEM_ENI	99,999,912.20-	0017
	04/06/2005	TableViewItera...	TableViewIterato	422.94 USD	ES	☐		9.00	0017
	05/04/2005	/sap/bc/bsp/sa...	/sap/..	422.94 USD	TR	☐		8.00	0017
	06/01/2005	TableViewItera...	TableViewIterato	422.94 USD	DE	☐		12,122,293.99-	0017
	06/29/2005	TableViewItera...	TableViewIterato	422.94 USD	EN	☐		4,674,567.99-	0017

1 of 51

Figure 9.1 Extension Example – Complex Table Presentation

You can imagine the thousands of lines of HTML and JavaScript that it requires to render such a feature-rich table. The sheer complexity of such coding would make such an object seldom obtainable.

This is the very reason that the BSP extension technology exists. In essence, BSP extensions take this complex rendering and make it reusable and easy to use by hiding the details. Instead of interacting with thousands of lines of coding, you instead only have to deal with a handful of customization attributes.

9.1.1 Extension Technology

A BSP extension is really just a high-level group for a set of UI elements. An example of an extension might be HTML Business (HTMLB) extension. This extension is delivered by SAP and contains nearly 50 individual elements. A single element, for example, might be `<htmlb:button>`.

Every BSP element is implemented via an ABAP class. This class contains the coding necessary to generate the required HTML and JavaScript.

Although you can create your own BSP extensions and elements (a technique covered in Chapter 11), SAP delivers nearly 200 elements of its own. The idea is that these elements cover the common aspects of UI development for business applications. As you create your BSP applications, you already have a rich set of UI components to draw from.

The combination of the technology implementation of extensions and the delivered set of elements has a number of advantages for BSP development:

- Unlike raw HTML and JavaScript, the syntax of BSP elements is known to the BSP compiler and can be checked at design time.
- Complex UI coding is only done once. Code reuse is maximized. This reduces the time and cost to testing and maintaining this code.
- Because SAP delivers so many UI components, BSP application development can be done by developers who do not have extensive knowledge of HTML or JavaScript.
- The extension framework streamlines implementations where the use of specific browsers is required. SAP's elements currently support several different mainstream browsers. Use of the elements instead of low-level coding provides applications with browser independence.
- All of SAP's delivered elements share a common look and feel. This design has been done by professionals to make the resulting applications highly usable.
- SAP spends a considerable effort ensuring that its delivered elements meet the highest standard for security and accessibilty.

9.1.2 Using BSP Extensions

Let us examine how easy it is to put the BSP extension technology to use. Insertion of BSP extensions into a BSP page has two parts. First the extension directive must be declared at the beginning of your page.

```
<%@extension name="htmlb" prefix="htmlb" %>
```

This directive tells the compiler which BSP extensions you are going to be using and what prefix you will use to identify the extension as you code the use of individual elements.

Once we have the directive in place, we insert the call to the BSP element itself.

```
<htmlb:button id   = "BuyBook"
              text = "Buy Book" />
```

This coding begins with the element prefix which should match with our directive to define the extension we will be using. This is followed by the element name itself. Finally, we have two attributes in use for this element: a unique ID and the text we wish to appear on the button itself.

The structure of the BSP element call is that of a markup language, just like HTML. Ultimately the contents of a BSP page layout are parsed via XML, including the BSP element definitions. This means that elements can have inner content between beginning and ending designators. In the example above, the button has no inner content and designates the end of the button definition with the "/" before the closing bracket.

We could just as easily have an `<htmlb:link>` element that wraps around its inner content.

```
<htmlb:link id        = "BookExampleLink"
            reference = "http://www.sap-press.com" >
  Sample Link to SAP PRESS
</htmlb:link>
```

9.1.3 Finding Details about the Extensions

With several different SAP-delivered extensions, each containing quite a few elements, a developer could get overwhelmed without some tools to organize and document the available functionality. Luckily, there are several ways to get to this information within the ABAP Development Workbench.

First, there is a special navigation view within the development workbench; called *Tag Browser*. This view allows you to see all the BSP extensions, their elements, and the element attributes. Elements and attributes can be inserted into BSP pages via Drag&Drop from this view. If there is online documentation for an element, it can be accessed by double-clicking on the element name.

In addition to the Tag Browser, shown in Figure 9.2, the ABAP workbench also allows you to view BSP elements from within the *Repository Browser*, as shown in Figure 9.3.

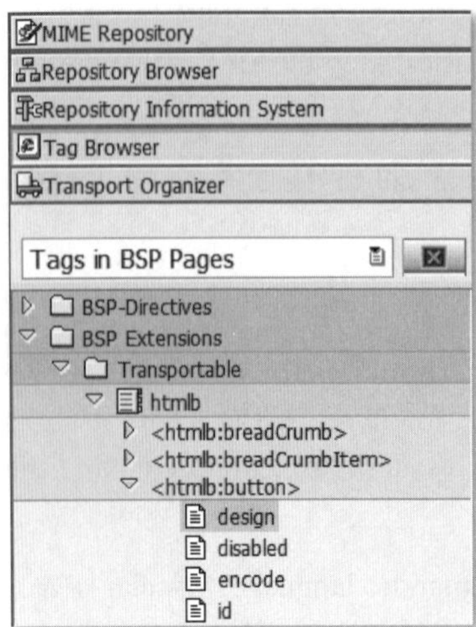

Figure 9.2 Tag Browser View in the ABAP Workbench

You can see the full technical view of the element attributes from here as well as the implementing ABAP class. For even easier access to the technical view of an element, you can simply double-click on the element in your application coding, and you will be forward-navigated to its definition.

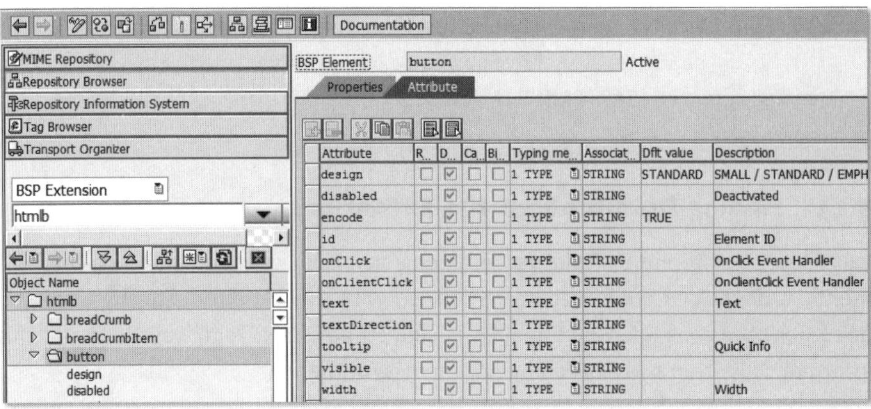

Figure 9.3 Element Attribute View from the ABAP Workbench

There is important information about each element attribute that can only be gathered from this view.

First, you see a row of four checkboxes after the attribute name. Each of these checkboxes controls a setting that affects how your application can interact with this current attribute. Here are expanded definitions for those four checkboxes:

- **Required**
  This checkbox defines whether an attribute is required. Quite often, the unique identifying attribute of the element (usually named "id") is the only required attribute.

- **Dynamic Value Allowed**
  This checkbox controls if the value for the attribute can be supplied dynamically via an ABAP variable or must be a static string. Nearly all element attributes support dynamic values. Dynamic values are supplied to attributes using a special BSP expression (`<%=...%>`).

  We can now adjust our simple button example to supply the text for the button via a dynamic value.

  ```
  <% data: book_text type string value 'Buy Book'. %>
  <htmlb:button id    = "BuyBook"
                text = "<%= book_text %>" />
  ```

- **Call by Reference**
  ABAP by default already uses a pass-by-reference, copy-on-write architecture. So even for a large internal table being passed into the `<htmlb:tableView>` element, it would have been no problem had we passed in the table itself directly. The problem is more that of generics. The `<htmlb:tableView>` needed to support rendering of any type of table. Thus it needed a data type that could be used to accept any table, and only with the `data` type this is possible. However, this type can only be used in a `ref to data` mode. Thus, the only reason for this style of coding in the `<htmlb:tableView>` was to get the generics correct.

  But the `<htmlb:tableView>` is actually a very special case. The real reason this option exists is to enable passing/transferring of data out of the tag back to the rendering page.

  For this setting, the corresponding *Type Method* must be set to `TYPE REF TO`.

  Behind the BSP page is ABAP code interpreting the element and attribute definitions. This ABAP code must map these attributes into the underlying ABAP class that represents the element. In order to prepare an ABAP data object for this *Call-by-Reference* operation, a generic reference must be created for the object. The following code sample shows what the BSP page interpreter has to do to complete this operation. This example will be important later, once you learn how to call BSP elements directly via the ABAP implementing class.

  ```
  data itab type ref to data.
  get reference of items into itab.
  ```

▶ **Bindable**

The **Bindable** checkbox defines whether an attribute supports Model View Binding. Data-binding is an important aspect of the Model View Controller design pattern (covered in detail in Chapter 13). This functionality allows a developer to connect the business data object to the corresponding UI element.

In this example, we can see the bindable option in use. The text for the hyper link is now supplied via an attribute that is filled from a binding string.

```
<htmlb:link id        = "BookExampleLink"
            reference = "http://www.sap-press.com"
            text      = "//model/sample_text" />
```

9.1.4 Available Extensions

SAP delivers three main extensions. They are HTMLB, XHTMLB, and PHTMLB. You might sometimes see these core extensions all referred to generically as HTMLB or the HTMLB family.

HTMLB, short for "HTML for Business", was the first extension delivered. It contains your most elementary User Interface components, such as buttons, links, or images. XHTMLB—Extended HTMLB— was added at a later date mostly to meet the specialized requirements of one of SAP's in-house development groups. It has extended functions such as a toolbar, button group, and an updated tabstrip. The most recent extension is PHTMLB, or Pattern HTMLB. This extension is focused on the delivery of UI pattern elements. Perhaps the best example of one of these new patterns is the form layout contained in PHTMLB.

Each of these major extensions has a delivered application (`SBSPEXT_HTMLB`, `SBSPEXT_XHTMLB`, and `SBSPEXT_PHTMLB`) that demonstrates its capabilities. These example applications provide excellent coding examples, and demonstrate the possible values for each element attribute.

There are several other specialized extensions: btf, Benchmark, Graphics, and bsp. These extensions and their use are discussed in detail in Chapter 12.

9.1.5 Extensions Designs

SAP currently ships three different design options for the HTMLB family of extensions: CLASSIC, DESIGN2002, and DESIGN2003. The choice of design affects the look and feel as well as some of the functionality of these inner elements. This is demonstrated in Figure 9.5. In this example we have an `<htmlb:tray>` with some inner content comprised of `<htmlb:textView>`, `<htmlb:button>`, and `<htmlb:dropdownListBox>`.

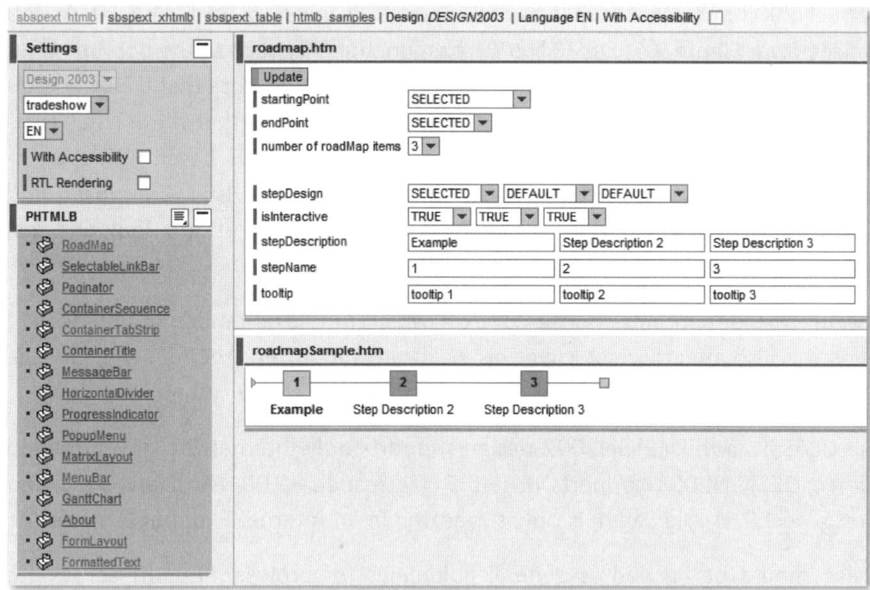

Figure 9.4 Example Application SBSPEXT_PHTMLB

There were absolutely no changes to the coding of inner elements between these three images. All of the changes in look, feel, and functionality come about automatically just by changing the design.

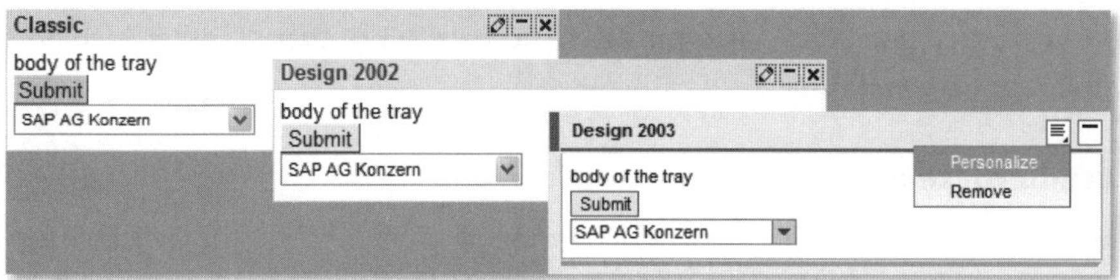

Figure 9.5 Examples of the different Designs.

Different BSP extensions have different requirements for which design they can run within. The HTMLB extension supports all three designs (CLASSIC, DESIGN2002, and DESIGN2003), whereas the newer XHTMLB extension only supports DESIGN2002 and DESIGN2003. The most recent BSP extension, PTHMLB, only supports the DESIGN2003 option.

Of the design options, DESIGN2003 is the most recently developed and most advanced and should really be the only design used for any new development. In a very near-future release, SAP is extremely likely to completely drop support for CLASSIC and DESIGN2002 all together.

DESIGN2003 became available as of Support Package 32 of Web AS 6.20. As you can see from Figure 9.5, DESIGN2003 has functionality such as the pop up menu that the other designs do not have. It is also important to note that DESIGN2003 is built upon what SAP calls *Unified Renderer*. This means that the HTML, JavaScript, and style sheets behind the scenes of DESIGN2003-based BSP applications will be the same as those of the Enterprise Portal, Visual Composer, and Web Dynpro-based application. This gives your BSP application a look and feel that is consistent with all of SAP's other UI technologies.

Because the design you choose controls which low-level rendering libraries are used, this also affects which client browsers are supported. The following are the latest supported browsers based upon a Web AS 6.40 SP13 system.

The CLASSIC and DESIGN2002 design supports only Internet Explorer 5.50 and higher. DESIGN2003 supports IE >=5.5, Netscape >=7.00, Mozilla >=1.7.5 and Firefox >=1.0. Apple Safari, is only supported in an Internet Explorer 6 mode.

These should be viewed as general guidelines for browser support across the designs. However, support for different browsers is constantly changing to meet market and customer demands. For the most recent information, always refer to OSS note 598860.

9.1.6 High Level Elements

A BSP page that is going to use BSP HTMLB-family of extensions must include a few high-level elements that form the basic framework that all other elements within the page will run in.

<htmlb:content>

The first of these elements is `<htmlb:content>`. This must be the first BSP element inserted into your page. All BSP elements that you want to use must be included inside this element. This next code sample demonstrates how all BSP Element and regular HTML content for a page is included inside the `<htmlb:content>` element.

```
<%@page language="abap" %>
<%@extension name="htmlb" prefix="htmlb" %>
<htmlb:content design="design2003" >
  <htmlb:page title="BSP Book Example" >
    <htmlb:form>
      <htmlb:link id        = "BookExampleLink"
                  reference = "http://www.sap-press.com"
                  text      = "Sample Text for link" />
```

```
      <b><i>Some more raw HTML sample text</b></i>
    </htmlb:form>
  </htmlb:page>
</htmlb:content>
```

The <htmlb:content> element has the important responsibility of setting the rendering context for the current page. Its primary role is for setting the design that will be used by all the inner BSP elements. The value for the design attribute will determine which rendering library will be used.

As if this was not enough functionality to draw from this one little attribute, the chosen design also influences the version of SAP's Enterprise Portal that is supported. Enterprise Portal 5.0 only supports the older two designs, CLASSIC and DESIGN2002). Enterprise Portal 6.0 supports all three designs.

To support this variation across the Enterprise Portal versions, the <htmlb:content> tag allows you to supply multiple design values. The runtime will then choose the best design to match the version of the Enterprise Portal that is in use. You should note, however, that this option does not remove any of the design requirements on BSP extensions (such as the PHTMLB requirement for DESIGN2003).

```
<htmlb:content design="DESIGN2002+DESIGN2003" >
```

Given this code, the BSP runtime would analyze the version of the Enterprise portal that it was running in. If it was not running within the portal, it would choose DESIGN2003. If it was inside a portal of version 5.0, it would choose DESIGN2002. Finally, in Enterprise Portal 6.0, it would choose DESIGN2003.

The <htmlb:content> element has attributes that control aspects other than setting the design for the application. One of these is controlRendering. This attribute, which is only supported under DESIGN2003, further allows you to affect the look and feel of your application. There are some UI controls, such as the <htmlb:dropdownListBox>, that—when rendered with HTML—retain the design of the hosting browser or the surrounding operating system. This attribute allows you to specify whether you want the Browser to continue to control this aspect of the rendering, or if you want to switch to the SAP rendered control (default). Figure 9.6 shows the differences in the rendered output for our earlier DESIGN2003 example when the two different possible options for controlRendering are used.

The forceEncode attribute causes all inner BSP elements to perform an HTML encoding or escaping of their attribute values. This means that certain characters that would otherwise have special meaning within HTML or that are not available in the plain ASCII character set are replaced with a special escape sequence. For instance, if you actually want to use a less than sign (<) in an attribute value and you do not want it to be interpreted as an HTML opening tag, you would replace this character with the escape sequence <. The use of encoding also eliminates the vulnerability to cross-site scripting attacks (for more details, refer to CERT® Advisory CA-2000–02: Malicious HTML Tags Embedded in Client Web Requests).

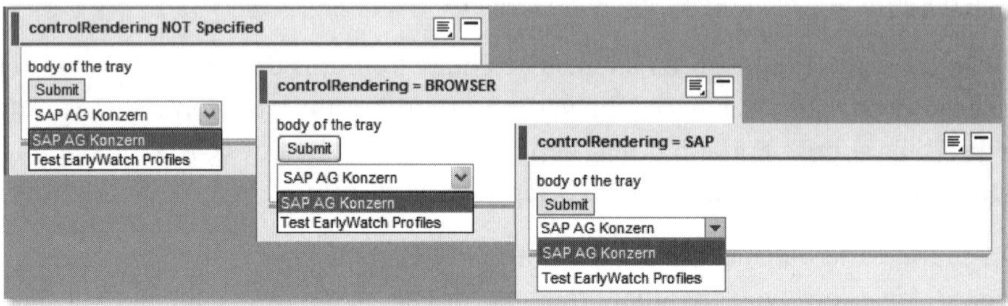

Figure 9.6 Examples of Control Rendering under DESIGN2003

The sessionManagement attribute allows you to specify if you want your application's session to be managed by the Enterprise Portal. Setting this attribute really only makes sense if you have a stateful application; otherwise, there is no session to manage.

Certain languages, such as Arabic and Hebrew, are written right to left. The BSP runtime supports right to left (RTL) rendering for Internet Explorer under DESIGN2003. You can active RTL rendering support via the rtlAutoSwitch attribute, although this does not actually trigger the RTL mode. It is just the signal to the rendering engine that the application has been tested with RTL, and if it detects a RTL based language (using the logged on language), it should switch. If the RTL attribute is set, and the browser is using a RTL language, then it automatically switch into RTL mode. One way you can force the switch to RTL regardless of the language setting is by calling the SET_RIGHT_TO_LEFT method of the BSP Runtime or via the URL parameter sap-rtl='X'.

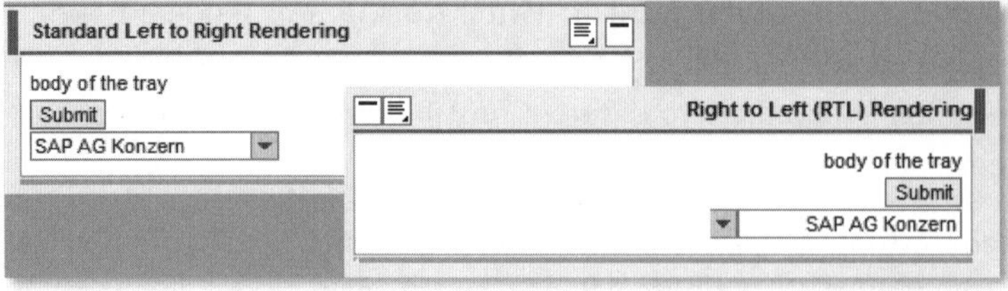

Figure 9.7 Right to Left (RTL) rendering

When rendering with DESIGN2003, field labels are prefixed with a small notch to set them out. This visual identification allows the label to stand out. However, there could be circumstances where you need more control over the look of the application and therefore want to disable this function. The attribute `labelDesignBar` will disable this functionality if it is set to *LIGHT*.

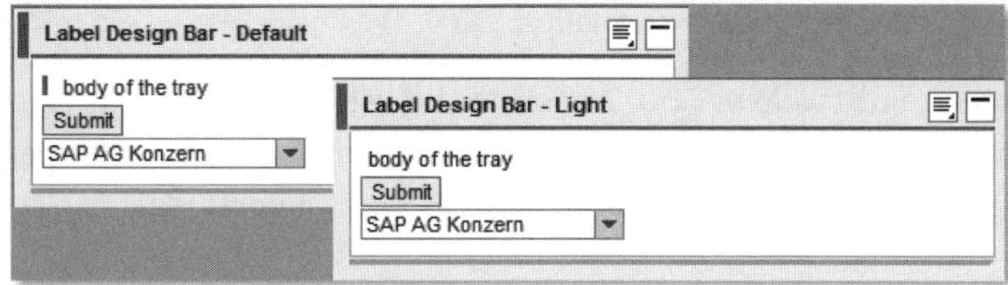

Figure 9.8 labelDesignBar STANDARD and LIGHT examples

The discussion around `<htmlb:content>` has centered heavily on the look and feel of the resulting page. When using DESIGN2003, an additional piece—themes—is added to the look-and-feel puzzle. A theme is a set of colors and fonts that complement the overall design. The topic of creating and changing themes is discussed in detail in Chapter 17.

The concept of themes is central to the Enterprise Portal. You might create a company-branded theme that you want all your applications to share. The attribute `themeRoot` allows you to specify one of these themes for your application.

<htmlb:page>

Whereas the `<htmlb:content>` element was very specific to the functionality of BSP, the remaining high-level elements all have close approximations in standard HTML. In BSP pages that are going to use extension elements, we must follow up the `<htmlb:content>` with one of two different header elements.

The first alternative is `<htmlb:page>`. This is the less extensive of the two options, allowing for only a small amount of control over the document structure. This element will be wrapped around all our inner BSP elements or plain HTML content.

The `<htmlb:page>` element has four attributes that control the document margins on all sides (`marginBottom`, `marginLeft`, `marginRight`, and `marginTop`). It also has an attribute, `title`, which allows you set the document title that will appear in your browser's title bar.

The `onLoad` attribute allows the specification for a client-side script that you write, usually in JavaScript, to be executed when the document loads. This client script will be executed once the document is finished loading within the browser.

With the attribute reposition, a page should be able to retain the cursor position even after a server event. It saves the scrollX and scrollY coordinates of the document body before submitting the form. If these values are received by the HTMLB library, it will also generate a scrollTo call on next-page rendering, so that the browser shows the same section of the screen as in the previous call. This attribute defaults to TRUE, so you only need to add it to the <htmlb:page> element if you want to disable this functionality.

Finally, the attribute scroll allows you to disable the use of scroll bars in your page. However, the browser should only enable scroll bars if necessary for proper navigation. Disabling the scroll bars via this attribute is rarely a good idea.

<htmlb:document>

For greater control over the document structure, SAP offers a separate set of BSP elements that can be used instead of <htmlb:page>. The document elements work as a set in which you combine the use of <htmlb:document>, <htmlb:documentHead>, <htmlb:headInclude>, and <htmlb:documentBody>. This technique is especially required if additional CSS or JS files must be included into the header of the HTML document. In the following code sample, we have adjusted the code example for the beginning of the chapter to now be structured using the document elements.

```
<%@page language="abap" %>
<%@extension name="htmlb" prefix="htmlb" %>
<htmlb:content design="design2003" >
  <htmlb:document>
    <htmlb:documentHead title="BSP Book Example" >
      <%-- load here additional includes --%>
      <htmlb:headInclude/>
    </htmlb:documentHead>
    <htmlb:documentBody>
      <htmlb:form>
        <htmlb:link id        = "BookExampleLink"
                    reference = "http://www.sap-press.com"
                    text      = "Sample Text for link" />
        <b><i>Some more sample text</b></i>
      </htmlb:form>
    </htmlb:documentBody>
  </htmlb:document>
</htmlb:content>
```

All the same attributes that are exposed by the <htmlb:page> element are also represented through the use of the document elements. They are simply spread out across the different individual elements. The <htmlb:documentHead> gets the title attribute. The element <htmlb:documentBody> gets all the remaining attributes.

In addition to all the other attributes exposed by the <htmlb:page>, the <htmlb:documentBody> also has the powerful attributeBee attribute. This attribute accepts a BSP Element Expression (BEE—discussed in detail in Chapter 10) that will be rendered in-line as the element builds the HTML body element. This is especially useful if you wish to hook your own JavaScript client scripts onto any of the additional document events.

<htmlb:form>

The <htmlb:form> element is built right on top of the basic HTML FORM construct. Any inner content that has user input or events will require the <htmlb:form> element. It is this element that is ultimately responsible for setting up all communications between the browser and the server.

The action, target and method attributes come right from the definition of HTML FORM. Action allows you to specify the URI destination for input form data. Most of the time in BSP, you simply do not specify a value for this attribute. If you do, input will be brought back to the page where it originated.

Method determines the type of HTTP request that will be sent back to the server. The options are POST or GET, with POST as the default value. GET passes all input information appended to the request URL. This makes all input values visible in the address bar of your browser. However, this can also be a big problem, because now your input is limited in size to the maximum length of a request string (typically two to four KB). POST, on the other hand, imbeds all input information in the body of the request object. This allows for the greatest flexibility and keeps the browser address bar clean.

The target attribute further defines the destination for input form data. With target, you might specify the name of a HTML FRAME or you might choose one of the special targets such as _blank. _blank will cause the creation of a new browser window. A common example of the use of target in the context of frames is to click in one frame that has a navigation tree. The corresponding results are then loaded into a separate frame. For a good example of this concept in BSP, have a look at the sample program SBSPEXT_HTMLB.

There are two attributes of <htmlb:form>, doValidate and validationScript, that are marked in documentation as reserved for future implementation. However, the inner coding of the `<htmlb:form>` does reveal that these attributes will generate HTML code for calling some sort of validation scripting on input. Furthermore, placing a JavaScript alert in the `validationScript` attribute does appear to fire correctly.

```
<htmlb:form validationScript="alert('Hi!')">
```

The `autoComplete` attribute is intended to activate or deactivate the Internet Explorer auto-complete functionality for form fields. However, this feature is not supported with the new DESIGN2003 rendering and also does not work with MVC applications. The reason is that IE `autoComplete` runs on the `name` attribute of input fields, and that for MVC applications the name attribute is prefixed with the controller and model of the data, thus invaliding any form of semantic names that would have been required to make this work. As an example, a field `<input name="mail">` will give you a list of items you typed into fields with the name "mail." The value set of the `autoComplete` feature is grouped by the name's value. Think of a number of mail fields within a table. Certainly they all have different "names" because of the way that the data binding ties the data of each row to a different table row using the name attribute. The user will be surprised that he or she cannot choose the mail address that he or she typed into the first mail field (mailrow1) in the second mail field (mailrow2). Only after the table is filtered and the previous mailrow2 becomes mailrow1 can the user choose the value previously typed in mailrow1.

The `encodingType` attribute specifies the content type that will be used to send data back to the server. The default type is *application/x-www-form-urlencoded*. This type is normally sufficient. In a situation where you need to support the `<htmlb:fileUpload>` element, you should instead use *multipart/form data*.

9.2 HTMLB Event System

9.2.1 Event Dispatching

It does not do you much good to render BSP elements with server events if you do not know how to catch and thereby respond to those events.

For this purpose, we will examine a small example. With this example we can see the three different ways that events can be trapped and responded to.

In this example, a small stateful BSP page will contain two buttons, inside a `<xhtmlb:buttonGroup>`. These two buttons will simply either increment or decrement an index between the values of 1 and 7. When the upper or lower bounds of the index are reached, the corresponding navigation button will be disabled.

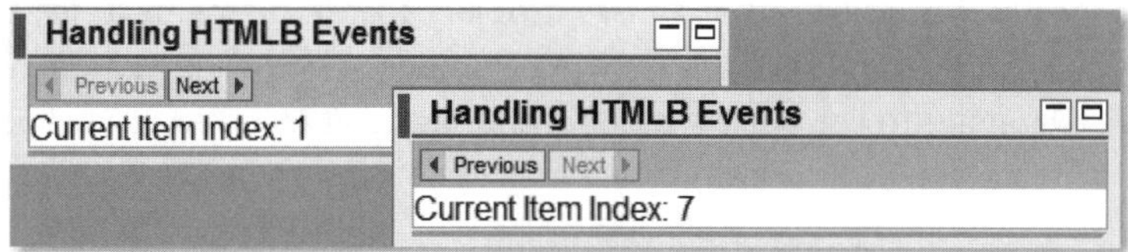

Figure 9.9 Handling HTMLB Events Example Application

The <xhtmlb:buttonGroup> has two buttons for moving to the previous or next item. Notice that only one event is registered for the complete button group, and that it will be fired regardless of which button is pressed.

```
<xhtmlb:tabStrip id                      = "ts"
          renderSingleTabAsHeading = "TRUE" >
 <xhtmlb:tabStripItem title = "Handling HTMLB Events"
                      name  = "tsil" >
  <xhtmlb:buttonGroup id      = "btngrp"
                      onClick = "ButtonPager" >
   <xhtmlb:buttonGroupItem key = "prev_item"
                 text     = "Previous"
                 design   = "PREVIOUS"
                 disabled = "<%= vIndex_prev_disabled %>" />
   <xhtmlb:buttonGroupItem key = "next_item"
                 text     = "Next"
                 design   = "NEXT"
                 disabled = "<%= vIndex_next_disabled %>" />
  </xhtmlb:buttonGroup>
  Current Item Index: <%= vIndex %>
 </xhtmlb:tabStripItem>
</xhtmlb:tabStrip>
```

9.2.2 Manually Handling Events

The first approach to HTMLB event-handling is to retrieve the event and then simply investigate what type of event it is. This type of coding is usually done in the OnInputProcessing handler of a BSP page.

The incoming event is retrieved with the method call cl_htmlb_manager=>get_event_ex. In all cases, only this new method must be used. The older get_event method is obsolete and not supported for the XHTMLB and PHTMLB libraries. Note that this method can be called more than once within the same input cycle, and will always return the same event.

The get_event_ex method will return an event object that implements at least the IF_HTMLB_DATA interface. This interface has a number of interesting parameters that can be examined to see what type of event has been received.

IF_HTMLB_DATA Attribute	Description
event_class	The name of the class that decoded this event (example: cl_xhtmlb_buttongroup).
event_name	The name of the element that fired the event (example: buttonGroup).
event_type	The type of event that was triggered for the specific element. Typically a button is "clicked", an entry is "selected" in a drop-down listbox, and a tree will be "expanded" or "collapsed".
event_id	The ID of the element that fired the event (example: btngrp).
event_server_name	The string that was specified in the onClick handler. This string has no further meaning to the event handling system and is transported verbatim (example: ButtonPager).
event_defined	Usually an event can contain additional parameters. However, the IF_HTMLB_DATA interface has to be cast to the correct event handler class, and the parameters retrieved from there. Many events only require one small string to return, and will use the event-defined string. For our example, the button-Group will place the key of the actual button that was clicked into the event_defined string. (example: prev_item or next_item from <xhtmlb:buttonGroupItemkey/>).

Table 9.1 Parameters of Interface IF_HTMLB_DATA

Once the event is available, it can still be a bit of a guessing game to know the possible values for event_name and event_type. A detailed overview is required to determine what elements can fire what events.

This information is available in the *classes* HTMLB_EVENTS, XHTMLB_EVENTS and PHTMLB_EVENTS. These classes contain constant strings of all elements that can fire events (the values to match against event_name), plus a list of all the different types of events that each element will fire (the values to match against event_type).

For this example, we wish to check that we have received a <xhtmlb:buttonGroup> event of type click.

```
data: event type ref to if_htmlb_data.
event = cl_htmlb_manager=>get_event_ex( request ).

if  event is not initial
and event->event_name = xhtmlb_events=>buttongroup
```

```
and event->event_type = xhtmlb_events=>buttongroup_click.
  case event->event_defined.
    when 'prev_item'.
      vindex = vindex - 1.
      if vindex < 1. vindex = 1. endif.
    when 'next_item'.
      vindex = vindex + 1.
      if vindex > 7. vindex = 7. endif.
  endcase.
endif.
```

Class Interface: XHTMLB_EVENTS — Implemented / Active

Properties | Interfaces | Friends | Attributes | Methods | Events | Types | Aliases

Filter

Attribute	Level	Visi...	Rea...	Typing	Associ...		D...	Initial value
LIBRARY	Constan	Public		Type	STRING			'xhtmlb'
BUTTONGROUP	Constan	Public		Type	STRING			CL_XHTMLB_BUTTONGROUP=>CO_EVENT_NAME
BUTTONGROUP_CLICK	Constan	Public		Type	STRING			CL_XHTMLB_BUTTONGROUP=>CO_EVENT_CLICKED
BUTTONGROUP_TOGGLE	Constan	Public		Type	STRING			CL_XHTMLB_BUTTONGROUP=>CO_EVENT_TOGGLED
PAGER	Constan	Public		Type	STRING			CL_XHTMLB_PAGER=>CO_EVENT_NAME
PAGER_EVENT	Constan	Public		Type	STRING			'event'

Figure 9.10 XHTMLB_EVENTS Class

This approach of event-handling is very fast to program, especially on a BSP page. The disadvantage of this approach is that the code quickly explodes once events for many controls must be handled.

Dispatching Events via IF_HTMLB_EVENTS

The HTMLB rendering libraries also contain a technique to dispatch events to a handler class. For this, use the `cl_htmlb_manager=>dispatch_event_ex` method. One of the parameters is a handler class that will accept the incoming event and process it. Typically, this can be a separate developed class, a controller class, or even the application class.

In this example, we will use a handler class that has been developed separately. On the BSP page, in the `OnInputProcessing` method, the event-handling code now reduces to a few lines. All that is required is an instance of the handler class, and then the dispatcher is called.

```
DATA: handler TYPE REF TO YCL_BSP_BOOK_HANDLING_EVENTS.
CREATE OBJECT handler.
cl_htmlb_manager=>dispatch_event_ex(
   request       = request
```

```
    page_context  = page_context
    event_handler = handler ).
```

The benefit of this approach is that the event-handling code is placed in a separate class, where the full strength of the ABAP workbench can be used. This approach also reduces clutter in BSP pages. In addition, if new elements are added, no further event handling code is required on the BSP page. All events will be dispatched by this one call. Especially when using the model-view-controller (MVC) paradigm, the standard approach is to implement all event handlers for a view in the corresponding controller class.

The important questions are: How will the handler class know what events are available, and what parameters each event handling method must have? The interface `IF_HTMLB_EVENTS` is defined to solve this. This interface contains all the possible events that can be fired by the HTMLB library. Each method contains the correct parameters with which it will be called. Similar interfaces `IF_XHTMLB_EVENTS` and `IF_PHTMLB_EVENTS` exist for the other two major libraries.

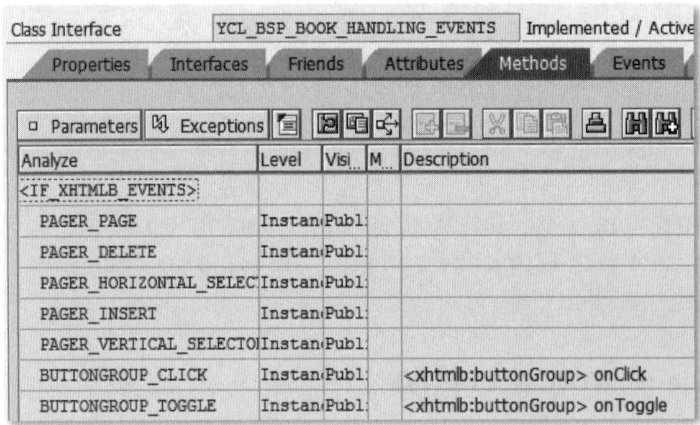

Figure 9.11 Event Handler Class Implementing the IF_XHTMLB_EVENTS Methods

The handler class must now just implement these interfaces.

```
class ycl_bsp_book_handling_events definition public.
public section.
  interfaces if_htmlb_event .
  interfaces if_htmlb_events .
  interfaces if_xhtmlb_events .
...
endclass.

class YCL_BSP_BOOK_HANDLING_EVENTS implementation.
  method IF_XHTMLB_EVENTS~BUTTONGROUP_CLICK.
```

```
  case buttonclicked.
    when 'prev_item'.
      vindex = vindex - 1.
      if vindex < 1. vindex = 1. endif.
    when 'next_item'.
      vindex = vindex + 1.
      if vindex > 7. vindex = 7. endif.
  endcase.
  endmethod.
endclass.
```

For this example, the `if_xhtmlb_events~buttongroup_click` method is implemented. It will be called by the dispatch method with one interesting parameter: `buttonClicked`. This will contain the key of the button that was clicked.

The advantage of this technique is that event-handling coding can be placed in normal classes and broken down per event type. Each method receives all of its parameters correctly unpacked. The biggest disadvantage of this technique is still that events are grouped according to their event types. Thus, for all buttons on a page, the method `if_htmlb_events~button_click` will be called. In this method, you might still have to look at the ID to decide which button was clicked. Further, this technique still groups large blocks of event-handling code into one method. Another disadvantage: One should theoretically implement all the event methods with at least a minimal empty body, which can involve some work.

Dispatching Events via OnClick Handlers

It would be nice if the save button would call the save method on the event handler. The `cl_htmlb_manager=>dispatch_event_ex` method contains such additional functionality.

It will first examine the event handler class to see if it implements the `IF_HTMLB_EVENTS` interface. If so, it will then dispatch the event via this interface, as previously described. If this interface is not implemented by the event handler class, it will blindly call an event handling method based on the `event_server_name` string. This string is usually supplied to the `onClick` handlers.

In the initial layout, the `<xhtmlb:buttonGroup>` was specified as follows:

```
<xhtmlb:buttonGroup id = "btngrp" onClick = "ButtonPager">
```

In a new event handler class, we now define method `ButtonPager` that has one importing parameter. The parameter is `event_object TYPE REF TO if_htmlb_` data. It is important to note that this parameter must be specified exactly like this. The existence of the parameter and both the name and type of the parameter are critical for the event-dispatching to work.

In the event handler class, ensure that none of the IF_HTMLB_EVENTS family of interfaces is implemented. Instead, define a new method ButtonPager, and implement it.

```
class YCL_BSP_BOOK_HANDLING_EVENTS2 definition public.
    public section.
      METHODS ButtonPager IMPORTING
         event_object TYPE REF TO if_htmlb_data.
  endclass.

CLASS ycl_bsp_book_handling_events2 IMPLEMENTATION.
    METHOD ButtonPager.
      CASE event_object->event_defined.
       WHEN 'prev_item'.
         vindex = vindex - 1.
         IF vindex < 1. vindex = 1. ENDIF.
       WHEN 'next_item'.
         vindex = vindex + 1.
         IF vindex > 7. vindex = 7. ENDIF.
     ENDCASE.
   ENDMETHOD.
ENDCLASS.
```

Keep in mind that this technique of event dispatching is only triggered if the IF_HTMLB_EVENTS interface is *not* implemented in the event handler class.

The benefit of this approach is that you can actually implement the code to handle each event in its own method. The only disadvantage is that, because of the dynamic nature of the call, no compiler checks are done to ensure that the method is specified correctly. The actual call itself is protected inside a try sequence, to ensure that non-existing methods do not break the BSP application. The fired event will then just be lost.

9.3 Common Extension Elements

With SAP delivering nearly 200 BSP extension elements, it would be impractical to cover the use of every one of them in this text. Instead, this section will attempt to address a few of the most commonly used and most important elements.

9.3.1 <htmlb:tableView>

The ability to have a rich UI control for interacting with tabular data is critical to any business-application environment. In the classic ABAP Dynpro world, this need is fulfilled by the ALV Grid. The ALV Grid, especially in its control-based version, has a considerable amount of functionality that goes beyond the basic tabular display. If you are a long-time ABAP programmer and have used the ALV Grid, you will probably approach BSP with some fairly high expectations for equivalent functionality.

The BSP solution is the `<htmlb:tableView>`. Overall, this element does a good job of matching up functionality-wise to its thick-client big brother. You will not find a one-for one-match for every piece of functionality in the ALV Grid, but a close approximation of most of the critical functionality is present.

As you might imagine, this element is so large and flexible that it deserves an example BSP application all of its own. This application, `SBSPEXT_TABLE`, covers a wide range of different topics, including row selection, column filters, editable data, and data navigation.

It is important to note that the most advanced techniques involving the `<htmlb:tableView>` will probably require the use of an iterator class. This is a special rendering class that gives the developer control over even individual cell creation. The use of the table-view iterator is discussed in detail in Chapter 10.

The most important attribute of the `<htmlb:tableView>` is the `table` attribute. With this attribute you supply the single ABAP internal table that will contain the data represented in the table view for rendering.

It would be easy to be overwhelmed by all the attributes of the `<htmlb:tableView>` element. Instead of looking at all the possible attributes, let us instead focus on a small sample of the table view that demonstrates some of the most commonly used attributes.

This simple example will read data from table `t002t`. This is the system configuration table that contains all the languages supported by SAP and their descriptions.

To start our example, we will use only the two required attributes of the `<htmlb:tableView>`, `id` and `table`.

```
<htmlb:tableView id     = "TableExample"
                 table  = "<%= it002t %>" />
```

This results in a simple, yet plain looking tabular representation of the data in the given table.

Language	Language	Language
EN	SR	Serbian
EN	ZH	Chinese
EN	TH	Thai
EN	KO	Korean
EN	RO	Romanian
EN	SL	Slovenian
EN	HR	Croatian
EN	MS	Malaysian
EN	UK	Ukrainian

Figure 9.12 Simple <htmlb:tableView> Example

Now we are ready to use a few attributes to spice up the table view a bit. First we will make our table output a little more readable by using the `design` attribute with a value of *ALTERNATING* to produce a look that is similar to the ALV Grid stripped pattern.

Next we want to allow the user to have the option to sort or filter the data in the table view. To activate these abilities, we will set both the `filter` and `sort` attributes to *SERVER*. Although this element allows you to program the filtering and sorting using either client-side scripting or server-side events, you also have the option of just letting the element provide this basic functionality for you. If you do not specify the server event names in attributes `onHeaderClick` or `onFilter`, then the element will respond to the events for you.

Finally, we want to add a table header with a brief description of what we are displaying. We can activate the table header by setting the attribute `headerVisible` to *TRUE*. To supply the text for the header, you use attribute `headerText`.

Please note that the first blank row that is now rendered in our table output is the filter row. This empty row of input areas is where the user can place the values that they wish to filter their output results by.

The coding of our example now looks like this:

```
<htmlb:tableView id = "TableExample"
    table          = "<%= it002t %>"
    design         = "ALTERNATING"
    filter         = "SERVER"
   sort            = "SERVER"
    headerVisible  = "TRUE"
    headerText     = "SAP Language Table" />
```

Now we need to do something with the column definitions. To start with, we do not really need the first column. It is showing us which language we are using to display the description. Since this example is programmed to only pull descriptions matching the logon language, this column is unnecessary and confusing. We should also change the description on the columns and deactivate sorting on the language key field.

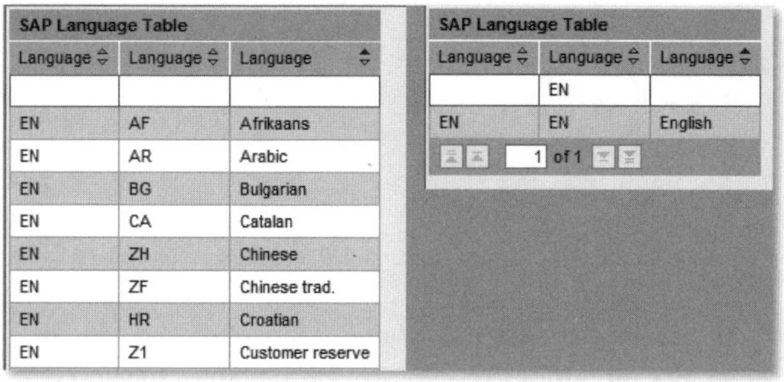

Figure 9.13 <htmlb:tableView> Example with Sorting and Filtering

To accomplish these changes, we have three options. First, a table-view iterator class has functionality to control the table column definitions. This will be discussed in Chapter 10. The second option is to supply all the column definitions via an ABAP internal table of type TABLEVIEWCONTROLTAB to the attribute columnDefinitions. The final option, and the one we will use here, is to use the inner BSP elements <htmlb:tableViewColumns> and <htmlb:tableViewColumn> to define the column layout in our page.

```
<htmlb:tableView id = "TableExample" ... >
    <htmlb:tableViewColumns>
      <htmlb:tableViewColumn
         columnName = "SPRSL"
         sort       = "NONE"
         title      = "Language Key" />
      <htmlb:tableViewColumn
         columnName = "SPTXT"
         sort       = "SERVER"
         title      = "Language Description" />
    </htmlb:tableViewColumns>
</htmlb:tableView>
```

The last thing we want to do to our table is to address navigation. Currently, a user would have to scroll within the browser to see the entire contents of the table view. This is fine when the table view is the only element on the page (and is not too large!). However, quite often you have a restricted amount of space in which to display the table. Or you also might want to reduce the amount of data that has to be rendered for large tables and sent to the client, in order to conserve bandwidth and rendering time.

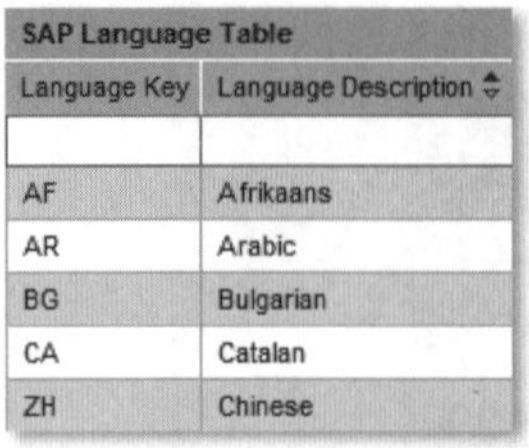

SAP Language Table	
Language Key	Language Description
AF	Afrikaans
AR	Arabic
BG	Bulgarian
CA	Catalan
ZH	Chinese

Figure 9.14 <htmlb:tableView> Example with Custom Column Definitions

To do all this, we will need to limit the number of rows that are displayed initially and then give the user a navigation tool to page through the table. To supply the number of rows we want displayed at one time, we have the attribute `visibleRowCount`. Simply by supplying a value to this attribute, we have not only limited the amount of rows displayed, but we also now have navigation tools in the footer of our table view that allow the user to move through the data. To provide a consistent length to our table view we will also use the attribute `fillUpEmptyRows` to even out any odd table rows on the last page.

```
<htmlb:tableView id = "TableExample"
   table           = "<%= it002t %>"
   design          = "ALTERNATING"
   filter          = "SERVER"
   sort            = "SERVER"
   headerVisible   = "TRUE"
   headerText      = "SAP Language Table"
   visibleRowCount = "7"
   fillUpEmptyRows = "TRUE" >
```

SAP Language Table	
Language Key	Language Description
Z1	Customer reserve
AF	Afrikaans
IS	Icelandic
CA	Catalan
SH	Serbian (Latin)
ID	Indonesian
6 of 6	

Figure 9.15 <htmlb:tableView> Example with Page Navigation

There is an alternative to allowing the table view to provide its own navigation. The BSP element <xhtmlb:pager> allows greater control over the look and feel as well as the placement of the navigation UI (typically in a toolbar above the table view). It can interact with the table view by supplying a value for the <htmlb:tableView> attribute visibleFirstRow. However this approach requires more programming, as the developer is also responsible for the server events of the <xhtmlb:pager>.

The following demonstrates the code required to create a custom <xhtmlb:pager>. A complete example is also shipped in the BSP application SBSPEXT_PHTMLB.

```
<htmlb:tableView id = "TableExample"
   table           = "<%= it002t %>"
   ...
   footerVisible   = "FALSE"
   visibleRowCount = "8"
   visibleFirstRow = "<%= vindex * 8 - 7%>" >

<%  data vmax type i.
    data remainder type i.
    vmax = lines( it002t ) / 8.
    remainder = lines( it002t ) mod 8.
    if remainder ne 0 and remainder < 4.
      vmax = vmax + 1.
    endif. %>

<xhtmlb:pager id     = "pager"
        text   = "Page [$vIndex$] of $vMax$"
        onPage = "pager_onPage"
        vMax   = "<%= vmax %>"
        design = "VERTICAL_SIMPLE+INDICATOR" />
```

Listing 9.1 Custom <xhtmlb:pager> layout coding

```
  DATA: pager TYPE REF TO cl_xhtmlb_pager.
  pager ?= cl_htmlb_manager=>get_data( request = request
           name    = 'xhtmlb:pager'
           id      = 'pager' ).
  vindex = pager->vindex.
```

Listing 9.2 Custom <xhtmlb:pager> event handler

9.3.2 <htmlb:tree>

It is not uncommon to display data in a hierarchical view, for example in a navigation area. Quite often, navigation is grouped by the concept of folders and items. This need is fulfilled by the BSP element `<htmlb:tree>`.

The `<htmlb:tree>` is very similar to the classic dynpro control `CL_GUI_SIMPLE_TREE`. It allows for the building of a tree by supplying all data nodes and the parent/child relationship between nodes. Unfortunately, the data that you can represent within a node on the tree is output as a single area. In other words there is no approximation to the `CL_GUI_COLUMN_TREE`, which allows more complex data representation per node. The only close approximation of this functionality is provided by a hierarchy column in an `<htmlb:tableView>`.

The `<htmlb:tree>` element itself is relatively simply. It has attributes such as `height`, `width`, `title`, `showTitle`, and `tooltip` that control the basic formatting of the element. The attribute `onTreeClick` allows you to set a server side event handler for whenever any node text is clicked on.

The `restoreViewState` controls how the tree reacts to server events. By default, the tree element will remember which nodes were opened or closed by the user and restore these same settings back after the server event. However, you may want the ability to reset all node statuses back to their initial state by setting `restoreViewState` equal to *FALSE*.

The powerful attribute `toggle` controls what happens when the user expands or collapses a node. In the default `FALSE` state, only the visible nodes will be rendered to the client. When the client opens a new node that has children, a server event will occur to retrieve the details for these children nodes. This reduces the size of the content that must be sent to and rendered in the browser. However, the user may experience a delay while waiting for the server round trip to finish.

The other option is to set this attribute to *TRUE*. If the client's browser has sufficient support, all the nodes will be sent to the browser initial. The expansion or collapse then can occur on the client, providing a better visual experience at the cost of the higher initial load.

There are two ways to supply the nodes to the `<htmlb:tree>`. The first is to simply imbed them into the page layout using the inner element of `<htmlb:treeNode>`. This works nicely for a small number of nodes that are relatively static, such as a simple navigation area. `<htmlb:treeNode>` Elements can be nested within each other to create the folder/item hierarchy. The following example shows a simple tree with a single folder and two inner items.

```
<htmlb:tree id="exampleTree" >
   <htmlb:treeNode id    = "node1"
                   text = "Folder1" >
      <htmlb:treeNode id    = "node2"
                      text = "Item1" />
      <htmlb:treeNode id    = "node3"
                      text = "Item2" />
   </htmlb:treeNode>
</htmlb:tree>
```

Figure 9.16 Simple <htmlb:tree> Example

The other option is to supply the nodes via attributes of the `<htmlb:tree>` element. The attribute `table2` accepts an internal table of type `TVIEW2` containing the nodes and their relationships. Passing the nodes via an internal table obviously has advantages for trees that will contain a large number of nodes or where you need to supply the nodes dynamically.

Each record in the node internal table supports the same attributes that you could supply to the `<htmlb:treeNode>`. Attributes such as `img`, `text`, and `tooltip` allow you to specify the output content for the node. Since the `<htmlb:tree>` is a natural way of building navigation structures, the nodes themselves have special attributes, `link` and `target`, that allow for turning your node content into a hyper link. You also have the ability to control the `toggle` attribute and to specify a server `onClick` event at the node level.

When creating the nodes via the `<htmlb:treeNode>` method, you can simply create hierarchies by nesting the elements. On the other hand, our internal table is a flat structure. Therefore, the relationship between records must be created by specifying a `parentid` and `childid` on each node. To demonstrate this, let us recreate the earlier example now using the `table2` attribute to supply the nodes.

```
<htmlb:tree id     = "exampleTree"
            table2 = "<%= nodes %>" />
```

Listing 9.3 Page Layout

```
nodes type tview2
```

Listing 9.4 Page Attributes

```
FIELD-SYMBOLS: <wa_node> LIKE LINE OF nodes.

APPEND INITIAL LINE TO nodes ASSIGNING <wa_node>.
<wa_node>-treeid  = 'exampleTree'.
<wa_node>-childid = 'node1'.
<wa_node>-text    = 'Folder1'.

APPEND INITIAL LINE TO nodes ASSIGNING <wa_node>.
<wa_node>-treeid   = 'exampleTree'.
<wa_node>-parentid = 'node1'.
<wa_node>-childid  = 'node2'.
<wa_node>-status   = 'FINAL'.
<wa_node>-text     = 'Item1'.

APPEND INITIAL LINE TO nodes ASSIGNING <wa_node>.
<wa_node>-treeid   = 'exampleTree'.
<wa_node>-parentid = 'node1'.
<wa_node>-childid  = 'node3'.
<wa_node>-status   = 'FINAL'.
<wa_node>-text     = 'Item2'.
```

Listing 9.5 OnCreate Event

9.3.3 <phtmlb:matrix>

The `<phtmlb:matrix>` element is a close equivalent of the standard HTML table. Unlike the `<htmlb:tableView>`, which is concerned with the output of a single internal table, the `<phtmlb:matrix>` is used to layout content. For example, you might have a number of input fields and labels that you want to align. The `<phtmlb:matrix>` allows you to setup these elements within an invisible grid so that everything is lined up and well readable.

There is actually an older BSP element called `<htmlb:gridLayout>` that was commonly used in the past for this same functionality. However, the `<phtmlb:matrix>` is superior to the older element in that it is easier to program and has considerably better rendering performance.

The `<phtmlb:matrix>` has several attributes (`height`, `width`, `marginLeft`, `marginRight`, `marginTop`, and `marginBotton`) that allow you to control the overall size of the entire matrix.

Individual cell spacing and padding are controlled by two additional attributes, `separation` and `design`. The `separation` attribute controls the column spacing in addition to allowing you to specify a vertical separator between cells. By default, there are no separators or additional spacing. You have the additional values of SMALL, SMALLWITHLINE, LARGE, and LARGEWITHLINE. The attribute design is concerned with cell padding. The default value is to have cell padding on the right, top and bottom. There are also values for LRNOPAD (cell padding only top and bottom), LPAD (cell padding left, top, and bottom), LRPAD (cell padding right, left, top, and bottom), PADLESS (no cell padding).

The cells themselves can be supplied to the <phtmlb:matrix> in two ways. The most common method is to use the inner element <phtmlb:matrixCell>. In this case the <phtmlb:matrix> and <phtmlb:matrixCell> simply wrap around the additional content that you are grouping. The other option is to supply all the cells and their content dynamically via an internal table. This table of type PHTMLB_MATRIXCELLS is passed to the attribute cells. Although potentially very complex to program, because all the inner content within the matrix must be included, this is a powerful capability that assists you in creating dynamically generated user interfaces.

One final attribute in the <phtmlb:matrix> is the cellWidths. Normally the matrix is based upon the size of the content within its columns. However, if you want to set specific column widths in advance, you can supply them all here as a single string of lengths separated by commas.

The inner <phtmlb:matrixCell> element has many of the formatting options that you might expect, such as the ability to wrap the inner content (attribute wrapping), to specify the alignment (attributes hAlign and vAlign for horizontal and vertical alignment respectively), and to specify column spacing (attribute separation). There is also the option for a single cell to cover more than one column or row with the attributes colSpan and rowSpan.

Now we come to the real power of the <phtmlb:matrix> compared to the <htmlb:gridLayout>. In the <htmlb:gridLayoutCell>, you are required to supply a specific row and column index number. This can make your layouts inflexible, because you have to renumber all later elements when you add something new in the middle.

<phtmlb:matrixCell> attempts to solve this problem by giving you several options when supplying the values for the attributes col and row. You can still use the absolute column and row specifications; but now you also have the ability to use relative positioning. With this, you specify via +N the number of columns or rows that you wish to move relative to the last one rendered. You can even not specify a column or row at all. If no column is specified, then the inner content is placed automatically in the next column. If no row is specified, the content is automatically placed in the same row as the last cell. It is important to remember that you can only use ascending values whenever incrementing columns or rows.

The example in Figure 9.17 places several images in a matrix using only relative positioning.

Figure 9.17 <phtmlb:matrix> Example

```
<phtmlb:matrix width="50%" >
   <phtmlb:matrixCell/>
     <htmlb:image src="ICON_SAP" />
   <phtmlb:matrixCell col="+1" />
     <htmlb:image src="ICON_DECEASED_PATIENT" />
   <phtmlb:matrixCell col="+1" />
     <htmlb:image src="ICON_SYMBOL_FEMALE" />
   <phtmlb:matrixCell row="+1" /> <%-- col auto reset --%>
     <htmlb:image src="ICON_SYMBOL_MALE" />
   <phtmlb:matrixCell col="+1" />
     <htmlb:image src="ICON_STATUS_CRITICAL" />
</phtmlb:matrix>
```

Notice from the example how the coding is cleaner and more condensed than the corresponding code would be if we had used an `<htmlb:gridLayout>`. This is because of the unique nature of the `<phtmlb:matrixCell>`. Instead of having to wrap our content in beginning and ending elements, the `<phtmlb:matrixCell>` simply works as delimiters between the content.

9.3.4 <xhtmlb:protectDoubleSubmit>

When browser-based applications need to return to the server for processing or loading of data, the user has very little information about the progress of that processing and loading. There is nothing stopping the user from getting impatient and submitting the server event again. This can lead to all kinds of problems on the backend, perhaps even duplicate postings of the same information.

In all likelihood, you have visited a website where you finish your shopping and are ready to hit the submit button to complete your order, only to have the website inform you that you need to be patient and not hit "submit" more than once—or else you might receive multiple orders. It seems as though there should be a way to prevent duplicate data without having to rely upon end users not to accidentally do something.

The BSP element <xhtmlb:protectDoubleSubmit> solves this problem. The element can be used within any BSP page that utilizes the <htmlb:form> element. When an event is sent to the server, all screen input is immediately blocked by placing a transparent .gif over the screen. This ensures that users can not submit another event to the server while the first is still processing. After a certain amount of processing time has passed without receiving a response, the element produces a pop up window asking the user to please wait.

This element only has four attributes. The first is `active`. This determines if the element will function on the next response cycle. That way, you can disable or activate the <xhtmlb:protectDoubleSubmit> element dynamically in code. With the attributes `text` and `title` you can customize the UI of the pop up window. Finally the attribute `timer` allows you to set the amount of wait time on the client before the popup is activated. This attribute is measured in milliseconds and defaults to 2,500 or 2.5 seconds. 2.5 seconds is a practical duration that allows for quick server roundtrips to still fire with no disruption to the user. However, you have the ability to override and set this timer shorter or longer.

In the following example, we have simply placed an ABAP `WAIT` statement in the event handler of the page to simulate some extended processing so that the <xhtmlb:protectDoubleSubmit> element can be demonstrated.

```
<htmlb:form>
   <xhtmlb:protectDoubleSubmit
     title = "Customized Double Submit"
     text  = "This demonstrates a customized Double Submit"
   />
   <% WAIT UP TO 3 SECONDS. %>
   <htmlb:textView text   = "Customized Double Submit"
                   design = "EMPHASIZED" />
   ...
</htmlb:form>
```

9.3.5 <phtmlb:containerTabStrip>

Tabstrips are important UI elements that allow us to simplify an application by reducing the amount of navigation that the user needs to perform. Tabstrips have been a part of standard ABAP development since Basis release 4.0, so it is not surprising that the functionality for tabstrips within BSP is considerable.

There are actually three different sets of elements that can be used to produce a tabstrip: <htmlb:tabStrip>, <xhtmlb:tabStrip> and <phtmlb:containerTabStrip>.

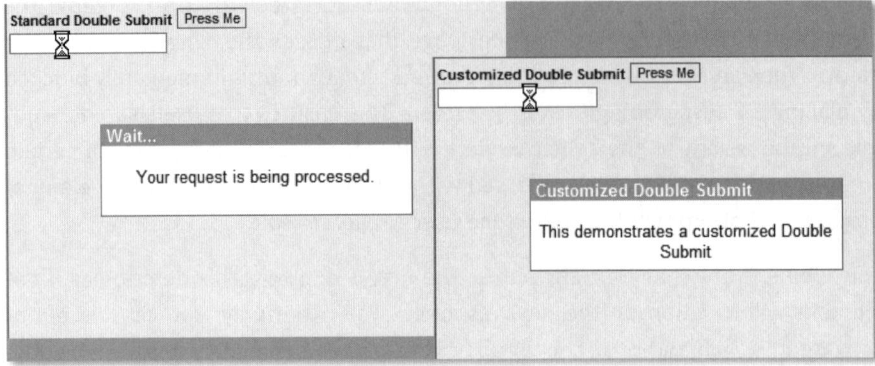

Figure 9.18 Two <xhtmlb:protectDoubleSubmit> Examples: Default Attributes and Attributes Customized by Program

Each new version of the tabstrip produced greater functionality. Therefore, we will take a closer look at the latest version with the most functionality and flexibility: `<phtmlb:containerTabStrip>`.

To create a complete tabstrip there are really three BSP elements involved. The first is the `<phtmlb:containerTabStrip>` itself. This element has the attributes that affect the entire tabstrip. The attributes `collapsed` and `collapsible` and `onCollapse` all work to together to support collapsible tabstrip areas. `<phtmlb:containerTabStrip>` defaults to `collapsible` being `TRUE`, however, for this to work you must also supply an `onCollapse` event handler. Within that handler, you should trap the collapsed state and then feed that back to the element through the attribute `collapsed`.

The `<phtmlb:containerTabStrip>` gets considerable functionality via the `items` attribute. This attribute allows the inner content of the tabstrip, including all the UI elements that will be rendered into each tab, to be supplied dynamically via an ABAP internal table of type `PHTMLB_CONTAINERTABSTRIPITEM`. This is another example of how BSP supports dynamic UI creation.

The `maxVisibleItems` attribute allows you to control how many of the tabs are visible in the strip area. If the total number of tabs exceeds this value, navigation controls will be generated to allow the user to page through multiple sets of tabs. By default, the element will generate and control this paging for you. You could also build a custom options menu, perhaps to further support navigation or to allow for removal of personalization of the tabstrip, via the attribute `optionMenuId`. You actually define a separate `<phtmlb:popupMenu>` element in your page. You then connect this to your tabstrip in the strip area by supplying the `<phtmlb:popupMenu>` element id to the `optionMenuId` attribute.

Finally we have the attribute selectedIndex. This attribute must to be set to control which tab is the active one. This attribute expects an integer value for the index of the tab that you wish to be active. If this attribute is not supplied or has an initial value, no content will be displayed in the tabstrip area. When the user clicks on a changed tabstrip, a server event is fired. It is the responsibility of the application to trap this event and place the new selected tab index into a variable that will be passed back into this attribute.

Each tab is defined with <phtmlb:containerTabStripItem>. For this element you can set the ID, title and tooltip that will appear for the tab in the strip area. You can also disable a single tab with the attribute enabled and control the scrolling mode of the inner content with the attribute scrollingMode.

Once again, we have the ability to supply the inner content of a tab dynamically. The attribute contentItems allows for dynamic elements to be supplied via an internal table of type PHTMLB_CONTAINERCONTENTITEM.

Finally, we reach the inner most element in our tabstrip, the <phtmlb:containerContentItem>. Each tabstrip item can contain one or more of these <phtmlb:containerContentItem> elements. The inner UI elements, such as input fields or text views, are all rendered within this element. We can set a scrolling mode that overrides the one specified at the tabstrip item level using the attribute scrollingMode. At the content level, you can also control visual elements such as cell padding, attribute hasPadding, and bordering, attribute border with a default value of FALSE.

The following example shows a simple tabstrip with three items, the third of which has been disabled. The example also has the event-handling necessary to support the switching of the active tab.

```
<phtmlb:containerTabStrip id = "TabStrip"
        selectedIndex         = "<%= selected_tab %>"
        firstVisibleItemIndex = "2" >
  <phtmlb:containerTabStripItem id    = "Tab1"
                                title = "Tab 1" >
    <phtmlb:containerContentItem>
      <htmlb:textView>Inner Content of Tab 1
      </htmlb:textView>
    </phtmlb:containerContentItem>
  </phtmlb:containerTabStripItem>
  <phtmlb:containerTabStripItem id    = "Tab2"
                                title = "Tab 2" >
```

```
    <phtmlb:containerContentItem>
      <htmlb:textView>Inner Content of Tab 2
      </htmlb:textView>
    </phtmlb:containerContentItem>
  </phtmlb:containerTabStripItem>
  <phtmlb:containerTabStripItem id      = "Tab3"
                                title   = "Tab 3"
                                enabled = "FALSE" >
  </phtmlb:containerTabStripItem>
</phtmlb:containerTabStrip>
```

Listing 9.6 Layout

```
DATA: event TYPE REF TO if_htmlb_data.
event2 = cl_htmlb_manager=>get_event_ex( request ).
IF event->event_type = phtmlb_events=>containerts_tab_selected.
  selected_tab = event->event_server_name.
ENDIF.
```

Listing 9.7 OnInputProcessing

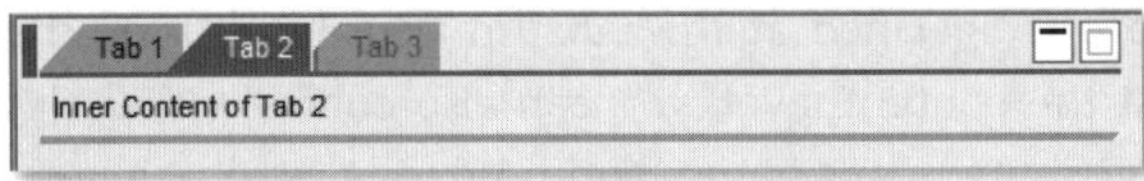

Figure 9.19 <phtmlb:containerTabStrip> Example

9.3.6 <phtmlb:formLayout>

As a BSP application developer, you will be spending a lot of time creating form layouts. A good portion of that time will be spent designing the complex matrixes to align input fields and their labels so that data input is attractive. Even with the advances that the `<phtmlb:matrix>` makes over the `<htmlb:gridLayout>`, the creation and maintenance of large forms can still be daunting.

However this task does not have to be that difficult, thanks to the `<phtmlb:formLayout>` element. The `<phtmlb:formLayout>` does all this work for you by creating the label, input element, and supporting matrix structure, all from the definition of a single element.

The best way to learn about the `<phtmlb:formLayout>` is to begin with a simple example and then dissect it. In this example, we will have a small form that will request input of a person's first name, family name, and email address.

```
<phtmlb:formLayout>
  <phtmlb:formLayoutInputField id = "FName"
          label = "First Name"
          value = "<%= name1%>" />
    <phtmlb:formLayoutInputField id = "SName"
            label = "Family Name"
            pos   = "asNeighbour,tiedTo=FName"
            value = "<%= name2%>" />
    <phtmlb:formLayoutInputField id = "Email"
            label = "Email Address"
            pos   = "skipRow,colspan=2"
            value = "<%= email %>" />
    <phtmlb:formLayoutItem idOfItem = "Submit"
            pos      = "skipRow" >
      <htmlb:button id      = "Submit"
             onClick = "Submit"
             text    = "Submit" />
    </phtmlb:formLayoutItem>
</phtmlb:formLayout>
```

Figure 9.20 <phtmlb:formLayout > Example

The `<phtmlb:formLayout>` element itself has just a few attributes that give you some control over the design of the form. Our example keeps all the default values for these attributes, but you can control the spacing between the form elements and their labels using the attribute `fieldToLabelFactor`. You can also insert a vertical separator between columns using attribute `verticalLineSeparation` and you can move the labels to be right aligned using `labelAlignment`.

But looking at the example, you can see that the real details come from the inner elements of the `<phtmlb:formLayout>`. What SAP has done is to create a few of the most used data input elements in simplified versions for use in the `<phtmlb:formLayout>`. These elements follow the 80/20 rule: that 20% of the functionality is used 80% of the time. True to that rule, these inner elements do not have all the functionality of the originals; however, they do contain the most used and useful functions.

SAP implements four of these simplified inner elements: <phtmlb:formLayoutInputField>, <phtmlb:formLayoutDropDownListBox>, <phtmlb:formLayoutCheckBox> and <phtmlb:formLayoutTextEdit>. Obviously there are going to be times when you need one of the more specialized attributes of the elements that are wrapped within the <phtmlb:formLayoutX> items. Or perhaps you need to include a BSP extension element other than input fields, dropdown list boxes, check boxes, or text edit boxes. For this, we have a generic form layout item called <phtmlb:formLayoutItem>. As you can see from the example, we have used this generic item to insert an <htmlb:button>.

Use of the form layout items immediately addresses one concern laid out to begin with: the generation of input elements with matching labels. That is only part of the value we gain by using the <phtmlb:formLayout>. The other time saving aspect is the positioning of elements relative to one another.

All of the positioning options are set by the single attribute pos. This single element has a considerable amount of functionality packed into. At its most basic form the attribute pos allows you to set the relative values of the row and the column for the element separated by a comma. For example pos= ="row+1,col=0" means new row, same column. Likewise to move to the next column in the same row you would use pos="row=1,col=+1".

In addition to directly specifying the positioning via a row and column value, there are also special positioning directives for two of the most common actions. These are NEWCOLUMN and SKIPROW. Use NEWCOLUMN to move to the next column in the same row. For instance, you have finished all output for the current column, and through the use of NEWCOLUMN output now goes to the next column. SKIPROW results in an empty row. It is effectively row=+2.

For large input elements, such as the email-address input field in our example, you may want to take up more than one column or row. For this activity we can use the pos attribute addition of COLSPAN or ROWSPAN. Our email element pos of pos="colspan=2" produced an element on the next row that covered two columns.

You may also want to ensure that two or more fields are always aligned next to each other regardless of what happens to the relative positioning of the elements around them. In our example, we wanted this functionality for the first name and family name elements. Instead of using relative positioning or the NEWCOLUMN pos value, we used the ASNEIGHBOUR directive.

It turns out that positioning and simplified interface are only two of the three major factors when working with <phtmlb:formLayout>. There is also layout customization functionality. Similar to the way that you can customize the R/3 application using the IMG, any <phtmlb:formLayout> allows you to give the ability to your business users to do code free customization of the form layout.

To support customization, you must first change the definition of the <phtmlb:formLayout> and add a value for the attribute customizationKey. This is the key value that will be used later to match up with the customization settings. You can imagine how you might generate a key for different organizational structures, such as company code or plant. The business would then have the flexibility to configure different input options along these lines.

This customization is made possible via the use of three database tables. The developer of the application must first create an entry in two of these tables, PHTMLB_FLI and PHTMLB_FLI_TEXT, in order to expose each element of their form layout where customization is possible. The first table, PHTMLB_FLI, has two keys. The first key, NS_APPL_PAGE, requires you to specify the BSP application namespace, application name and page/view. An example might be: SAP/Y_PHTMLB_TEST/test_page.html. The other key, FLI_ID, is a value that must match up with the ID given to each form layout item.

The second table, PHTMLB_FLI_TEXT, allows the developer to supply a language-dependent description for each item in PHTMLB_FLI. You should note, however, that this description is only used during the customization activity; it will *not* be used to supply the label for the form element at runtime.

The final table, PHTMLB_FLI_CUST, is where the actual customization values are stored. It has the same two key fields as PHTMLB_FLI for matching up to the BSP page and form layout element. It also has a key called VARIANT_KEY that should match the customizationKey attribute of the <phtmlb:formLayout>. Finally we have the field called MODIFIER that sets the customization option for the element in question. The following are the possible customization values.

Attribute Value	Definition
As Defined	The inner element is rendered exactly as defined in the original coding. This is the default configuration option.
Invisible	The inner element is not rendered at all, nor is a space reserved for it. All later elements are moved up a position to fill its space.
Hidden	Although similar to Invisible in the effect that it has on the element in question, Hidden affects the elements around it differently. With Hidden the space for the element continues to be reserved. However, entire empty rows are still removed. As you can see, with the use of Invisible and Hidden, the earlier pos attribute value of ASNEIGHBOUR becomes even more important.

Table 9.2 Possible Values for MODIFIER

Attribute Value	Definition
`Required`	If this value is set, during the rendering of the label for the element a required indicator, visualized as a small red star, is output. This only affects the visual rendering of the label. The application is still responsible for actually checking to make sure a value was supplied.
`Optional`	If the application had set in code an element to be required, this customization now can set it to be optional. Just as with the Required customization option, this value only affects visualization and not application logic.
`Read Only`	The inner element is displayed in a Read Only mode.

Table 9.2 Possible Values for MODIFIER (cont.)

It is important to note that SAP does not deliver any user interface for maintaining these customization tables. Standard table maintenance has been generated, so updates are possible using the SAP GUI transaction SM30. This is fine for the entries that the application developer must maintain in `PHTMLB_FLI` and `PHTMLB_FLI_TEXT`. However, you are more likely to have to create a custom application or build a personalization screen into your application to support business-level customization of table `PHTMLB_FLI_CUST`.

The discussion on customization does bring us back around to one final value for the attribute `pos`. Going back to our example where we wanted to make sure that first name and family name were always kept together, it also makes sense that customization options should apply to both fields. It does not really make sense to allow someone to hide one field without the other. Therefore, the `tiedTo` option can be added to the `pos` string. This will allow the form item to inherit whatever customization is set for the field it is tied to.

10 BSP Element Expressions and Iterators

The most powerful aspect of BSP development is the fact that that as a developer you are not locked into a ridged framework. SAP has given us the ability to work outside its rendering libraries. Even more important are the opportunities that BSP Element Expressions (BEEs) and tableView Iterators provide to alter the rendering within the existing framework.

Any rendering library is like a corset. It does the work it was designed for, but does not allow the flexibility to break out where required. The most interesting example is custom-rendering for specific `<htmlb:tableView>` cells. Sometimes you would like to render something special inside such a cell, for instance an icon to indicate a status, depending on the values of three other fields in the table row. This chapter discusses the building blocks used to group small parts of rendering code into a generic interface that then can be used to custom-render specific areas of the layout.

10.1 BSP Element Expressions

10.1.1 What is a BEE?

Effectively, a BEE can be described as an interface with one method `RENDER( )`. The complete interface (ignoring the trivial second `RENDER_TO_STRING` method) is:

```
INTERFACE IF_BSP_BEE.
  METHODS render IMPORTING page_context
     TYPE REF TO if_bsp_page_context .
ENDINTERFACE.
```

Any class can implement the interface. Once it comes to rendering, the `RENDER` method receives the page context as an import parameter. The page context contains information about the current BSP page being rendered and the current writer active, and provides methods to handle rendering of BSP elements.

Given a class that implements the `IF_BSP_BEE` interface, a simple element `<bsp:bee>` is also available to render such a class inline anywhere on a BSP page, if required.

```
bee->RENDER( page_context = me->m_page_context ).
```

In summary, a BEE is any class that implements the `IF_BSP_BEE` interface, and that can render itself when requested.

10.1.2 N=1, Using Any BSP Element as BEE

BEEs were initially designed for custom-rendering one specific cell in an <htmlb:tableView>. It was sufficient to specify one BSP element, for example an <htmlb:inputField> or <htmlb:image>. All HTMLB elements had to implement the IF_BSP_BEE interface to be usable as BEEs.

The simple solution was to implement this interface in the base class for all BSP elements (CL_BSP_ELEMENT). With this small change, it suddenly became possible to use any BSP element for custom-rendering as a BEE.

You will need a general understanding of how BSP elements are used inside a BSP page. There are three steps involved:

- Create an instance of element class.
- Set all attributes.
- Process BSP element.

The BSP compiler can look up what class is associated with a specific BSP element. It then will generate roughly the following code:

```
DATA: tagI TYPE CL_<class_name>.
CREATE OBJECT tagI.
TagI->A1 = V1.
...
TagI->An = Vn.
... process tagI ...
```

If you wish to use any BSP element as a custom-renderer at a later stage, you only have to complete the first two steps. Each BSP element has the interface IF_BSP_BEE via the base class, and the render method of this interface knows how to "process" the BSP element at the right time.

The matching class name can easily be looked up via the ABAP Workbench as shown in Figure 10.1.

However, using the above technique of setting attributes is still slightly error-prone. You have to keep all attributes in mind, their names and types, and especially remember to set all required attributes. For this reason, a factory method is also generated for each BSP element to handle all the hard work. Therefore, the above code would reduce to the following form:

```
DATA: tagI TYPE CL_<class_name>.
TagI = CL_<class_name>=>FACTORY( A1 = V1 ... An = Vn ).
... process tagI ...
```

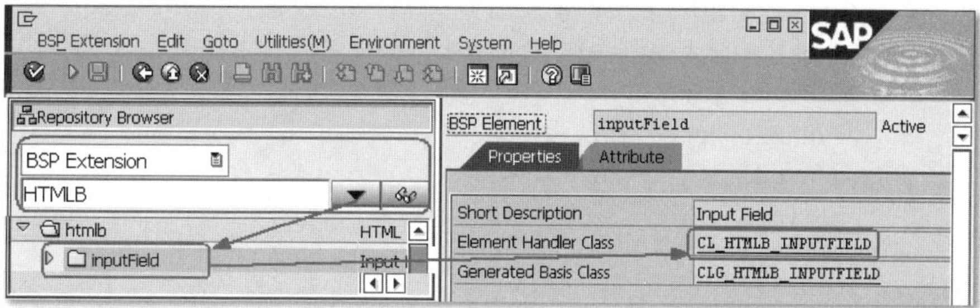

Figure 10.1 Class Name Lookup Using the Workbench.

The benefit of this approach is that the ABAP compiler is used to check all attributes during the compile phase. If you are uncertain about the available attributes, a simple double-click on the `FACTORY` brings you immediately to the definition of the method.

In order to demonstrate the effectiveness of the BEE, we will build a simple test program. We know that there are four supported techniques for using BEEs. So the test program must show four buttons, and it must provide an open piece of canvas into which we can render anything at runtime. The complete coding is:

```
<%@page language="abap"%>
  <%@extension name="bsp"    prefix="bsp"%>
  <%@extension name="htmlb"  prefix="htmlb"%>
  <%@extension name="xhtmlb" prefix="xhtmlb"%>
  <%-- general document structure --%>
  <htmlb:content design="design2003">
   <htmlb:page>
    <htmlb:form>
    <%-- button group with four test cases --%>
    <xhtmlb:toolbar id="tbbgl" >
      <xhtmlb:toolbarItem>
        <xhtmlb:buttonGroup        id    = "buttons"
                                onClick = "buttonPressed" >
          <xhtmlb:buttonGroupItem  key  = "single"
                                   text = "Single" />
          <xhtmlb:buttonGroupItem  key  = "html"
                                   text = "HTML"   />
          <xhtmlb:buttonGroupItem  key  = "table"
                                   text = "Table"  />
          <xhtmlb:buttonGroupItem  key  = "xml"
                                   text = "XML"    />
```

```
    </xhtmlb:buttonGroup>
   </xhtmlb:toolbarItem>
  </xhtmlb:toolbar>
  <%-- dynamic rendering --%>
  <bsp:bee bee = "<%= bee %>" />
  </htmlb:form>
 </htmlb:page>
</htmlb:content>
```

For the program, three page attributes are defined:

```
bee        TYPE REF TO IF_BSP_BEE
text       TYPE STRING (auto fill)
url        TYPE STRING (auto fill)
```

The `bee` is the actual instance of rendering code that will be rendered. The `text` and `url` fields are used for our small example. We would like to render two input fields below one another. This first allows us to specify some text for a URL. The URL will be displayed in the second (disabled) input field.

Finally, the `onInputProcessing` event-handling code must be as follows:

```
url = 'http://www.sap.com'.
DATA: event       TYPE REF TO if_htmlb_data,
      buttongroup TYPE REF TO cl_xhtmlb_buttongroup.
event = cl_htmlb_manager=>get_event_ex(
      runtime->server->request ).
IF event IS NOT INITIAL
AND event->event_name = cl_xhtmlb_buttongroup=>co_event_name.
  buttongroup ?= event.
  CASE buttongroup->buttonclicked.
    WHEN 'single'.      "* TO DO
    WHEN 'html'. "* TO DO
    WHEN 'table'.       "* TO DO
    WHEN 'xml'. "* TO DO
  ENDCASE.
ENDIF.
```

This code just sets the URL, static for our example, and then checks for an event from the HTMLB library. For button-group events, the corresponding action is taken.Given our test harness, we have a "hole" in the layout that we wish to fill with one BEE. We know that each BSP element can function as a BEE. So let us use an `<htmlb:inputField>` as a BEE. Keep in mind that we only must create the BEE. The actual "processing" is done later by the `<bsp:bee>` element.

The code is only a few lines (where variable bee is of type IF_BSP_BEE):

```
WHEN 'single'.
  DATA: tag_if TYPE REF TO cl_htmlb_inputfield.
  tag_if = cl_htmlb_inputfield=>factory(id = 'text'
              value = text ).
  bee = tag_if.
```

A new <htmlb:inputField> is declared and then instantiated via its factory method. Thereafter, the <htmlb:inputField> is ready to be rendered. For this, we assign the instance to the bee page variable. This works because each BSP element implements the IF_BSP_BEE interface via the base class.

The code can be reduced to:

```
WHEN 'single'.
  bee = cl_htmlb_inputfield=>factory( id = 'text'
        value = text ).
```

With the first button now completed, we run the BSP page again, and look at the output in Figure 10.2.

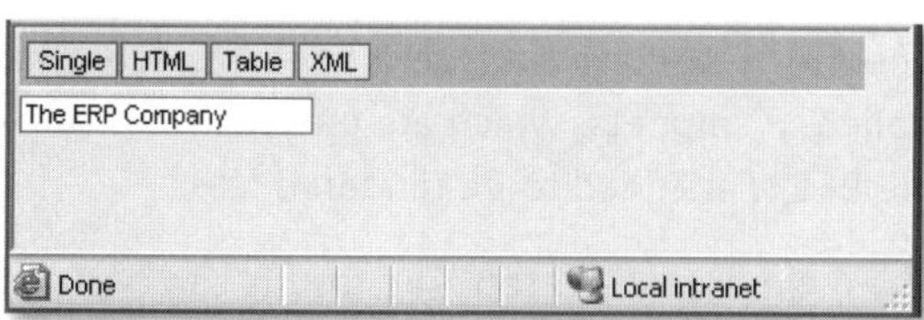

Figure 10.2 Starting Point of the Example

It works as designed! Even with the BSP element declared in one place, the rendering at a later stage during the layout phase works perfectly. And with this, nearly 80 % of the work is done for the <htmlb:tableView> custom-rendering.

10.1.3 HTML BEE

Using BSP elements to fill "holes" is interesting, but sometimes greater rendering control is required. For this, there is nothing better than pure, raw HTML.

For raw HTML, a second BEE is available. This class, CL_BSP_BEE_HTML, also implements the IF_BSP_BEE interface and therefore can be rendered later. Its primary goal is to store HTML sequences and render them out later.

For this example, we want to have two input fields, one for the text and the second to display a URL. Here is the code:

```
WHEN 'html'.
  DATA: bee_html TYPE REF TO cl_bsp_bee_html.
  CREATE OBJECT bee_html.
  bee_html->add(
    html1 = `<input name="text" id="text" `
    html2 = `title="Inputfield for text" `
    html3 = `value="`
    html4 = text
    html5 = `">`
    html6 = `<BR>` ).

  bee_html->add(
    html1 = `<input name="url" id="url" `
    html2 = `title="Inputfield for url disabled" `
    html3 = `value="`
    html4 = url
    html5 = `" `
    html6 = `readonly style="background-color:#ABABAB">` ).
  bee = bee_html.
```

In the first step, an instance of the HTML BEE is allocated. The add method is called twice, once for each input field. The add method has a handy feature that allows the HTML string to be supplied in snippets, which are internally concatenated together. In the last step, the BEE is assigned to be rendered later.

We run the test page again, and press the HTML button. The results can be seen in Figure 10.3.

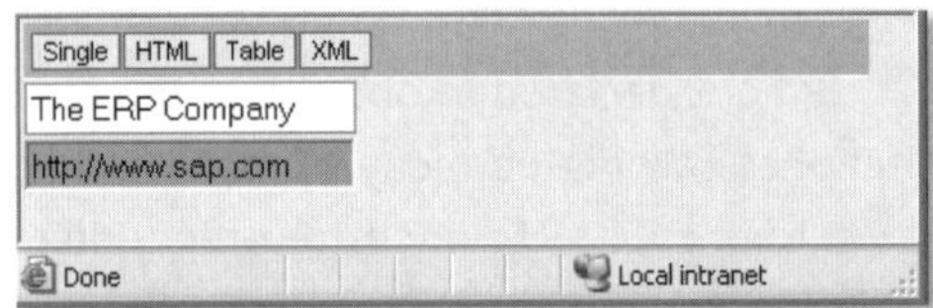

Figure 10.3 HTML BEE Example

The HTML is rendered in the "hole," as expected.

WARNING Using raw HTML is not recommended for the faint of heart. In principle, HTML coding is easy to understand and use. However, once it is written, you must also accept responsibility that the code will work in other supported browsers, for example Netscape. Even more important, you must handle all accessibility aspects, at a minimum setting the title attribute correctly.

10.1.4 Table BEE

The N=1 case was powerful, but did not go very far. What is really required is a set of BSP elements that can be rendered together: effectively, an expression!

For our stated problem, we could have written the following code directly in the layout of the BSP page:

```
<htmlb:gridLayout columnSize  = "1" rowSize  = "2">
  <htmlb:gridLayoutCell columnIndex = "1"
                        rowIndex    = "1">
    <htmlb:inputField    id    = "text"
                         value = "<%=text%>" />
  </htmlb:gridLayoutCell>
  <htmlb:gridLayoutCell  columnIndex = "1"
                         rowIndex    = "2">
    <htmlb:inputField    id       = "url"
                         value    = "<%=url%>"
                         disabled = "TRUE" />
  </htmlb:gridLayoutCell>
</htmlb:gridLayout>
```

However, we wish to process something similar dynamically. We already know how to create an instance of any BSP element via its factory method. Now all we need are techniques to put all these BSP elements into one expression, and still keep the relationship among them. For this, the table BEE—shown below—was designed.

```
WHEN 'table'.
  DATA: bee_table TYPE REF TO cl_bsp_bee_table.
  CREATE OBJECT bee_table.

  DATA: tag_if_text  TYPE REF TO cl_htmlb_inputfield,
        tag_if_url   TYPE REF TO cl_htmlb_inputfield.
  tag_if_text = cl_htmlb_inputfield=>factory( id = 'text'
              value = text ).
  tag_if_url  = cl_htmlb_inputfield=>factory(id = 'url'
              value = url disabled = 'TRUE' ).
  DATA: tag_gl       TYPE REF TO cl_htmlb_gridlayout,
        tag_glc_text TYPE REF TO cl_htmlb_gridlayoutcell,
        tag_glc_url  TYPE REF TO cl_htmlb_gridlayoutcell.
  tag_gl        = cl_htmlb_gridlayout=>factory(
            ColumnSize  = '1' rowSize  = '2' ).
```

```
tag_glc_text = cl_htmlb_gridlayoutcell=>factory(
            columnIndex = '1' rowIndex = '1' ).
tag_glc_url  = cl_htmlb_gridlayoutcell=>factory(
            ColumnIndex = '1' rowIndex = '2' ).

bee_table->add( level = 1 element = tag_gl ).
bee_table->add( level = 2 element = tag_glc_text ).
bee_table->add( level = 3 element = tag_if_text ).
bee_table->add( level = 2 element = tag_glc_url ).
bee_table->add( level = 3 element = tag_if_url ).
bee = bee_table.
```

First the table BEE is created. The next part of the code just uses the factory methods of the different BSP elements to create all the BSP element instances required. Then each BSP element is added in the sequence that it will be processed.

Very special care must be taken with the level attribute. This is an integer number used later during processing to determine if the next BSP element in sequence is a child of the current BSP element, or must be processed at the same level. The `RENDER` method of the table BEE knows how to render such a complex expression.

The final output can be seen in Figure 10.4.

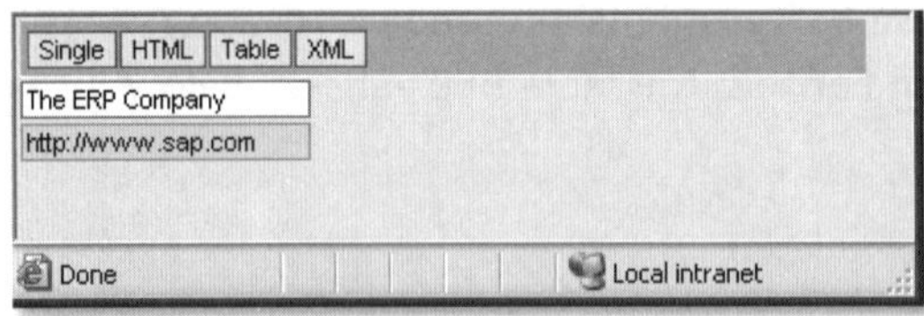

Figure 10.4 Table BEE Example

With this, we now achieve complete dynamic rendering of a "hole" with a sequence of BSP elements (the expression).

10.1.5 XML BEE

Writing all this code by hand can be complex. Imagine instead loading the complete sequence from a string, possibly even one stored in the database. A string is easy to write, can easily be understood, and can be changed to dynamically define an overriding layout for a specific part of the screen.

So the final example takes an XML string containing a BSP element expression and renders it into the "hole."

```
WHEN 'xml'.
  DATA: xml_string TYPE STRING.
  CONCATENATE
    '<bee:root> '
    '  <htmlb:gridLayout columnSize ="1" rowSize ="2"> '
    '    <htmlb:gridLayoutCell columnIndex="1" '
    '                          rowIndex="1"> '
    '      <htmlb:inputField   id ="text" '
    '                          value ="<%=text%>" /> '
    '    </htmlb:gridLayoutCell> '
    '    <htmlb:gridLayoutCell columnIndex="1" '
    '                          rowIndex="2"> '
    '      <htmlb:inputField   id ="url" '
    '                          value   ="<%=url%>" '
    '                          disabled = "TRUE"/>'
    '    </htmlb:gridLayoutCell>  '
    '  </htmlb:gridLayout> '
    '</bee:root> '
  INTO xml_string.

  DATA:           xml_parms  TYPE TABLE_BSP_BEE_PARMS.
  FIELD-SYMBOLS: <xml_parm> TYPE BSP_BEE_PARM.

  INSERT INITIAL LINE INTO TABLE xml_parms ASSIGNING
         <xml_parm>.
  <xml_parm>-name  = 'text'.
  <xml_parm>-value = text.

  INSERT INITIAL LINE INTO TABLE xml_parms ASSIGNING
         <xml_parm>.
  <xml_parm>-name  = 'url'.
  <xml_parm>-value = url.

  DATA: bee_xml TYPE REF TO cl_bsp_bee_xml.
  CREATE OBJECT bee_xml.
  bee_xml->set( EXPORTING xml        = xml_string
                          parms      = xml_parms
                IMPORTING xml_errors = xml_errors ).
  bee = bee_xml.
```

The first block of code just "writes" the BSP page code dynamically into a string. With a few small exceptions, this is written exactly as in the layout part of any BSP page.

The next block of code handles the dynamic attributes. These attributes are stored in a table, from which the values can be looked up when the BEE is processed.

The last block creates a new XML BEE and sets both the XML string and dynamic parameters.

The final output—in what might at first seem like a slight anti-climax—looks exactly like that of the table BEE. That is quite simply because exactly the same BSP elements are executed!

Although the table and XML BEEs achieve the same goal, they still have slightly different dynamics. For the table BEE, some form of code must be known beforehand, and written, in order to fill the table.

The XML BEE is completely dynamic. It also has the benefit that configuration-like layout sequences can be read from the database.

WARNING This flexibility comes at a high price. The XML BEE was rewritten three times by one of the best programmers in the ABAP Language Group. However, this still does not help with the fact that XML is parsed, interpreted, and code-executed dynamically. This technique will always be slow and only recommended for very special cases.

What Can be Used in the XML String?

Most important, the `<bsp:root>` node must be used as root node. This is just a pseudo-node added to enable a valid XML DOM for parsing.

Another pseudo-node that is supported is `<bee:html>`. It can be used to pack HTML text into the string. Although the inner HTML text does not conform to XML rules, this is a user-friendly way of writing. The HTML block is internally placed into a CDATA section before the DOM is parsed.

All other XML nodes in the DOM are considered to be BSP extension elements. No dynamic prefixes are supported. The prefixes used must match directly the BSP extension IDs, not to be confused with the recommended default IDs.

BSP elements with "element-dependent" bodies are not supported. There are no such elements within all HTMLB rendering libraries, so this should not be a problem.

Dynamic expressions from BSP pages (<%...%>) are not supported.

Any CDATA section is printed verbatim onto the output stream.

10.1.6 Errors and Error Handling

Of course, this small program was completed quickly and worked flawlessly. Unfortunately on the first pass through when creating this sample, the XML BEE failed! No output was rendered. An hour was spent chasing this error down (for the gory details of one small XML bug revealing a BEE bug, see OSS/CSN note 674230).

The lesson is to not ignore the return codes of method calls. The bee_xml->set( ) method returns a list of XML errors. These where ignored originally. Had we considered this table immediately, the hour of debugging would have been saved.

To show the power of the BEEs, the ultimate solution was extended. In case of an error, we now replace the output with an error table, as shown below. Please note that xml_errors is defined as a page attribute of type TIXMLTERR in order to keep the data reference alive even after onInputProcessing has been completed:

```
IF LINES( xml_errors ) > 0.
   DATA: table_ref TYPE REF TO DATA.
   GET REFERENCE OF xml_errors INTO table_ref.
   bee = CL_HTMLB_TABLEVIEW=>FACTORY( id = 'tview'
          table = table_ref ).
ENDIF.
```

If an error occurred, the <htmlb:tableView> would be used as a BEE to render out the error table. This shows the importance of error-handling and the strength of the custom-rendering provided by the BEEs.

Final Note

Like all powerful tools, BEEs must be used with care. For rendering small parts of the layout, they are excellent and highly recommended.

10.2 Table View Iterators

Often, you must influence the rendering of the <htmlb:tableView>. Maybe more (virtual) columns are required. Or perhaps the presentation of the data should not be done as text, but rather as icons or input fields.

For this, the <htmlb:tableView> supports the concept of an iterator. The <htmlb:tableView> will use this callback interface during rendering for each row and cell to allow you to control the exact rendering.

In order to demonstrate the table view iterator, we will create a very small BSP application that will display an <htmlb:tableView>.

```
TYPES: TABLE_SFLIGHT TYPE TABLE OF SFLIGHT.
```

Listing 10.1 Type Definitions:

```
flights   TYPE          TABLE_SFLIGHT
iterator  TYPE REF TO   IF_HTMLB_TABLEVIEW_ITERATOR
```

Listing 10.2 Page Attributes

```
SELECT * FROM SFLIGHT INTO TABLE flights.
```

Listing 10.3 OnCreate Event

```
<%@page language="abap"%>
<%@extension name="htmlb"  prefix="htmlb"%>
<htmlb:content design="design2003"
               controlRendering = "SAP">
  <htmlb:page>
    <htmlb:form>
     <htmlb:tableView id              = "tv1"
                      visibleRowCount = "10"
                      selectionMode   = "lineEdit"
                      table           = "<%=flights%>"
                      iterator        = "<%=iterator%>" />
    </htmlb:form>
  </htmlb:page>
</htmlb:content>
```

Listing 10.4 Layout

For this test, we will display some information from the SFLIGHT table. We define a type table of sflight, and then declare a page attribute of this table type to hold all records from the database. In the layout section, the <htmlb:tableView> is used to display the table.

The output, as shown in Figure 10.5, is as expected, although not very exiting.

	Clt	ID	No.	Date	Airfare	Curr.	Plane	Capacity in economy class	Occupied economy class	Booking total
	088	AA	0017	11/17/2004	422.94	USD	747-400	385	374	192,124.98
	088	AA	0017	12/15/2004	422.94	USD	747-400	385	372	193,148.41
	088	AA	0017	01/12/2005	422.94	USD	747-400	385	374	192,556.44
	088	AA	0017	02/09/2005	422.94	USD	747-400	385	371	191,164.88
	088	AA	0017	03/09/2005	422.94	USD	747-400	385	374	195,622.64
	088	AA	0017	04/06/2005	422.94	USD	747-400	385	373	192,420.96
	088	AA	0017	05/04/2005	422.94	USD	747-400	385	373	193,199.26
	088	AA	0017	06/01/2005	422.94	USD	747-400	385	367	190,039.79
	088	AA	0017	06/29/2005	422.94	USD	747-400	385	363	189,071.40
	088	AA	0017	07/27/2005	422.94	USD	747-400	385	0	0.00

1 of 41

Figure 10.5 Basic <htmlb:tableView> Output

With the help of the table view iterator, we are going to do some rendering improvements to this output.

- Render a new column in the beginning with a little airplane icon.
- Instead of having available and occupied columns for first, business, and economy class seats, we would like to render one column of the format "Occupied/Max."
- In edit mode, the currency should be picked from an `<htmlb:dropDownListBox>`, and it should be possible to edit the occupation for the different seats individually, even if they are displayed only in summed format.

10.2.1 What is a Table View Iterator?

In principle, a table view iterator is any class that implements the interface `if_htmlb_tableview_iterator`.

```
INTERFACE if_htmlb_tableview_iterator PUBLIC.
  METHODS get_column_definitions ...
  METHODS render_row_start ...
  METHODS render_cell_start ...
ENDINTERFACE.
```

This interface supports three methods. The `get_column_definitions` method is called once at the beginning of rendering, to allow an update or complete specification of all column definitions. This is very similar to the classic ABAP ALV Grid Field Catalog.

The row and cell start methods are called at the start of a new row and cell respectively. The complete parameter list will be discussed later.

Let us complete the last part of our test program. We need an iterator to enable custom-rendering of the <htmlb:tableView>. For this, we use transaction SE24 or SE80, and create a new class that implements the iterator interface. All methods are implemented initially as empty.

Our iterator class looks like this:

```
CLASS ycl_bsp_book_iterator DEFINITION PUBLIC CREATE PUBLIC.
  PUBLIC SECTION.
      INTERFACES if_htmlb_tableview_iterator .
ENDCLASS.

CLASs ycl_bsp_book_iterator implementation.
  METHOD
       if_htmlb_tableview_iterator~get_column_definitions.
  ENDMETHOD.
  METHOD if_htmlb_tableview_iterator~render_cell_start.
  ENDMETHOD.
  METHOD if_htmlb_tableview_iterator~render_row_start.
  ENDMETHOD.
ENDCLASS.
```

As a final step, we extend the onCreate event to also instantiate such an iterator.

```
  SELECT * FROM sflight INTO TABLE flights.
  CREATE OBJECT iterator TYPE ycl_bsp_book_iterator.
```

Listing 10.5 OnCreate Event

It is unfortunately not possible to implement local classes inside a BSP page. Therefore we must implement the iterator interface in a separate class. For this example, a new global class is created to implement the interface. If the <htmlb:tableView> is used in the context of Model View Controller, another idea is to implement the iterator interface in the calling controller class. Alternatively, you could also place the iterator inside the application class. However, this approach becomes difficult when more than one iterator is required. The recommendation in such cases would be to use local classes housed within your application class.

10.2.2 Method GET_COLUMN_DEFINITIONS

The method GET_COLUMN_DEFINITIONS is called at the beginning of the rendering. It receives the list of existing column definitions, and can update the list. This method has three parameters:

Parameters	Comments
P_TABLEVIEW_ID Importing STRING	The ID of the current table being rendered is supplied, for the situation in which the same iterator implementation is used for more than one table.
P_COLUMN_DEFINITIONS Changing TABLEVIEWCONTROLTAB	The columns definition is actually the most interesting parameter. It contains the content of all <htmlb:tableViewColumn> BSP elements. For a detailed description of all fields, please refer to the documentation of this BSP element and/or see DDIC definition for this structure.
P_OVERWRITES Changing TABLEVIEWOVERWRITETAB	This parameter allows the iterator to fill a table of special BEEs that will be rendered at the specific row and column indexes. However, the overwritten BEEs must all be created in advance, without even knowing if they will be used. The recommendation is to ignore this attribute in most cases.

Table 10.1 Parameters of Method GET_COLUMN_DEFINITIONS

Usually, column definitions are done with the inner tags <htmlb:tableViewColumn> or supplied via the <htmlb:tableView> attribute columnDefinitions. This is still possible. The already configured columns will be listed in the column-definition table. However, setting the column definitions dynamically cleans up the layout, and allows the flexibility to decide at runtime which columns should be rendered.

For our example table, the complete coding is:

```
METHOD if_htmlb_tableview_iterator~get_column_definitions.
  FIELD-SYMBOLS: <def> LIKE LINE OF p_column_definitions.
  APPEND INITIAL LINE TO p_column_definitions ASSIGNING <def>.
    <def>-COLUMNNAME = 'ICON'.
    <def>-TITLE      = ' '.

  APPEND INITIAL LINE TO p_column_definitions ASSIGNING <def>.
    <def>-COLUMNNAME = 'CARRID'.

  APPEND INITIAL LINE TO p_column_definitions ASSIGNING <def>.
    <def>-COLUMNNAME = 'CONNID'.

  APPEND INITIAL LINE TO p_column_definitions ASSIGNING <def>.
  <def>-COLUMNNAME = 'FLDATE'.   <def>-EDIT = 'X'.

  APPEND INITIAL LINE TO p_column_definitions ASSIGNING <def>.
  <def>-COLUMNNAME = 'PRICE'.    <def>-EDIT = 'X'.

  APPEND INITIAL LINE TO p_column_definitions ASSIGNING <def>.
  <def>-COLUMNNAME = 'CURRENCY'. <def>-EDIT = 'X'.
```

```
  APPEND INITIAL LINE TO p_column_definitions ASSIGNING <def>.
  <def>-COLUMNNAME = 'PLANETYPE'.

  APPEND INITIAL LINE TO p_column_definitions ASSIGNING <def>.
  <def>-COLUMNNAME = 'SEATS'.
  <def>-TITLE      = 'Seats'(001).
  <def>-EDIT       = 'X'.
ENDMETHOD.
```

The column-definition structure provides us with many options for fine-tuning the display of each column. However, for this example, only a few options will be sufficient.

As our first step, we add a new column called **ICON**. As this column does not even exist in the table, it cannot be rendered by the `<htmlb:tableView>`. Instead we will have to create the custom-rendering for this column ourselves.

In the next block, only those columns that must be displayed are listed. The names used match column names defined in the table. For some columns, we set the `EDIT` flag to indicate that these columns are editable. By default, no columns can be edited. Also, no title information is set. Not specifying a title means that it will be read for us directly from data dictionary.

Last, we add our new **SEATS** column that will be the sum of all values.

The new output shown in Figure 10.6 demonstrates a dramatic improvement:

Figure 10.6 Enhanced <htmlb:tableView> Output

10.2.3 Method RENDER_ROW_START

The method `RENDER_ROW_START` is called once at the beginning of each row. The biggest benefit from this call is to dynamically load relevant data for only those rows that will be rendered. It is important to note that this method is only called for rows actually rendered. Keep in mind that in our layout, we defined that the <htmlb:tableView> would only have ten visible rows at a time. Our SFLIGHT internal table could potentially have thousands of rows.

This method has a number of parameters, of which the most interesting is the data reference to the actual row. Because the <htmlb:tableView> works generically with tables, it cannot supply a typed reference. However, the iterator usually should know the type and can cast this reference into the correct type. This is the fastest way to access the current row data.

The complete list of parameters is:

Parameter	Comments
P_TABLEVIEW_ID Importing STRING	The ID of the current table being rendered is supplied, for the situation in which the same iterator implementation is used for more than one table.
P_ROW_INDEX Importing I	The table index of the row that will be rendered.
P_ROW_KEY Importing STRING	If a key column has been defined, the key for the row will be supplied.
P_ROW_DATA_REF Importing REF TO DATA	This is a reference to the current row to be rendered. Probably the most important parameter. It is not necessary to reload the data.
P_EDIT_MODE Importing XFELD	Indicator whether this row is in edit mode.
P_SKIP_ROW Returning XFELD	Flag that can be set to indicate that this row should not be rendered. It can be used to implement user-defined filters.

Table 10.2 Parameters of Method RENDER_ROW_START

For our example program, we will only use RENDER_ROW_START to store the reference to the actual data row. For this, we define a new class attribute m_row_ref TYPE REF TO SFLIGHT in the iterator class.

```
method IF_HTMLB_TABLEVIEW_ITERATOR~RENDER_ROW_START.
  m_row_ref ?= p_row_data_ref.
endmethod.
```

That little question mark is not a mistake, but a cast operator in ABAP. It is a little know feature of ABAP that like object references you can cast data references. We have now cast our untyped data reference into a typed one without ever copying any memory.

10.2.4 Method RENDER_CELL_START

The RENDER_CELL_START method will be called for each and every cell that will be rendered, including those cells in virtual columns. In all cases, it is highly recommended that you not implement any code in RENDER_CELL_START for any cell in which you simply want to enable the default rendering of the <htmlb:tableView>.

This method supports a large number of parameters. The most significant ones are listed below. Note that many parameters are equal to those of RENDER_ROW_START. Of course, it is optimal to do the work only once for the entire row. The parameters that are the same as RENDER_ROW_START are not listed again.

Parameter	Comments
P_CELL_ID Importing STRING	The correct (HTML) ID that has been computed for this cell. This value contains the tableView ID, the row and column index.
P_CELL_BINDING Importing STRING	This value is only set if the table has been bound using Model View Controller. This is the binding path for the cell being rendered. It can be used in your customer rendering of new BSP elements.
P_COLUMN_INDEX Importing I	Index of current column relative to column definitions.
P_COLUMN_KEY Importing STRING	Name of the column being rendered.
P_REPLACEMENT_BEE Exporting REF TO IF_BSP_BEE	If this value is left initial, the default <htmlb:tableView> rendering action will be taken. However, with this exporting parameter, it is possible to set a new BEE that will then be rendered into the current cell. This new BEE can, but does not have to, keep the current EDIT mode in mind.

Table 10.3 Parameters of Method RENDER_CELL_START

The best approach to using RENDER_CELL_START is to always implement only the absolute minimum needed. Leave the default rendering to the <htmlb:tableView>. For our example, we wish to custom render the ICON and SEAT fields. For the FLDATE and CURRENCY fields, we want to accept the default display handling, and use a different rendering only for editing.

The skeleton code will begin as:

```
METHOD if_htmlb_tableview_iterator~render_cell_start.
  CASE p_column_key.
    WHEN 'ICON'.
    WHEN 'CURRENCY'.
```

```
      IF p_edit_mode IS NOT INITIAL.
      ENDIF.
    WHEN 'SEATS'.
  ENDCASE.
ENDMETHOD.
```

In the next step, we wish to complete the code for these columns. In all cases, when we require direct access to the data from the row that is currently been rendered, we use the row reference which we stored earlier using method RENDER_ROW_START. This is fast, clean, and safe. Specifically, no dynamic programming is done with this type of access, and the compiler can completely check at compile time that we are referencing the correct data in the correct format.

For the ICON column, we require a small icon at all times. So an <htmlb:image> is created and returned as BEE.

```
WHEN 'ICON'.
  p_replacement_bee = CL_HTMLB_IMAGE=>FACTORY(
         id = p_cell_id
         src = 'ICON_WS_PLANE' ).
```

For currency, we are only interested in handling the Edit mode. For this, we want to render an <htmlb:dropDownListBox>. There are a number of techniques to fill the data. For this example, we created a name/value table, type TIHTTPNVP, in the class constructor and already filled it with the currencies that we support. A reference to this table is stored in class's attribute m_currencies_ref (ABAP statement GET REFERENCE OF var INTO ref).

```
WHEN 'CURRENCY'.
  IF p_edit_mode IS NOT INITIAL.
     p_replacement_bee = CL_HTMLB_DROPDOWNLISTBOX=>FACTORY(
       id                  = p_cell_id
       selection           = m_row_ref->CURRENCY
       table               = m_currencies_ref
       nameOfKeyColumn     = 'NAME'
       nameOfValueColumn = 'VALUE' ).
  ENDIF.
```

For the **SEATS** column, our work is slightly more complex. For the display part, we need to show only the final totals of the form "Occupied/Max." The work boils down to calculating the values for the current row that has been rendered, and placing them into a string. An <htmlb:textView> is used to render the string. It is important to note that this display was not selected to be functionally perfect, but rather to have a little complexity in order to show data manipulation directly against the selected table row. For this reason, the achieved layout is not really recommended.

The code for edit mode is only slightly more complex. For this example, we will show all three values directly inline, each in its own input field. The complete coding consists of creating three `<htmlb:inputField>`, and using a table BEE to build them into one expression.

```
WHEN 'SEATS'.
  IF p_edit_mode IS INITIAL.
   DATA: max TYPE string, occ TYPE string,
         value TYPE string.
   max = m_row_ref->seatsmax + m_row_ref->seatsmax_b
         + m_row_ref->seatsmax_f.
   occ = m_row_ref->seatsocc + m_row_ref->seatsocc_b
         + m_row_ref->seatsocc_f.
   CONDENSE: max, occ.
   CONCATENATE occ ` / ` max INTO value.
   p_replacement_bee = cl_htmlb_textview=>factory(
         text = value ).
  ELSE.
   DATA: if_first TYPE REF TO cl_htmlb_inputfield.
   if_first = cl_htmlb_inputfield=>factory(
         id = p_cell_id  id_postfix = '_first'
         type = 'INTEGER' size = '4' ).
   if_first->value = m_row_ref->seatsocc_f.

   DATA: if_bus   TYPE REF TO cl_htmlb_inputfield.
   if_bus    = cl_htmlb_inputfield=>factory(
         id = p_cell_id  id_postfix = '_bus'
         type = 'INTEGER' size = '4' ).
   if_bus->value = m_row_ref->seatsocc_b.

   DATA: if_econ  TYPE REF TO cl_htmlb_inputfield.
   if_econ = cl_htmlb_inputfield=>factory(
            id = p_cell_id  id_postfix = '_econ'
            type = 'INTEGER' size = '4'  ).
   if_econ->value = m_row_ref->seatsocc.

   DATA: seats_bee TYPE REF TO cl_bsp_bee_table.
   CREATE OBJECT seats_bee.
```

```
    seats_bee->add_html(      html    = '<table><tr><td>' ).
    seats_bee->add( level = 3 element = if_first ).
    seats_bee->add_html(      html    = '</td><td>' ).
    seats_bee->add( level = 3 element = if_bus ).
    seats_bee->add_html(      html    = '</td><td>' ).
    seats_bee->add( level = 3 element = if_econ ).
    seats_bee->add_html(      html    = '</td></tr></table>' ).
    p_replacement_bee = seats_bee.
  ENDIF.
```

In the code above, there are three important aspects. The first is that the `FACTORY` parameter `id_postfix` is used to create new IDs for each input field relative to the supplied cell id. The postfix string is appended onto the supplied ID by the factory method. The other significant aspect is that value is not set during the factory call. It is not possible to supply `INT4` values to `STRING` parameters. The values are set directly after the factory call in order to use ABAP `MOVE` conversion semantics. This way of initializing a BSP element is completely acceptable. Finally, we had to use a small amount of HTML around the input fields in order to align them correctly within the cell.

10.2.5 Finished Output

The finished output, shown in Figure 10.7, is just what we expected.

Figure 10.7 Final <htmlb:tableView> Version

Nearly all the work for rendering cells, in both display and input mode, is done by the `<htmlb:tableView>`. We only had to add about 100 lines of code to get the special cases rendered correctly. Using BEEs and the table-view iterator together greatly enhances the final rendering. This can be considered a critical part of any BSP programmer's toolbox.

11 Creating your own BSP Extension Element

We already have seen in the last few chapters how powerful the BSP Extension Framework is. Fortunately, this is also an open technology framework that allows SAP's customers to build their own BSP extensions and to combine existing extensions to create composite elements.

11.1 Creating a BSP Extension Element

In Chapter 9, we took a close look at how BSP extension elements are structured in order to better understand how to use them. However, this only scratched the surface of what lies within the BSP extension element. Before we begin the process of writing our own elements, it is important to study in detail the most important part of an extension element: its element-handler class.

11.1.1 Extension Framework Hierarchy

The element-handler class actually represents an inherited hierarchy of class objects that all come together to form the extension framework. It is important to build this inheritance hierarchy correctly, because much of the functionality we will code within our handler will be placed inside of redefinitions of inherited methods.

The core extension framework comprises two objects, `IF_BSP_ELEMENT` and `CL_BSP_ELEMENT`. `IF_BSP_ELEMENT` defines all the core methods and attributes for the extension framework. `CL_BSP_ELEMENT` implements the `IF_BSP_ELEMENT` interface and provides the basic functions that support all BSP extension elements.

There are two more objects within this hierarchy, both specific to the individual extension element. The first is a generated basis class, usually created with the following naming standard:

```
(Z)CLG_<EXTENSION>_<ELEMENT>
```

This class is automatically generated by the BSP development environment. When you define attributes for your extension element inside the BSP extension editor, these attributes will be generated as public attributes of this basis class. This class should also inherit from `CL_BSP_ELEMENT` and provide the specific constructor for the element. By dynamically generating this class, all the attributes of your element can be strictly typed and checked at compile time.

The final object is the core handler class itself. It should inherit from the generated basis class, and its name is completely user definable. However it is probably good form to following a naming standard such as the following:

```
(Z)CL_<EXTENSION>_<ELEMENT>
```

This class is where you will be spending most of your time as an element author. This class has the method redefinitions and any specific methods or attributes needed to implement the element.

11.1.2 User-Defined Validation

BSP extension elements are unique among the ABAP language tools in their approach to input validation. The extension runtime gives you the opportunity to code different validation routines that will be executed at runtime and compile time. That means that the syntax check of a BSP page will fire validation code that you can write. This gives you the ability to throw compiler errors for your own elements.

In order to implement user-defined validation, we must redefine two methods in our handler class that were inherited down from IF_BSP_ELEMENT.

The first method is COMPILE_TIME_IS_VALID. This is where we will code our compile time checks. SAP provides a series of validation methods (in class CL_BSP_ELEMENT_CT_ATTR_VALID), which assist in this process. In addition to providing simple checks, these methods also properly convert attribute-input string values into Boolean and integers values where necessary.

What follows are coding examples for the validation routines of a fictional BSP Extension Element. They contain common types of checks in order to demonstrate the different possible techniques.

```
METHOD if_bsp_element~compile_time_is_valid .
  validator->to_enum( name = 'Color'
    enums = 'RED/BLUE/GREEN' ).
  validator->to_enum( name  = 'alignment'
    enums = 'LEFT/RIGHT' ).
  validator->to_boolean( name = 'disabled' ).
  validator->to_integer( name = 'size' ).
  valid = validator->m_all_values_valid.
ENDMETHOD.
```

We also have the method RUNTIME_IS_VALID. This method is useful for checking attribute values that are supplied dynamically, such as through BSP expressions

(<%=...%>) only at runtime, or for attributes whose values are transformed into another data type.

```
METHOD if_bsp_element~runtime_is_valid.
 get_class_named_parent(
       class_name = 'CL_HTMLB_CONTENT' ).
  IF runtime_parms = '/*/' OR runtime_parms CS 'alignment'.
   alignment = m_validator->to_enum(
        name  = 'alignment'
        value = alignment
        enums = 'LEFT/RIGHT'
        required = space ).
  ENDIF.
  IF runtime_parms = '/*/' OR runtime_parms CS 'disabled'.
   disabled  = m_validator->bindable_to_boolean(
        name  = 'disabled'
        value = disabled
        binding_path = _disabled
        page_context = m_page_context ).
  ENDIF.
  IF runtime_parms = '/*/' OR runtime_parms CS 'size'.
   size = m_validator->bindable_to_integer(
        name  = 'size'
        value = size
        binding_path = _size
        page_context = m_page_context ).
  ENDIF.
ENDMETHOD.
```

The first line in the runtime validation method checks that this BSP element is used with an `<htmlb:content>` element. It is not possible to check this at compile time, as different elements can be used in different views, and these are compiled separately. We surround each of our dynamic value checks with an `IF` check for performance. That way we only perform validation routines on attributes that actually have values set dynamically.

It is important to note that these two validation methods will only be called if the **User-Defined Validation** option is selected in the **BSP Element Properties**. That way, if you have no validations that you wish to perform in your element, you can save the time that it would have taken for the framework to make calls into simply empty methods.

11.1.3 Element Content

Three methods in our element-handler class control the flow of creation of element content. They are DO_AT_BEGINNING, DO_AT_ITERATION and DO_AT_END.

DO_AT_BEGINNING is always accessed by the runtime at the beginning of the element processing. You can control the flow of processing after DO_AT_BEGINNING by setting the return parameter RC. If your processing is simple and only requires logic in the DO_AT_BEGINNING, you can set RC to CO_ELEMENT_DONE. Processing is then completed and returned to the BSP runtime. However setting RC to CO_ELEMENT_CONTINUE will allow processing to move on to the body of the element.

This means that all inner tags are given the change to render themselves. A small example might be that within a tabstrip there are many <lib:tabStripItem> elements. But, only one tabstrip item is required and must be rendered. Consequently, each item checks whether it is active and visible. Those that are not active are set rc to CO_ELEMENT_DONE to skip the processing of all inner elements, as this not needed for rendering. Only the one active tab strip item will actually continue with processing of its inner tags to generate the required HTML.

If the option **Iteration Through Element Content** was selected in the element properties screen, the method DO_AT_ITERATION can be called following DO_AT_BEGINNING. This method allows the element handler to make several passes over its inner content.

The method DO_AT_END is accessed after all other processing is completed. At this point, all the element content is available and can be further manipulated. This method is especially useful for BSP elements that contain inner elements.

The combination of DO_AT_BEGINNING and DO_AT_END methods are very similar to the structure of basic HTML. They are most useful for their ability to render before and after their inner content.

Let us assume the following example:

```
<htmlb:link href="http://www.sap-press.com" >
  SAP PRESS
</htmlb:link>
```

In this example, the DO_AT_BEGINNING method of the <htmlb:link> element will render out the HTML <a href="http://www.sap-press.com"> and then set CO_ELEMENT_CONTINUE.

This causes the runtime to process the inner body, which in this case only outputs the string "SAP PRESS". Thereafter, the DO_AT_END method is called, which corresponds very much to the end tag in HTML. This method will render out the HTML

</a> sequence. Here the two methods very much reflect the way that HTML is structured with leading/trailing markup, allowing for efficient rendering.

11.2 Writing a Composite Element

Very often, we find the same pattern repeated on some or all of our BSP pages. Although such coding can be easily placed on all pages with cut-and-paste programming, it quickly becomes tedious and error-prone. Modifications suddenly require code updates over all BSP pages.

One approach to this problem, is to place the specific pattern into a page fragment and simply include it on every page where required. This has the advantage that changes are only required once in the page fragment. However, it still has the disadvantage that the code inside the page fragment is expanded inline into each BSP page. This increases the size of each page and can result in a `GEN_BRANCHOFFSET_LIMIT` error when generation limits are reached.

11.2.1 Designing a New Composite Element

What we most would like to have is a principle of *composition*. Usually these reusable patterns are just a collection of HTMLB elements. Would it not be nice if we could combine such a collection into one composite element? Well, we can, by creating our own BSP Extension Element.

Let us first look at an example application that could benefit from a redesign with composite elements in mind. This example shows the typical process of navigating back and forth inside a simple form. Normally, this can be done by using the `<htmlb:button>` element, with the new previous and next designs. Let us assume that we would like to place two navigation buttons at the bottom of each page.

Figure 11.1 Composite Element Example

```
<%@extension name="htmlb" prefix="htmlb"%>
<%@extension name="phtmlb" prefix="phtmlb"%>
<htmlb:content design="design2003">
 <htmlb:page>
```

```
   <htmlb:form>
      ...body comes here...
    <phtmlb:horizontalDivider hasRule          = "TRUE"
                             separationHeight = "LARGE" />
    <phtmlb:matrix width = "100%" >
      <phtmlb:matrixCell hAlign = "RIGHT" />
        <htmlb:button    text           = "Page In-1"
                         design         = "PREVIOUS"
                         onClick        = "pageIn-1.bsp" />
        <htmlb:button    text           = "Page In+1"
                         design         = "NEXT"
                         onClick        = "pageIn+1.bsp" />
    </phtmlb:matrix>
   </htmlb:form>
  </htmlb:page>
 </htmlb:content>
```

The goal is to replace this entire navigation rendering with one simple element. The expected final code on each BSP page would then be:

```
<%@extension name="htmlb"   prefix="htmlb"%>
<%@extension name="ybook"   prefix="ybook"%>
<htmlb:content design="design2003">
 <htmlb:page>
  <htmlb:form>
     ...body comes here...
   <ybook:pager prev = "Page In-1" next = "Page In+1" />
  </htmlb:form>
 </htmlb:page>
</htmlb:content>
```

We want one element that takes a previous and/or next attribute with the text to display. As we are slightly lazy in this example, we assume that pages are named exactly the same as the descriptive text, except that they are without spaces, and terminated with our typical `.bsp` extension.

The definition in the workbench, transaction SE80, of the new BSP element is quickly done. It has only two string attributes. Once this BSP element has been defined and activated, the above example BSP page will actually compile and run. It will just not yet render any output.

BSP Element pager Active

Properties | Attribute

Short Description: Previous/Next Navigation
Element Handler Class: YCL_BSP_BOOK_EXTENSION_PAGER
Generated Basis Class: ZCLG_YBOOK_PAGER

Element: content
Data
Blank

Attribute	R...	D...	Ca...	Bi...	Typing ...	Associated Type
next	☐	☐	☐	☐	1 TYPE	STRING
prev	☐	☐	☐	☐	1 TYPE	STRING

Further options
☑ "PAGE DONE" is not returned at end of BSP element

Figure 11.2 BSP Element Properties and Attributes

11.2.2 Processing Other BSP Elements

Now that we have defined our new `<ybook:pager>` element and already written the test program, it is time to complete the code for the composite element itself. Before processing other elements, it is important to understand how elements are processed on BSP pages. It is only possible to use existing BSP elements within our new element in this way.

A BSP element is written on a page using an XML format. As a first step, the BSP compiler must map the XML name onto a specific handler class. This class name can be seen in the workbench, when looking at the BSP element. The compiler generates code to create a new temporary variable to hold the reference to the handler class (`data:` statement), and then to create an instance of this BSP element-handler class. Next, the compiler generates the source code to initialize each attribute with its specified value. Finally, the BSP element is pushed onto a stack, which contains all elements that are currently in process, and the `do_at_beginning` method is called.

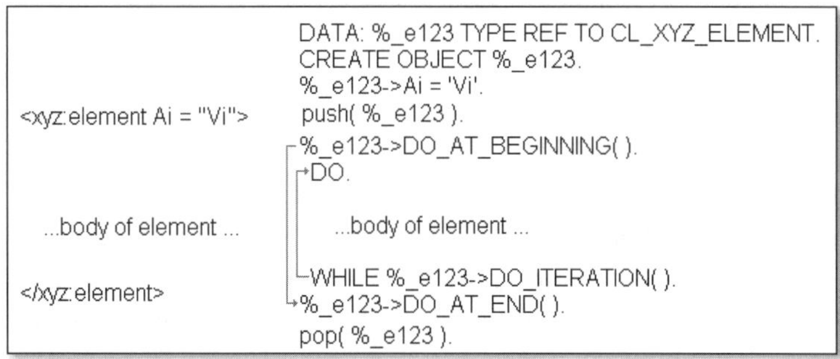

<xyz:element Ai = "Vi">
...body of element ...
</xyz:element>
DATA: %_e123 TYPE REF TO CL_XYZ_ELEMENT.
CREATE OBJECT %_e123.
%_e123->Ai = 'Vi'.
push(%_e123).
%_e123->DO_AT_BEGINNING( ).
DO.
...body of element ...
WHILE %_e123->DO_ITERATION( ).
%_e123->DO_AT_END( ).
pop(%_e123).

Figure 11.3 Element Processing Flow

In the simplest case, the element has no body or is defined as empty. In this case, the `do_at_end` method is called directly afterwards. If the element has a body, it is processed between the two method calls. It is also possible for the BSP element to request that the body be skipped, for example if you have an inactive tabstrip body. In the most extreme case, the BSP element can request that it reiterates over its body, which results in the body being processed as long as the `do_iteration` method requests that this be done.

In principle, it is difficult to know the exact code required to process each specific BSP element. It can also happen that, the BSP element is changed over time, and then has a different execution sequence.

You can break down the element-processing parts into the following phases.

- Each BSP element is first instantiated, and then its attributes are set correctly. This coding is very specific for the BSP element and will be different for each one.
- Thereafter, preamble coding is required to get the element onto the stack and process the `do_at_beginning` method call. This generic code is the same for each element.
- The body is processed. The body depends completely on the element being used. It can contain more BSP elements, or even raw HTML code can be rendered.
- More coding is required either to complete the processing of the BSP element, or to set it up correctly for a new iteration.

Specifically the fact that a BSP element can iterate over its body implies that some form of loop will be required. In addition, framework coding is required before and after the body to ensure correct processing. In order to encompass all these aspects, the following processing model was designed:

```
... user written factory and attribute initialization code ...
WHILE m_page_context->element_process( the_element )
    = CO_ELEMENT_CONTINUE.
    ... body of element ...
ENDWHILE.
```

This approach leaves the programmer the freedom to initialize the specific BSP element correctly. Thereafter, only one `WHILE` construct is required to process any BSP element in any of its variations. The `element_process` method will be called as many times as required to ensure that the BSP element is processed correctly.

Important Do not attempt to process BSP elements any other way! Such an attempt will fail, and it will not be supported by SAP. This WHILE construct is the only correct method.

Let us now look at a few detailed examples of processing existing elements. For our first example, let us assume that we have the following code on our BSP page:

```
<htmlb:button   text     = "Page In-1"
                design   = "PREVIOUS"
                onClick  = "pageIn-1.bsp" />
```

Then the correct code to process this <htmlb:button> dynamically would be:

```
DATA: myBtn TYPE REF TO CL_HTMLB_BUTTON.
CREATE OBJECT myBtn.
myBtn->text     = 'Page In-1'.
myBtn->design   = 'PREVIOUS'.
myBtn->onClick = 'pageIn-1.bsp'.
WHILE m_page_context->element_process( element = myBtn )
   = CO_ELEMENT_CONTINUE.
ENDWHILE.
```

The workbench must be used to find the correct class that implements this specific BSP element.

Alternatively, you can use the factory method that is automatically generated onto all BSP elements. The benefit of the factory method is that you can double-click on it to see the exact list of required parameters, and the ABAP language compiler is used to enforce required attributes.

```
DATA: myBtn TYPE REF TO CL_HTMLB_BUTTON.
myBtn = CL_HTMLB_BUTTON=>FACTORY( text     = 'Page In-1'
                                  design   = 'PREVIOUS'
                                  onClick = 'pageIn-1.bsp' ).
WHILE m_page_context->element_process( element = myBtn )
    = CO_ELEMENT_CONTINUE.
ENDWHILE.
```

Now let us look at a slightly more complex example. Assume that we are using an <htmlb:link> element that contains, as body, both an <htmlb:image> element and normal text. The source code on a BSP page would be:

```
<htmlb:link id = "lnk" reference = "http://www.sap.com" >
  <htmlb:image src = "logo.gif" />
```

```
  SAP
</htmlb:link>
```

To process this sequence dynamically, the correct coding would be:

```
DATA: myLnk TYPE REF TO CL_HTMLB_LINK.
myLnk = CL_HTMLB_LINK=>FACTORY( id = 'lnk'
        reference = 'http://www.sap.com' ).
WHILE m_page_context->element_process( element = myLnk )
    = CO_ELEMENT_CONTINUE.

  DATA: myImg TYPE REF TO CL_HTMLB_IMAGE.
  myImg = CL_HTMLB_IMAGE=>FACTORY( src = 'logo.gif' ).
  WHILE m_page_context->element_process(
        element = myImg ) = CO_ELEMENT_CONTINUE.
  ENDWHILE.

  DATA: out TYPE REF TO IF_BSP_WRITER.
  out = m_page_context->get_out( ).
  out->print_string( 'SAP' ).

ENDWHILE.
```

The WHILE loop to process the <htmlb:image> is placed inside the WHILE loop of the <htmlb:link>. This reflects the fact that the image is part of the body of the link. In addition, text or raw HTML can be rendered as body of an element being processed. This is done by obtaining a reference to the active writer at the top of the stack and writing the relevant text.

Do not attempt to cache this writer reference. In all cases, always do the get_out call again after any element_process call. It is always possible for any new element on the stack to also push an additional writer onto the stack. The get_out call always returns the active writer.

In later support packages, there is a helper method called print_string that should be inherited from the super class CL_BSP_ELEMENT. This method already contains the logic to correctly retrieve the writer reference, allowing you to simplify your coding. In the example above, you could replace the text output with the following single line of code.

```
print_string( 'SAP' ).
```

Often, while writing the code to process a BSP element dynamically, you get weird error messages from the compiler. For example, the code snippet below produced the error "*Field WHILE unknown*."

```
* <htmlb:image src = "logo.gif" />
myImg->src = "logo.gif".
WHILE ...
```

The reason for this is very subtle. Inside BSP elements, strings are written using XML syntax with double quotes. Typically, code is cut-and-pasted from BSP pages directly into an ABAP class for the processing sequence. However, the double-quote character in ABAP starts a comment sequence that extends up to the end of the line. So, in the above source, the ABAP compiler will see `myImg->src = WHILE`.

The correct coding is:

```
* <htmlb:image src = "logo.gif" />
  myImg->src = 'logo.gif'.
  WHILE ...
```

11.2.3 Writing the Composite BSP Element

We already defined a test page that shows us the required rendering. Furthermore, we defined a new BSP element. As this will be an empty BSP element, we redefine only the `do_at_beginning` method and paste the code from the test page into this method. The code changes become straightforward, given the examples above.

Below is an extract of the code.

```
METHOD if_bsp_element~do_at_beginning.
    ... <phtmlb:horizontalDivider/> ...
* <phtmlb:matrix width = "100%" >
  DATA: phtmlb_matrix TYPE REF TO cl_phtmlb_matrix.
  phtmlb_matrix = cl_phtmlb_matrix=>factory(
            width = '100%' ).

  WHILE m_page_context->element_process(
         element = phtmlb_matrix ) = co_element_continue.

*   <phtmlb:matrixCell hAlign = "RIGHT" />
    phtmlb_matrix->mc_halign = 'RIGHT'.
    phtmlb_matrix->do_set_data(
         element_name = 'matrixCell' ).
        ... prev button ...
*   space between two buttons
        me->PRINT_STRING( ' ' ).
       ... next button ...
```

```
* </phtmlb:matrix>
  ENDWHILE.
* Set return code to done (empty element)
  rc = co_element_done.
ENDMETHOD.
```

Notice the use of a WHILE statement around the code that represents the body of the <phtmlb:matrix>. Another important fact: When a very small piece of raw HTML is required, we obtain the active writer at the moment that we require it. We have not yet explained the do_set_data call.

11.2.4 Handling of Inner Data BSP Elements

Often we will find constructs where child BSP elements are used to feed information into the parent BSP element for later rendering. A typical example is <htmlb:breadCrumb>.

```
<htmlb:breadCrumb id = "myBreadCrumb0">
  <htmlb:breadCrumbItem key="k1" value="text1" />
  <htmlb:breadCrumbItem key="k2" value="text2" />
  <htmlb:breadCrumbItem key="k3" value="text3" />
</htmlb:breadCrumb>
```

Each item has only stub code for finding the parent and supplying the configured parameters:

```
METHOD if_bsp_element~do_at_beginning .
    DATA: breadcrumb  TYPE REF TO cl_htmlb_breadcrumb.
    breadcrumb ?= get_class_named_parent(
          'CL_HTMLB_BREADCRUMB' ).
    breadcrumb->append_item(
          key   = key
          value = value ).
    rc = co_element_done.
ENDMETHOD.
```

However, for each item on the BSP page, code must be generated to instantiate a new <htmlb:breadCrumbItem>, set its attributes, and then to process the element. This is very high overhead for simply adding additional configuration information to the parent item. To improve the performance for this typical usage pattern, a new BSP element of type Data was created.

Effectively, the name of the parent handler class is specified for the new BSP element. The BSP library generator will then place all the attributes of the data element onto the parent element, using the camel-case abbreviation of the name as key to prefix the attributes. For example, for `<phtmlb:matrixCell>`, the camel-case abbreviation will be `mc_`. The `<phtmlb:matrixCell>` has at least two attributes: `col` and `row`. For these defined attributes, new attributes `mc_col` and `mc_row` are generated on the handler class of the parent.

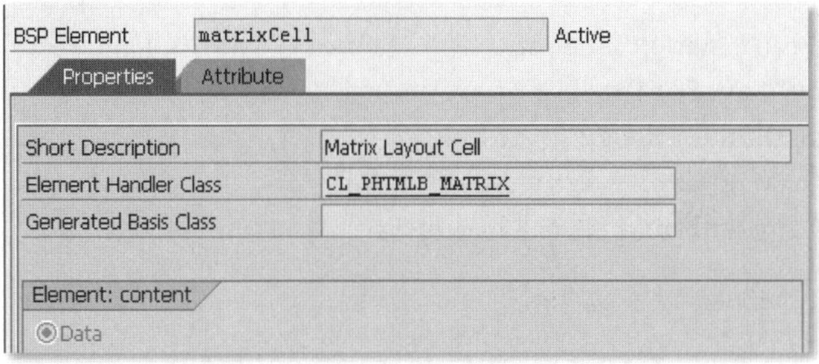

Figure 11.4 DATA BSP Element Type

When the `<phtmlb:matrixCell>` is used on a BSP page, the BSP compiler keeps a list of the surrounding BSP elements. It sees that `<phtmlb:matrixCell>` is a `data` element attached to the class `cl_phtmlb_matrix`. As a result, the following code is generated:

```
%_matrix_6->mc_col = 1.
%_matrix_6->mc_row = 2.
...
%_matrix_6->DO_SET_DATA( element_name = 'matrixCell' ).
```

The `%_matrix_6` is the outer instance of type `<phtmlb:matrix>`. The attributes are set on the parent class, and the `DO_SET_DATA` call is placed, giving the name of the actual data element being processed. This way, data can be moved into the parent element with better performance.

11.3 A Deeper Look at BSP Extensions Events

11.3.1 Introduction to BSP Extension Events

HTML/HTTP does not support the concept of server events. At the lowest level, the only building block that is available is forms in HTML, which can be submitted to a server. When a form is submitted, all input fields—including hidden input fields—are transported to the server. Therefore, event-handling in the browser is reduced to setting up specific predefined input fields, usually `type="hidden"`, with values that reflect the event to be sent to the server, and then submitting the form.

When using the HTMLB family of rendering libraries, it is very seldom that any raw HTML is required. The rendering libraries already have sufficiently extensive sets of controls. However, once some HTML is required, you are immediately faced with a few perplexing problems. One is the question of transporting events from the browser to the server.

```
<htmlb:form id="myform" >
  <input type="hidden" name="s_event_id" value ="TEST"/>
  <SCRIPT language="JavaScript">
    function myEventHandler(event_id) {
      document.myform.s_event_id.value = event_id;
      document.myform.submit(); }
  </SCRIPT>
  <button id="Test"
          onclick="myEventHandler('button_clicked');">
    Submit! </button><br>
  Event = <%= server_event_id %>
</htmlb:form>
```

Listing 11.1 Triggering a "Server Event" via the HTML form submit

The HTMLB library comes with its own event-handling system, which also includes a large piece of JavaScript code. If native HTML code, such as the code listing above, is added on a page that bypasses the HTMLB event system, the HTMLB library could be negatively affected.

One typical example is the `<xhtmlb:protectDoubleSubmit>` element. This item hooks into the HTMLB event system in the browser and will display a wait message once an event is sent to the server. Therefore, it is helpful for other library writers, and for people writing native HTML, to use the HTMLB event system for their event handling as well.

11.3.2 Rendering Events

During rendering, each element might require one or more events. This is usually done by wiring the HTML `onClick` attribute with some JavaScript code that will handle the event. This specific, required JavaScript code is obtained by a call to the method `cl_htmlb_manager=>render_event_call`.

This method will return a sequence of JavaScript code, which consists of one or more calls to the different JavaScript functions that are available for event handling in the browser. The output of this method is for internal use only. This output has been improved a number of times. Do not try to concatenate this Java-

Script output together directly, as this will cause problems if the underlying event-handling code is modified.

Rendering Phase:

```
<htmlb:button id="myBtn" onClick="button_clicked"/>
... CL_HTMLB_BUTTON
      ... event = CL_HTMLB_MANAGER=>RENDER_EVENT_CALL(...).
      ... render onclick="htmlbSubmitLib(...)"
```

In the above examples, the JavaScript function htmlbSubmitLib is shown. However, the exact call that will be generated depends on a number of factors, for example whether a client-side event is also involved, or whether the event is listed in a predefined dictionary. Consider the output of the RENDER_EVENT_CALL method as a black box.

In the browser, once a control event is triggered, the JavaScript code in the onClick handler is executed. This code calls the defined JavaScript code, which packs the relevant event information into hidden input fields and then submits the form:

In Browser:

1. User clicks on button
2. onclick is triggered, calls htmlbSubmitLib(...)
3. Sets up a number of input fields with correct values
4. Calls form.submit();

RENDER_EVENT_CALL Method

The render_event_call can only be used within a BSP element. One of the checks that this method does is to see if it is used within an HTMLB form. This is verified by checking the processing stack of all BSP elements, looking for an <htmlb:form> element. This method has a relatively complex interface that is discussed below in detail.

Parameter Name	Description
bsp_element IF_BSP_ELEMENT	This is the actual element that is rendering the event. From this interface, the library name, the element name and the ID will be used for event-rendering. The first two values are generated into the base class of the element. The ID string must be set by the element.

Table 11.1 Parameters of Method RENDER_EVENT_CALL

Parameter Name	Description
event_type STRING	This string indicates what type of event was fired by the element. Typically, a button could fire a click event, a pager could fire page up or down events, and a table could fire a row-select or header-click event. This string has no further meaning for the HTMLB event system, and is transported transparently.
server_event STRING	This string is defined by the user of the element for the event. A typical example would be to write `<htmlb:button onClick="myHandler"/>`. This string can contain information to help the user to handle the event correctly. This string has no further meaning for the HTMLB event system, and is transported transparently.
client_event STRING	This string reflects the typical `onClientClick` attribute used on many elements. It must contain valid JavaScript code that will be executed in the browser. This string is not returned to the server. At a minimum, one of the server or client events must be specified. Otherwise, no event-handling code will be generated.
client_event_inlined XFELD Default SPACE	Initially, it was up to the control to render out a JavaScript function that had a predefined name containing the `client_event` code. However, during HTML-parsing, small JavaScript functions cause a high overhead for the HTML-rendering. Thus, the inline flag leaves the rendering of the JavaScript code to the HTMLB manager class. It only creates a JavaScript function if this event should actually be triggered. We highly recommend that you set the value always to "X".
event_defined STRING Default 'null'	Many events require a minimal string to contain additional information for the event. Instead of using additional parameters, you can use this one string for carrying the information. This string has no further meaning for the HTMLB event system, and is transported transparently.
param_count I	Number of parameters that will be transported in this event. This value must be set correctly for the `render_event_call` method.
param_string STRING	A comma-separated string of parameters (strangely starting with a comma!). This list of parameters is copied verbatim into the generated event handling function. It is also possible to imbed the names of JavaScript variables in the event - parameter string with this format, which is then automatically used during the event-handling.
param_1 ... _9 STRING	An alternative option is to specify the `param_string` string as single parameters from `param_1` to `param_9`. The parameters are copied together during the rendering of the event. If the parameters are supplied individually, each parameter is considered to be a constant string, and will be rendered with quotes.

Table 11.1 Parameters of Method RENDER_EVENT_CALL (cont.)

Parameter Name	Description
return_value STRING	Keep in mind that the actual generated JavaScript is placed inside an HTML onclick sequence. In HTML, it is important to keep event- bubbling in mind. One typical instance occurs when an anchor is used to render a control. If the onclick does not return false, the <a href> will be triggered as well. By default, all JavaScript contains a "return false" as the last instruction. This parameter can be either true or false to set the value to be returned, or blank to prevent the rendering of a return value. This is unfortunately a very complex aspect of HTML rendering; when in doubt, leave the default value.

Table 11.1 Parameters of Method RENDER_EVENT_CALL (cont.)

11.3.3 Handling Incoming Events

On the server, the event-handling system will look at the incoming HTTP request. If it detects form fields with well-known names, for example all HTMLB element-event input fields having a prefix htmlbevt_, it will signal an HTMLB event. The runtime then unpacks the relevant fields into an event object.

On Server:

```
event = CL_HTMLB_MANAGER=>GET_EVENT_EX( request )
```

- ... examines HTTP request for fields matching htmlbevt_*
- ... creates event object cl_htmlb_button, unpacks fields

This action of unpacking the relevant fields into an event object is done by the class cl_htmlb_manager. It will map the event onto the correct class, which is by default the same class used for rendering the BSP element. It instantiates a new copy of this class and then does a query for the if_htmlb_data interface.

The method event_initialized will be called with all the standard attributes of an HTMLB event. The values are restored onto the event attributes defined on the interface if_htmlb_data. The last call will be to event_set_parameters with all additional parameters that were available in the incoming HTTP request. These are also restored into the class attributes.

11.3.4 Rendering an Event via the <bsp:htmlbEvent> Element

It is useful to understand the way to directly interact with the CL_HTMLB_MANAGER=>RENDER_EVENT_CALL method if you are going to create your own custom BSP elements. This method call can be included in the rendering code of your ABAP class.

What if you simply want to render an event in-line in your BSP page and attach it to some standard HTML or another BSP Element? For this task, SAP provides the <bsp:htmlbEvent> element. This element can either return the event JavaScript code for later use, or it can generate a JavaScript function that, when called, will fire an event back to the server.

For example, the control can be used as:

```
<bsp:htmlbEvent name="fireMyEvent" p1="a" p2="b" />
```

It will write into the output stream the following:

```
<script> function fireMyEvent(a,b) {...} </script>
```

This function can now be called directly from HTML or JavaScript:

```
<button onclick="return fireMyEvent('myButton',123)">
 myButton</button>
```

With this design, it is actually possible to use the HTMLB event system, without even knowing what is rendered out. The <bsp:htmlbEvent> element renders out a wrapper function that can be called directly, and it even allows additional parameters to be transported.

Another approach is to request that the <bsp:htmlbEvent> element return the JavaScript code for direct use. By flagging an attribute on the element as a reference attribute, it will get a reference to a local variable, and then can write back the information. In the example below, event_code will be updated by the <bsp:htmlbEvent> element with the final generated JavaScript code, and the code can now be used directly inline when writing HTML.

```
<% DATA: event_code TYPE string. %>
<bsp:htmlbEvent event_defined="myBtn2"
                event_code="<%=event_code%>" />
<button onclick = "<%=event_code%>">myButton2</button>
```

11.4 Event Handling in Composite Elements

Earlier in this chapter, we built a composite element, but you may have noticed that the example did not fire any events and was not tied into the HTMLB event manager. Now that we have studied the HTMLB event manager in detail, we are ready to return the earlier example and improve it by changing the fired <htmlb:button> events into real native events from this element. In addition, we will add support for a data interface.

11.4.1 Extending the Design of the Composite Element

As the names of all IDs and events used in the previous example were hard coded, it was not possible to use two pagers on the same HTML page. For example, this could be interesting in scenarios where a split screen showing two logical independent sequences is used, and can be paged separately. Thus, we need to begin our enhancements by adding an `ID` attribute

In addition, one never knew what the current page was. The pager only handled the previous and next pages. We will also add a `current` attribute, which is the name of the current page. This will also be rendered left-aligned on screen.

Last, we are adding an `onPage` attribute to allow us to configure the event handler that must be called on return. Note that we will have both `pagePrevious` and `pageNext` events. The `onPage` is just a string that is the user's handle for the event. Although in most elements we define an `onX` per event, it is not required. Using one such `onX` string for a number of events is perfectly acceptable.

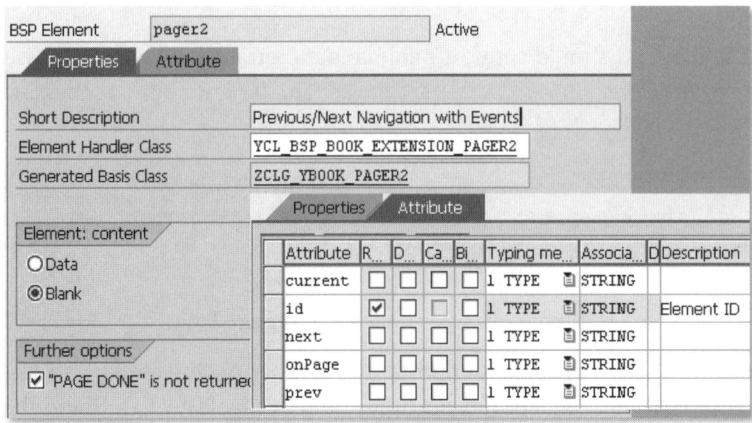

Figure 11.5 BSP Element Properties and Attributes

As Figure 11.5 demonstrates, we have created a new element for these enhancements so as to keep the older example for reference. But it is also possible simply to change the original code.

11.4.2 Using the Composite Element

Before we start looking under the hood at the code that will be needed to complete the work, let us first use the new element. This will give us a good idea of what must be supported. The test program will be similar to that used previously. We only have to set additional attributes for the element.

For each page, we define the following source code:

```
<htmlb:content design="design2003"><htmlb:page><htmlb:form>
   ...body comes here...
    <ybook:pager2 id      = "<any id string>"
                  prev    = "<name of previous page>"
                  current = "<name of this page>"
                  next    = "<name of next page>"
                  onPage  = "<name of event handler>" />
 </htmlb:form></htmlb:page></htmlb:content>
```

For the `onInputProcessing` code, we would now like to use code that is similar to that of the HTMLB library:

```
DATA: event TYPE REF TO if_htmlb_data.
event = cl_htmlb_manager=>get_event_ex( request ).
IF event IS NOT INITIAL AND event->event_id = 'myPager'.
  navigation->goto_page( event->event_defined ).
ENDIF.
```

In addition, the element should support minimal data retrieval, where it is possible to query the previous, current, and next pages. The typical code for the data call is:

```
DATA: pager TYPE REF TO ycl_bsp_book_extension_pager2.
pager ?= cl_htmlb_manager=>get_data( request = request
           name     = 'ybook:pager2'
           id       = 'myPager' ).
* use here pager->current, pager->next, pager->prev
```

Notice that for the `get_data` call it is important to also supply the library and element name. The HTMLB manager has no other help available to determine the correct handler class. The library name is not that of the prefix used in the layout, but the original name under which the library was created. This allows the HTMLB manager to again determine the correct handling class.

We see from the above coding that we wish to achieve a new pager element that will work transparently with the HTMLB manager. Any consumer of our new element should not be able to see a difference between it and any other standard SAP-delivered element.

11.4.3 Use of IDs

The first significant aspect is the handling of the element ID. Once we allow the option that the same element can be used multiple times on the same page, each must have a unique ID. First, the element was given a new required ID attribute.

The pager element itself does not really do any rendering. Primarily, it uses two <htmlb:button> elements. Each of these buttons requires an ID. This at first was solved by just hard coding the ID string.

```
htmlb_button = cl_htmlb_button=>factory(
                 id            =  'ybook_pager_next'
                 ... )
```

With the new approach, we would like to have IDs that are unique and independent of the usage count. This goal can be achieved by using the ID of the element as the basis for creating new IDs. All new IDs will typically be of the form <id>__<sub string>.

This is such a common pattern when building composite elements that the factory methods were extended to handle the concept of an id, plus a postfix string that must be attached.

```
htmlb_button = cl_htmlb_button=>factory(
                  id            = id
                  id_postfix    = '__Previous'
                  ... ).

htmlb_button = cl_htmlb_button=>factory(
                  id            = id
                  id_postfix    = '__Next'
                  ... ).
```

The factory method will concatenate the id and id_postfix strings together to create the new ID for the specific button.

11.4.4 Integrating into the HTMLB Manager

The HTMLB manager interacts with the element-handler class via the if_htmlb_data interface. The interface has four methods used for the data and event handling.

Method	Description
RESTORE_FROM_REQUEST	This method is called by the HTMLB manager to restore view state from the incoming request. This is always triggered by the get_data call.
EVENT_INITIALIZE	The get_event_ex call will result in a call to this interface, with the event data already decoded. The code has to fill the event_* attributes of the if_htmlb_data interface.

Table 11.2 Methods of Interface IF_HTMLB_DATA

Method	Description
EVENT_SET_PARAMETERS	Called directly after event_Initialize to set the additional event parameters p1 to p9.
EVENT_DISPATCH	If the HTMLB manager is used to dispatch the event and the target handler has also implemented at least the if_htmlb_event interface, then this method will be called with the handler object to dispatch the event using a typed method call.

Table 11.2 Methods of Interface IF_HTMLB_DATA (cont.)

When implementing these methods, the biggest problem is the interaction between data and events. For example, assume that we have an <htmlb:group> element and that the minimize button was pressed. Using only the get_data call, the view state would actually indicate that the group container is still maximized. After restoring the previous view state, you therefore must check whether the incoming event must be applied onto the data. Similarly, if only the get_event_ex call is used, it is usually practical that the rest of the view state data is also restored, so that no additional get_data call is required.

For this reason, we always implement the event_iniatilize code to also call the restore_from_request method, thereby simulating a get_data call. The restore_from_request code uses the event_id as a flag to determine whether it is called from the event-handling code, in which case it continues to restore data, or whether it is triggered from a get_data call, in which case it will use an HTMLB manager call to apply an event if required.

```
METHOD if_htmlb_data~event_initialize.
* Initialize event_* parameters
    me->if_htmlb_data~event_* = ...
* Restore all data from the request
    me->if_htmlb_data~restore_from_request(
         request = p_request
         id      = if_htmlb_data~event_id ).
   ...now apply event onto restored data...
ENDMETHOD.

METHOD if_htmlb_data~restore_from_request.
* Use event_id as flag to check whether we also have an
* event. Let it do work.
    IF me->if_htmlb_data~event_id IS INITIAL AND
       CL_HTMLB_MANAGER=>CHECK_AND_INITIALISE_EVENT(
                           instance          = me
                           request           = request
```

```
                        event_id_expected = id
                        class_name        = m_class_name
                  ) IS NOT INITIAL.
      RETURN. " means an event found and restored
* (recursively called here)
    ENDIF.
    ...restore values from request...
  ENDMETHOD.
```

11.4.5 Data-Handling

We require the pager to be able to restore the values of the previous, current, and next pages. We must keep in mind that any control on the page can trigger an event to the server, and thus it is not always possible to retrieve this information from the event data.

The best technique for storing the view state within an HTML page is to use hidden input fields. This information is not rendered and will be returned to the server when the form is submitted.

The following code is used within the `do_at_beginning` method to render the view state into the response, so that it will be returned to the server on the next request:

```
DATA: html TYPE STRING.
CONCATENATE
  `<input type="hidden" name="` id `__valPrev"
    value="` prev    `">`
  `<input type="hidden" name="` id `__valCurrent"
    value="` current `">`
  `<input type="hidden" name="` id `__valNext"
    value="` next    `">`
INTO html.
print_string( html ).
```

Notice the use of the ID with sub strings to create new names for each hidden input field. The values are taken from the current element attributes.

To restore the values, the code below is used in the `restore_from_request` method:

```
me->id = id.
CONCATENATE me->id `_valPrev` INTO name.
me->prev = request->get_form_field( name ).
```

```
CONCATENATE me->id `_valCurrent` INTO name.
me->current = request->get_form_field( name ).

CONCATENATE me->id `_valNext` INTO name.
me->next = request->get_form_field( name ).
```

Notice again the use of the ID to compute the actual names of the form fields that hold the data in the incoming HTTP request.

11.4.6 Event-Handling

Event-handling is slightly more complex. The pager element uses two `<htmlb:button>` elements. As such, when one of these buttons is pressed, a HTMLB button-clicked event is returned to the server. What we actually want is to present a pager event.

The problem is that the HTMLB manager has the class `cl_htmlb_button` defined as handler class for the button-click. We want our new pager class defined as the handler for these events. For this, the HTMLB manager supports an escape mechanism. Usually events are encoded in the HTML in the form:

```
htmlb:button:click:null
```

But, it is also possible to add an additional handler classes onto this string, using "::" as separator sequences.

```
htmlb:button:click:null::<handler_class>::<event_defined>
```

This means that even although a button-click event is received, the newly specified handler class must be called to decode the event. As it is not possible to configure these escape strings when processing another element, the HTMLB manager will also accept these escape sequences when they are attached to the event-server name, `onX` strings.

```
DATA: htmlb_button TYPE REF TO cl_htmlb_button.
htmlb_button = cl_htmlb_button=>factory(
                        id          = id
                        id_postfix  = '__pagePrevious'
                        text        = prev
                        design      = 'PREVIOUS' ).
CONCATENATE onPage '::YCL_BSP_BOOK_EXTENSION_PAGER2::'
            prev '.bsp'
       INTO htmlb_button->onclick.
WHILE m_page_context->element_process( htmlb_button )
                                    = co_element_continue.
ENDWHILE.
```

In the previous example we have hard-coded the class name. This approach is simple but can lead to problems if you rename your handler class. If you want to use the element handler as the event handler, it is best to retrieve the class name dynamically using the CLG (base) class.

```
CONCATENATE onPage '::' me->m_class_name '::'
            prev '.bsp'
       INTO htmlb_button->onclick.
```

Instead of just writing `onClick = onPage`, we are now adding our `YCL_BSP_BOOK_EXTENSION_PAGER2` class into the escape string to function as the handler for this specific button-click event. We use our event-defined string to carry the name of the previous page. With this small change, our handler class will always be called when one of the buttons is pressed.

For an incoming event, the `event_initialize` method will be called with the information about the button click. First, we set up all the `event_*` attributes. Afterwards, we would like to map a button-click event onto a pager `pagePrevious` or `pageNext` event.

Our first step is to set the new event name to the name of this BSP element (`pager2`). As a next step, the `ID` has to be set correctly. Remember that the initial `ID` was post-fixed with a constant string `__<direction>`. Therefore, we split the string at "__" to get the original `ID` again and the event type, which was effectively encoded as a sub string in the `ID`.

```
METHOD if_htmlb_data~event_initialize .
* Copy those parameters which we keep verbatim
  if_htmlb_data~event_id              = p_event_id.
  if_htmlb_data~event_type            = p_event_type.
  if_htmlb_data~event_class           = p_event_class.
  if_htmlb_data~event_name            = p_event_name.
  if_htmlb_data~event_server_name     =
        p_event_server_name.
  if_htmlb_data~event_defined         =
        p_event_defined.
  if_htmlb_data~event_intercept_depth =
        p_event_intercept_depth.
* The pager uses two <htmlb:button> elements. Massage the
*  event to be pager event.
* Event name will be 'button', should be our 'pager2'.
* Event Id will be <id>__pageNext or <id>__pagePrevious
* Event Type will be click from the button. The actual value
```

```
* we want, was already encoded into the ID before.
    if_htmlb_data~event_name = me->m_name.
    SPLIT if_htmlb_data~event_id AT '__'
     INTO if_htmlb_data~event_id
          if_htmlb_data~event_type.
* Restore view state from the request
    if_htmlb_data~restore_from_request( request = p_request
          id       = if_htmlb_data~event_id ).
ENDMETHOD.
```

With the above changes, events are now presented as `pager2` events, as shown in Figure 11.6

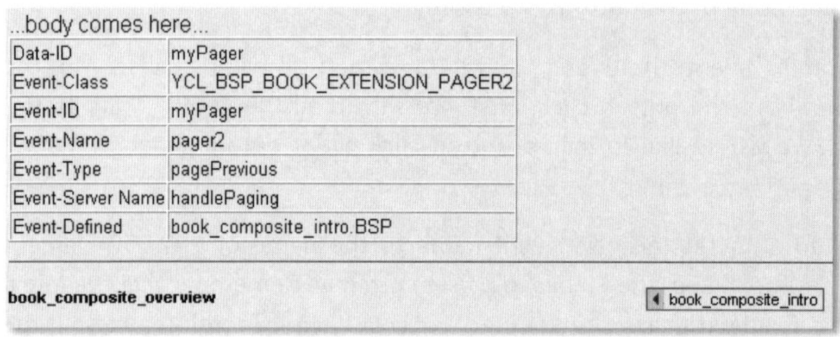

Figure 11.6 Intercepted Events

12 Additional BSP Extensions

Although a Web AS is delivered with nearly 200 BSP extension elements, there are a few that stand out as being unique in function or application. In this chapter, we will examine some of these more specialized elements.

12.1 Business Text Framework

We begin our examination of these special-purpose BSP elements with the extension library called *Business Text Framework* (BTF). This extension exposes a text editor that represents a considerable improvement over the old SAPscript technology or plain-text editors.

Unlike SAP's previous versions of text editors, this new editor is not based upon any proprietary internal format. This new editor is actually an easy-to-use WYSIWYG (What you see is what you get) HTML-based editor. Therefore, the documents produced by this editor are especially simple to integrate into BSP or other Web-based applications. Such integration makes an excellent foundation for creating HTML-based emails.

SAP has two implementations of this editor. One is for the use in traditional Dynpro screens via the Control Framework Technology. This editor is accessed via ABAP class `CL_BTF_EDITOR`. SAP also has exposed this same editor technology to BSP pages via the BSP extension `BTF`, BSP element `editor`.

Before we even get into this section on the BTF editor, the reader should we aware that the implementation of the BTF editor is really only fully functional in the Internet Explorer browser. In other browsers that BSP supports, a simple text editor exposing the raw HTML tags is displayed instead of the user-friendly WYSIWYG editor. The reason for this is that the BTF editor uses proprietary features of Internet Explorer.

In short, if you are concerned about cross-browser support, then you are probably going to have to skip the BTF editor. However, if you know you have an internally facing application that only needs to support Internet Explorer, then learning about the BTF editor is well worth your time.

12.1.1 SAP Example

Besides the examples put forth in this text, SAP delivers an example BSP application named `BTF_EXT_DEMO`. This example, although limited in scope, does provide the basics of loading a document into and retrieving a document from the editor. Because the editor generates HTML code, the example application also demonstrates how easily the resulting text can be displayed inline in a BSP application.

12.1.2 BTF Functionality

Before we get involved with any code, let us first have a look at the BTF editor in action and discuss some of its advantages and hidden features.

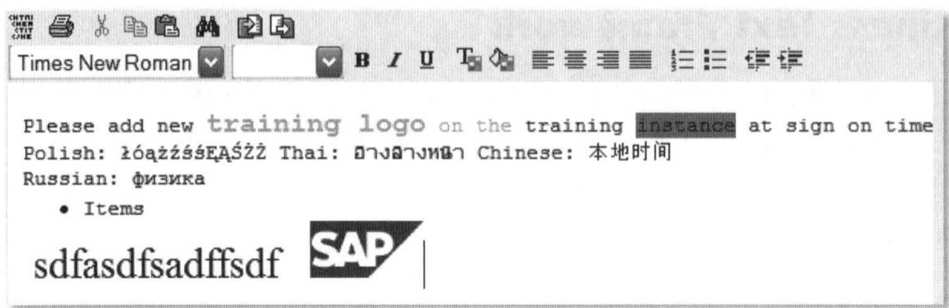

Figure 12.1 BTF Example

BTF Toolbar

Going through the user interface icons, you get an idea of the basic functionality of the BTF editor. The first button (which can be hidden by an attribute) allows the user to switch back and forth between the WYSIWYG editor and a raw HTML code editor. This is a nice feature to expose in case you have users who aren't scared off by HTML.

Next, we have a **Print** icon. This allows us to print the contents of the BTF editor using the user's PC. This means that the list of printers users will have to choose from, will be the ones installed on their client machines, not your SAP server printers. It is possible to use the BTF editor in display-only mode, just so you can expose this print functionality.

Next come the expected **Cut**, **Copy**, and **Paste** functions. Because this is a HTML editor, the ability to paste in elements from other richly formatted locations is quite powerful. You can even copy and then paste in links to images from other Web-based sources.

This is followed by a **Find** and **Replace** feature for mass editing. For the last icons on the first bar we have an **Upload** and **Download** function. This is again a nice feature that you wouldn't necessarily expect in a Web-based HTML editor.

The second row gives us the tools we will need to control the text formatting and alignment. We have basic text formatting, such as **Font**, **Size**, **Bold**, **Italics**, **Underline**, **Text Color**, and **Background Color**.

Next up, we have a set of buttons that allow us to set the **Text Justification** (left, centered, right, and full). Finally, we have four buttons for setting up lists. The first two turn on either **Numbered** or **Bulleted** lists. The last two buttons move the text indentation **Left** or **Right**.

Content Example

A look at the content the example contains also tells a story of the BTF editor's capabilities.

You can see the effects that altering the text size, color, font, and other formatting options has on the output. You can also see in the middle of the editor that there is a link to a Web image. This was done by pasting in the image from the original source.

Finally, we come to what is one of the most important aspects of the BTF editor. The BTF editor supports the editing of Unicode[1] documents, even if your backend SAP system is not Unicode.

As you can see from the example, we have a mixture of languages from a variety of codepages. The system this example was built on is neither MDMP[2] nor Unicode, yet we have no problem processing and storing this data.

How is all this possible? The BTF editor expects to receive and return its document data via a binary string. This allows your back-end SAP system to store the Unicode document without any character corruption regardless of the codepage the system runs under. Of course Unicode isn't your only option. You can also set the document content to any single codepage. We will look at the coding for the use of Unicode in detail in this example.

12.1.3 Database Storage

We will start by looking at how the example application stores the content that is generated within the BTF editor. As stated earlier, the BTF editor expects its data to be received and returned as a binary string. Therefore the simplest way to store the data is by writing the data into the database as a binary string.

1 The Unicode Standard is the universal character encoding standard used for representation of text for computer processing. The Unicode Standard provides the capacity to encode all of the characters used for the written languages of the world. To keep character-coding simple and efficient, the Unicode Standard assigns each character a unique numeric value and name. *http://www.unicode.org*.

2 MDMP: an SAP Specific technology that predates Unicode. MDMP (**M**ultiple **D**isplay **M**ultiple **P**rocessing) allows for the processing of multiple codepages within a single system instance and database; however only one codepage can be processed at a time.

Luckily this is now a possibility as of Web AS 6.x. We can have strings and binary strings of undetermined length stored as database fields. Figures 12.2 and 12.3 demonstrate what this table layout can look like.

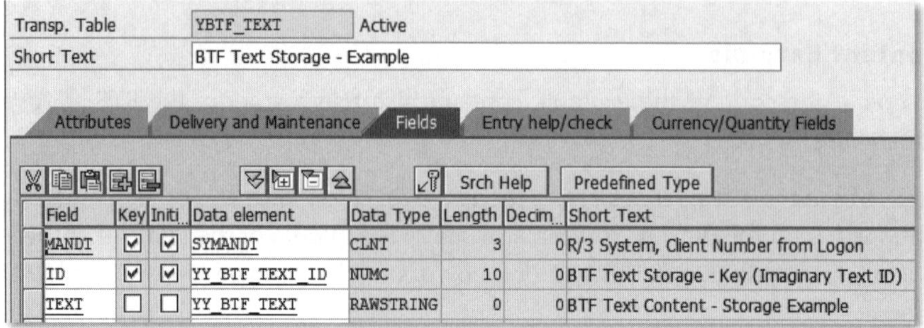

Figure 12.2 Example Database Table for String BTF Content

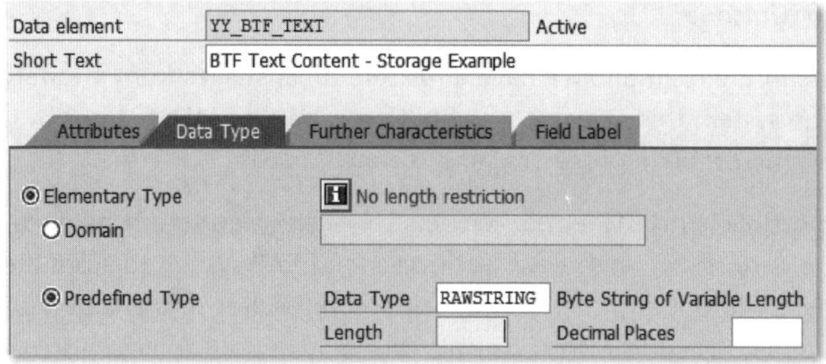

Figure 12.3 Binary String Data Element

12.1.4 BSP Extension Element

The BSP extension element for the BTF editor has only a handful of fairly simple attributes. The content of the document itself is the most important attribute. For this attribute, you must pass an instance of a class that implements the interface `IF_BTF_DOCUMENT`.

Name	Description
`id` (mandatory)	Unique indentification for the BSP element
`document` (mandatory)	The pointer to the BTF Document Object itself. This object must implement the `IF_BTF_DOCUMENT` interface. This is how the content within the BTF editor gets passed to the extension element.

Table 12.1 BSP Element Editor Attributes

Name	Description
disabled	This attribute sets the BTF editor into Edit or Display only mode. Allowed values are FALSE (default value) and TRUE.
width	This attribute sets the display width of the BTF editor
height	This attribute sets the display height of the BTF editor
onClientInsertImage	This attribute sets a client-side event handler, which you are responsible for coding in JavaScript, that will be called whenever the **Insert Image** button is clicked. The button will not be shown in the editor unless an event handler is specified here.
onClientInsertLink	This attribute sets a client-side event handler, which you are responsible for coding in JavaScript. The event handler will be called whenever the **Insert Link** button is clicked. The button will not be shown in the editor unless an event handler is specified here.
sourceView	This attribute controls whether the BTF Document is displayed in the editor in WYSIWYG mode or raw HTML Source. The possible values are FALSE (default value) and TRUE.

Table 12.1 BSP Element Editor Attributes (cont.)

12.1.5 BTF Editor in the Page Layout

Inclusion of the <btf:editor> extension into a BSP page layout is simple. In the following example, the document object comes from the BSP application class. Although this element-attribute value could just as easily have come from a model class or page attribute, you should note that none of the <btf:editor> attributes support Model View Binding. Be careful with the document attribute however. If the document attribute contains a null pointer, you will get a short dump for passing an invalid object reference.

Also please notice that in order to properly support the <btf:editor> element, the default value for encodingType of the <htmlb:form> element must be set to multipart/form-data. This is done so that the <btf:editor> element can support the upload of content from the client.

```
<%@page language="abap" %>
<%@extension name="htmlb" prefix="htmlb" %>
<%@extension name="btf" prefix="btf" %>
<htmlb:content design="design2003" >
  <htmlb:page title="Sample BTF editor Page " >
    <htmlb:form id           = "myFormId"
                method       = "post"
                encodingType = "multipart/form-data" >
      <btf:editor id       = "btf1"
```

```
          document = "<%= application->btf_document %>"
          height   = "100px"
          width    = "400px" />
     <br/>
     <htmlb:button id       = "Submit"
            onClick = "Submit"
            text    = "<OTR>Submit</OTR>" />
   </htmlb:form>
  </htmlb:page>
</htmlb:content>
```

Listing 12.1 BTF Page Layout Example

12.1.6 Preparing the BTF Document

In the following section of code, we will prepare a BTF document and either set an initial message into this document or the one we loaded from the database earlier. You can trigger this logic in the `DO_REQUEST` method of a controller class if you have a MVC application. In a non-MVC page, you would most likely want to do this in the `onInitialization` event handler.

We start our processing by getting a pointer to the BTF itself. Then we create a BTF document class instance if we don't already have one.

```
****btf is type ref to if_btf.
  if btf is initial.
    btf = cl_btf=>get_reference( ).
  endif.
****btf_document is type ref to if_btf_document
  if btf_document is initial.
    btf_document = btf->create_document( sy-langu ).
  endif.
```

Listing 12.2 BTF Initialization Example

12.1.7 Retrieving BTF Content on Input

Now we are ready to look at the process for getting the edited content back out of the BTF editor. For every server event, regardless of what the event does, you need to capture the data that is returned by the BTF control. This is necessary for you to have the content to send back out via the BTF element as the layout is rebuilt. Even inside a stateful BSP application, you must treat the BTF editor and its document content as though it is stateless.

For Model View Controller based application in this example, we perform this action in the DO_HANDLE_DATA method of the controller class. In a non-MVC application this same logic could be applied in an OnInputProcessing routine.

We will start the processing by getting a pointer to a BTF editor (class CL_BTF_BSP_EDITOR) by requesting one from the special event handler class for BSP BTF (CL_BTF_BSP_MANAGER).

```
****Cast a pointer to my application class
  data: appl type ref to ycl_es_bsp_appl_main.
  appl ?= application.
****Read data from editor:
  data: editor type ref to cl_btf_bsp_editor.
  editor ?= cl_btf_bsp_manager=>get_data( request = request
            name      = 'editor'
            id        = 'btf1' ).
```

Listing 12.3 BTF Editor Pointer Retrieval Example

In the next code sample, we first will make sure that a valid editor pointer was passed back. Only an active BTF editor should be processed. Next, we will ask the BTF editor to give back its content, supplying the binary string, language, and encoding. Use a test condition to see if you have an encoding returned. If you do, then you know you have a valid document in the editor class.

If you pass all of these checks, you can then pass the document from the BTF Editor into the document class and store it there.

```
if editor is not initial.
    data: l_encode type string.
    data: l_lang   type spras.
    editor->document->get_content( importing text = appl->text
            encoding = l_encode
            language = l_lang ).
    if l_encode is not initial.
      appl->btf_document = editor->document.
    endif.
endif.
```

Listing 12.4 Extract the Document Content From the Editor Example

You might experience slight irritation with the HTML that the BTF editor creates, as it inserts a XMP tag into the HTML code. This tag tends to mess up the display of the generated HTML under certain circumstances. One solution to this might be to go back and strip out all occurrences of this tag after the content is retrieved.

The editor returns its content in a Unicode binary string. So first you need to convert this Unicode binary string into a Unicode character string. The SAP function module SCP_TRANSLATE_CHARS provides one possible way of doing this. You can then do a `replace all occurrences of` to remove the offending tag. Finally, you turn the Unicode string back into a Unicode binary string, also with the function module SCP_TRANSLATE_CHARS. This forms a nice example of how you can manipulate the content generated by the BTF editor within ABAP.

12.2 Internet Graphics Service

Eventually most developers will encounter a business requirement for some sort of analytical application that requires a graphical presentation. In other development environments, you might be forced to look to a third-party tool to support such requirements. Luckily, SAP delivers a tool in the Web AS that supports the easy generation of complex graphs and charts. This tool is called the *Internet Graphics Service* (IGS).

The IGS is not a new tool, nor is it specific to BSP. The IGS has been around for a few years and already has integration points with the Enterprise Portal, classic ABAP Dynpro and the Internet Transaction Server (ITS). It is available on the Server Tools disc or via download from the SAP Service Marketplace. In Web AS 6.40 the IGS is now available as an integrated kernel component.

The IGS only takes a few minutes to install. The software then listens on HTTP and/or RFC ports. It accepts the input data and formatting via Unicode XML streams. It then returns your graphic as a binary data stream.

12.2.1 IGS Setup and Administration

Before beginning any coding in BSP, it would be wise to make sure that your Web AS has a proper IGS installation connected to it.

The first place to check is transaction SM59 (RFC Destination Maintenance). There should be a RFC destination set up under type **TCP/IP Connections** called IGS_RFC_DEST. SAP requires that you use this name. Some older SAP GUI applications are hard-coded to only use this destination name. A simple test connection on this RFC destination should confirm that you have a correct IGS installation.

If you need to do more than verify that the IGS is installed correctly and want a full administration tool, look at the ABAP program GRAPHICS_IGS_ADMIN. This tool gives you full view into the health and state of your IGS application. You can also track statistics on its use from there.

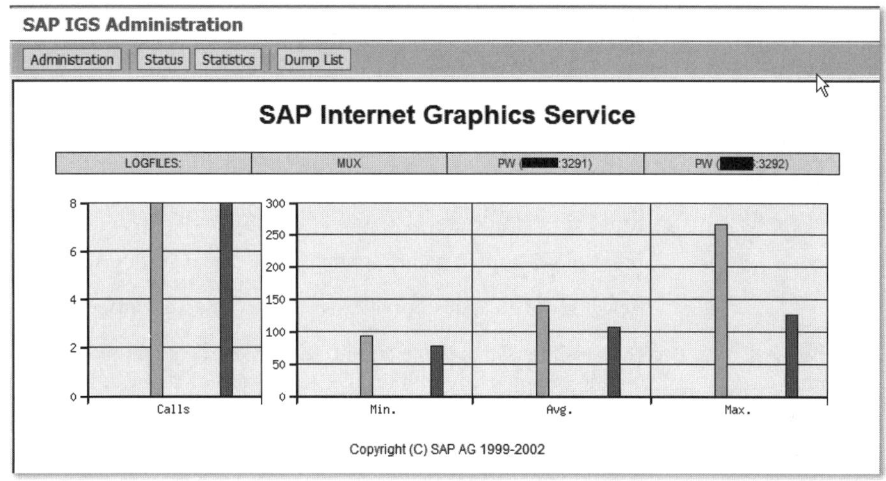

Figure 12.4 IGS Administration Program

12.2.2 SAP Examples

In addition to the administration application, SAP also delivers several example and test applications that all begin with the name GRAPHICS_IGS*. If you need to study IGS examples for use in BSP, have a look at the BSP applications GRAPH_BSP_TEST, GRAPH_TUT_CHART, and GRAPH_TUT_JNET.

12.2.3 IGS BSP Extension

Once you have established that the IGS is connected to your system and functioning properly, it is time to look at it in the context of BSP. For that we have a single BSP extension called graphics.

This extension has 13 elements that allow for a wide range of functionality. You might want a simple bar chart or graph with hard-coded values. However, these elements also allow for interactive charts with a complex number of different series of data all supplied dynamically via XML.

For the purpose of this example, we will focus on a single element of this extension call <graphics:chart>. This main element exposes the majority of the basic charting and graphing functionality that you would want to work with. Even as we look at the attributes of this element, it becomes apparent that this element controls the overall look and feel of the generated graphic.

Name	Description
id	Unique indentification for the IGS chart element
charttype	The overall graphical type of the chart. Depending upon the release you are on, there are about 25–27 options here. Some examples are columns, bars, area, pie, etc.
dimension	Allows you to choose between 2D, 2.5D, and 3D look for the resulting chart.
font_familiy	This attribute specifies the default font that will be used for texts in the generated graphic. If not specified, Arial will be used.
format	The graphical format of the resulting image (JPG, GIF, Bitmap, etc).
height	Height specified in number of pixels for the generated image.
igs_rfc_destination	This attribute allows you to specify the RFC destination that will be used to communicate with the IGS. It does default to the destination named IGS_RFC_DEST.
language	The language used during image generation.
onclick	Name of the server side event that will be raised if the user clicks on the image. This event will return the series and the data point that were selected, allowing for simple image interactivity.
style	This attribute allows you to specify style sheet information that overrides the default presentation of the generated image.
transparent_color	The attribute that allows you to mark a color as transparent in the generated image. It should be specified as a RGB string. Example: RGB(255,64,25)
width	Width specified in number of pixels for the generated image.

Table 12.2 BSP Element <graphics:chart> Attributes

12.2.4 Chart Data

If you study the attributes of the <graphics:chart> element, you might notice something is missing: a way to get actual data into IGS to use as a basis for image generation. So far, all we have seen are attributes that affect the overall look and feel of the generated image.

This is where some of the other elements in the graphics extension come into play. Elements such as <graphics:data> and <graphics:nativexml> can be imbedded between the chart-begin and chart-end tags in order to pass data to the IGS. The structuring of multiple imbedded BSP extension elements is a little different from the way that most other standard extensions work.

Looking at the following simple example, we can see this interaction between the elements. In this case, the data for image generation will be passed via native XML in line in the BSP page. The raw XML data has been removed for demonstration purposes.

```
<graphics:chart width="300" height="300" format="JPG" >
  <graphics:data>
    <graphics:nativexml>
     ... Raw XML
    </graphics:nativexml>
  </graphics:data>
</graphics:chart>
```

Listing 12.5 Chart with nativexml inner element

So, now we know how to format the BSP parts of the equation. To produce a finished image, we will need to study the way that the IGS expects its XML data steam formatted. For this we will look at the example image in Figure 12.5.

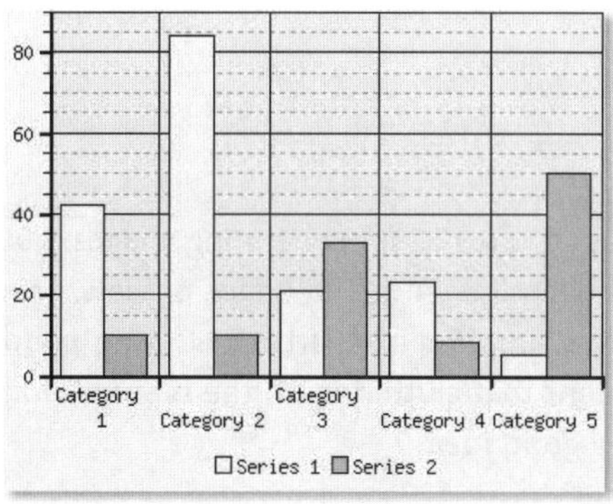

Figure 12.5 IGS Sample Image

This example is helpful because in its simplicity it represents the three major elements of the XML stream structure for the IGS. These three elements are categories, series, and data points.

In this bar chart example, you can see that one or more categories define the x axis of the chart. We then have one or more series that correspond to individual bars within each category. This is where we can build useful comparisons between two objects within the same category. Finally, data points represent the value of an individual series within the given category. Therefore in our example chart, the data point value for category 1, series 1 is 42.

The raw XML to build this simple example looks like the example below. Note that there is no well-defined connection between the categories and series. Everything is simply processed in the order received and aligned as it is input.

```
<?xml version="1.0" encoding="utf-8"?>
      <SimpleChartData>
        <Categories>
          <C>Category 1</C>
          ...
          <C>Category 5</C>
        </Categories>
        <Series>
          <S>42</S>
          ...
          <S>5</S>
        </Series>
        <Series>
          <S>10</S>
          ...
          <S>50</S>
        </Series>
      </SimpleChartData>
```

12.2.5 Chart Model Classes

We have seen how to build the XML to pass to the IGS for generating images, but so far all the XML content has had to be built inline in the BSP page or view. This approach is really only appropriate for the simplest of charts. Following good design practices, it quickly becomes apparent that cluttering up the presentation layer with a lot of XML coding just is not a good idea.

Luckily there is another, cleaner approach to passing data to the IGS. Looking closer at the `<graphics:data>` element, you can see that there are two attributes that can be used to pass the XML data to the IGS rather than embedding it in the BSP page.

The first attribute is `url`. To use this attribute, simply supply a URL that will return the required XML stream when called via HTTP. This could be effective if the data you want to process is already available via XML on another system.

The more likely attribute to be used is the `model` one. This attribute requires a reference to any ABAP class that implements the interface `IF_GRAPH_DATA_MODEL`. With this approach you can encapsulate all your data retrieval, manipulation, and conversion to XML into its own class.

The `IF_GRAPH_DATA_MODEL` interface has a single method that must be implemented called `GET_DATA_XML`. This method returns your XML to the calling IGS classes as a binary string.

If we take the simple example chart from earlier, we can now create that same XML inside a class with the following coding. The code has been trimmed to demonstrate specifically how to create each type of element (`category`, `series`, and `data point`) and then convert to XML.

```
DATA: ixml TYPE REF TO if_ixml,
          document TYPE REF TO if_ixml_document,
          root TYPE REF TO if_ixml_element.
DATA: s TYPE string.
DATA: categories TYPE REF TO if_ixml_element.
DATA: series1 TYPE REF TO if_ixml_element.

DATA: streamfactory TYPE REF TO if_ixml_stream_factory,
      ostream TYPE REF TO if_ixml_ostream.
ixml = cl_ixml=>create( ).
document = ixml->create_document( ).
root =
  document->create_element( name = 'SimpleChartData' ).
document->append_child( new_child = root ).
categories = document->create_simple_element(
    name = 'Categories'
    parent = root ).
document->create_simple_element(
    parent = categories
    name = 'C'
    value = 'Category 1' ).
...
Series1 = document->create_simple_element(
    parent = root
    name = 'Series' ).
document->create_simple_element(
    parent = series1
    name = 'S'
    value = '42' ).
...
streamfactory = ixml->create_stream_factory( ).
ostream = streamfactory->create_ostream_xstring( xml ).
document->render( ostream = ostream recursive = 'X' ).
```

12.2.6 IGS Customizing

So far we have a nice-looking chart in this example, but it is rather plain. The `<graphics:chart>` element had some basic formatting options that can be applied to the entire image, but more fine granular customizing is often necessary. Once again the IGS solution provides an opportunity to control the image generation to a considerable degree.

The same way that you can pass the raw data to the IGS via XML, you also can pass customizing settings. This XML can be added inline like in the following example.

```
<graphics:custom><graphics:nativexml>
      <?xml version="1.0" encoding="utf-8"?>
      <SAPChartCustomizing version="1.0">
        <GlobalSettings>
          <Defaults>
            <FontFamily>Arial Unicode MS</FontFamily>
          </Defaults>
        </GlobalSettings>
       ...
      </SAPChartCustomizing>
    </graphics:nativexml></graphics:custom>
```

Also, just like the `<graphics:data>` element, the `<graphics:custom>` has the `model` and `url` attributes. The model is set up to accept a class that implements `IF_GRAPH_CUSTOM_MODEL` interface. In the end, you can generate your XML for the customizing just as we just did for the data.

On the other hand, there are potentially thousands of options that can be set. The IGS allows you to customize look-and-feel down to the individual data point level. A developer would easily be overwhelmed by the complexity of generating this XML without a nice visual chart-design tool. Luckily, SAP delivers several different versions of just such a tool.

The first tool option is a standalone chart-designer executable program available as a free download from SAP Developer Network. This tools starts off with a simple wizard that walks you through the most common customization options. Then it opens up a complete editor that allows the full range of customization options. From Figure 12.6, you can see that we have taken our simple little chart example and made some drastic changes to its visual design.

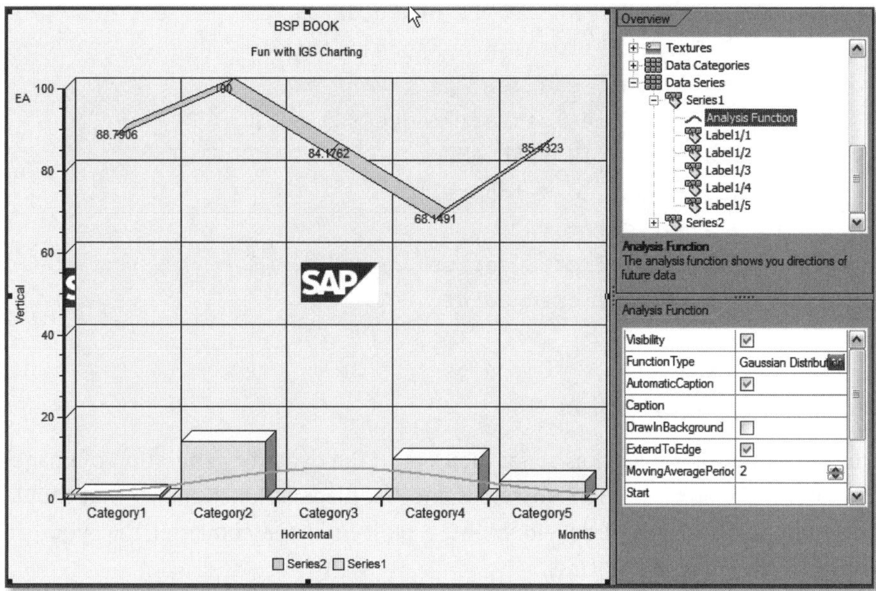

Figure 12.6 IGS Standalone Chart Designer

If you are on Release 6.40, there is another option in the form of a chart designer implemented in ABAP. This program name is `GRAPHICS_GUI_CE_DEMO`. However both the standalone tool and the ABAP tool require a recent patch level of the 6.20 or 6.40 SAP GUI because that is where the chart designer ActiveX control actually gets installed.

12.2.7 Image Click Event Handling

Now that our example has a custom look-and-feel to it, we are ready to enhance it further by adding interactivity. Graphs and charts are great ways of presenting summarized data to a user; but if you really want to give your users a powerful analytical tool, you should consider giving them the option to drill into the details behind the graphical summary.

Earlier in the discussion of the attributes of the `<graphics:chart>` element, we saw that there was an attribute called `onClick`. In order for the IGS to generate server-side events when the user clicks on an area in the graphic, all you must do is supply the name of the event you want it to raise through this attribute.

Catching and processing the event is quite easy as well. In your event handler, you will just want to cast the event data into an object of type `CL_GRAPH_CHART_EXT`. You can query this object to access the series and data point that the user clicked on.

```
DATA: event_data TYPE REF TO if_htmlb_data.
DATA: chart1 TYPE REF TO cl_graph_chart_ext.
event_data = cl_htmlb_manager=>get_event_ex(
               runtime->server->request ).
IF event_data IS NOT INITIAL AND
   event_data->event_id = 'chart1'.
  chart1 ?= event_data.
  series = chart1->clicked_series.
  point  = chart1->clicked_point.
ENDIF.
```

12.2.8 Image Conversion

Our discussion of the IGS has so far focused on the dynamic generation of images as charts and graphs. The IGS possesses another piece of functionality that should be of interest during BSP development: a built-in image converter that you can interact with via an ABAP class.

Let us say, for instance, that you have images that you want to include in a BSP application. The images are delivered to you as bitmaps. You could sit down with a desktop image converter and change the file format on the images to something a little more bandwidth-friendly. As a developer, though, you surely have better things to do with your time then convert a bunch of images.

The IGS can do the job for you on the fly. SAP delivers a sample program called `GRAPHICS_IGS_IMGCONV_DEMO` that shows how you can convert from a TIF, JPG, or Bitmap to a GIF image.

12.3 BSP Library

Tucked away in the BSP extensions library is an unimposing little extension with the name of `bsp`. This extension provides a series of helpful utilities that do not really have a home of their own but that offer some of the most powerful functionality you will find.

12.3.1 findAndReplace Element

The first element we will look at is `<bsp:findAndReplace>`. This amazingly powerful element gives the developer the freedom to alter the raw rendering stream of a BSP page. This means that you not only have access to the JavaScript and HTML produced by other BSP extensions, but you also have the opportunity to alter this rendered code.

Obviously any such technique that allows low-level interaction with already rendered code comes with a warning. If you change the rendered output of other SAP elements, you are responsible for the consequences. The code you are changing could be different based upon which browser the end-user has. This code is obviously subject to change from release to release and even across support packages.

In the end, this element can lead to dangerous programming hacks that could break at any minute. However, to solve a problem, you sometimes need just this kind of access to the low-level system.

In the following very simple example, you can see how this element is used to convert bold HTML tags to italics.

```
<bsp:findAndReplace find1="<b>"  replace1="<i>"
                    find2="</b>" replace2="</i>">
     <htmlb:textView text="<br><b>original text</b>"/>
</bsp:findAndReplace>
```

12.3.2 htmlbEvent Element

One of the powerful benefits to using BSP is the ease with which events can be handled with server-side coding and thus by the ABAP programming language. Many of the SAP-delivered BSP elements already contain the code necessary to trigger these server-side events. However, if you ever wanted to code your own event trigger, the `<bsp:htmlbEvent>` element is how you could do it.

This element will generate the client-side JavaScript function that is necessary for triggering a server event and passing parameters from the front end to the server during this event.

The best way to learn about this element is to study a simple example. Let us say for instance that you want to implement value help for an input field. The standard HTMLB input field only has a client-side event for `onValueHelp`. In our fictional situation, we really decide that we want a server event instead of a client event. This is exactly where `<bsp:htmlbEvent>` come to the rescue.

The following code from a BSP page will generate the necessary JavaScript to fire a server-event `onValueHelp` request.

```
<bsp:htmlbEvent onClick      = "specialEvent"
                id           = "specialEvent"
                name         = "bspEventTrigger"
                return_value = "TRUE" />
```

```
<htmlb:inputField id          = "EventTest"
                  value       = "<%= value1%>"
                  onValueHelp = "bspEventTrigger();"
                  showHelp    = "TRUE"/>
Event Name: <%= event_name %>
```

With the following little bit of event-handling code, you can catch your custom server-side event and even query-parameter values for the CL_BSP_HTMLB_EVENT class.

```
DATA: event_data TYPE REF TO if_htmlb_data.
DATA: htmlb_event TYPE REF TO cl_bsp_htmlb_event.

event_data = cl_htmlb_manager=>get_event_ex(
       runtime->server->request ).
IF event_data IS NOT INITIAL AND
     event_data->event_id = 'specialEvent'.
  htmlb_event ?= event_data.
  event_name = htmlb_event->onclick.
ENDIF.
```

12.3.3 Portal Integration

BSP technology is designed for easy integration into the SAP Enterprise Portal. The bulk of this integration is activated by simply setting a check mark on the properties tab of the BSP application.

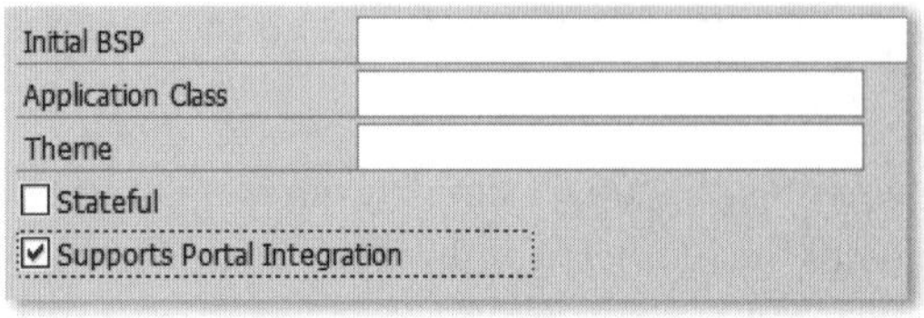

Figure 12.7 Activate Portal Integration

This magical little checkbox puts your application under the state-management control of the portal. It also allows your application to inherit the theme (look-and-feel) from the portal. That is quite a lot of functionality for just one click of the mouse.

But once you are ready to create an application that truly interacts with the portal, you will want to have a look at a few of the extension elements that SAP supplies.

Portal Eventing

The first element is the <bsp:portalEvent>. This element allows your application to subscribe to a portal event via the Enterprise Portal Client Framework, or EPCF. The EPCF is a component of the Enterprise Portal written in JavaScript and Java applets that allow for inter-iView communication and eventing. The supplied BSP element simply allows your application to hook into this portal JavaScript by supplying the namespace and name of the event you wish to subscribe to.

These portal events can then be trapped and responded to by BSP server-side event handlers. The HTMLB event manager will return details about the Portal event. The key here is to look for any event name called portalEvent.

```
DATA: event TYPE REF TO if_htmlb_data.
event = cl_htmlb_manager=>get_event_ex(
          runtime->server->request ).
IF event IS BOUND.
  IF event->event_name EQ 'portalEvent'.
    event_dataobject = event->event_server_name.
    event_sourceid   = event->event_defined.
    SPLIT event->event_id AT ':'
       INTO event_namespace event_name.
  ENDIF.
ENDIF.
```

SAP does not supply a BSP extension element for raising a portal event since this would not make sense. All you really need is the JavaScript function that exposes this functionality from the portal. All the necessary JavaScript functions are rendered out by the method CL_HTTP_EXT_BSP_HTMLB->EVENTS_JS and included in your application automatically.

This means that all you will have to code is the call to the JavaScript function portalFireEvent. This call to a JavaScript function can be added to any existing BSP extension element that supports an onClientClick attribute.

For instance, you might create an <htmlb:button> and in the onClientClick attribute place the call to the required JavaScript function. Keep in mind that this JavaScript executes from the client browser not the SAP server. Therefore, any data that you wish to pass along to the event must be accessed via JavaScript and the browser.

This example code demonstrates the possibility of raising a portal event from BSP through the press of an <htmlb:button>. It also shows how to pass data from an <htmlb:inputField> into the event.

```
<htmlb:inputField id     = "bookTitle"
                  value = "BSP for Fun and Profit" />
      <htmlb:button id            = "fireBuyBook"
                    text          = "Buy Book"
               onClientClick = "portalFireEvent('myBooksEvents',
                 'fireBuy',document.getElementById('bookTitle').
                 value);" />
```

Portal Navigation

If you choose to create an iView using BSP that must control navigation to separate content within the portal, whether that addition content is BSP or not, you can do this through another set of BSP-extension elements. The elements `<bsp:portalNavigationAbsolute>`, `<bsp:portalNavigationRelative>`, and `<bsp:portalNavigationToObject>` expose the critical navigation APIs of the EPCF.

`<bsp:portalNavigationAbsolute>` requires that you specify the full path name of the component that you are calling using the attribute `navigationTarget`.

The attribute `navigationMode` has three possible values `SHOW_INPLACE`, `SHOW_EXTERNAL`, and `SHOW_EXTERNAL_PORTAL` with `SHOW_INPLACE` being the default value. `SHOW_INPLACE`'s actual outcome depends upon the setting in the Portal *WorkProtect* feature. Depending upon the value of the *dirty indicator* in the WorkProtect, the new content is either opened in a new window or on the current portal desktop. `SHOW_EXTERNAL` always opens the target in a new window that has no Portal header or navigation bar. `SHOW_EXTERNAL_PORTAL` does just the opposite. It opens the target in a new window, but with the Portal header and navigation bar.

The attribute `windowFeatures` allows you to control the look-and-feel of the new window if the content is to be opened that way. This attribute should receive its values via a comma-separated list with no blank. The syntax of these values should match that of the JavaScript method `window.open`.

With the attribute `windowName`, you can specify a window title if the content is to be opened in a new window.

The attribute `historyMode` has three possible values: `ALLOW_DUPLICATIONS`, `NO_DUPLICATIONS`, and `NO_HISTORY`. The value `NO_HISTORY` is the default value.

The attribute `targetTitle` will set the title for the page title bar. However, if the navigation target is sent through an integrator, the title will then be the integrator tile.

Both the `businessParameters` and the `launcherParameters` attributes allow you to specify URL parameters for the navigation target. These Name/Value pairs will simply be appended to the end of the `navigationTarget` URL.

With the element `<bsp:portalNavigationRelative>`, you can specify a navigation target relative to the location of the current navigation node. This element supports the same basic attributes as the absolute navigation element. It does have three addition attributes used to determine the absolute navigation path from the relative one.

The `baseURL` attribute specifies your starting point—in other words, the current node URL. The `levelsUp` attribute allows you to specify the number of hierarchy levels to step up through. This attribute only accepts integers. Finally, we have the `pathList` attribute. In this attribute you can supply all the names of the children nodes relative to the node that you want to navigate to.

Object-based navigation, using the element `<bsp:portalNavigationToObject>`, takes a completely different approach from that of the other navigation elements we have already looked at. This element allows for navigation based upon the business object in your back-end system. These business objects must be exposed to the portal via iView `implementers`. With this functionality, you are not required to know the technical URL for your navigation target, just some identifying metadata about it.

The attribute `system` allows you to specify a system alias that has been pre-configured in the portal. This will be the business-application system that houses the business object you wish to call.

The `objectType` attribute specifies the business object name that you need to navigate to. If your business object has more than one method that can be executed, you can pick the one you want with the `operation` attribute.

The `objectValue` attribute represents any data that needs to be sent to the navigation target. The `objectValue` and the `businessParameters` attribute will be added to the navigation target as URL parameters.

13 MVC—Model View Controller

As you begin to develop large BSP applications, you may find you need a better organizational structure for the application components than simple BSP pages can provide. The Model View Controller design approach is the answer to that problem.

13.1 MVC Design Paradigm

Model View Controller (MVC) is not a specific technology, nor is it unique to the SAP, ABAP, or the BSP environments. MVC is a design pattern or paradigm that, like so many modern programming techniques and technologies, originated from the Smalltalk programming language.

The core concept of MVC is the separation and encapsulation of the three major components of an application. The model component represents all application data and the logic necessary to retrieve or manipulate that data. The view is the visual representation of this data, generally regarded as the user-interface layer. Finally the controller houses the logic that affects the program flow. It is responsible for responding to events and user input and for dispatching the resulting changes to the view or the model.

Not only does MVC offer a clean organizational structure, but by separating the sections logically it creates better maintenance opportunities. Because the layers of MVC are separated the way they are, you can make changes to the user interface without having to touch or see the coding of your business logic. Of course the opposite is true as well, in that alterations to the business logic can be isolated. Theoretically, this should also reduce the amount of testing needed as changes are made.

So far nothing discussed about MVC is specific to Web development. Both the traditional Microsoft Foundation Classes and the Java Swing Library are based upon MVC. However, the difficulties of managing large modern Web applications have pushed MVC into the spotlight and made the design pattern nearly synonymous with Web development. Some of the more popular Web development frameworks outside of the SAP environment, such as JavaServer Faces, Jakarta Struts, and Ruby on Rails, heavily support MVC.

13.2 Application Structure

The BSP implementation of MVC relies heavily upon the concepts of ABAP object orientation. If you have never taken the time to get really comfortable with some of the more advanced topics of ABAP OO, such as inheritance and polymorphism, now is the time to do so. MVC is likely to push your OO skills to a whole new level.

The model implementation is so decoupled from the rest of the MVC framework within BSP that you do not even see the model objects within the navigation tree of the ABAP Workbench. Within a BSP application node in the navigation tree, only controllers, views, pages with flow logic, and multipurpose Internet mail extensions (MIMEs) are displayed. As you become serious about MVC BSP development, you find yourself switching the view that you use within the Workbench Navigator from BSP application to package.

Grouping a BSP application and all its implementing classes together into one package is the only way to get the complete view to all the objects within the workbench navigator. In Figure 13.1, you can see that by working at the package level we have quick access to and visibility of the underlying controller classes, the application class, the model class, and all the inherent BSP application components.

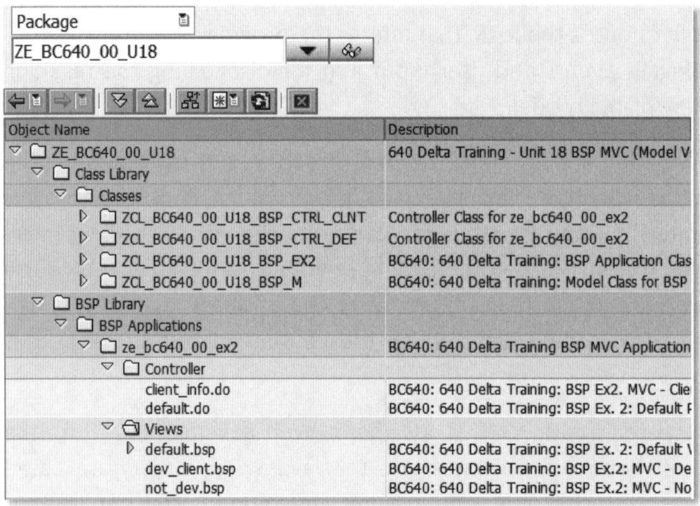

Figure 13.1 Package View of an Entire MVC BSP Application

13.2.1 Model

The model object is represented directly by a single ABAP Class that inherits from `CL_BSP_MODEL`. The ABAP workbench and the BSP design tools do not really have aspects specific to the model object. To create a model, you create a class in the workbench just as you would any other class, setting the inheritance from `CL_BSP_MODEL` manually.

For now, we will keep our example very simple. We will use our model class as our container for our business data and logic. Later, we will look at the more advanced techniques possible with MVC, such as the model binding and getter/setter methods.

We start our example by creating a normal ABAP class that inherits from CL_BSP_MODEL. We will then expose our business data directly from the model class by creating public instance attributes. For this example we will have two attributes. The first is an internal table called ISFLIGHT with all fields from the database table SFLIGHT. This attribute will be displayed later in an <htmlb:tableView>. The second attribute, called CARRID, will be used later in an <htmlb:dropDownListBox> to narrow the selection of data from SFLIGHT.

ISFLIGHT	Instance	Public	☐	Type	SFLIGHT_TAB1	⇨	SFLIGHT Internal table
CARRID	Instance	Public	☐	Type	S_CARR_ID	⇨	Airline Code

Figure 13.2 Model Class Attributes

While in our model, we will add one public instance method called READ_SFLIGHT that will select the data from the database with the selection criteria of CARRID.

```
METHOD read_sflight.
  SELECT * FROM sflight
    INTO TABLE isflight
   WHERE carrid = carrid.
ENDMETHOD.
```

13.2.2 Controller

The controller is represented in BSP as two separate entities. First, you have the controller object that is part of your BSP application. The controller object contains the attributes of the controller, such as stateful/stateless, caching, compression, HTTPS, etc. This is also the only object within MVC that is addressable via URL. It is this controller object, and its name that for navigation is the equal to the standard BSP page.

Controller	book_mvc.do	Active
Description	Simple MVC Example	
Controller Class	YCL_BSP_CTRL_BOOK_SIMPLE	

Figure 13.3 Controller Object

The controller object definition also lists the name of a controller class, however. This ABAP class is actually the heart of the controller logic. This is where all the ABAP code for implementing the many controller responsibilities will reside. Creating this class is a little simpler than creating your model was. You can just type in the name you want to give the class in the controller object screen. When you double click on the class name or save the controller, a class with the proper inheritance will be generated for you.

Controllers should inherit from the class CL_BSP_CONTROLLER2. This is the inherited class that will be used by default in the automatic generation of controller classes.

You may find after a little time developing MVC that you are writing a lot of the same code within your controller. Different development groups will often come up with their own internal standards and ways of doing such tasks as event handling or model initialization. This is the perfect opportunity to use the OO structure of MVC to its maximum. Do not be afraid to create your own framework of controller classes that inherit from CL_BSP_CONTROLLER2. You can easily change the generated inheritance on the controller class to use any such controller framework you like, as long as CL_BSP_CONTROLLER2 is in the inheritance hierarchy.

Controller Methods

At first, you might be overwhelmed by the sheer number of inherited methods and attributes within your new controller class. Do not worry. Many of these methods are internal to the processing of the controller. There are also a few methods supplied to help with your processing of code.

Let us instead focus on some of the methods that address the flow logic of the controller. There are several methods whose purpose corresponds to the event handlers of your traditional BSP page. These methods are delivered empty through inheritance, but with the correct interfaces. The MVC runtime will call the correct method for the event at hand. Your job is to redefine the methods for the events that you want to add coding for.

Redefinition is done via the ABAP Class Builder. You must select the inherited method you wish to add coding to and then hit the redefinition icon.

So, how do these controller methods match up to the event handlers that you are probably already familiar with from BSP pages? The OnCreate and OnInitialization event handlers have direct replacements in the form of methods DO_INIT and DO_INITATTRIBUTES respectively.

Figure 13.4 Redefinition of Controller Methods

The `OnRequest`, `OnInputProcessing`, `OnLayout`, and `OnManipulation` page event handlers all map more or less onto the single controller method `DO_REQUEST`. This controller method, `DO_REQUEST`, is very important because it is responsible for the main flow of input and output. Let us look at the following sample controller `DO_REQUEST` method to demonstrate this.

```
data: view type ref to if_bsp_page.
dispatch_input( ).
if is_navigation_requested( ) is not initial.
  return.
endif.
view = create_view( view_name = 'book_mvc_simple.htm' ).
call_view( view ).
```

The processing starts with a call to the controller method `dispatch_input`. This internal method triggers all the input processing. It is responsible for performing any input-data binding and triggering of input events. It also calls three more controller methods that can be redefined to add code to the input processing.

The first method that it will call is the `DO_HANDLE_DATA`. This method is charged with retrieving data from the input event. If left with its default coding, it will automatically map all input form fields into their corresponding model attributes (this is the input part of model binding).

More complex operations also can be performed here. Perhaps you also have input elements that do not support model binding, and you want to retrieve their values as well. The fact that this method has an input parameter, `FORM_FIELDS`, that is an internal table of input form fields, makes this process very simple. However if you redefine this method and you also want to support data binding as well, remember to include the call to the super-class in your redefined code.

```
super->do_handle_data( form_fields      = form_fields
                       global_messages = global_messages ).
```

The next method called is `DO_HANDLE_EVENT`. This is the method that you can redefine in order to program event handling. To help you with your event-handling coding, this method already has input parameters such as HTMLB_EVENT_EX of type IF_HTMLB_DATA, which has the details about the incoming event. This saves the developer from having to code to get this information, as he or she would have to do in the classic BSP page event handler.

The final method is DO_FINISH_INPUT. This method is mainly used when you have a set of nested controllers. The controller handling the current event can set the GLOBAL_EVENT attribute during the DO_HANDLE_EVENT method. This GLOBAL_EVENT will then be passed into any sub-controllers so that they can react to this event as well.

Getting back to the processing in the DO_REQUEST method, we can see that after we return from the inner call to DISPATCH_INPUT; there is a check to see if navigation was requested within the event handling. If a navigation redirection was already set, there is no reason to continue with the navigation logic within this controller.

Assuming that we do continue with the navigation logic, you can see that the controller initializes an instance of the view that it will navigate to and performs the navigation with the CALL_VIEW method. This example was a rather simple 1:1 controller to view relationship. However, in complex real world applications, you often have multiple views that can be called from a single controller. For instance, you might have different views depending whether you are in create, change, or display mode in your application.

Model Lifetime

So far we have seen how the controller is responsible for the flow of logic and data from input to output. However, the controller has another major mission. It is responsible for the model object's instantiation and lifetime.

After the controller creates one or more model instances, it keeps track of them internally as attributes. Because of the way the model instances are tracked and used automatically during controller input processing, MVC is generally used only in stateful applications. This way the model instance is retained within the controller class through the lifetime of the application. This does not mean that stateless MVC is not possible within BSP. Stateless MVC simply requires some special techniques to restore any model instances at the correct point in time. Later in this chapter, we will look at these techniques. For now, we will keep with our simple example that is stateful.

This listing of models is kept in the protected attribute M_MODELS. There are public methods, SET_MODEL, CREATE_MODEL, DELETE_MODEL, and GET_MODEL, of the controller that allow for manipulation of this list of models.

For this example, we will want easy access to the model instance within the controller logic as well. The model references in the M_MODELS attribute are stored as references to the super-class CL_BSP_MODEL. In order to work with our specific model implementation, we must be able to cast the reference into our exact class type. Therefore we will create a single private attribute called MODEL of TYPE REF TO YCL_BSP_MODEL_BOOK_SIMPLE that will be easily available for this casting operation. This action of casting between generic and specific object implementations is referred to as polymorphism.

For the creation of the model instance we now will redefine the coding of the controller method DO_INIT. Remember that this method corresponds to our OnCreate event handler in BSP page processing. Therefore, it is only called once for a stateful application.

We will accomplish several things with the logic given below. With the single call to CREATE_MODEL, we manage to create the instance of our model class. We also place a reference to this instance into our M_MODELS attribute under the ID "MS". We can use this id to refer to this exact instance in calls to the other controller's method manipulation. Finally, we also place a reference into our model attribute for easy access to the specific implementation of this single model.

```
METHOD do_init.
  IF model IS INITIAL.
    model ?= create_model( model_id = 'MS'
                class_name = 'YCL_BSP_MODEL_BOOK_SIMPLE' ).
  ENDIF.
ENDMETHOD.
```

Eventing

Although the process of responding to events within the controller is relatively unchanged from the same processing in BSP page event handlers, it is interesting to study how we can use some of the additional functionality within the controller to save ourselves time.

The main difference within the controller is that that we do not have to make the call to CL_HTMLB_MANAGER=>GET_EVENT_EX. One of the attributes passed into DO_HANDLE_EVENT is an object of type if_htmlb_data. For more details on this object and how to use it for HTMLB eventing, see Section 9.2.

For this simple example, we need to respond to the input event on the drop down list box and load the new corresponding data.

```
METHOD do_handle_event.
  CHECK event IS NOT INITIAL.
  IF htmlb_event_ex->event_name =
       htmlb_events=>dropdownlistbox
  AND htmlb_event_ex->event_type =
        htmlb_events=>dropdownlistbox_select.
          model->read_sflight( ).
  ENDIF.
ENDMETHOD.
```

Subcontrollers and Components

For large, complex applications even breaking your application into a single controller with multiple views really is not enough granularity. For these applications you can create components—a nesting of a single high level controller and one or more subcontrollers.

It is important to note that the very powerful and important DISPATCH_INPUT method only needs to be called from within the DO_REQUEST method of the highest level controller. The MVC framework coding will make sure that the corresponding methods in all the subcontrollers will be called correctly. This simple approach allows for nesting of event handlers within the controller hierarchy.

This nesting of controllers can be created using two different methods. The first approach is to create the sub controller with ABAP coding from within the highest level controller. This is done with a call to the controller method CREATE_CONTROLLER.

In this example we will create a subcontroller and send it our current model instance to be its model as well.

```
DATA: model TYPE REF TO zcl_bsp_m_doc_srch_list.
DATA: docdetails TYPE REF TO cl_bsp_controller2.
model ?= create_model(
      class_name = 'zcl_bsp_m_doc_srch_list'
      model_id = 'ml' ).
docdetails ?= create_controller(
      controller_name = 'docdetails.do'
      controller_id = 'dd' ).
docdetails->set_model( model_id = 'ml'
                       model_instance = model ).
```

The other way to create a subcontroller is from the view coding.

Similar to the way a controller keeps a listing of all methods under its influence, a listing is made of all subcontrollers. We can do this using the special BSP extension element <bsp:call>. This approach is particularly useful when creating tabstrips. It seems logical to use subcontrollers to represent the inner content of each tab. This also allows you greater dynamic flexibility for your tab content and enables you to separate the event handling of each tab.

```
<phtmlb:containerTabStrip id = "TabStripUpdate1"
        selectedIndex = "<%= model->SELECTED_tab %>" >
   <phtmlb:containerTabStripItem id     = "T1"
           title = "Basic Data" >
     <phtmlb:containerContentItem />
        <bsp:call url      = "header_form.do"
                  comp_id = "hd" />
     </phtmlb:containerContentItem>
    </phtmlb:containerTabStripItem>
    <phtmlb:containerTabStripItem id     = "T2"
            title = "Materials" >
     <phtmlb:containerContentItem >
         <bsp:call url      = "materials_form.do"
                   comp_id = "mt" />
    </phtmlb:containerContentItem>
   </phtmlb:containerTabStripItem>
</phtmlb:containerTabStrip>
```

Subcontrollers can also be dynamically activated and deactivated so that processing does not have to pass through them unnecessarily. This is an efficient way to handle hidden or out-of-scope subcontrollers. The controller method CONTROLLER_SET_ACTIVE allows for this control.

The following code would deactivate the subcontroller that we created in the first example.

```
controller_set_active( controller_id = 'dd'
                       active = 0 ).
```

13.2.3 View

Of the three parts that make up Model View Controller, the view is probably the area where developers accustomed to BSP pages will feel the most at home.

The view is very much like the BSP page. Working with the presentation logic is exactly the same in the view as from the page. The main difference you will notice is the lack of interface for coding any event handlers. Of course all of this logic is replaced by the methods within the controller that we have already discussed.

Another important aspect to keep in mind is that the view is not an object than can be addressed via a URL. Views are constructs that have no meaning to the client browser. Only the controller can be addressed by the client browser.

However, views can still have attributes similar to the page attributes. All of these attributes must be mapped in via the controller. The most common attribute to fill on a view is a reference to the model class. This model attribute is necessary to have within the view for model binding. Let us change the coding of the controller in our example to pass in the model instance through an attribute to our view.

```
view = create_view( view_name = 'book_mvc_simple.htm' ).
view->set_attribute( name = 'MYMODEL'
                     value = model ).
call_view( view ).
```

13.3 Model Binding

Model binding is an important benefit, yet a part of MVC that many people often overlook. Model binding reduces the amount and complexity of the coding in your typical application; thereby lowering the cost of development and maintenance.

The work done by binding is twofold. First, when you bind model attributes to BSP extension elements, metadata about the objects is automatically read from the binding. For instance, when you bind an attribute to an `<htmlb:label>`, you do not have to supply the label text. If available, the language-specific text will be pulled automatically from the data-dictionary definition of the attribute that the element is bound to.

The second reason for binding is the automatic transfer of input and output values between model attributes and elements and their form fields. No longer in input processing do you have to map values back from the http form fields. All this logic is performed for you by the MVC runtime and proper placement of the `DISPATCH_INPUT` controller method.

Figure 13.5 shows the definition of the `mymodel` view attribute. This view attribute connects the model instance from the controller to the view.

```
<phtmlb:matrix width="100%" >
   <phtmlb:matrixCell/>
   <htmlb:label for="//mymodel/carrid" />
```

```
    <htmlb:dropdownListBox helpValues = "//mymodel/carrid"
                           selection  = "//mymodel/carrid"
                           onSelect   = "Submit" />
    <phtmlb:matrixCell row="+1" />
    <htmlb:tableView id               = "tbl1"
           visibleRowCount = "10"
           table           = "//mymodel/isflight" />
  </phtmlb:matrix>
```

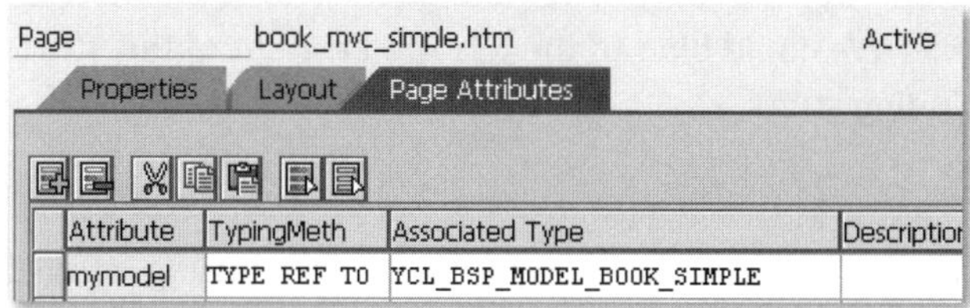

Figure 13.5 MVC—View Attributes

In this example, we supply very few attributes for the `<htmlb:label>` or `<htmlb:dropdownListBox>`. No text is supplied for label, nor do we have an internal table of possible values for the drop down list box. Yet we are able to produce the application interface shown in Figure 13.6.

Airline: Lufthansa

American Airlines
Air Berlin
Air Canada
Air France
Alitalia
British Airways
Continental Airlines
Delta Airlines
Air Pacific
Japan Airlines
Lufthansa
Lauda Air
Northwest Airlines
Qantas Airways
South African Air.
Singapore Airlines
Swiss
United Airlines

Clt	ID	Airfare	Curr.	Plane	Capacity in economy class	Occupied economy class
088	L	666.00	EUR	A310-300	280	271
088	L	666.00	EUR	A310-300	280	267
088	L	666.00	EUR	A310-300	280	268
088	L	666.00	EUR	A310-300	280	267
088	L	666.00	EUR	A310-300	280	267
088	L	666.00	EUR	A310-300	280	271
088	L	666.00	EUR	A310-300	280	261
088	L	666.00	EUR	A310-300	280	264
088	L	666.00	EUR	A310-300	280	269
088	L	666.00	EUR	A310-300	280	261

Figure 13.6 Model Binding Example

You might be wondering about the strange values that were placed in the attributes `for`, `helpValues`, etc. Instead of directly passing a reference to the model attribute, we need to use a special binding string.

These strings have several different formats in order to address single attributes, fields within structures, and fields within an internal table.

The most basic form of the binding string points to a single attribute. It consists of the model class identifier followed by the model attribute name. The string `//mymodel/carrid` represents a view attribute named `model` that is a valid reference to your model instance. This is followed by `carrid`, the name of the attribute within the model.

In complex applications, you would not want to create attributes in your class for every field in a large structure. You can avoid this by binding to single elements within a structure as well. For example, let us say we defined a work area called `wa_sflight` as an attribute in our model class to hold one selected record from our `isflight` internal table. We could bind to the `carrid` element of this structure with the following binding string.

```
//model/wa_sflight.carrid
```

The final variation of the binding string is the one required for processing internal tables. Naturally, we would need a way to bind to a particular row and a particular element within an internal table. Let us now change the binding string of our example to point to row 5 of the `isflight` table, element `carrid`.

```
//model/isflight[5].carrid
```

The entire possible syntax for binding strings can be represented by the following syntax:

```
"//" model_name "/" attibute [ "[" row "]" ] [ "." column ]
```

13.3.1 Getter/Setter methods

Another nice advantage to using model binding is the ability to create getter and setter methods in your model class. These methods will be automatically fired by the MVC runtime during input and output binding and during the retrieval of metadata.

Providing these override methods gives developers the opportunity to code their own methods for the input and output model binding. But equally important are the special metadata getters. They are called during the retrieval of any metadata, such as field length and data type, as part of the MVC process. Later in Chapter 18, we will see the incredible power of MVC and custom getter/setters as we build a BSP version of `SELECT-OPTIONS`.

Because these methods are called dynamically by the runtime, it is important that their parameter interface matches what is expected. Therefore, you should always copy your methods from the templates that SAP provides as part of the interface `IF_BSP_MODEL_SETTER_GETTER`.

The templates for metadata getters are:

- ▶ _GET_M_S_XYZ for structures
- ▶ _GET_M_T_XYZ for tables
- ▶ _GET_M_XYZ for simple attributes

The templates for getters are:

- ▶ _GET_S_XYZ for structures
- ▶ _GET_T_XYZ for tables
- ▶ _GET_XYZ for simple attributes

The templates for setters are:

- ▶ _SET_S_XYZ for structures
- ▶ _SET_T_XYZ for tables
- ▶ _GET_XYZ for simple attributes

When you copy the method, you must rename it so that the naming will match the name of the attribute you creating it for. The XYZ in each of the template names must be replaced with the name of the attribute. Also you remove the leading underscore. Therefore to create a metadata getter for our attribute CARRID, we would copy _GET_M_XYZ and rename it GET_M_CARRID.

The following is a sample implementation of the model getter GET_M_CARRID. In this example, we will override the English label text that is determined by default. In a more complex situation, you might even decide to use your own metadata class that inherits from CL_BSP_METADATA_SIMPLE. You then could redefine methods such as the GET_VALUELIST to provide your own application-specific logic.

```
DATA: l_field_ref      TYPE REF TO data,
      l_dfies_wa       TYPE dfies,
      l_rtti_elem      TYPE REF TO cl_abap_elemdescr.

l_field_ref = if_bsp_model_binding~get_attribute_data_ref(
    attribute_path = attribute_path ).
l_rtti_elem ?= cl_abap_elemdescr=>describe_by_data_ref(
    l_field_ref ).
l_dfies_wa = l_rtti_elem->get_ddic_field( ).
IF l_dfies_wa-langu = 'E'.
  l_dfies_wa-scrtext_m = 'Override Text'.
ENDIF.
CREATE OBJECT metadata TYPE cl_bsp_metadata_simple
  EXPORTING info = l_dfies_wa.
```

13.4 Dynamic Model Binding

We have already seen how powerful data binding can be. Besides the benefits already put forward for using it, data binding really shines when it comes to creating dynamic UI elements.

For an example of the power of the dynamic model binding, let us examine a situation that would be very difficult to reproduce in classic ABAP dynpro. We will start with a structure that represents a reduced number of fields in a database table. We want to expose each one of these fields as individual input fields with their own labels.

Of course we could manually design the UI for our structure, creating each individual element by hand. This could become time consuming depending upon the size of the structure at question. Also every time we add or remove fields from the structure, we have to return to the user interface and adjust it as well.

Would it not be much simpler if we could just supply the data object for the structure to the user interface and let it dynamically build all the necessary input fields, with metadata pulled from the structure and automatic field-input retrieval? Well, that is exactly what model binding makes possible.

We will start this example by creating a structure that is a subset of the fields in the table `SFLIGHT`. For now, we will throw out `MANDT` and all the fields that break down first class and business class. Our structure leaves us with about three-quarters of the original fields.

Structure: YBSP_SFLIGHT_LITE — Active
Short Text: Reduced Version of the SFLIGHT Table

Attributes | Components | Entry help/check | Currency/quantity fields

Predefined Type — 1 / 9

Component	RT...	Component ...	Data Type	Length	Decim...	Short Text
CARRID	☐	S_CARR_ID	CHAR	3	0	Airline Code
CONNID	☐	S_CONN_ID	NUMC	4	0	Flight Connection Number
FLDATE	☐	S_DATE	DATS	8	0	Flight date
PRICE	☐	S_PRICE	CURR	15	2	Airfare
CURRENCY	☐	S_CURRCODE	CUKY	5	0	Local currency of airline
PLANETYPE	☐	S_PLANETYE	CHAR	10	0	Aircraft Type
SEATSMAX	☐	S_SEATSMAX	INT4	10	0	Maximum capacity in economy class
SEATSOCC	☐	S_SEATSOCC	INT4	10	0	Occupied seats in economy class
PAYMENTSUM	☐	S_SUM	CURR	17	2	Total of current bookings

Figure 13.7 Reduced SFLIGHT Structure

From here on we will keep everything as dynamic as possible so that if we want to extend our user interface, all we have to do is add or remove fields from this YBSP_SFLIGHT_LITE structure. Our model class will have a public attribute of type of the structure we just created. It also will have the logic to select a single record from the database table SFLIGHT for the corresponding fields of this attribute.

Inside of our view, we are ready to start our dynamic element creation. The first thing we will need to do is retrieve a listing of the fields in our structure using the ABAP Runtime Type Services or RTTS.

```
DATA: descriptor TYPE REF TO cl_abap_structdescr.
descriptor ?= cl_abap_structdescr=>describe_by_data(
              model->isflight ).
DATA: flddescr TYPE ddfields.
flddescr = descriptor->get_ddic_field_list( ).
```

Now, we are going to be able to loop through our field listing and create a label and input field for each entry. What we would like to do is just build our binding string into a variable and give that variable to the BSP elements. However, when working within pages or views, BSP elements do not expose separate attributes for the bound and unbound values. Therefore, if we send a dynamic binding string into a BSP element attribute as a variable, it will incorrectly interpret that action. The element will assume that we are taking the value directly from the variable instead of trying to read it as a binding string.

One might also think that completing the binding string dynamically, as in the following example, would also be possible.

```
<htmlb:label
       for="//model.isflight.<%= <wa_field>-fieldname %>" />
```

By design the BSP runtime can not identify this example as a direct value assignment. Effectively for each attribute X that can also be bound, we have an additional _X attribute that is the binding string. If you look at for example the <htmlb:tableView>, you find that the table attribute is a REF TO DATA, and it is not possible to write a binding string into this attribute.

This is the reason why we have both X and _X for all bindable attributes. So in the normal writing of <lib:tag INT = "//model/..."/> already the compiler must make a very hard decision to generate code of the form o->x = string, where ABAP move semantics will do a string to integer conversion, or o->_x = string, where we want to save the binding string. This is the reason why binding strings are enforced to be static, so that compiler can do its magic. Of course, once you want to do dynamic binding, you must also assume the role of the compiler and then must know about this additional complexity.

If you create the BSP element directly via the ABAP class, the separate X and _X attributes are exposed for unbound and bound values. For instance, in the <htmlb:label> the implementing class, CL_HTMLB_LABEL, has two attributes—for and _for. The attribute that will expect a binding string always comes with the underscore.

Within our view we will now generate the BSP elements directly via code much as we did when creating a composite BSP element (see Chapter 11). We can then render the BSP element using its factory method and output that element via the <bsp:bee> element.

```
<% data: descriptor type ref to CL_ABAP_STRUCTDESCR.
 descriptor ?= CL_ABAP_STRUCTDESCR=>describe_by_data(
     model->isflight ).
 data: flddescr type DDFIELDS.
 flddescr = descriptor->GET_DDIC_FIELD_LIST( ).
 field-symbols: <wa_field> like line of flddescr.
 data: label type ref to cl_htmlb_label.
 data: input type ref to CL_HTMLB_INPUTFIELD.
 data: binding_string type string.
 loop at flddescr assigning <Wa_field>.
 clear label.
 clear input.
 concatenate '//model/isflight.' <wa_field>-FIELDNAME
 into binding_string.
 label ?= cl_htmlb_label=>factory( _for = binding_string ).
 input ?= cl_htmlb_inputfield=>factory(
       _value = binding_string ).  %>
```

We will use the flexibility of the <phtmlb:matrix> to support our dynamic user interface.

```
<phtmlb:matrixCell row    = "+1" vAlign = "TOP" />
  <bsp:bee bee="<%= label %>" />
<phtmlb:matrixCell col    = "+1" vAlign = "TOP" />
  <bsp:bee bee="<%= input %>" />
```

With only a handful of lines of code, we have generated our nine fields from our simplified SFLIGHT structure. Moreover, the same number of lines of code could have just as easily created 90 input fields and their labels. And the same code works for different structures, making it the typical type of code to integrate into a new tag for automatic form layout!

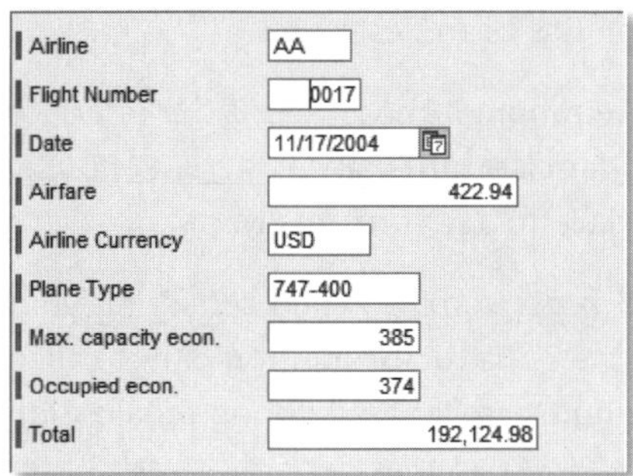

Figure 13.8 Dynamic Model Binding Output

13.5 Stateless MVC

SAP's implementation of MVC is designed to be used within stateful applications. There are two inherent assumptions made that require a stateful application. The first is the assumption that the model class itself will persist between request/response events. If you must recreate your model instance during every event, any data retrieval or manipulation must be repeated before the input data binding to ensure consistency.

This is complicated by the second assumption: that the controller class instance will also persist. The controller class contains the table of references to all of its models and is responsible for triggering the model binding. In a stateless application, all models would have to be reset into the controller before binding occurred.

These difficulties can be overcome, as can the general inefficiencies that come from having to reread and reprocess the same data over and over.

The goal is to create a situation where our model-class instance, which should contain all of our business data, persists without having to maintain the entire session state. This way, we avoid the overhead of the total size of the session state, the management of the session state, and the unnecessary re-retrieval of data from the underlying business system. In short you end up with the benefits of both stateless and stateful applications without the downsides of either.

13.5.1 XML Serialization of ABAP Objects

But how best can we accomplish this persistence of the model class? The first technology we will look to is the XML serialization of ABAP Objects. The ABAP runtime has built-in support for the conversion of data and class objects to XML. But more important is its ability to restore object instances from these XML representations at a later time. This technique allows any object to live on in another form even after its in-memory representation has been destroyed.

In order for an ABAP object to support serialization, it must inherit the interface IF_SERIALIZABLE_OBJECT. The normal model-class inheritance, CL_BSP_MODEL, does not contain this interface, so you will have to add it manually.

There are a couple of important aspects to keep in mind when serializing your model class. The first is to remember that the constructor method is not called when the object is restored. Also, static attributes are ignored during serialization and de-serialization. Finally, if you have inner ABAP classes declared as attributes of your class, these can be serialized and restored along with your object. However, for this occur; these inner classes, too, must implement the IF_SERIALIZABLE_OBJECT interface.

```
DATA: ostream TYPE string.
CALL TRANSFORMATION id
           SOURCE model = model
           RESULT xml ostream.
```

Listing 13.1 XML Serialization of a Model Instance

13.5.2 Server Cookie Storage of the XML Stream

Using this XML technique, we can convert the entire object instance to a string and then store this string in memory, in the database, or even in the file system of the application server.

Within the context of BSP, however, there is an even simpler approach to storing this XML representation of your model class, namely the server cookie. The theory of the server cookie is very similar to that of standard browser cookies; the main difference being that server cookies are stored in the back-end database instead of within the client's browser.

Server cookies are tied to the BSP application that created them, as well as being user- and session-ID specific. Keep in mind that even stateless applications will still have a unique session ID.

Server cookies contain expiration times and are cleaned up by the scheduling of the ABAP program BSP_CLEAN_UP_SERVER_COOKIES. They also can be viewed with the program BSP_SHOW_SERVER_COOKIES.

```
cl_bsp_server_side_cookie=>set_server_cookie(
 name = i_name
 application_name = runtime->application_name
 application_namespace = runtime->application_namespace
 username = sy-uname
 session_id = runtime->session_id
 data_name = i_name
 data_value = ostream
 expiry_time_rel = '1200' ).
```

Listing 13.2 Server Cookie creation example

13.5.3 Controller Modifications to Support Serialized Models

So far, we have not had to make very many changes to the model class to support this stateless approach. The simple inclusion of the IF_SERIALIZABLE_OBJECT interface has been the extent of the modifications. It appears that it must fall to the controller class to be responsible for the saving and proper restoration of the model instance before data binding occurs.

The first thing to consider if you are going to implement this technique is how best to reuse the logic for model-class serialization and restoration. It would be impractical to code this over and over in each of your controller classes. Instead you might want to create your own controller super-class that inherits from CL_BSP_CONTROLLER2. You could then code reusable SAVE_MODEL and READ_MODEL methods into your controller framework.

These methods should be designed with generic processing in mind. For example, your SAVE_MODEL method would probably want an input parameter for the cookie data name. You would also have an input parameter for your model class instances. You can make your method reusable by not specifying the exact type reference for your model class. Instead, only specify the type from the inheritance, CL_BSP_MODEL. Using the OO concept of polymorphism, your more specific model instance can still be passed into this parameter and processed within.

Method parameters SAVE_MODEL

Methods | Exceptions

Parameter	Type	Pa...	O...	Typing Method	Associated Type	Default value	Description
I_NAME	Importing	☐	☑	Type	STRING	'model'	
I_MODEL	Importing	☐	☐	Type Ref To	CL_BSP_MODEL		BSP: Model Basis Class

Figure 13.9 SAVE_MODEL Method Interface

Once the serialization logic is written and exposed to the controller class, we are ready to concentrate on the model's lifetime within the controller flow. Since we want to be able maintain our ability to data bind to the model class, the order in which we place our code within the controller class becomes very important.

The first thing we will want to do is attempt to restore our model instance. If we are able to restore the model instance from the server cookie, then we need to re-initialize it into the controller's listing of models. If, however, we are not able to restore the model class, then we might assume that this is the first time this page is being called for this session. Therefore we will create the model and run any necessary model-initialization methods.

```
model ?= read_model( ).
IF model IS NOT INITIAL.
   model->if_bsp_model~init( id = 'BB' owner = me ).
   set_model( model_id = 'BB'
              model_instance = model ).
ELSE.
   model ?= create_model( model_id = 'BB'
            class_name = 'YCL_BSP_M_BOOK_XML_EXP' ).
   model->initialize_data( ).
ENDIF.
```

Once the model is restored, the controller can make the call to its internal method DISPATCH_INPUT. It is this method that will trigger all input data binding and event handling. If our serialization and restoration of the model class was successful, then the inner binding and eventing methods should notice no difference between a normal stateful model and this stateless one.

After returning from the DISPATCH_INPUT method, we probably want to take this opportunity to save our model instance. This will ensure that new input values brought in through data binding or new data retrieved because of an event are captured within a new snapshot of our model class. The server cookie will be overwritten each time with the new XML representation of our model class.

Keep in mind, however, that if you directly change attribute values of your model during any view coding, these changes will not be retained unless you force another serialization of your model class. Since your view should only contain presentation logic, it is always a good idea to avoid such direct manipulation of the model class.

13.6 Building a Pattern Engine with MVC

Employee Self Services (ESS) is one of the hottest new developments in the intranet environment. Most companies attempt to streamline processes by having employees complete simple administrative processes directly themselves. Typical examples are holiday scheduling, address changes, or ordering office supplies. These processes are all targeted at occasional use, and must be simple to use. The typical approach is to use a fixed pattern that all ESS applications follow, so that the casual user will be able to complete the process easily.

In order to demonstrate building a pattern engine, we would like to write an ESS application for holiday/vacation scheduling. First, we will write a pattern engine that does all of the generic work and handles the overall layout. Then, we will write our small ESS application.

> **Note** The work presented here does not come from any SAP product. The words ESS and pattern engine are used here in a generic way, and do not reflect any specific SAP product development work.

We would like to have the same layout for all our ESS applications, At the top should be the title. A roadmap will be used to give an overview of all the steps to be followed, plus the current active step. Navigation buttons must be placed at the bottom of the page. All ESS processes will have at a minimum an introduction page to explain how to complete the process, the actual work pages, and a save page giving a summary of the entered data, plus a final confirmation page.

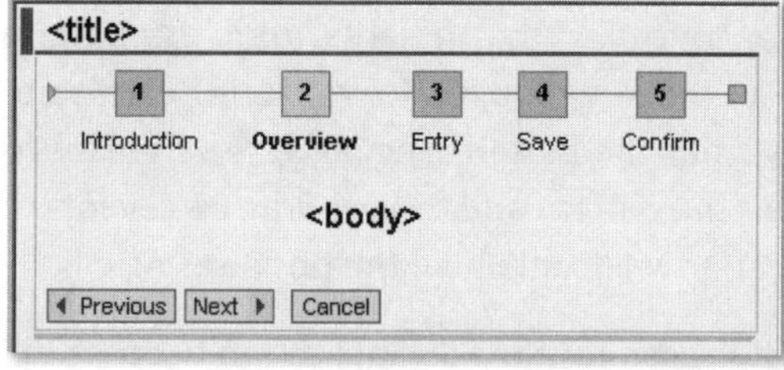

Figure 13.10 Sample Output of the Pattern Engine

One might assume that a good approach would be to use a composite element to handle the complete layout, wrapped around the body of the ESS application. While BSP elements are excellent at handling rendering, they are not appropriate for complex logic. In this case, we would have required additional data structures to hold configuration information and extra classes to handle events.

Using a controller has many benefits. The code for the controller is placed in a separate class. Adding the controller into a BSP application is just one data entry. The same controller can then be used many times within one BSP application. As a controller is effectively a normal ABAP class, it is possible to place all the type declarations and event handling into this class. Furthermore, it is possible to use the same techniques employed in composite elements, in controllers as well. In this way, the controller can contain rendering code and is quite capable of processing BSP elements.

For our design, we have one controller that will be the pattern engine. The pattern engine is responsible for handling the complete layout, determining the current active step, and displaying it. In addition, the pattern engine will offer a number of events, mapped onto method calls, to help the ESS application.

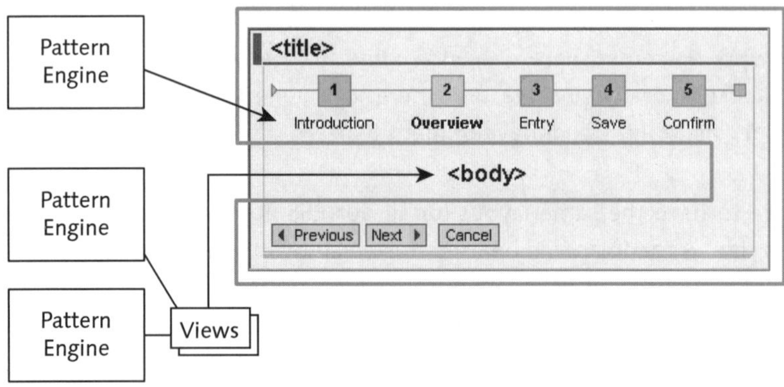

Figure 13.11 Application Breakdown

The ESS application will comprise a controller that inherits from the pattern engine, a model class, and all the views that are required for rendering each step. Because the ESS application inherits from the pattern engine, it is very easy to complete the configuration data about the pattern and to overwrite any events of interest. Furthermore, the ESS application will contain all the business logic.

The use of a model class is optional. It is used for the ESS application because the model binding makes it easier to have the data from the incoming request automatically returned to the model. The model class also handles the conversion between internal and external representation. A typical example is the conversion of a date from YYYYMMDD into any of the several display versions, such as YYYY-MM-DD and MM/DD/YYYY.

For each step in the ESS application, one view is written. The view itself will only contain the BSP elements that represent that actual ESS step. Everything else will be done by the pattern engine.

13.6.1 The Final ESS Application

Before looking at the actual code, let us first look at what we want to achieve. This will make the actual code much easier to understand.

Our small ESS application will have five steps. The first is an introduction page, which explains the complete process quickly. The second step will give an overview of the holidays that have been taken this year and list the available holidays.

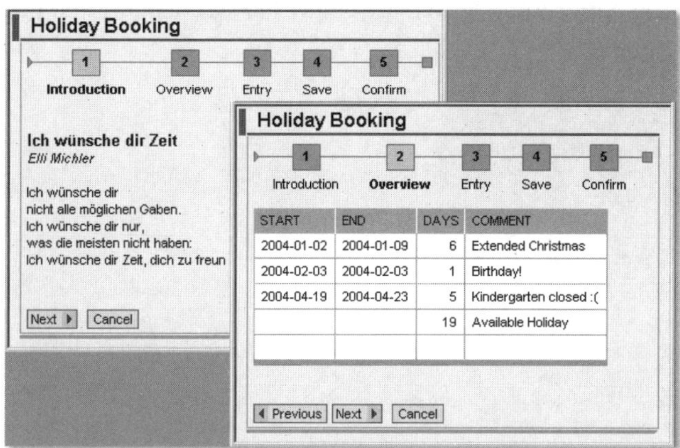

Figure 13.12 Steps One and Two of the Sample Application

The next step will be to enter the data for the next holiday. After the data has been verified as correct, it will be presented in read-only mode in step four, with a confirm button. Up to this step, it's always possible to navigate back to the previous steps, or to cancel the process.

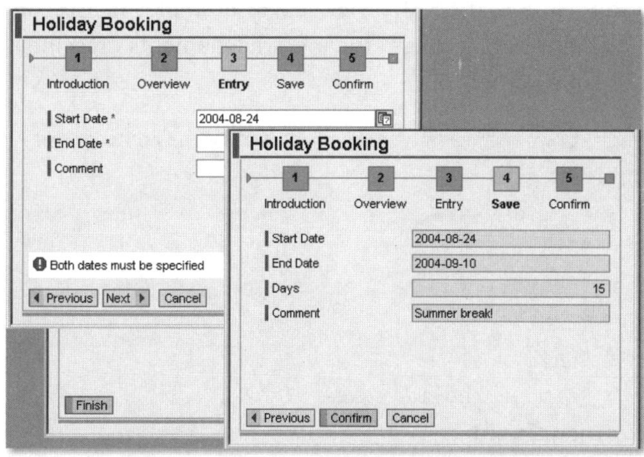

Figure 13.13 Steps Three and Four of the Sample Application

In the last step, a final confirmation shows that the holiday has been booked. Now the only navigation option is to press the finish button. For typical ESS applications, this exit URL will be configured to return to a small portal that contained all the different ESS applications.

13.6.2 Writing the ESS Application

Before looking at the more complex pattern engine, let's first look at the work required to develop the ESS application. We create a new BSP application that has one controller and five views.

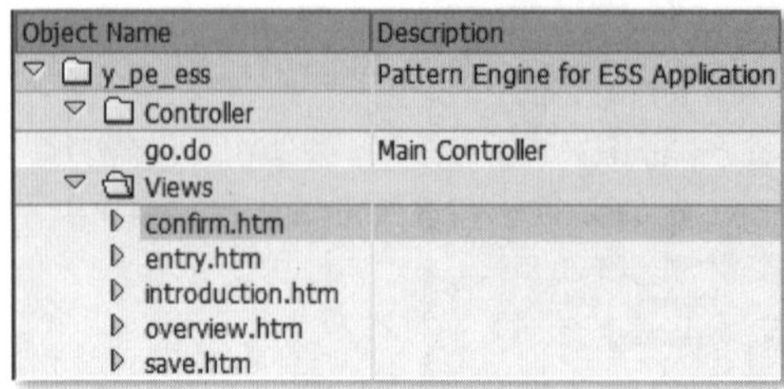

Figure 13.14 Object Overview

Each view will have two attributes, which will be set automatically by the pattern engine. The first will be a reference to the defined model class; the second is a reference onto the pattern engine (pe) controller.

```
model    TYPE REF TO   ycl_pe_ess_model
pe       TYPE REF TO   ycl_pe_ess_controller
```

Given that all the data is stored in the model class, the views themselves are very simple, and quickly written. Here is the entry view as an example. It uses the <phtmlb:formLayout> element to quickly get the required elements on screen. The other views are of the same complexity.

```
<%@extension name="phtmlb" prefix="phtmlb" %>  <phtmlb:formLayout>
    <phtmlb:formLayoutInputField
            id       = "holiday_start"
            label    = "Start Date"
            required = "TRUE"
            showHelp = "TRUE"
            type     = "DATE"
            value    = "//model/holiday_start" />
    <phtmlb:formLayoutInputField
            id       = "holiday_end"
            label    = "End Date"
```

```
            required = "TRUE"
            showHelp = "TRUE"
            type     = "DATE"
            value    = "//model/holiday_end" />
    <phtmlb:formLayoutInputField
            id       = "holiday_comment"
            label    = "Comment"
            type     = "STRING"
            value     = "//model/holiday_comment" />
  </phtmlb:formLayout>
```

The model class is required to hold all relevant information. For our ESS application, we need a table that contains a list of all holidays taken, plus a few data values for the new holiday to be booked, such as days available, start and end dates, and comment string. Everything needed to make model binding work, is done by the base class (`cl_bsp_model`). The model class is just a data holding class, as well as the constructor to fill the `holidays_taken` table.

```
CLASS ycl_pe_ess_model DEFINITION
      INHERITING FROM cl_bsp_model.
  PUBLIC SECTION.
    TYPES: BEGIN OF t_holiday,
             start   TYPE d,
             end     TYPE d,
             days    TYPE i,
             comment TYPE string,
           END OF t_holiday,
           t_holidays TYPE STANDARD TABLE OF t_holiday.
    DATA holidays_taken    TYPE t_holidays.
    DATA holiday_start     TYPE d.
    DATA holiday_end       TYPE d.
    DATA holiday_days      TYPE i.
    DATA holiday_comment   TYPE string.
    DATA holiday_available TYPE i.
    METHODS constructor. " fill table holidays_taken  ENDCLASS.
```

In our final step, the ESS controller is required. It contains the code necessary to configure the pattern engine, plus the business logic to book the actual holiday. The most important aspect is the fact that this controller will inherit from the pattern engine.

```
CLASS ycl_pe_ess_controller DEFINITION
      INHERITING FROM ycl_ess_pattern_engine.
  DATA model TYPE REF TO ycl_pe_ess_model.
  METHODS do_init          REDEFINITION.
  ...
  METHODS do_handle_data   REDEFINITION.
  METHODS pe_confirm       REDEFINITION.
ENDCLASS.
```

The `do_init` method is used to create our required model class and to configure the pattern engine. The most interesting code is the filling of the `pe_steps` table. This table contains a list of all views in sequence. With this, the pattern engine can render the required roadmap to give an overview of all steps, call the correct view for each step, and control the navigation buttons.

```
METHOD do_init.
* Create our model object
  model ?= create_model( class_name =
          'YCL_PE_ESS_MODEL' model_id   = 'm' ).
* Setup Pattern Engine
  pe_model    = model.
  pe_title    = 'Holiday Booking'(001).
  pe_exit_url = 'http://sdn.sap.com'.
  APPEND 'Introduction'(100) TO pe_steps.
  APPEND 'Overview'(101)     TO pe_steps.
  APPEND 'Entry'(102)        TO pe_steps.
  APPEND 'Save'(103)         TO pe_steps.
  APPEND 'Confirm'(104)      TO pe_steps.
* Initialize also pattern engine
  super->do_init ( ).
ENDMETHOD.
```

Data handling is done via the model class. However, some sanity checking is required to ensure that the entered holiday booking is actually acceptable. For this, we just overwrite the `do_handle_data` method. Once we see the entry view (step three), we quickly check that the entered data range is valid. In case of problems, an error message is added and the flag is set to prohibit navigation to the next step.

```
METHOD do_handle_data.
  super->do_handle_data( form_fields = form_fields
                    global_messages = global_messages ).
```

```
  IF pe_step_current = 3. " Entry
      IF model->holiday_start IS INITIAL
      OR model->holiday_end IS INITIAL.
        messages->add_message( condition =
           'start || end INITIAL'
           message   = 'Specify both dates'(100) ).
        pe_step_next_prohibited = ABAP_TRUE.
        RETURN.
    ENDIF.
    ...
    model->holiday_days = model->holiday_end
                              - model->holiday_start + 1.
* do additional complex logic to for weekends  ENDIF.
ENDMETHOD.
```

Lastly, our ESS application must book the holiday. The pattern engine maps its own events onto methods. These methods can be overwritten where required. We overwrite the `pe_confirm` method and add the logic required to book the holiday.

```
METHOD pe_confirm.
* save data
* ...complex steps to dump data from model onto
* database...
  super->pe_confirm( event_object = event_object ).
ENDMETHOD.
```

Although the above section suggests a lot of work is involved in writing the ESS application, the truth is that once the pattern engine is done, ESS applications of this complexity can be written in less than one hour!

Let's recap the steps needed so far.

- Create a model class with the relevant data.
- Create a controller to configure the pattern engine.
- Add validation logic and coding for the final business logic.
- Create the relevant views.

13.6.3 Writing the Pattern Engine

Although the pattern engine is not very complex, it does involve a lot of code. Only small extracts will be shown here. Most important, the pattern engine is also a BSP controller, and as such must inherit from the class `cl_bsp_controller2`.

A number of configuration parameters are required for the pattern engine. These are all declared as protected data, so that the actual ESS application can fill the data. We need to display a title and a typical exit URL. Lastly, we require a list of all the steps that the application contains.

A number of event methods are defined. These will be called to handle events from the navigation buttons. It enables the ESS application to easily handle specific events via redefinition.

```
CLASS ycl_ess_pattern_engine DEFINITION
   INHERITING FROM cl_bsp_controller2.
  PROTECTED SECTION.
    DATA pe_title       TYPE string.
    DATA pe_exit_url    TYPE string.
    DATA pe_steps       TYPE string_table.
    ...
    METHODS pe_next     IMPORTING event_object TYPE REF TO
            if_htmlb_data.
    METHODS pe_previous IMPORTING event_object TYPE REF TO
            if_htmlb_data.
    METHODS pe_cancel   IMPORTING event_object TYPE REF TO
            if_htmlb_data.
    METHODS pe_finished IMPORTING event_object TYPE REF TO
            if_htmlb_data.
    METHODS pe_confirm  IMPORTING event_object TYPE REF TO
            if_htmlb_data.
ENDCLASS.
```

The most complex part of the pattern engine is the `do_request` method. Usually, when writing controllers, this method will just decide the next view and call it. However, using views to also contain the layout of the pattern engine would make it more complex to use and reuse. In addition, these layout views would have to be copied into the current ESS application. Instead, the complete rendering is done by processing other BSP elements, as if we are writing a composite element.

The actual coding is straightforward, although tedious. As if we were writing the BSP elements on a page, they are all systematically processed. Notice that the method of writing the code reflects exactly the same structure as the elements would display on a page.

```
METHOD do_request.
*<htmlb:content>
```

```
DATA: content TYPE REF TO cl_htmlb_content.
content = cl_htmlb_content=>factory(
          design = 'design2003' ).
WHILE page_context->element_process( element = content )
      = co_element_continue.
* <htmlb:page>
  DATA: page TYPE REF TO cl_htmlb_page.
  page = cl_htmlb_page=>factory( ).
  WHILE page_context->element_process( element = page )
        = co_element_continue.
*   <htmlb:form>
     ...
*    <phtmlb:containerTitle>
      ...
*     <phtmlb:containerContentItem>
       ...
*      <phtmlb:roadmap/>
        ...
*       Actual content, call correct view
          DATA: view TYPE REF TO if_bsp_page.
          READ TABLE pe_steps INDEX pe_step_current
                INTO name.
          view = create_view( view_name = name ).
          view->set_attribute( name = 'pe'    value = me ).
          view->set_attribute( name = 'model'
                               value = pe_model ).
          call_view( view ).
*       <phtmlb:messageBar/>
          IF messages->num_messages( ) > 0.
           ...
          ENDIF.
*         <htmlb:button/>
          DATA: button TYPE REF TO cl_htmlb_button.
          IF me->pe_step_current > 1 AND me->pe_step_current
             < me->pe_step_max.
             button = cl_htmlb_button=>factory(
              id            = 'sdn_pattern_engine_previous'
              text          = 'Previous'(001)
              design        = 'PREVIOUS'
              onclick       = 'PE_PREVIOUS' ).
                WHILE page_context->element_process(
```

```
                    element = button ) =
                    if_bsp_element=>co_element_continue.
                  ENDWHILE.
            ENDIF.
****Additional Button Processing
*       </phtmlb:containerContentItem>
*      </phtmlb:containerTitle>
*     </htmlb:form>
*    </htmlb:page>
*   </htmlb:content>
ENDMETHOD.
```

The most interesting part of the above coding is the code to call the correct view. After the roadmap has been processed, a specific view must be rendered out. Here, the current step is used as the index into the steps table; the view is created; the two standard attributes, controller and model are set, and the view is rendered. Then the rest of the pattern layout is completed.

Another important part of the pattern engine is the way that events are handled. From Chapter 9, we know that the `onX` event string specified by the user is transported back transparently as the event server name. We will use this string to call a specific method to handle the event. The `do_handle_event` will have been called with the correct HTMLB event. We just have to do the dynamic call to the correct event method.

```
METHOD do_handle_event.
  IF htmlb_event_ex IS NOT INITIAL.
     DATA: method TYPE STRING.
     method = htmlb_event_ex->event_server_name.
     TRANSLATE method TO UPPER CASE.
     TRY.
        CALL METHOD me->(method)
          EXPORTING event_object = htmlb_event_ex.
     CATCH CX_ROOT.
     ENDTRY.
  ENDIF.
ENDMETHOD.
```

The event methods themselves are small, each handling the interaction of one button. As a typical example, we will look at the code for the **Next** and **Finished** buttons. For the next event, the current step will be incremented. For the finished button, a navigate-to-the-exit-URL will be done. Using the `exit` method here ensures that our session is also cleaned up.

```
METHOD pe_next.
  IF pe_step_next_prohibited = ABAP_TRUE.
   RETURN.
  ENDIF.
  pe_step_current = pe_step_current + 1.
ENDMETHOD.
...
METHOD pe_finished.
  navigation->exit( pe_exit_url ).
ENDMETHOD.
```

In the end, the use of a BSP controller enabled us to write a pattern engine that is simple and elegant to use. With this building block, it is easy to develop similar ESS applications within hours, all of them with the same look and feel. If the layout for all ESS applications needs changing, this is done in one method only.

The placement of all rendering code within the controller, instead of a view, makes the actual code slightly difficult to write once, but makes this pattern very easy to use. With this approach, usage reduces to declaring a new controller with the BSP application, which then derives from the pattern engine. No further work is required, and this same controller can reused extensively. If the layout code was placed in a view, then this view had to be copied into each BSP application where the pattern engine is used. This small project shows the power of switching between layout code that the compiler generates code for, and just hand writing the equivalent code.

14 Help Systems

If you are developing BSP applications as replacements for SAP GUI business transactions, you probably will miss certain help systems, like the F1 Field Help and F4 Value Help. In this chapter, we will look at ways to provide similar functionality in BSP.

You should be aware in advance that this chapter is a little different from most in this book. Because SAP does not deliver full solutions for field help or value help, we are going to look at some solutions that you can build yourself. These should just be considered as starting points to get your own development moving in the right direction.

The complete source code for all solutions is available on the book CD; therefore, not all coding is presented in line in this text. These examples use highly generic and flexible coding that can be integrated into just about any application. By necessity, generic coding is often complex and lengthy. We will try to hit all the important architecture elements of the examples without spending too much time on each line of code.

14.1 F1—Field Level Help

Long-time SAP GUI transaction users will probably automatically reach for the F1 key when they find fields in their applications that they do not understand. Some form of context-sensitive help is a sorely missed feature in BSP.

The goal of this example is to recreate not just the context help but also the technical information about the field that is exposed in the classic dynpro.

As you develop large and complex BSP applications, especially very dynamic ones, you will badly want some mechanism to identify what part of the code houses a particular element.

14.1.1 The Help UI

In the SAP GUI environment you really get all of this functionality *for free*, in that no special coding is required to attach this functionality to your field. For this example, we wanted to have a similarly non-intrusive approach to existing coding. The addition of the field help should be easy to implement. On the other hand, the use of this help should be intuitive even to users who have never worked with a SAP GUI transaction.

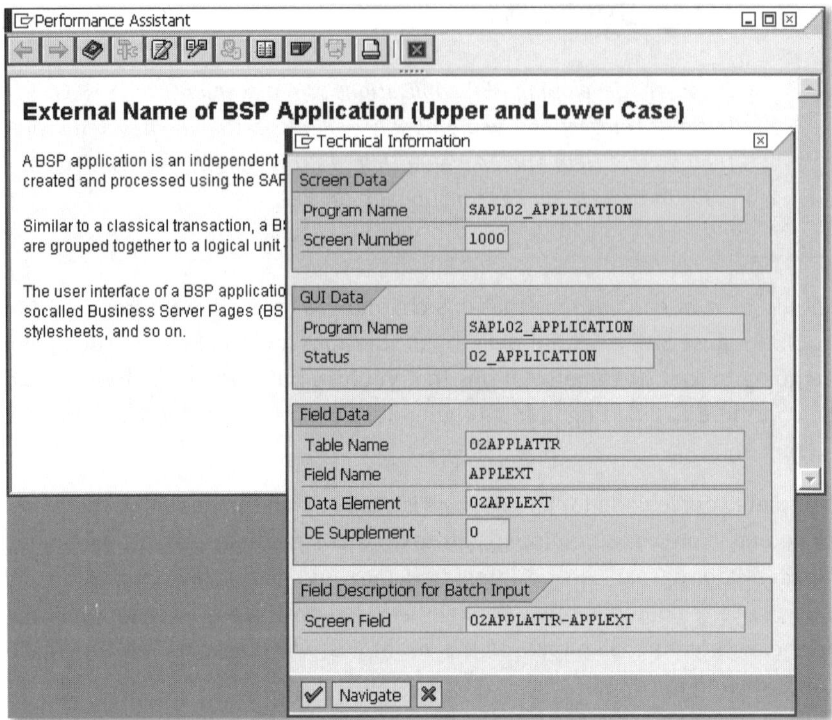

Figure 14.1 Typical Context Help with Technical Information in the Classic SAP GUI

To that end, this example was designed to wrap its functionality so as to fire the field help around the `<htmlb:label>` element. It will generate a hyperlink that will open the context help in a modeless window when clicked.

We hope the resulting solution ends up being so simple to implement in your code that all you have to do is change the name of the element from `<htmlb:label>` to `<yourextension:flLabel>` if you are using Model View Binding.

If you are not using binding or if you want to override the data element from the binding attribute, you only need to add one attribute to the standard label attributes to provide this data element name.

The ease with which this new element can be introduced into existing applications is especially important if we consider the amount of code that you might want to go back and retrofit with this new functionality.

Figure 14.2 demonstrates `<htmlb:labels>` that have been wrapped by this example and now have hyperlinks.

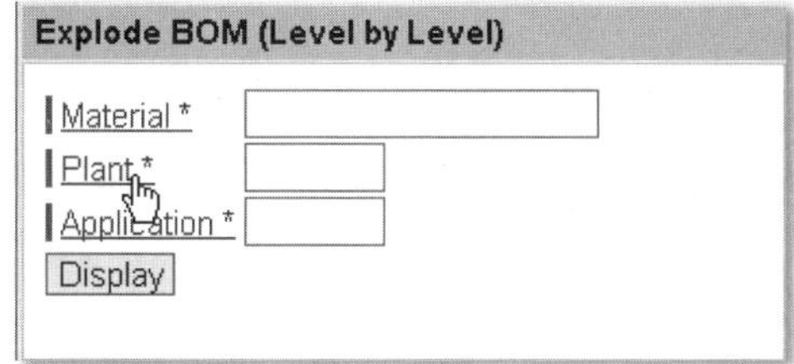

Figure 14.2 Label Element with Hyperlink to Context Help

Figure 14.3 shows that when you click on the label hyperlink you get a basic browser modeless window where there are two tabs. In the first and default tab, there is the Data Element Help itself. The Internal ITF (SAPscript) format for the Help has been converted to HTML for this display.

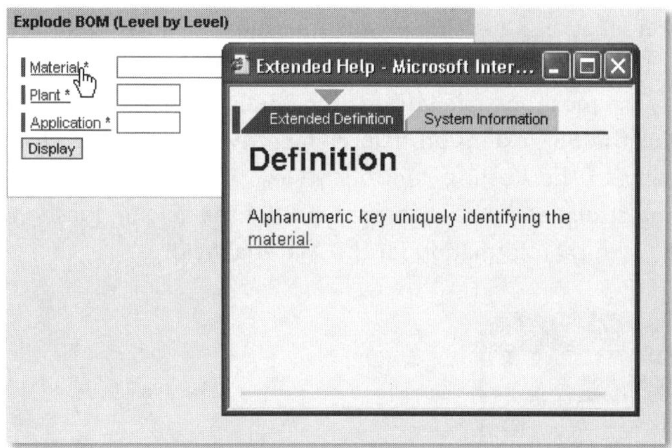

Figure 14.3 Context Help; Extended Definition

Notice the internal hyperlink in the example help for Material. In the converted HTML, this link actually points to a `SAPEVENT`. If you have ever done any programming for HTML content in the SAP GUI HTML viewer, you might remember that this is a special event that will be caught and returned to dynpro-event processing (see Chapter 7).

However, this `SAPEVENT` link is useless in the BSP context. Therefore, the BSP help solution will have to convert this to a normal hyperlink to make it functional. Also, most of these internal links point to glossary entries instead of data-element texts. Therefore, this solution will also need internal processing to support the navigation and output of both types of help objects. Figure 14.4 shows the help after we navigate through the Material link.

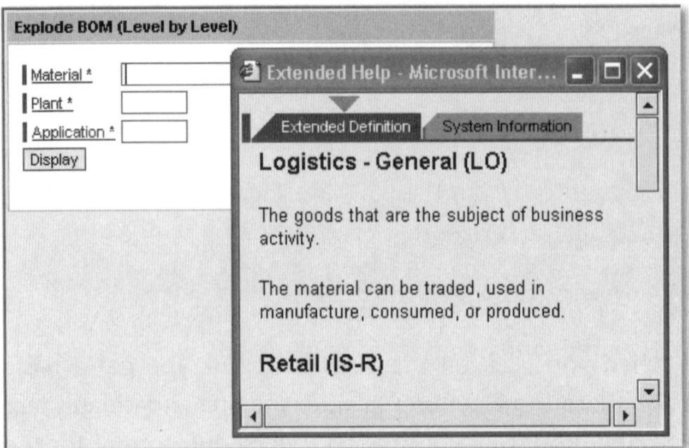

Figure 14.4 Internal Help Navigation to a Glossary Item

The second tab is the one that, as a developer, you are probably more interested in. This is the tab that displays the technical information about the field in question. In order to display the most possible information here, you will want to use Model View Binding for the BSP extension help element we are creating. That way it will have visibility to the hosting controller, view, model-class, model-attribute, model-binding-string, and data-element types for the field in question. Figure 14.5 shows the technical information for the **Material** field.

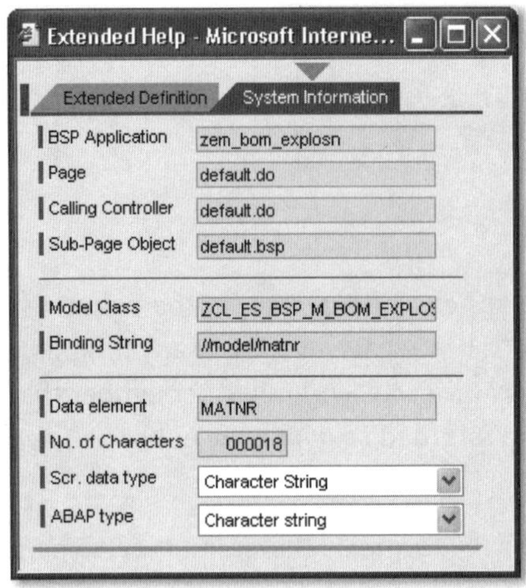

Figure 14.5 Help System Information

Before we dig into the coding for the example solution, let us have a look at the small amount of code that gets inserted into the host page to produce the screens we have seen.

```
<zbook:f1Label for      = "//model/matnr"
               required = "TRUE" />
```

14.1.2 Implementing the BSP Extension Element

The solution has two major parts. The first is the BSP extension element itself. This element will be responsible for all the rendering of the label with the surrounding hyperlink. The second part is a BSP MVC application for displaying the extended help in the popup modeless window. This application will be stateless and anonymous so that it can be integrated with any type of hosting BSP application.

In this design, our BSP extension element will be responsible for creating the model class that will be used later in the popup dialog. This is necessary so that the field's runtime information can be easily passed from the hosting application to the help-dialog one. After creating and initializing the model class, the BSP extension element will serialize it to XML and then write it into a server cookie. The keys for retrieving this model class later will be the only information that we will actually pass to the dialog application via the URL.

As you might see by now, this example builds upon many of the technologies we have introduced in past chapters. Be sure to have read Chapter 9, *BSP Extensions*; Chapter 11, *Writing a Composite Tag*; and Chapter 13, *Model View Controller*, before attempting to recreate this example.

14.1.3 BSP Element Properties

We will start our example by creating a new BSP element in an existing BSP extension. If you are creating your first extension, just make sure that it uses the `CL_HTMLB_ELEMENT` class as its generated Basis class (**Very Important**: This is in the extension, not the element!).

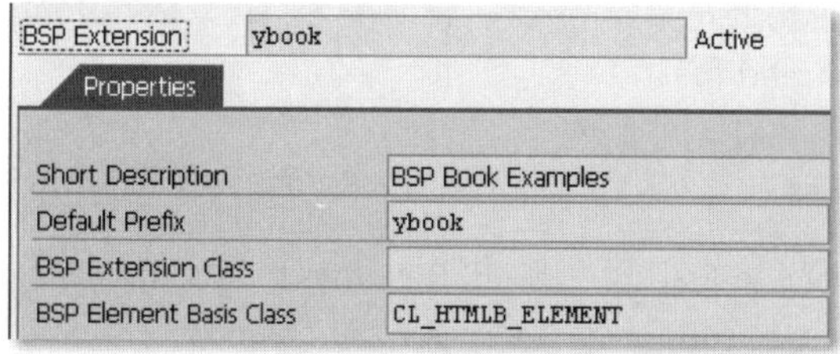

Figure 14.6 Extension Properties

For the element properties, be sure to check **User Defined Validation**. We will use this later to write our own compiler check for one of the element attributes.

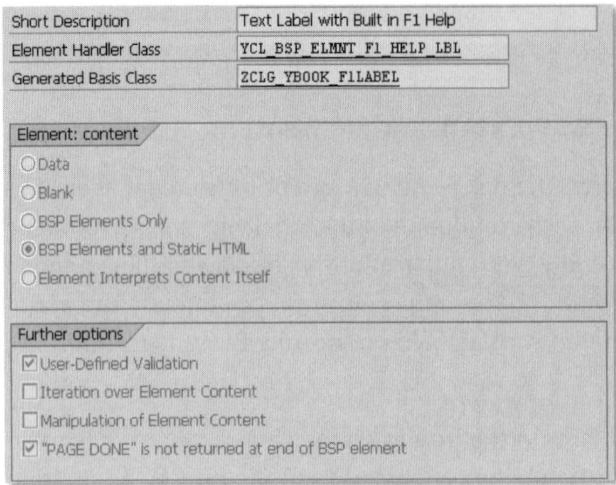

Figure 14.7 Extension Element Properties

14.1.4 BSP Element Attributes

Because we are wrapping our element around the standard SAP `<htmlb:label>` element, we will want to include all the attributes of the inner element. You could either cut and paste to bring these over from the `<htmlb:label>` element or just start by copying the entire `<htmlb:label>` element .

The first additional attribute is `dataElement`. If you are not using Model View Binding, then you will have to explicitly state the data element that you want to use for the field-level help. This is also useful if your model field is of a generic type and does not point to a particularly helpful data-dictionary element.

The second attribute to add is `rfcDest`. Now, we are going to mark this as not yet implemented. In the future you might want to be able to read the help from remote systems. For now, however, we will use this element to demonstrate how you can program a compiler check to throw an error if anyone does try to use this attribute before we have programmed for it.

14.1.5 Element Handler Class

We only have one attribute that we will add to the BSP element class. This is an attribute that will store an instance of model class that we are creating.

The first method that we will inherit and redefine is `compile_time_is_valid`. This is where we can code our compiler checks for this extension element. We only want to check and make sure that no one uses the `rfcDest` attribute before we have coded for it. Figure 14.10 shows the error that this routine generates in the editor if someone does use the `rfcDest` attribute.

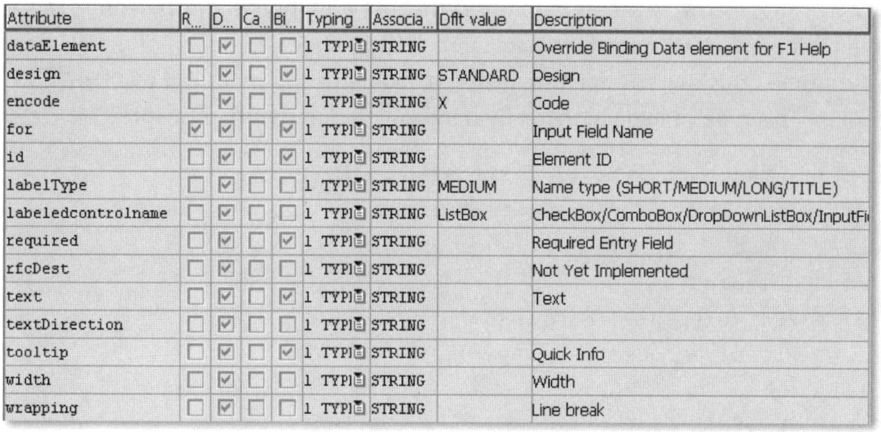

Attribute	R...	D...	Ca...	Bi...	Typing...	Associa...	Dflt value	Description
dataElement	☐	☑	☐	☐	1 TYPI	STRING		Override Binding Data element for F1 Help
design	☐	☑	☐	☑	1 TYPI	STRING	STANDARD	Design
encode	☐	☑	☐	☐	1 TYPI	STRING	X	Code
for	☑	☑	☐	☑	1 TYPI	STRING		Input Field Name
id	☐	☑	☐	☑	1 TYPI	STRING		Element ID
labelType	☐	☑	☐	☐	1 TYPI	STRING	MEDIUM	Name type (SHORT/MEDIUM/LONG/TITLE)
labeledcontrolname	☐	☑	☐	☐	1 TYPI	STRING	ListBox	CheckBox/ComboBox/DropDownListBox/InputFi
required	☐	☑	☐	☑	1 TYPI	STRING		Required Entry Field
rfcDest	☐	☑	☐	☐	1 TYPI	STRING		Not Yet Implemented
text	☐	☑	☐	☑	1 TYPI	STRING		Text
textDirection	☐	☑	☐	☐	1 TYPI	STRING		
tooltip	☐	☑	☐	☑	1 TYPI	STRING		Quick Info
width	☐	☑	☐	☐	1 TYPI	STRING		Width
wrapping	☐	☑	☐	☐	1 TYPI	STRING		Line break

Figure 14.8 Extension Element Attributes

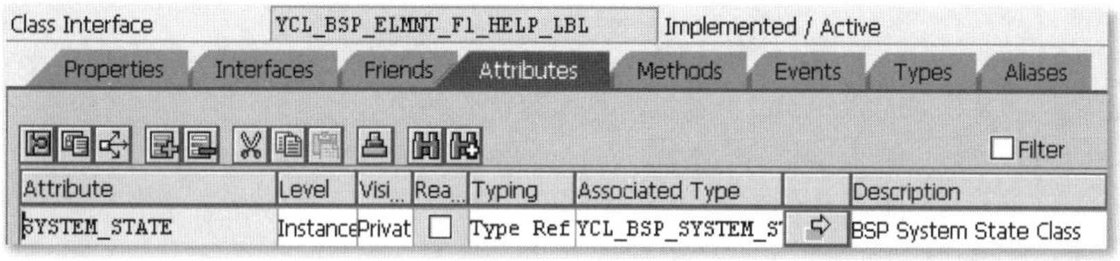

Class Interface YCL_BSP_ELMNT_F1_HELP_LBL Implemented / Active

Properties | Interfaces | Friends | Attributes | Methods | Events | Types | Aliases

☐ Filter

Attribute	Level	Visi...	Rea...	Typing	Associated Type		Description
SYSTEM_STATE	Instance	Privat	☐	Type Ref	YCL_BSP_SYSTEM_S	⇨	BSP System State Class

Figure 14.9 Extension Element Handler Class Attributes

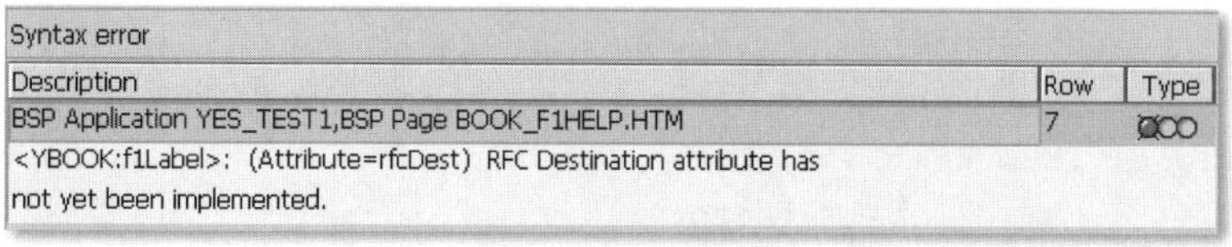

Syntax error

Description	Row	Type
BSP Application YES_TEST1,BSP Page BOOK_F1HELP.HTM	7	
<YBOOK:f1Label>: (Attribute=rfcDest) RFC Destination attribute has not yet been implemented.		

Figure 14.10 Custom Syntax Error

```
DATA: value TYPE string.
value = element_data->get_attribute( name = 'rfcDest' ).
IF value <> cl_bsp_element_data=>co_no_attribute_value.
  validator->error(
    name = 'rfcDest'
    msg  = 'RFC Destination attribute has yet been
            implemented'(c01) ).
  valid = validator->m_any_value_in_error.
ELSE.
  valid = validator->m_all_values_valid.
ENDIF.
```

do_at_beginning is the next method that we will inherit and redefine. This is the method that will control the actual rendering-code generation of the element at runtime. This method for the most part contains the inner call to CL_HTMLB_LABEL. This type of logic has already been covered in depth in Chapter 11.

```
DATA: javascript_link TYPE string.
DATA: link TYPE REF TO cl_htmlb_link.
CREATE OBJECT system_state.
****Model Bind?
IF me->dataelement IS INITIAL.
  me->resolve_model_binding( ).
ELSE.
  IF id IS INITIAL.
    CONCATENATE for '_1' INTO id.
  ENDIF.
ENDIF.
****Serialize the System State and pass the Keys on the URL
javascript_link = me->record_system_state( ).
****Initialize the Link Object
link ?= cl_htmlb_link=>factory(
       id             = me->id
       onclientclick = javascript_link
       target         = '_Top' ).

WHILE m_page_context->element_process(
                    element = link ) = co_element_continue.
  DATA: label TYPE REF TO cl_htmlb_label.
  label ?= cl_htmlb_label=>factory(

   ... Rendering Logic
```

In addition to the inherited methods that we will be redefining in the BSP element class, we will add two methods. The first, record_system_state, is responsible for completing the model class. It then serializes it to XML and writes the XML string into a server cookie for later consumption. Finally, the method creates the URL with keys included for reading the server cookie that will point to the field help BSP application.

To record the model class in the server cookie, we need a unique id in order to avoid overlaying data from another field on the screen that might have the same data element. If we do not have data about our model class, then we can go ahead and just record the details according to the data element.

```
METHOD record_system_state.
*  ReturningVALUE( R_JAVASCRIPT_LINK )TYPE STRING
  DATA: data_name TYPE string.
****If we didn't record the system state from the model,
****then our only key is the data element name.
  IF system_state->rollname IS INITIAL.
    system_state->rollname = me->dataelement.
    data_name =              me->dataelement.
  ELSE.
****System State came from the model, therefore we will
****create a unique ID for each entry.
    IF STRLEN( me->id ) GT 30.
      DATA: guid_22 TYPE guid_22.
      CALL FUNCTION 'GUID_CREATE'
        IMPORTING ev_guid_22 = guid_22.
      MOVE guid_22 TO data_name.
    ELSE.
      MOVE me->id TO data_name.
    ENDIF.
  ENDIF.
```

In this section of code, we look up some of the details about the BSP application we are running within. We use the page-context object to find most of these details.

```
****Record the system state - BSP Page and Application
system_state->o2applext = me->mc_runtime->application_name.
system_state->o2pageext = me->mc_runtime->page_name.
DATA: page_context TYPE REF TO cl_bsp_page_context.
TRY.
   page_context ?= me->m_page_context.
   IF page_context IS NOT INITIAL.
      system_state->sub_page = page_context->m_page_name.
      IF page_context->m_caller IS NOT INITIAL.
         DATA: parent_controller
                 TYPE REF TO cl_bsp_controller.
         parent_controller ?= page_context->m_caller.
         IF parent_controller IS NOT INITIAL.
            system_state->sub_controller =
                 parent_controller->controller_name.
         ENDIF.
```

```
      ENDIF.
    ENDIF.
CATCH cx_sy_move_cast_error.
ENDTRY.
```

This next section will serialize the model object to XML and write the data into the server cookie. Notice that we do not set any application name or namespace. This allows details for the same data element to be used across applications.

```
DATA: ostream  TYPE string,
      xslt_err TYPE REF TO cx_xslt_exception.
TRY.
   CALL TRANSFORMATION id SOURCE model = system_state
                          RESULT XML ostream.
   cl_bsp_server_side_cookie=>set_server_cookie(
        name = data_name
        application_name = ''
        application_namespace = ''
        username = 'F1HELP'
        data_name = data_name
        data_value = ostream
        expiry_time_rel = '1200' ).
CATCH cx_xslt_exception INTO xslt_err.
ENDTRY.
```

This final section will create the URL for calling the popup window, passing the data keys in the URL.

```
  DATA: url  TYPE string, page TYPE string.
  page = 'F1_Help.do'.
  DATA:  params TYPE tihttpnvp.
  FIELD-SYMBOLS: <wa_params> LIKE LINE OF params.
  APPEND INITIAL LINE TO params ASSIGNING <wa_params>.
  <wa_params>-name = 'DOCUOBJECT'.
  CONCATENATE 'DE' me->dataelement INTO <wa_params>-value.
  ... <wa_params>-name = 'SESSION_ID'. ...
  ... <wa_params>-name = 'RFCDEST'. ...
  ... <wa_params>-name = 'DATA_NAME'. ...
****Copy over the current theme to the popup window
  DATA: selection TYPE string.
  selection = mc_runtime->get_external_theme_root( ).
  IF selection IS INITIAL.
```

```
    selection = 'sap_standard'.
  ENDIF.
 ...<wa_params>-name = 'sap-themeRoot'. ...
****Use your application name here
  CALL METHOD
    cl_bsp_runtime=>construct_bsp_url
    EXPORTING  in_application = 'yes_test1'
               in_page        = page
               in_parameters  = params
    IMPORTING  out_local_url  = url.
  CONCATENATE `newDialog = window.open("` url
    `", "_blank", "resizable=yes,height=300,width=300");`
    INTO r_javascript_link.
```

The second method, `resolve_model_binding`, will be used to process a data-binding string and turn it into a data reference. It will determine the class and attribute that correspond to the provided binding string. This method will also use the Runtime Type Services (RTTS) to determine information about the model class and details about the model attribute data type.

```
METHOD resolve_model_binding.
  DATA: l_for TYPE string.
  DATA: model            TYPE REF TO if_bsp_model_binding,
        metadata         TYPE REF TO if_bsp_metadata_simple,
        metadata_base    TYPE REF TO if_bsp_metadata,
        value_path       TYPE string.
  DATA: class_name TYPE string.
  model  = m_page_context->get_model( _for ).
  CALL METHOD
    cl_bsp_model=>if_bsp_model_util~split_binding_expression
    EXPORTING binding_expression = _for
    IMPORTING attribute_path     = value_path.
  CHECK value_path IS NOT INITIAL.
  system_state->model_string = _for.
  IF model IS NOT INITIAL.
    DATA: class_desc TYPE REF TO cl_abap_typedescr.
    class_desc = cl_abap_classdescr=>describe_by_object_ref(
          model ).
    class_name = class_desc->get_relative_name( ).
  ENDIF.
  l_for = model->get_attribute_name(
```

```
    attribute_path = value_path ).
  IF id IS INITIAL.
    CONCATENATE l_for '_1' INTO id.
  ENDIF.
****Get Data Reference to bound data object
  DATA: l_data TYPE REF TO data.
  l_data = model->get_attribute_data_ref(
      attribute_path = value_path ).
  CHECK l_data IS NOT INITIAL.

****Get the RTTI Drescriptor for this data reference
  DATA: descriptor TYPE REF TO cl_abap_elemdescr.
  descriptor ?= cl_abap_elemdescr=>describe_by_data_ref(
        l_data ).
****Read Data Dictionary information for this reference
  DATA: flddescr TYPE dfies.
  flddescr = descriptor->get_ddic_field( ).
  me->dataelement = flddescr-rollname.
  system_state->rollname = me->dataelement.
  ...
ENDMETHOD.
```

14.1.6 BSP F1 Help Controller Method—DO_REQUEST

Inside a stateless anonymous BSP application, we will fill our F1 Help popup starting with a new controller. For this controller, we will have a fairly normal DO_REQUEST method to control the flow of our application. As with most any high-level controller, we will have logic to initialize our model class.

However this initialization will be different from the normal model-view-controller (MVC) method. If the model is initial, which in stateless applications will always be true, we will need to read our keys from the URL with request->get_form_field. Then the model is restored with a call to cl_bsp_server_side_cookie=>get_server_cookie followed by the de-serialization.

14.1.7 Implementing the BSP F1 Help Application—Model

The final component in our help BSP application is the model class. This class has all the logic to read our field help or glossary entry. It also has the logic to convert the SAPEVENT hyperlinks. Do not forget to include the IF_SERIALIZABLE_OBJECT interface in this class definition. This is the interface that will allow us to convert the class instance to XML.

You can explore the complete logic to this class on the CD for this book. Although not related directly to BSP, it contains the logic for reading the help or glossary and converting the internal SAP ITF format to HTML.

14.2 Dialog Windows

In our first solution, we were able to open a new browser window with the JavaScript call `window.open`. This approach actually matches the SAP GUI solution fairly well. Users are able to minimize or move the help-off screen. You do have the disadvantage that if you close the browser window with your application, the help window still remains.

However this solution really is not optimal for a Value Help solution. With the popularity of the so-called popup blocker on the Internet, the technologies to create floating IFrames, which are movable and resizable using JavaScript, have also become quite popular. This design is really closer to what we are looking for in a Value Help solution.

Thanks to the open nature of BSP, you should be able to find most any JavaScript/DHTML example on the Internet that meets your needs and hook it into the BSP event system. For this text we are going to take an even more drastic approach. Web Dynpro will have just such dialog windows. SAP has already developed the JavaScript libraries for Web Dynpro, we will just need to adapt them for BSP. The JavaScript libraries in question are shipped for customer use as of Web AS 6.20 SP56 and 6.40 SP15 and can be found in the MIME repository—`/sap/bc/ur/design2002/js/popup*.js`.

How better to expose this Web Dynpro element than as its own BSP extension element. We start with a rather simple header element that has the responsibility of hooking into the event system for the dialog. It has three attributes. These attributes are an element ID, a server-side event ID named `onClick`, and a client side event JavaScript function named `onClientClick`.

The Web Dynpro JavaScript coding already has a hook to fire a custom JavaScript on the **Hide Dialog** event. We just need to connection our events into this hook. For this we have the following code. This allows us to create a JavaScript function that will fire an event on the client side, the server side, or both.

```
data: event_script type string.
data: id       type string value 'Parameter1'.
data: popup_id type string value 'Parameter2'.
event_script =
   cl_htmlb_manager=>render_event_call(
          bsp_element          = me
```

```
event_type          = 'click'
server_event        = me->onclick
client_event        = me->onclientclick
param_count         = 2
param_1             = id
param_2             = popup_id
client_event_inlined = 'X' ).
```

As we render out the JavaScript callback function within our element processing, we can just call the JavaScript function we just rendered.

```
concatenate html_out
  `<script>`
     `function ptrOnHideModalDialog(id,popupId)`
     `{`
       `if(typeof(id)=="undefined")`
         `return true;`
       `var check=true;`
       `if (popupId==''){ } else {`
        event_script `;}`
       `return check;`
    `}`
     `ptrDialogObj=new Object();`
     `ptrDialogObj.popupIdArray=new Array();`
    `</script>`
    into html_out.
me->print_string( html_out ).
rc = co_element_done.
```

We can now create individual BSP extension elements that make the call to the JavaScript functions provided by SAP to initialize the different types of dialog windows. Mostly this involves exposing customizing settings such as width and height and concatenating them into the JavaScript function.

```
concatenate html_out
  `<script>`
     `function ` me->clientevent `()`
     `{`
     `ptrPopup.ptrModalDialogUrl(window,`
     `'` me->url    `',`
     `'` me->title  `',`
     `'` me->style  `',`
        me->width  `,`
```

```
            me->height `,`
        `'` me->id     `');`
        `}`
`</script>`
into html_out.
me->print_string( html_out ).
rc = co_element_done.
```

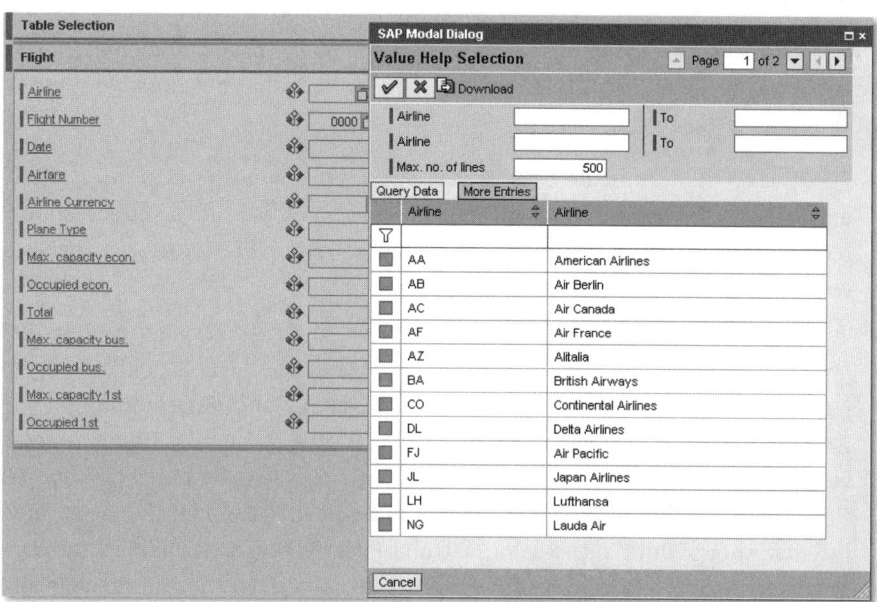

Figure 14.11 Dialog Window

Figure 14.11 demonstrates the rich UI that this dialog window functionality from SAP provides. You have window maximizing, resizing, dragging—basically everything that you would expect with any dialog window. However, this frame is not a separate window within the browser. Therefore it shares the same system state; if you close the browser window or navigate away from the application, it will close as well.

Not only does this solution fit nicely into the Value Help solution, but it also demonstrates how powerful the openness of BSP is. We were able to take an external JavaScript library that was originally designed for Web Dynpro and adapt this to BSP. You could have just as easily have integrated one of hundreds of open-source code samples from the Internet as well.

14.3 F4—Value Help

If you have worked in the classic ABAP Dynpro world, you probably learned to take for granted just how powerful and easy to use is the built-in functionality for Value Help. It is not until you begin BSP development that you realize just how much you miss all that functionality that you never really gave a second thought to.

14.3.1 Value Help Requirements

Once again, we are looking in the standard functionality provided by BSP for one possible way to fill this gap. Here are the requirements that this possible solution would need to meet.

- First this solution must be easy to use. We want only to have to insert a BSP extension in the source pages in order to use it. We want it to support model binding directly. So, to start we are going to have a BSP extension that is a wrapper around the `<htmlb:inputField>`.
- We wanted more than just a simple selection of data dictionary Help values from the local Web AS System. Simple value/description pairs could already be created easily with an `<htmlb:dropDownListBox>` and data binding on the `helpValues` attribute. The solution has to be able to support more complex value selections. An example of this is the common selection of User in reports. Just listing User ID or even User Name is not enough. We want to have a value list that shows **Building**, **Business Unit**, **First Name**, **Last Name**, etc. This means the value selection routine needs to have a powerful exit mechanism, similar to ABAP search helps, so that each consuming application can control the value list. It also needs to support complex search helps with one or more inner element search helps. Furthermore, it is rather common to have a separate Web AS for the backend data system, such as a separate R/3 system. This means that we also need to be able to retrieve the help values from a remote system via RFC.
- We want the **Help Values** display to be powerful but easy to use for the end user. The solution should have filtering and sorting capabilities on the value list. Therefore, the solution displays the Help Values in an `<htmlb:tableView>` element.
- The user needs to be able to choose more than one value from the help list. That means that our new BSP element will have to be a wrapper around `<htmlb:listBox>` as well as `<htmlb:inputField>`.
- The **Help Values** dialog needed to work in both stateful and stateless applications.

14.3.2 The Solution

Much as we did with F1 Field Help, we will create a new BSP extension element that will be a wrapper around existing elements. We will hook our own event into the `onValueHelp`.

When the user requests Value Help, this example will create a stateless, Model-View-Controller page that will be displayed in a floating IFrame dialog box. The solution will include the JavaScript that allows this IFrame to be dragged around the window like it was a modal dialog box.

Finally, this IFrame will write its selected values back into the source `<htmlb:inputField>` or `<htmlb:listBox>`. Figure 14.12 shows the most advanced version of this solution in action. This example is a complex search help with several elemental helps.

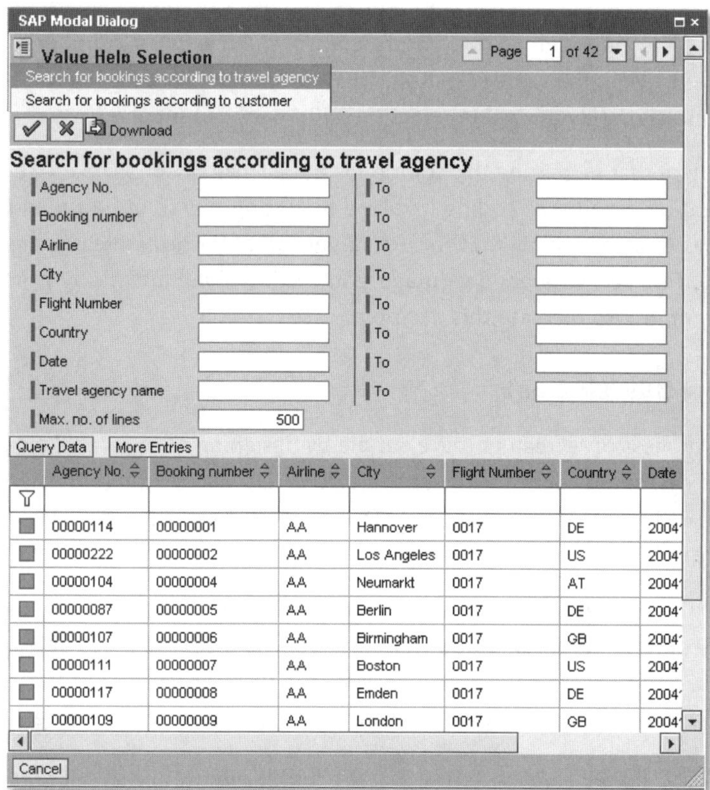

Figure 14.12 Value Help Example

At the top of the **Help Values** dialog we have a `<phtmlb:popupMenu>` that will be use to select elemental search helps if we are attached to a collective search help.

On the right side of this area, we also have navigation controls for moving through the result list that is displayed in an <htmlb:tableView>.

On the next line in the user interface we have the check-mark (for OK) and **Cancel** icons. Choosing the **OK** icon will fire the JavaScript to copy the selected value(s) back into the originating element. Selecting the **Cancel** icon, the **Cancel** button at the bottom of the dialog window, or the "X" Icon in the top right corner of the dialog window will all close the window without copying back any values. The final item on this line is the **Download** menu. This is actually another custom BSP extension element that will download the value results as Excel, XML, or HTML. This solution is discussed in detail in Section 16.5.

The next area shows input fields that can be used to narrow our selection. Although the value output is displayed in an <htmlb:tableView> with sorting and filtering turned on, we want to support more opportunities to reduce our value results than what a single filter could accept. Finally, we have an input field called **Max. no. of lines**. This input field allows you to control the maximum number of records that are returned in the value selection. This is helpful for keeping the runtimes low on the initial display of a value selection with many potential results.

We should state here that recreating this solution is not a small or simple exercise. There is a signification amount of coding involved in getting this solution up and running in your system. The coding for the current version of this example is available on the book CD. We strongly encourage you to download and study it in detail before attempting to recreate this example.

14.3.3 The New BSP Element

We will start the process of recreating this example by designing our new BSP element. As we said earlier, we want to trigger the Value Help dialog from either an <htmlb:inputField> or <htmlb:listBox>. Therefore, just as with the F1 Field Help solution, we will want to copy all the attributes from these inner elements.

Far more interesting, however, will be the new attributes that we must add to support the three different types of **Value Help** dialogs. The first type is the determination of the search help via data reference from the local system only. Of the three approaches, this is the one that we are going to look at in detail in this text.

To support this type of dialog, we will add one attribute called dataRef of type STRING. It must contain the name of the data dictionary field that we will use to determine the search help.

```
<% data: data2 type sflight-carrid.  %>
<ybook:inputHelp id       = "In2"
```

```
                    value    = "<%= data2%>"
                    dataRef = "SFLIGHT-CARRID" />
```

Although this method is simple to use, a better approach might be to also determine the `dataRef` value dynamically from the data object that is being passed into the `value` attribute. To do that, we really just need a static class method to look up the `help-id` for us.

```
method read_field_type.
* Input: FIELD                       TYPE ANY
* Returning: VALUE( DATAREF )   TYPE STRING
  describe field field help-id dataref.
endmethod.
```

Listing 14.1 Method READ_FIELD_TYPE of Class YCL_ABAP_UTILITIES

```
<% data: data2 type sflight-carrid. %>
<ybook:inputHelp id      = "In2"
                 value   = "<%= data2%>"
               dataRef   = "<%=
   YCL_ABAP_UTILITIES=>READ_FIELD_TYPE( data2 ) %>" />
```

Listing 14.2 Modified Use of our Value Help Element

14.3.4 Input Help Controller

Because the rendering logic of the BSP extension element is really very similar to the F1 Field Help, we will skip ahead and look instead at the application that resides inside the **Value Help** dialog.

Once again, we will create the content of the dialog as a separate stateless MVC application. Our entrance into this application will be through a controller. This controller will be responsible for reading the keys for the value selection from the URL and initializing the model class.

Because this is a stateless application, the instance of our model class is lost after each request/response cycle. We could have taken a similar approach to the F1 Field Help and serialized the model class to a server cookie. However, due to the nature of the processing when working with the search-Help function modules and/or BAPIs, doing this would not have provided much value. Therefore we simply recreate the model fresh for each cycle.

The most important role of the controller, however, will be choosing which of the three logic paths we want to take based upon the attributes that were set in the calling BSP element.

```
****Requested Simple Help Values
  if not model2->data_ref is initial.
    model2->get_helpvalues_complex( ).
****Requested Help Values Via an RFC Exit
  elseif not model2->rfcfunction is initial.
    model2->get_helpvalues_exit( ).
  elseif not model2->objtype is initial.
    model2->get_helpvalues_bapi( ).
  else.
    model2->message = 'Element ID can not be blank'(e03).
  endif.
```

14.3.5 Input Help View

For the most part, the view for the UI rendering is fairly standard. We use a `<xhtmlb:toolbar>` to lay out the first two rows of the dialog that contain the element search help popup, the `<htmlb:tableView>` navigation, and then the buttons.

The values of the elemental search help popup menu are built dynamically using an internal table that is filled during model processing.

```
<%   if lines( model->bapishlp ) > 1.
     data: popupitems type phtmlb_popupmenuitems.
     field-symbols <wa_menu> like line of popupitems.
     field-symbols <wa_bapishlp>
                   like line of model->bapishlp.
     loop at model->bapishlp assigning <wa_bapishlp>.
      append initial line to popupitems assigning <wa_menu>.
      <wa_menu>-text = <wa_bapishlp>-title.
      <wa_menu>-MENUITEMID = <wa_bapishlp>-shlpname.
      <wa_menu>-enabled = 'X'.  <wa_menu>-cancheck = ''.
      <wa_menu>-checked = ''.   <wa_menu>-hasseperator = ''.
     endloop. %>
<phtmlb:popupTrigger id = "shlpPop"
           popupMenuId = "shlpMenu" >
 <htmlb:image src="pop1.jpg" />
</phtmlb:popupTrigger>
<phtmlb:popupMenu id = "shlpMenu"
     maxVisibleItems = "30"
     items           = "<%= popupitems %>" />
<%  endif. %>
```

Unfortunately, an <xhtmlb:toolbarButton> does not support the display of an icon. However, in our output we wanted to emulate the classic SAP GUI Value Help dialog with the buttons that display the green check mark and red "X." To accomplish this, we just rendered the image directly into the text of the button.

```
<% data image type ref to cl_htmlb_image.
   data image_string type string.
   create object image.
   image->id = `UserCancel2`.
   image->src = cl_bsp_mimes=>sap_icon( `ICON_INCOMPLETE` ).
   image->tooltip = ``.
   image_string = image->IF_BSP_BEE~RENDER_TO_STRING(
         page_context ). %>
<xhtmlb:toolbarButton id = "UserCancel"
   onClientClick = “ptrPopup.ptrHideModalDialog('CANCEL');"
   text          = "<%= image_string %>" />
```

The internal table that we will use for the value results must be a generic type. At design time, we have no idea what kind of structure this table will need. In the model, we have declared this internal table as TYPE REF TO DATA. Later in the model-processing logic, you will see the code necessary to dynamically redefine this internal table. However, because this internal table is just a reference to a generic data object, we must pass it to the <htmlb:tableView> by first assigning it to a field symbol.

```
<% field-symbols: <tab> type table.
   assign model->idata->* to <tab>.
   if <tab> is assigned. %>
<htmlb:tableView id = "ml_users"
   ...
              table = "<%= <tab> %>"
   ... />
<% endif. %>
```

The last interesting aspect of the view is the dynamic creation of the input fields. Because the definition for the input fields varies depending upon the search-Help we are working with, the fields' UI coding must be dynamic as well. To simplify this process, we will rely upon model binding to bring our values back in from the browser on input. We will use the dynamic-binding-string approach that we learned about in Section 13.4.

```
<% field-symbols: <wa_mvc> like line of model->shlp_mvc.
   data: input_string type string.
```

```
   data: input2 type ref to cl_htmlb_inputfield.
   data: input_id type string.
   data: tabix type string.
   data: label type string. %>
<phtmlb:formLayout labelAlignment         = "LEFT"
                   design                 = "SOLID"
                   verticalLineSeparation = "TRUE"
                   fieldToLabelFactor     = "1.0"
                   customizationKey       = "ZE0002" >
<% loop at model->shlp_mvc assigning <wa_mvc>.
     move sy-tabix to tabix.
     condense tabix.
     create object input2.
     concatenate <wa_mvc>-select_fld tabix '_low'
           into input2->id.
     condense input_id no-gaps.
     input2->_value = <wa_mvc>-bind_low.
     input2->size   = 15.
     input2->maxLength = 30.
     label = <wa_mvc>-TITLE.
     input_string = input2->IF_BSP_BEE~RENDER_TO_STRING(
           page_context ). %>
    <phtmlb:formLayoutItem idOfItem = "<%= input2->id %>"
                           label    = "<%= label %>" >
     <%= input_string %>
    </phtmlb:formLayoutItem>
...
</phtmlb:formLayout>
```

There is one last thing that we will use model binding for. Remember that because our Value Help dialog application is stateless, our model instance will be lost. However, there is a small amount of data that we would like to retain about the state of the model. The simple approach to accomplishing this is to just write these items out to hidden input fields. The values will then be restored automatically thanks to data binding.

```
<htmlb:inputField value   = "//model/SHLPNAME"
                  visible = "FALSE" />
```

14.3.6 Input Help Model

The final piece to the puzzle in the Value Help example is the model class itself. We are only going to look in detail at the method, GET_HELPVALUES_COMPLEX, which supplies the logic for one of the three approaches that we support. Once you understand the processing of one of the three methods, you will see that the other two amount to slight variations in processing.

The goal of this method was to have all of the functionality of the GET_HELPVALUES_BAPI, but with much less complexity in its use. This method only runs locally, but requires just a data type. From this data type we will determine what Help values, if any, are available and process the results into the same output structures as used in GET_HELPVALUES_BAPI. We thus will not be requiring any changes to the UI coding to support both methods.

We start this method by setting a default 500 rows of returned values in case no value was supplied for max_rows. Next, we want to validate that the data_ref attribute was supplied and passed in. Both of these fields are required and validated in the extension element, but it never hurts to check.

```
METHOD get_helpvalues_complex .
  IF me->max_rows IS INITIAL.
    me->max_rows = 500.
  ENDIF.
  DATA: field TYPE REF TO data.
  TRANSLATE me->data_ref TO UPPER CASE.
  IF me->data_ref IS INITIAL.
    me->message =
      'Data Type of Value Help can not be blank'(e02).
    RETURN.
  ENDIF.
```

We now will dynamically create a variable of whatever type was passed in. This will allow us to further validate that we have a correct data type.

```
  DATA: error4 TYPE REF TO cx_sy_create_data_error.
  TRY.  CREATE DATA field TYPE (me->data_ref).
  CATCH cx_sy_create_data_error INTO error4.
      me->message = error4->get_text( ).
      RETURN.
  ENDTRY.
```

Next, we will use the ABAP Runtime Type Information (RTTI) classes to further check our data element, making sure it is a data-dictionary type. We will then also use the RTTI to query for the help id attached to the object. If this help id references a structure and a field we will need to split them in two, `tabname` and `fieldname`, before further processing.

```
DATA: rtti TYPE REF TO cl_abap_elemdescr,
      fixvalues    TYPE ddfixvalues,
      l_help_value TYPE shsvalstr2.
DATA: l_typename    TYPE dfies-tabname,
      l_compname    TYPE dfies-fieldname.
rtti ?= cl_abap_typedescr=>describe_by_data_ref( field ).
if rtti->is_ddic_type( ) = abap_false.
    MOVE 'Input type not DDIC Type'(e99) TO me->message.
    RETURN.
ENDIF.
DATA: l_helpid TYPE string.
IF me->data_ref CS '-'.
   l_helpid = me->data_ref.
ELSE.
   l_helpid = rtti->help_id.
ENDIF.
CONSTANTS: component_separator TYPE c VALUE '-'.
SPLIT l_helpid AT component_separator
   INTO l_typename l_compname.
```

In the next section, we get some help from some SAP-provided function modules. First, we call `DD_SHLP_GET_HELPMETHOD`. This will return whatever search help, complex or elemental, that is attached to our help ID.

This is another validation that there is Value Help attached to our element. If the object returned was a complex search help, we need to expand that object out so that we have all the details about its inner search helps as well.

It is safe to pass even an elemental search help through the function module `F4IF_EXPAND_SEARCHHELP`. It will only create an internal table with the single record for the elemental help. This way we have a common interface to work with through the rest of our processing.

```
DATA: shlp TYPE shlp_descr.
CALL FUNCTION 'DD_SHLP_GET_HELPMETHOD'
  EXPORTING  tabname                    = l_typename
             fieldname                  = l_compname
  CHANGING   shlp                       = shlp.
IF shlp-fielddescr IS INITIAL.
```

```
    MOVE 'No Help Values Available'(e98) TO me->message.
    RETURN.
  ENDIF.
  DATA: shlps TYPE shlp_desct.
  CALL FUNCTION 'F4IF_EXPAND_SEARCHHELP'
    EXPORTING shlp_top = shlp
    IMPORTING shlp_tab = shlps.
```

We next have a section to record the listing of inner-element search helps if we have a complex search help. We remove characters that are not HTML- safe from the search-help descriptions because we are using these descriptions in a `<phtmlb:popupMenu>` later.

```
  FIELD-SYMBOLS: <wa_bapishlp> LIKE LINE OF me->bapishlp.
  FIELD-SYMBOLS: <wa_shlp> LIKE LINE OF shlps.
  CLEAR me->bapishlp.
  IF LINES( shlps ) > 1.
    LOOP AT shlps ASSIGNING <wa_shlp>.
      APPEND INITIAL LINE TO me->bapishlp
             ASSIGNING <wa_bapishlp>.
      MOVE <wa_shlp>-shlpname TO <wa_bapishlp>-shlpname.
      MOVE <wa_shlp>-shlptype TO <wa_bapishlp>-shlptype.
      MOVE <wa_shlp>-intdescr-ddtext TO <wa_bapishlp>-title.
      REPLACE ALL OCCURENCES OF  '/'
           IN <wa_bapishlp>-title WITH space.
      ...
    ENDLOOP.
  ENDIF.
```

If the user has not selected a search help yet, or there is only one search help to choose from, we will initialize to the first record. Otherwise we will read our listing of elemental search helps to find a match to the one the user has selected.

```
  IF me->shlpname IS INITIAL.
    READ TABLE me->bapishlp ASSIGNING <wa_bapishlp>
         INDEX 1.
    IF sy-subrc = 0.
      me->shlpname = <wa_bapishlp>-shlpname.
      me->shlptype = <wa_bapishlp>-shlptype.
      me->shlpdesc = <wa_bapishlp>-title.
    ENDIF.
    READ TABLE shlps INTO shlp INDEX 1.
```

```
ELSE.
  READ TABLE me->bapishlp ASSIGNING <wa_bapishlp>
       WITH KEY shlpname = me->shlpname.
  me->shlptype = <wa_bapishlp>-shlptype.
  me->shlpdesc = <wa_bapishlp>-title.
  READ TABLE shlps INTO shlp
   WITH KEY shlpname = me->shlpname.
ENDIF.
```

Now, we come to the processing section, where we will take an input-selection criterion from the UI and turn it into a valid range.

```
FIELD-SYMBOLS: <wa_mvc> LIKE LINE OF me->shlp_mvc.
FIELD-SYMBOLS: <wa_sel> TYPE ddshselopt.
LOOP AT me->shlp_mvc ASSIGNING <wa_mvc>.
  APPEND INITIAL LINE TO shlp-selopt ASSIGNING <wa_sel>.
  MOVE-CORRESPONDING <wa_mvc> TO <wa_sel>.
  MOVE <wa_mvc>-select_fld TO <wa_sel>-shlpfield.
  <wa_sel>-sign = 'I'. "Inclusive
  IF <wa_sel>-high IS NOT INITIAL.
    <wa_sel>-option = 'BT'.
  ELSEIF <wa_sel>-low CA '*' or
         <wa_sel>-low CA '+'.
    <wa_sel>-option = 'CP'.
  ELSEIF <wa_sel>-low IS NOT INITIAL.
    <wa_sel>-option = 'EQ'.
  ENDIF.
ENDLOOP.
```

We are almost ready to call DD_SHLP_GET_HELPVALUE to actually perform our value selection. However, before we do, we will take a backup copy of the selection fields. We do this so that we can return our input parameters back to the screen with the results.

```
DELETE shlp-selopt  WHERE low IS INITIAL.
DATA: b_shlp TYPE zes_shlp_mvc_tbl.
b_shlp[] = me->shlp_mvc.
DATA: fcat TYPE lvc_t_fcat.
FIELD-SYMBOLS: <wa_fcat> LIKE LINE OF fcat.
DATA: fname TYPE lvc_fname.
CLEAR me->tbl_def.
FIELD-SYMBOLS: <wa_def> LIKE LINE OF me->tbl_def.
```

```
DATA: l_output TYPE TABLE OF seahlpres.
DATA: l_shlp LIKE shlp.
l_shlp = shlp.
CALL FUNCTION 'DD_SHLP_GET_HELPVALUES'
  EXPORTING maxrows       = me->max_rows
  TABLES    output_values = l_output
  CHANGING  shlp          = l_shlp.
CLEAR me->shlp_mvc.
DATA: new_shlp(1) TYPE c.
DATA: tabix TYPE string.
IF b_shlp IS INITIAL. new_shlp = 'X'.
ELSE. me->shlp_mvc[] = b_shlp[].
ENDIF.
```

We now will build a listing of all the input fields for the search help that was returned as well. This allows us to setup the table of input fields that we will dynamically generate in the output view.

```
FIELD-SYMBOLS: <wa_fields> LIKE LINE OF shlp-fielddescr.
LOOP AT shlp-fielddescr ASSIGNING <wa_fields>
 WHERE fieldname NE '_HIGH'.
  APPEND INITIAL LINE TO fcat ASSIGNING <wa_fcat>.
  APPEND INITIAL LINE TO me->tbl_def ASSIGNING <wa_def>.
  <wa_fcat>-col_pos =   <wa_fields>-position.
  <wa_fcat>-fieldname = <wa_fields>-fieldname.
  <wa_def>-columnname = <wa_fields>-fieldname.
  MOVE 'X' TO <wa_def>-sort.
  <wa_fcat>-datatype  = 'CHAR'.
  <wa_fcat>-inttype   = 'C'.
  <wa_fcat>-intlen    = <wa_fields>-leng.
  <wa_def>-title      = <wa_fields>-scrtext_m.
  IF new_shlp = 'X'.
    APPEND INITIAL LINE TO me->shlp_mvc
           ASSIGNING <wa_mvc>.
    <wa_mvc>-select_fld = <wa_fields>-fieldname.
    <wa_mvc>-title      = <wa_fields>-scrtext_m.
  ENDIF.
ENDLOOP.
```

We are now ready to build our internal table of input fields for the search help. First, we have code to process multiple input values for the same item. We want to make sure that we have at least one input field for each item that is empty and ready for input. This is where we will build a **More Values** item. Next, we build our binding string for the low and high values in our range.

```
DATA: last_field TYPE string.
DATA: last_value TYPE string.
LOOP AT me->shlp_mvc ASSIGNING <wa_mvc>.
  MOVE sy-tabix TO tabix.
  CONDENSE tabix.
  IF last_field = <wa_mvc>-select_fld AND
         <wa_mvc>-low IS INITIAL AND
         last_value IS INITIAL.
    DELETE me->shlp_mvc.
    CONTINUE.
  ELSEIF last_field = <wa_mvc>-select_fld.
    <wa_mvc>-title = '  ...More Values'(001).
  ELSE.
    READ TABLE shlp-fielddescr ASSIGNING <wa_fields>
      WITH KEY FIELDNAME = <wa_mvc>-select_fld.
    <wa_mvc>-title = <wa_fields>-scrtext_m.
  ENDIF.
  MOVE <wa_mvc>-select_fld TO last_field.
  MOVE <wa_mvc>-low        TO last_value.
  CONCATENATE '//model/shlp_mvc[' tabix
              '].low' INTO <wa_mvc>-bind_low.
  CONCATENATE '//model/shlp_mvc[' tabix
              '].high' INTO <wa_mvc>-bind_high.
ENDLOOP.
```

Next we will dynamically create an internal table that has the data structure of the returned values for the Search Help. For this example, we stayed with the CL_ALV_TABLE_CREATE method for creating the internal table so that the coding will be compatible with Web AS 6.20. If you are on Web AS 6.40, you are welcome to replace this with calls to the RTTS.

For simplicity, after creating our dynamic internal table, we query the structure of the internal table with a call to a static method in a helper class called YCL_ABAP_UTILITIES . The source code for this class is also available for download with the rest of this example.

```
CALL METHOD cl_alv_table_create=>create_dynamic_table
    EXPORTING  it_fieldcatalog = fcat
    IMPORTING  ep_table        = me->idata
```

```
             e_style_fname    = fname.
  FIELD-SYMBOLS: <tab>          TYPE table,
                 <wa>           TYPE any,
                 <f>            TYPE any.
  ASSIGN me->idata->* TO <tab>.
  APPEND INITIAL LINE TO <tab>.
  DATA: struct TYPE extdfiest.
  FIELD-SYMBOLS <wa_desc> LIKE LINE OF struct.
  CALL METHOD ycl_abap_utilities=>get_table_structure
    EXPORTING itab   = me->idata
    RECEIVING struct = struct.
```

Finally, we come to the most complex part of the processing in this method. We need to move the data from our generic search-help result structure into the dynamic internal table. To make sure that all data is displayed properly, we will need to look up and process any attached conversion exits for each field. To make matters even more complex, all the data in the search-help results is returned in a single string. Therefore, we have to dynamically parse out this string based upon the definition of receiving internal table.

```
  CLEAR <tab>.
  DATA: conv_exit(10) TYPE c.
  FIELD-SYMBOLS: <wa_values> LIKE LINE OF l_output.
  DATA: tabix_tmp TYPE sytabix.
  LOOP AT l_output ASSIGNING <wa_values>.
    APPEND INITIAL LINE TO <tab> ASSIGNING <wa>.
****For each component (field) in the table -Output the data
    LOOP AT struct ASSIGNING <wa_desc>.
      ASSIGN COMPONENT sy-tabix OF STRUCTURE <wa> TO <f>.
      CHECK sy-subrc = 0.
      READ TABLE shlp-fielddescr ASSIGNING <wa_fields>
            WITH KEY fieldname = <wa_desc>-fieldname.
      CHECK sy-subrc = 0.
      IF <wa_fields>-fieldname = '_HIGH'.
        tabix_tmp = sy-tabix + 1.
        READ TABLE shlp-fielddescr
             ASSIGNING <wa_fields> INDEX tabix_tmp.
        IF sy-subrc = 0.
          IF <wa_fields>-convexit IS NOT INITIAL.
            CLEAR conv_exit.
            CONCATENATE '==' <wa_fields>-convexit
```

```
                INTO conv_exit.
          WRITE <wa_values>-string+<wa_fields>-
                offset(<wa_fields>-leng) TO <f>
                USING EDIT MASK conv_exit.
        ELSE.
          WRITE <wa_values>-string+<wa_fields>-
                offset(<wa_fields>-leng) TO <f>.
        ENDIF.
      ENDIF.
      me->key_field = '_LOW'.
      RETURN.
    ELSE.
      ...
    ENDIF.
  ENDLOOP.
ENDLOOP.
```

We now only have to set the key field so that the JavaScript in the UI knows what element from the returned value list to pull out and pass back to the originating input field.

```
  IF me->key_field IS INITIAL.
    IF l_compname IS INITIAL.
      me->key_field = l_typename.
    ELSE.
      me->key_field = l_compname.
    ENDIF.
  ENDIF.
ENDMETHOD.
```

15 Internationalization

In today's global economy, successful businesses rarely operate in only one language or geographic region. With globalization comes many technical challenges. In this chapter we will look at the tools and techniques in BSP that will allow you to open your applications to a whole new world.

15.1 Multiple Language Support

SAP software has always been known for its strong support for internationalization. SAP's core product, R/3, is used around the world and is available in 40 country versions and 30 different languages. SAP currently has installations in 140 countries around the world.

BSP joins the rest of the ABAP toolset with its strong support for multiple languages and code pages. In this chapter, we will examine several aspects of BSP that support internationalization. Figure 15.1 demonstrates how the same BSP page can support multiple languages. This page receives much of its translated content automatically, using the techniques we will discuss in this chapter.

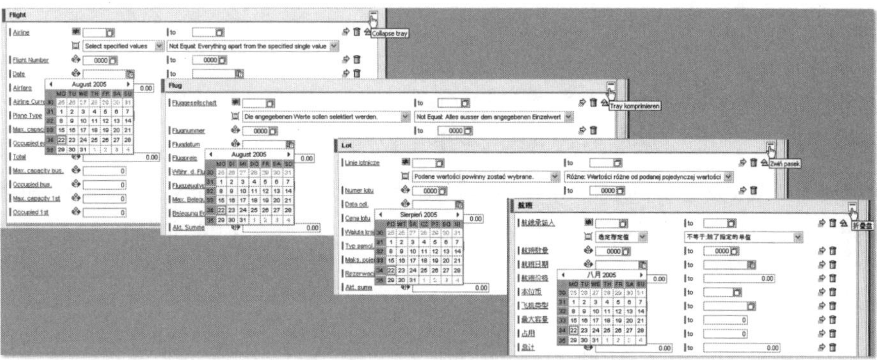

Figure 15.1 Multi-Language Example: English, German, Polish, Chinese

The most important aspects of supporting multiple languages require that you only use two of the BSP development techniques already discussed in this book: BSP Extensions and Model View Controller. As Figure 15.1 demonstrates, the tooltip for the expand/collapse button on the `<htmlb:tray>` is translated into each of the different languages, as is the calendar in the help for the input field. However, the developer did not have to perform this translation. Because this application reuses the SAP-delivered extension elements, SAP has already done the translation for you. This is just one more reason to rely upon the extension framework and SAP's delivered elements.

You might also notice that our `<htmlb:label>` and `<htmlb:dropDownListBox>` values were all translated as well. These translations are coming directly from their definitions in the data dictionary. SAP has supplied translations for these values as well. However, by using Model View Binding, we do not even need logic to pull the correct language versions of these descriptions. The data-binding logic will perform all the language-specific selections for us.

15.2 Logon Language

When you log onto the SAP system via the traditional SAP GUI method, you must select a language from the logon screen. This selection has two effects. First, it sets the language that will be used for the user interface. This effect is fairly obvious and probably the only thing that most people suspect is happening when they choose the logon language. However, the system could also be setting the correct code page to match your logon language. This allows processing of texts in order to be correctly stored in the database when your system is set up to work with multiple languages. All of this occurs provided that your system is not Unicode (see Chapter 15.3), in which case all languages are contained in a single code page.

BSP applications running in Web AS 6.40 and higher can be configured to have similar logon screens, as shown in Figure 15.2, but not every application will be configured to go through a manual logon screen. You might have configured Single Sign-On for instance; in which case no logon screen at all would be displayed.

There are actually several different ways that BSP applications can have their logon languages set. They are layered one on top of the other in a hierarchy of checks. The order that they are listed in this text is the order in which the BSP runtime processes them.

- In transaction SICF, if the service has the flag **Logon Data Required** set, the system uses the language that is entered in the **Anonymous Logon Data** area.
- If no setting is maintained in SICF, but the HTTP request contains the language in the HTTP header—either as a header or as a form field—this logon language will be used. The field that the runtime is looking for is called `sap-language`. You can supply a value to this field as an ISO language ID, such as EN for English or DE for German. If you want to test this field's abilities, simply add the field to the URL string in the browser after loading a BSP application:

  ```
  http://<host>/sap/bc/bsp/sap/ybsp/book.htm?sap-language=DE
  ```

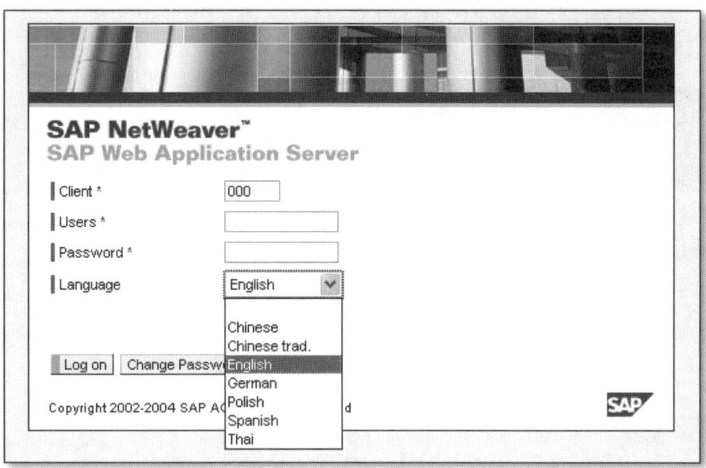

Figure 15.2 BSP Application Logon Screen

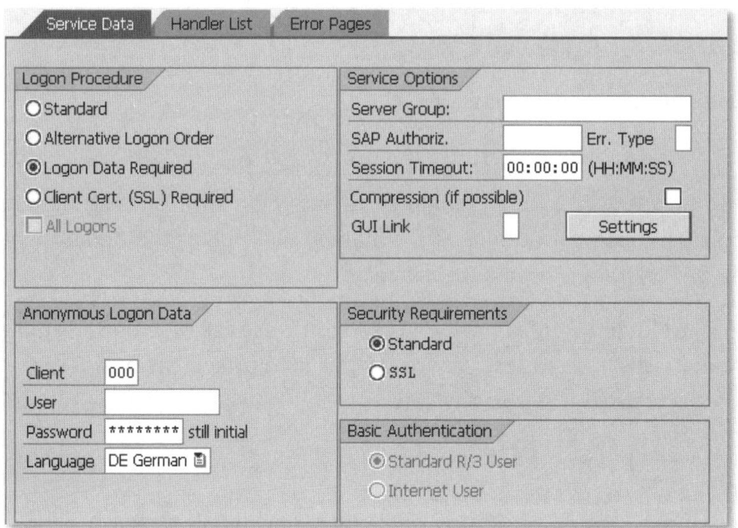

Figure 15.3 Language Determination via SICF

- If it is still impossible to determine a language, the system then will look at the browser settings. The system selects as the logon language the first language from the list in the browser that matches one of the installed installed languages in the SAP system. With Internet Explorer, you can set the language by choosing **Tools • Internet Options • Languages**. Technically, the browser transfers this value using the HTTP header field `accept-language`.

Figure 15.4 Language Setting in Internet Explorer

- If no language can be determined up to this point, the classic SAP system mechanisms are used. The logon language is based on the user settings, in transaction SU01. Finally, if nothing is maintained even here, the default language of the SAP system is used automatically.

You might find it useful to be able to switch the logon language of your BSP application programmatically. The easiest way to do this is to attach the `sap-language` header field to your URL as you navigate.

```
DATA:           params TYPE tihttpnvp.
FIELD-SYMBOLS: <wa_params> LIKE LINE OF params.
APPEND INITIAL LINE TO params ASSIGNING <wa_params>.
<wa_params>-name = 'sap-language'.
<wa_params>-value = 'DE'.
DATA: bsp_abs_url TYPE string.
CALL METHOD
     cl_bsp_runtime=>construct_bsp_url
  EXPORTING in_application = runtime->application_name
            in__page       = runtime->page_name
            in_parameters  = params
  IMPORTING out_abs_url    = bsp_abs_url.
```

```
currenttime = sy-uzeit.
CALL METHOD cl_http_server=>append_field_url
  EXPORTING name  = 'sap-unique'
            value = currenttime
  CHANGING  url   = bsp_abs_url.
navigation->exit( url ).
```

Listing 15.1 Switching the Logon Language to German

In the above listing, we have used two different techniques for appending a form field to the URLs (`cl_bsp_runtime=>construct_bsp_url` and `cl_http_server=>append_field_url`) in order to demonstrate their use. Also note that reloading the current application with a different logon language will require that, in a stateful application, we get a new session. Therefore we will lose access to any stateful data we had in memory.

That is also the reason we are attaching the `sap-unique` header field as well. If our application is stateful, it may be running within a frame that uses JavaScript to watch the URL for changes and destroy the session when no longer needed. However by only adding a different language to the URL, this JavaScript may not pickup the change. The addition of the `sap-unique` header can assist in this determination.

15.3 Unicode

15.3.1 What is Unicode?

A brief explanation of Unicode is in order here. Computers do not understand human language characters; they only understand numbers. A mapping table is therefore necessary to connect characters to numbers for output to human-readable displays.

Ideally, there would have been one single mapping that gave every character in every language a unique number of its own. This would have required more than one byte per character. Years ago, when computer memory was expensive, the overriding concern when it came to any design was the conservation of memory. Therefore different languages were separated in code pages and numeric values were reused from code page to code page. This allowed a single character from most languages to be represented by only one byte. However, it introduced the complexity that only one code page could be used at a time and consequently limited the number of languages that could be processed together.

With the advent of the Internet age and globally operating businesses, it is no longer possible to work in one or just a few languages. Today's applications need to be usable in just about any language known to man. This is where Unicode comes into play.

Unicode uses multiple bytes per character in order to have a single code page that holds every character from every modern language, and even some not- so-modern ones. One might think that this would solve all incompatibility problems when it comes to characters and code pages.

Unfortunately that is not the case. There are several different implementations of Unicode that use a different number of bytes per character, varying in use from one to four bytes. The three major flavors are UTF-8, UTF-16, and UTF-32. UTF-8 uses as little as 1 byte per character and as many as 4 bytes. UTF-16 uses a minimum of 2 bytes per character and as many as 4 bytes. Unlike UTF-8 and UTF-16, UTF-32 uses the same number of bytes (4) for every character. This has the advantage of not requiring any processing overhead for the variable byte conversion, but the disadvantage of requiring the largest amount of memory.

To complicate matters further, when you work with Unicode you also must consider the Byte Order Mark, or BOM. When you have two or more bytes representing a character, the processing program of these characters needs to know which byte is the significant one.

Significant byte has to do with how the underlying hardware architecture stores the bytes in memory. Big Endian means that the most significant byte is stored in the lowest memory address. Some architectures that use this approach are Motorola 68000 and SPARC. Little Endian means that the least significant or littlest byte is stored in the highest memory address. This method is used in Intel X86 and DEC VAX.

Therefore, a Unicode string should begin with a special BOM that signifies what byte order to use when processing the string. This BOM also can be used to determine the encoding as well. The following table lists the BOMs and explains what is meant by significant byte.

Bytes	Encoding Form
00 00 FE FF	UTF-32, Big-Endian
FF FE 00 00	UTF-32, Little-Endian
FE FF	UTF-16, Big-Endian

Table 15.1 Possible Values for the BOM

Bytes	Encoding Form
FF FE	UTF-16, Little-Endian
EF BB BF	UTF-8

Table 15.1 Possible Values for the BOM (cont.)

15.3.2 Unicode in BSP

Use of a Unicode Web AS clearly solves many problems for processing in multiple languages. If your Web AS is Unicode, it can process input or output data in any of SAP's supported languages.

But what if you are running on a system that has not yet been converted to Unicode? This is, after all, the more likely situation, given that Unicode conversions and installations for the Web AS are just now beginning to become common. Because of the higher memory requirements for Unicode, many customers will be putting off Unicode conversions for quite a few years.

However, there are some techniques that allow you to take advantage of Unicode within BSP even on a non-Unicode Web AS. You should use these techniques with caution, as their improper use could lead to data corruption.

The first technique is the use of the BTF WYSIWYG HTML editor. This BSP extension element supports the use of binary strings in Unicode format for transferring the data to or from the editor control in the browser. The `<btf:editor>` element was discussed in detail in Section 12.1.

But instead of a full blown HTML editor, let us say you only want to display some text strings. And, suppose these strings all come from a different code page in a back-end Multi Display Multi Processing (MDMP) system. MDMP is the pre-Unicode, SAP-specific technology that allows the processing of multiple code pages within a single system. However, MDMP has a major restriction in that only one code page can be processed at a time. Therefore in our situation, where we want to display descriptions from three different languages, we receive data corruption during the output, as shown in Figure 15.5.

Test
EN: Test - English
PL: Niezapamiêtane dane zostan± utracone w m
TH: ¶éÒ·èÒ¹ÂÑ§¤§·Ó¡ÒÃà¢éÒãªé§Ò¹â´ÂäÁè¨º¡ÒÃà¢

Figure 15.5 MDMP Display Data Corruption

We can start correcting this corruption by setting the MIME type on the **Properties** tab of the BSP page. With the MIME type setting, we override the default character set for the page generated by the system and force the ICM to publish the page as Unicode.

```
text/html; charset=UTF-8
```

This effectively sets the browser to Unicode encoding, but does nothing to the data stream itself. Therefore, as Figure 15.6 demonstrates, we now have corruption because the text streams are not Unicode encoded.

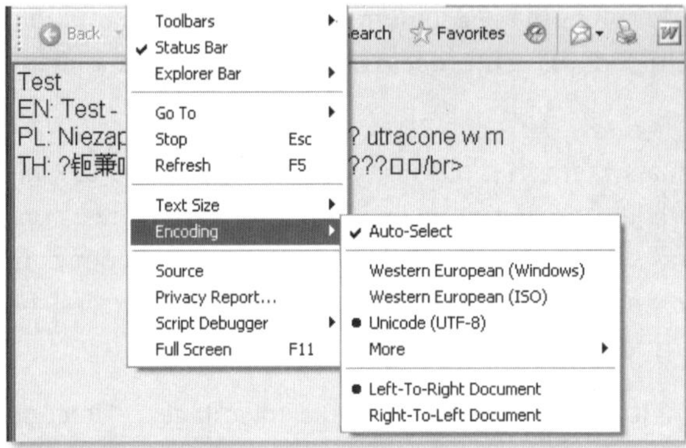

Figure 15.6 Browser Set to Unicode, But Corruption Still Occurs

Although we have taken a step in the right direction, we obviously need to do something to convert our individual text strings to Unicode as well. The first step in this process will be to create an RFC destination in transaction SM59 (Figure 15.7) for each language we want to read data from. This allows us to logon to that language and temporarily set our code page correctly to read the text string from the database.

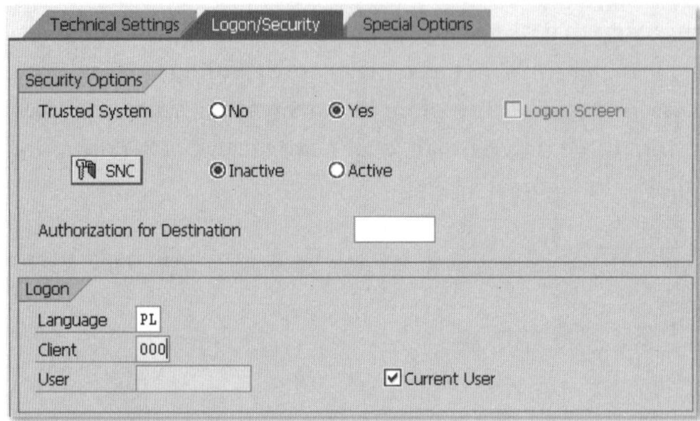

Figure 15.7 RFC Setup per Language

Inside the processing of our RFC that will be called through each destination, we will already be set to the correct code page. Therefore we can read the data from the database without corruption. To preserve the data while passing it back to the calling BSP page, we will convert the text string to a binary string before returning it.

```
FUNCTION y_e_rfc_lang_test1.
*"-----------------------------------------------------------
*"*"Local interface:
*" EXPORTING
*"     VALUE(O_XSTRING) TYPE  XSTRING
*"-----------------------------------------------------------
  DATA: dktxt TYPE dktxt.
  SELECT SINGLE dktxt FROM drat INTO dktxt
          WHERE dokar = 'ISS'
            AND doknr = '0000000010000000000002195'
            AND dokvr = '00'
            AND doktl = '000'
            AND langu = sy-langu.
  FIELD-SYMBOLS: <f> TYPE x.
  ASSIGN dktxt TO <f> CASTING TYPE x.
  MOVE <f> TO o_xstring.
ENDFUNCTION.
```

Once back in the processing of our BSP page, we have our binary string. Now we just need to convert that binary string into a Unicode text string. For that we will use the SAP function module SCP_TRANSLATE_CHARS. Before converting, however, we will cross-reference the standard external name of the code pages into the SAP internal numbers using the function module SCP_CODEPAGE_BY_EXTERNAL_NAME.

```
METHOD translate_pl.
  DATA: encoding TYPE string.
  DATA: codepage TYPE cpcodepage.
  encoding = 'iso-8859-2'.
  CALL FUNCTION 'SCP_CODEPAGE_BY_EXTERNAL_NAME'
    EXPORTING  external_name = encoding
    IMPORTING  sap_codepage  = codepage.
  DATA: codepage2 TYPE cpcodepage.
  encoding = 'utf-8'.
  CALL FUNCTION 'SCP_CODEPAGE_BY_EXTERNAL_NAME'
    EXPORTING  external_name = encoding
    IMPORTING  sap_codepage  = codepage2.
```

```
  DATA: xdocument_length    TYPE i.
  xdocument_length = XSTRLEN( me->pl_xstring ).
  CALL FUNCTION 'SCP_TRANSLATE_CHARS'
    EXPORTING  inbuff          = me->pl_xstring
               inbufflg        = xdocument_length
               incode          = codepage
               outcode         = codepage2
               substc_space    = 'X'
               substc          = '00035'
    IMPORTING  outbuff         = me->pl_string.
ENDMETHOD.
```

We can now output our Unicode text string to the BSP without any further special processing and receive the uncorrupted output as shown in Figure 15.8

```
<htmlb:form>
  <OTR>Test</OTR><br>
  EN: <%= application->en_string %></br>
  PL: <%= application->pl_string %></br>
  TH: <%= application->th_string %></br>
</htmlb:form>
```

Test
EN: Test - English
PL: Niezapamiętane dane zostaną utracone w m
TH: ถ้าท่านยังคงทำการเข้าใช้งานโดยไม่จบการเข

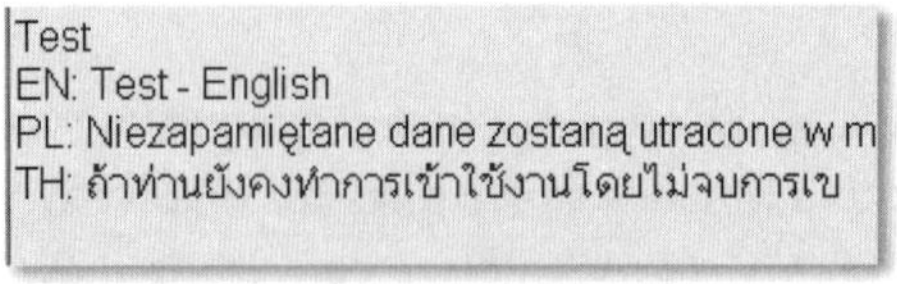

Figure 15.8 Normal Output Thanks to Unicode

15.4 Online Text Repository (OTR)

Through out this text you may have noticed the use of the following syntax:

```
<htmlb:textView text   = "<OTR>Hello!</OTR>"
                design = "HEADER1" />
```

Perhaps you were curious why text literals were quite often surrounded by the <OTR> tag. This technique is very similar to the following syntax in standard ABAP.

```
write:/ 'Hello!'(001).
```

Both techniques have the same purpose: to expose a text-literal string to translation.

The term OTR actually stands for *Online Text Repository*. By surrounding any text literal in your BSP application with OTR identifiers, you have in effect separated your text from the BSP coding. Not only is the text stored separately now, but it is stored in a language-dependent format. This means that for a single text string you could have several different language versions.

The BSP runtime will automatically retrieve the correct language version based upon the user's logon language. If no translated texts exist in that language, the BSP runtime will automatically substitute with the corresponding text version from the system language.

15.4.1 Types of OTR: Alias and Long

There are actually two different forms of OTR texts; Alias texts and Long texts. Alias texts are those texts that are reused frequently and are less than 255 characters. These texts are stored independently of the BSP page they are used on. This supports reuse and consistency from application to application. This also gives you the opportunity to reuse the thousands of terms that SAP has already translated in the standard system.

These texts are formatted a little differently when used in your BSP page.

```
<htmlb:textView text   = "<%= otr($tmp/ybook_test1) %>"
                design = "HEADER1" />
```

The downside is that you cannot display or maintain the text for your editing language from within the BSP page itself. You must double-click on the OTR string to even be able to view the text. This reduces the overall readability of your page coding.

When you do double click on the OTR string, an editor window is brought up (Figure 15.9). From here you must set the maximum length for the text across all translations. You can also set the text for the language in which you are currently editing your page.

OTR aliases also support the concept of contexts as well. This allows you to create variations of your text strings for a particular country or industry. However a system may only have one country and one industry context value set for it. That means that a single system cannot support both Spanish – Mexico and Spanish – Spain.

In Figure 15.10, we see how we might use the context to create a variation on the English greeting "Hello" that better suits our friends "down under."

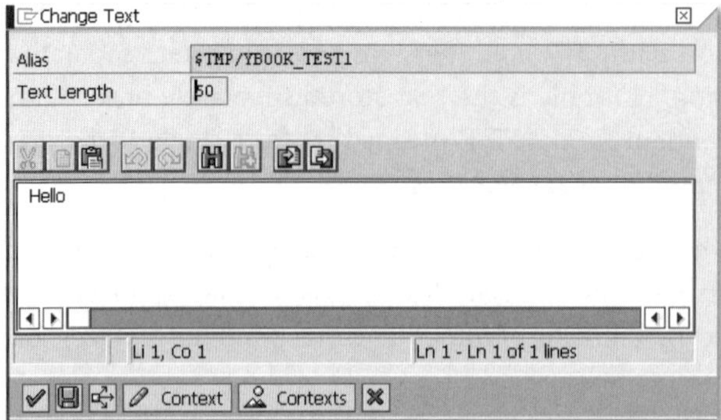

Figure 15.9 OTR Alias Editing

Contexts Display

Ctry	Indust.	ContextFl...	Text
		X	Hello
AU			G'day Mate

Figure 15.10 Australian Context for Hello

The other form of OTR is called the Long Text. This OTR type has the advantage of being able to maintain the texts directly from within the BSP page or view. However this also means that this text object is stored only with the page in question. These objects cannot be shared across multiple pages. This makes this variant of OTR suitable for longer strings, entire sentences instead of single words, that are not often used.

15.4.2 Working with OTR from ABAP Code

So far, we have looked at the OTR within the context of a BSP Page or view only. However, OTR texts actually can be used in any ABAP coding via a few supplied ABAP classes. This is useful for processing texts, such as error messages, within event handling or program flow.

To make OTR programming easy with BSP, the runtime object, class `CL_BSP_RUNTIME`, has a method called `GET_OTR_TEXT`. This method functions very similarly to the use of the OTR Alias in a page or view. You simply supply the OTR Alias, and a text stream with the results will be returned. The method handles the switch to the system language for you if the text is not available in the current logon language. If the method cannot find the alias, an error is not raised. The method simply returns an empty string in that situation.

```
METHOD get_otr_text
  IMPORTING alias TYPE string
  RETURNING text  TYPE string.
```

If you do not have easy access to the BSP Runtime object, you can also choose to use the class CL_BSP_GET_TEXT_BY_ALIAS. It has a single static method called GET_TEXT. The main difference between the runtime method and this one is that the CL_BSP_GET_TEXT_BY_ALIAS=>GET_TEXT also has an importing parameter that allows you to specify the language that you wish to retrieve the text for. This gives you the ability to get a text other than the one that matches your logon-language.

```
METHOD get_text
   IMPORTING language   TYPE sylangu
             alias      TYPE string
   RETURNING alias_text TYPE string.
```

15.4.3 Special Note about using OTR

There is special aspect of using OTR that should be made clear. If you create an OTR string and then translate it into two different languages, the lengths of the translation in two different languages often may be very different. Therefore, a long OTR string could have a very short translation in a different language.

However, the OTR system is so designed that it stores a length of the original text with the string and will always return the string filled with trailing spaces. This causes perfectly normal HTML rendering to produce some strange output. For example a button that is suddenly much too wide.

Luckily, there is a solution for this problem. There is a page directive that will have the BSP compiler automatically generate additional code to CONDENSE each <OTR> sequence after it has been looked up.

```
<%@page language="ABAP" otrTrim="true" %>
```

15.5 Translation

We have so far discussed the techniques for enabling our BSP applications to support multiple languages. However, this does not do us much good if we do not know how to translate our elements and in turn use those translations.

15.5.1 OTR

Although OTR texts can be translated using the Translation Workbench, transaction SE63, we do not really want to focus on the overall translation tool. The translation workbench may be worth studying on its own if you are serious about doing full blown translation projects. More likely, you will just want to translate a few texts within your own pages.

This simple translation effort can be performed directly in the ABAP Workbench. In the Workbench, we can choose menu **Goto · Translation**. In the context of a BSP page or view, we should have two options: one for OTR Long texts, and one for OTR short texts.

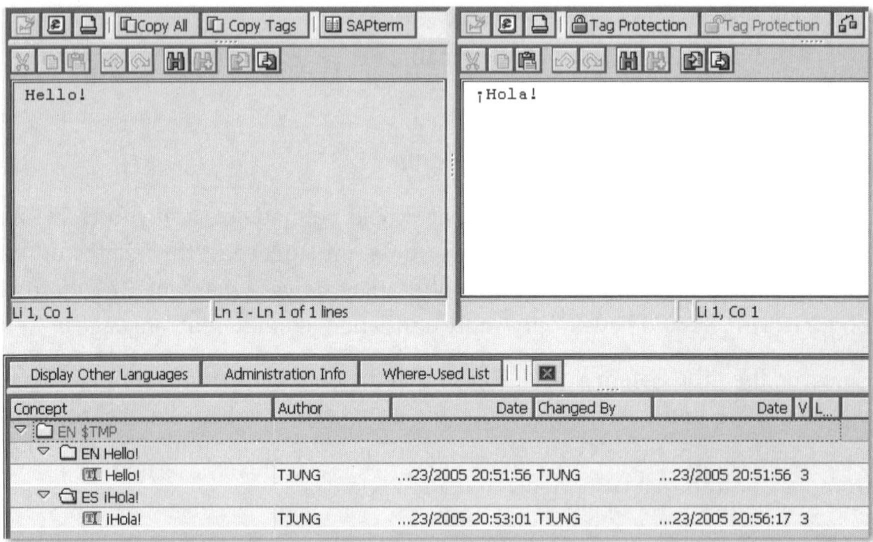

Figure 15.11 OTR Long-Text Translation Tool

The two tools do have slightly different user interfaces because of their different focuses. The Alias editor assumes you have a single word or small phrase. Therefore, it provides only the single-line input area for the translation.

The OTR Long Text supports larger groups of words and phrases. It is also designed to protect HTML tags that might be included amongst the text you are translating. Further, it allows language-dependent application of bold and italics attributes.

Figure 15.13 demonstrates the translated output of our two example OTR elements in English and in Spanish.

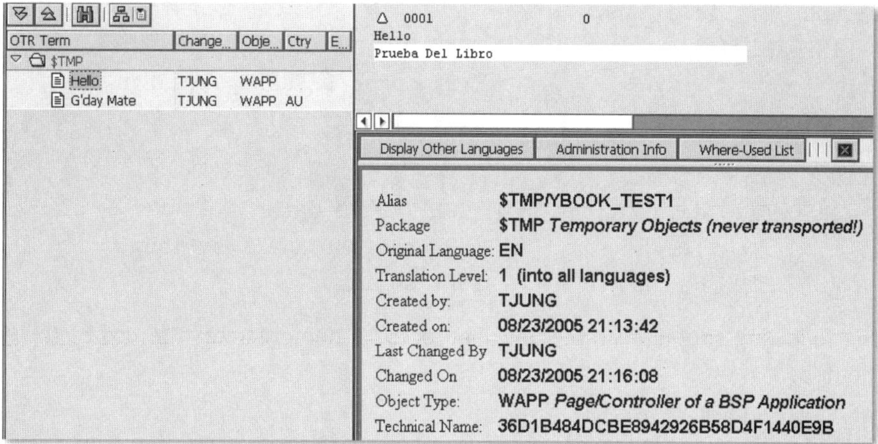

Figure 15.12 OTR Alias Text Translation Tool

Figure 15.13 Translation Output

15.5.2 Field Labels and Quick Info

As we use `<htmlb:inputField>` and `<htmlb:label>`, we quite often need to fill texts from the corresponding data-dictionary fields. Reusing the translations that already exist in the data dictionary will save you time and provide an even greater level of consistency than just using OTR texts alone.

As we noted earlier, if you use Model View Controller, the framework will automatically pull the correct language version of these kinds of texts for you.

But what if you are not using MVC? You could of course write your own custom SQL to read the texts directly from the database tables that house these texts. But repeating this custom logic all through out your applications is unnecessary. SAP has provided methods of the `DDIC_UTILS` object for retrieving texts for both Field Labels and Quick Info. The `DDIC_UTILS` object is already available in most parts of your BSP application as an attribute of the `RUNTIME` object instance.

For both methods you only need to supply a reference to any data object. You can also override the default logon language if you wish.

```
METHOD get_field_label
   IMPORTING data_object_ref TYPE REF TO data
             langu           TYPE spras DEFUALT sy-langu
   RETURNING label           TYPE string.

METHOD get_quickinfo
   IMPORTING data_object_ref TYPE REF TO data
             langu           TYPE spras DEFUALT sy-langu
   RETURNING quickinfo       TYPE string.
```

The following simple example and Figure 15.14 demonstrates the use of these methods.

```
<htmlb:form>
  <% DATA: l_matnr  TYPE matnr.
     DATA: data_ref TYPE REF TO data.
     GET REFERENCE OF l_matnr INTO data_ref.  %>
  <htmlb:label for      = "test"
        text     = "<%= runtime->ddic_utils->get_field_label(
                          data_ref ) %>"
        tooltip = "<%= runtime->ddic_utils->get_quickinfo(
                          data_ref ) %>" />
</htmlb:form>
```

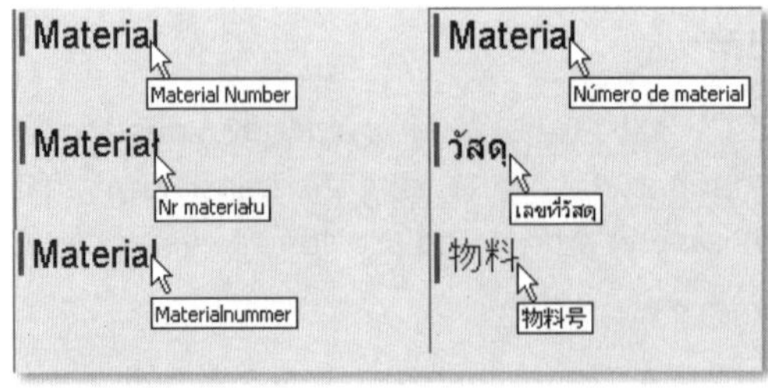

Figure 15.14 Automatic Field Label and Quickinfo Translation

15.6 Date Format

So far, our discussion about internationalization has focused on character strings and translation. However, the output format of dates is also an import aspect to consider as well. There are many different formats used around the world. Let us, for instance, consider two of these different formats: DD.MM.YYYY and MM/DD/YYYY. In this case 01.12.2000 is a very different date than 01/12/2000.

In order to support various date formats, ABAP stores dates internally as an eight-position character string:YYYYMMDD.

By using the BSP Extension Element <htmlb:inputField>, you can avoid any problems with the conversion from the internal to external date formats and automatically use the format that the user has selected in his or her SAP user profile.

```
<% DATA: current_date TYPE sydatum.
  current_date = sy-datum.
  DATA: data_ref TYPE REF TO data.
  GET REFERENCE OF current_date INTO data_ref. %>
  <htmlb:label for     = "AsString"
       text    = "<%= runtime->ddic_utils->get_field_label(
                      data_ref ) %>"
       tooltip = "<%= runtime->ddic_utils->get_quickinfo(
                      data_ref ) %>" />
  <htmlb:inputField id    = "AsString"
                    value = "<%= current_date %>"
                    type  = "STRING" /><br>
  <htmlb:label for     = "AsDate"
       text    = "<%= runtime->ddic_utils->get_field_label(
                      data_ref ) %>"
       tooltip = "<%= runtime->ddic_utils->get_quickinfo(
                      data_ref ) %>" />
  <htmlb:inputField id       = "AsDate"
                    value    = "<%= current_date %>"
                    showHelp = "TRUE"
                    type     = "DATE" />
```

In this code example and in Figure 15.15, you can see how setting the type of the <htmlb:inputField> to DATE triggers the extension to properly support various date formats.

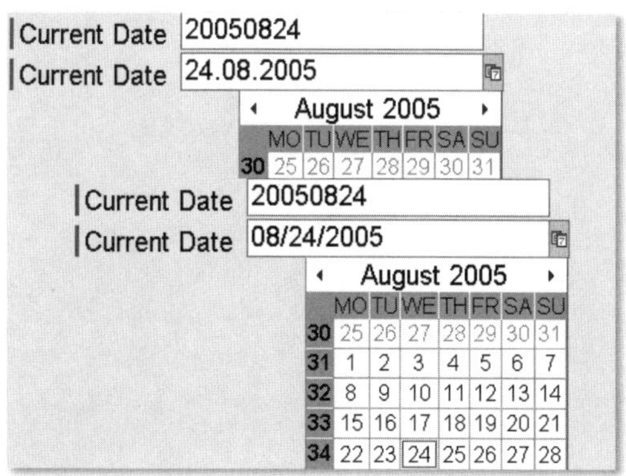

Figure 15.15 Different Date Formats for a German and English Logon User

16 Document Handling in BSP

Excel files, PDF documents, ZIP files, images: Before long you will need to process at least one of these document types within your BSP application. This chapter explains how to accomplish this for many non-HTML documents.

16.1 MIME Repository

BSP applications like any Web-based application are going to have a need reference existing MIME objects. Although MIME actually stands for Multipurpose Internet Mail Extensions, the term has come to represent any non-HTML or XML content such as images and style sheets.

To facilitate this need, SAP delivers the MIME repository as an integrated component of the ABAP Workbench. The MIME objects themselves are stored in the underlying database. However, they are represented through the MIME repository as a hierarchy of folders and items, much like the file system of a traditional Web server. This allows MIME objects to be referenced via relative path from within BSP applications.

```
<img src="../public/bsp_book/example.jpg">
```

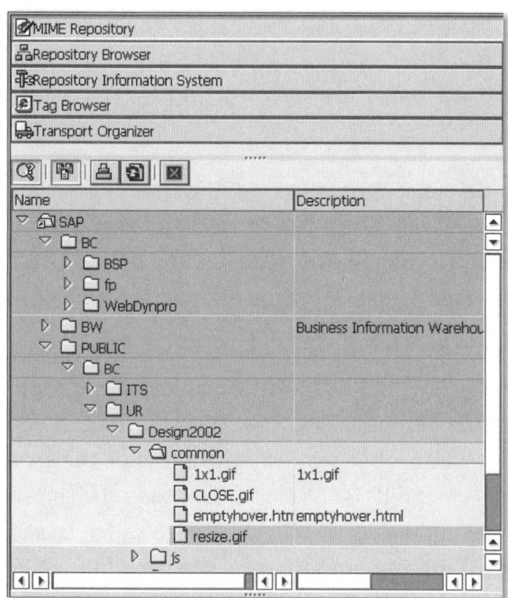

Figure 16.1 MIME Repository View in SE80

The MIME Repository browser, as shown in Figure 16.1, displays the complete hierarchy of all folders and items. Solutions other than BSP use the MIME Repository; however a new folder is automatically created for each BSP application.

MIME objects can also be created or imported for use in a specific BSP application without having to ever go through the MIME Repository. These objects are placed in the automatically created folder that represents each BSP application.

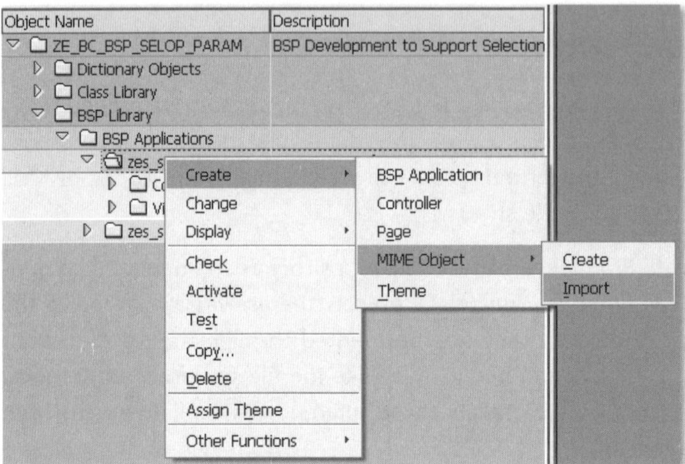

Figure 16.2 Import MIME Objects Directly into a BSP Application

Once you have one or more MIMEs attached to a BSP application, they will show up in the object browser along with the other components of the BSP application (shown in Figure 16.3). From this view, you can update or display the MIME objects as well.

All of the traditionally SAP GUI icons are also stored in the MIME repository and ready to use in BSP applications. However it is best not to refer to them directly via their relative path. SAP may decide to change this path at some point. Also if you want to support RTL (right-to-left) rendering, there are a separate set of icons with a different MIME path.

The best approach is to use the class `CL_BSP_MIMES` to retrieve information about the standard SAP Icons. There is a static method called `SAP_ICON` that allows you to retrieve the full path for an icon MIME object by supplying either the icon name, such as `ICON_CHECKED`, the ABAP icon ID, such as `@01@`, or the ABAP internal name, such as `@S_OKAY@`. The BSP application `IT00` has a page called `mime_sap_icons.htm` that does an excellent job of demonstrating the use of `CL_BSP_MIMES` as well as listing all possible icons with their IDs, internal names, icon names, and MIME names.

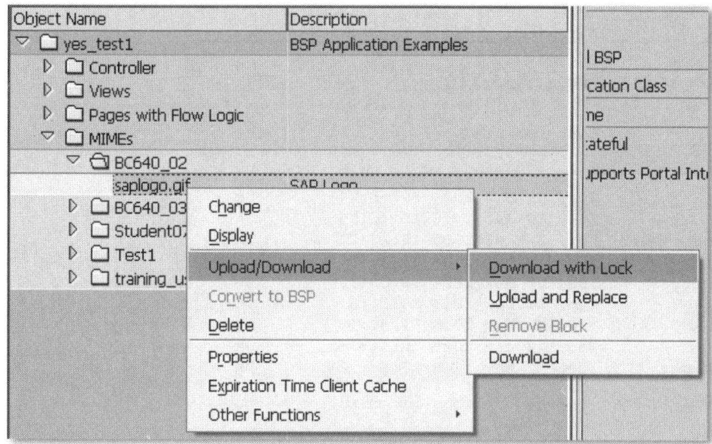

Figure 16.3 MIME Objects Inline in the BSP Application View

16.2 ICM File Handler

The MIME repository is great for storing and cataloging MIME objects that are necessary for use in our BSP applications. It supports the transport mechanism and translation. But sometimes we might need a simpler solution that does not require objects to be uploaded in advance and stored in the system's database.

The Internet Communication Manager (ICM) allows just such access to any file system accessible to the underlying operating system. You can map operating file system directories into ICM URL paths using the profile parameter icm/HTTP/file_access_<xx>.

If you have never maintained one of the system-profile parameters, now is good time to make friends with your Basis administrator. With the following additions to our instance profile and a quick restart of the ICM, we are now able to access file system directories via HTTP.

```
icm/HTTP/file_access_0 =
        PREFIX=/doc/, DOCROOT=/usr,BROWSEDIR=2

icm/HTTP/file_access_1 =
        PREFIX=/doc2/,
        DOCROOT=\\server\SAPPatches\Netweaver04,BROWSEDIR=2
```

In the first entry, we are just going to map to the local directory usr. We are able to control the user's options to browser a directory via the additional parameter BROWSEDIR. The possible values are: 0 – no browsing allowed, 1 – only file names are displayed, and 2 – file names along with their size and last change date are displayed.

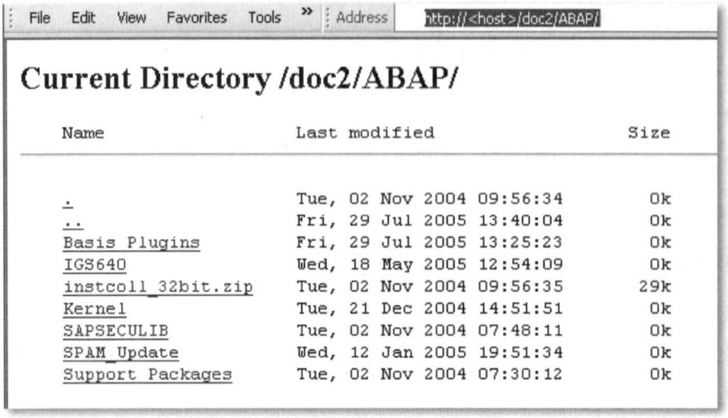

File Edit View Favorites Tools » Address http://<host>/doc2/ABAP/

Current Directory /doc2/ABAP/

Name	Last modified	Size
.	Tue, 02 Nov 2004 09:56:34	0k
..	Fri, 29 Jul 2005 13:40:04	0k
Basis Plugins	Fri, 29 Jul 2005 13:25:23	0k
IGS640	Wed, 18 May 2005 12:54:09	0k
instcoll_32bit.zip	Tue, 02 Nov 2004 09:56:35	29k
Kernel	Tue, 21 Dec 2004 14:51:51	0k
SAPSECULIB	Tue, 02 Nov 2004 07:48:11	0k
SPAM_Update	Wed, 12 Jan 2005 19:51:34	0k
Support Packages	Tue, 02 Nov 2004 07:30:12	0k

Figure 16.4 ICM FILE_ACCESS browse

The second entry really shows off the power of this profile parameter. We are able to expose a directory on a remote server via UNC paths. Of course the security on that directory would have to be open to allow read-and-browse access. There is also no real mechanism to apply security to the ICM URL for this file access node, so you will want to be careful what you expose through it.

16.3 Handling Non-HTML Documents

BSP pages contain, effectively, HTML. When binary objects are requested, they are placed in the MIME repository and referenced from there. However, it is often necessary to handle binary objects or documents during the runtime of the program. It is not feasible to place these runtime documents in the MIME repository. For any change in the MIME repository, transport records are written. This is usually not possible on a production system, and is relatively slow compared to the runtime requirements of the running BSP application.

Some real world examples are:

- For a personnel system, all colleagues' pictures are available in a database table and must be displayed as part of an HTML page.
- To use an ActiveX object, like Flash or SVG plug-in, the application dynamically generates XML data that is available for the plug-in via HTTP.
- Some internal data is converted into a PDF document that must be displayed in the browser.

Assume we are somewhere on a BSP page and we wish to display the complete document. A typical example: A button is pressed for a receipt, and then a PDF document must be displayed.

A slightly more complex example is to display the new document as part of an HTML page. This requires that the HTML page must be rendered back and then, on a second HTTP request, the document is fetched and displayed in the same page.

The last approach is to open a new window and display the document in the window.

16.3.1 Test Program

Our first step is to build a small test program to have a document available to display. As we do not feel like generating PDF documents on the fly or reading images from some database table for this simple example, we will instead just upload the test document from the client. In all cases, we assume that either an image (`.jpg`, `.gif` or `.png`) or some "known" document (`.pdf`, `.doc`, `.xls`, etc.) is specified.

After the document is uploaded, we have it "in our hands" and must do something with it. Keep in mind that after the response is processed, our session will be closed because this example is a stateless program.

First, we create a new BSP application and add a few page attributes:

```
file_length     TYPE  STRING
file_mime_type  TYPE  STRING
file_name       TYPE  STRING
file_content    TYPE  XSTRING
display_type    TYPE  STRING
display_url     TYPE  STRING
```

The four `file_*` attributes reflect the dynamic document that we "created" via an upload. Note that the content is of type XSTRING because we are working with binary documents.

The next step is to write the BSP application that will do the upload.

```
<%@page language="abap" %>
<%@extension name="htmlb" prefix="htmlb" %>
  <htmlb:content design="design2003" >
    <htmlb:page>
      <htmlb:form method       = "post"
                  encodingType = "multipart/form-data" >
        <htmlb:radioButtonGroup id="display_type" >
          <htmlb:radioButton    id = "inline"
```

```
            text="Display Inline" />
       <htmlb:radioButton    id = "html"
            text="Display Inside HTML Page" />
       <htmlb:radioButton    id = "window"
            text="Display In New Window" />
     </htmlb:radioButtonGroup>
     <htmlb:fileUpload id          = "myUpload"
                       onUpload    = "HandleUpload"
                       upload_text = "Display"
                       size        = "90" />
     <hr>
     <br>Name = <%= file_name%>
     <br>MIME-Type = <%= file_mime_type%>
     <br>Length = <%= file_length%>
   </htmlb:form>
  </htmlb:page>
</htmlb:content>
```

Listing 16.1 Layout

Here the <htmlb:*> BSP extension is used to create two elements on the web page. The first is a radio-button group to see which of the test cases to execute. The next is the file-upload element. The encodingType attribute set for the <htmlb:form> is very important! This is absolutely required for file uploading.

The last and most important aspect is to retrieve the uploaded document from the HTTP request and to fill our page attributes with the correct values. This is done in the onInputProcessing event handler.

```
DATA: fileUpload TYPE REF TO CL_HTMLB_FILEUPLOAD.
fileUpload ?= CL_HTMLB_MANAGER=>GET_DATA(
                       request = request
                       id      = 'myUpload'
                       name    = 'fileUpload' ).
file_name      = fileUpload->file_name.
file_mime_type = fileUpload->file_content_type.
file_length    = fileUpload->file_length.
file_content   = fileUpload->file_content.

DATA: radioButtonGroup TYPE REF TO
      CL_HTMLB_RADIOBUTTONGROUP.
radioButtonGroup ?= CL_HTMLB_MANAGER=>GET_DATA(
                       request = request
```

```
                         id       = 'display_type'
                         name     = 'radioButtonGroup' ).
  display_type = radioButtonGroup->selection.
```

Listing 16.2 OnInputProcessing

The final results in the browser are shown in Figure 16.5.

Figure 16.5 Test Application User Interface

16.3.2 Display Document Inline

With this simplest approach, we have an incoming HTTP request for an HTML page. Instead of processing the BSP page, thus rendering out HTML code, we just send out the dynamic document that we uploaded so that it is displayed inline.

What do we have to do? In essence, write the content that we already have available into the HTTP response, and set the correct content data. Finally, inform the BSP runtime that the response has been completely written and that no further processing is required.

```
   ... code previously displayed above ...
  IF display_type = 'inline' AND
     XSTRLEN( file_content ) > 0.
    DATA: response TYPE REF TO if_http_response.
    response = runtime->server->response.
    response->set_data( file_content ).
    response->set_header_field(
       name  = if_http_header_fields=>content_type
       value = file_mime_type ).
    response->delete_header_field(
       name = if_http_header_fields=>cache_control ).
    response->delete_header_field(
       name = if_http_header_fields=>expires ).
```

```
    response->delete_header_field(
       name = if_http_header_fields=>pragma ).
    navigation->response_complete( ).
    RETURN.
  ENDIF.
```

Listing 16.3 OnInputProcessing

The `IF` statement checks that it is the inline test and that we actually have content available to display. The `set_data()` method writes the complete `XSTRING` into the response. The "Content-Type" HTTP header field is set. This MIME type is critical so the browser knows what is coming down the pipe.

Theoretically we also want to set the "Content-Length" HTTP header field. It is good programming practice within our HTTP framework to never manually set the content length field. It is the kernel-serialize code's task to determine the actual serialized length. This may depend on various side effects such as compression.

One can also consider deleting the three HTTP headers "Cache-Control", "Expires" and "Pragma". As BSP pages are effectively HTML pages with business data, the BSP runtime already pre-set these HTTP headers to indicate that BSP pages must not be cached. However, we are now reusing the HTTP response for our binary document. We can delete these headers.

The last problem is that after the `onInputProcessing` method, the layout is also processed. As a result, all output from the layout is also written into the response. Consequently, the `response_complete()` call informs the BSP runtime that the response is completed and no further processing is required.

Figure 16.6 shows how the browser now displays only the returned image.

Figure 16.6 Document Display Inline

16.3.3 Display Document Inside HTML Page

Displaying the document inside the existing HTML page is slightly more complex. The problem is that in the response we must write HTML coding in order for the browser to render the page. The HTML coding must reference the dynamic document that we have available at this very moment. The question arises: Where should we park the dynamic document until the browser has time to fetch it? Keep in mind that once the response has been processed, the session will be closed and we will lose everything we had in memory.

The solution is actually very simple and elegant. The ICM supports an excellent HTTP cache. Whenever a MIME object is retrieved from Web AS, it is also added into the ICM cache. All other requests for the same document are served directly from the cache and do not require a call to ABAP. These requests are processed in the kernel.

When we have the dynamic document on-hand, we can write it into the ICM cache. Thus, any HTTP requests for the document, actually for this specific URL, will retrieve the document from the cache.

The first significant part of the code is to write the dynamic document directly into the ICM cache.

```
... code previously displayed above ...
IF display_type = 'html' AND
   XSTRLEN( file_content ) > 0.
  DATA: cached_response TYPE REF TO if_http_response.
  CREATE OBJECT cached_response TYPE CL_HTTP_RESPONSE
      EXPORTING add_c_msg = 1.
  cached_response->set_data( file_content ).
  cached_response->set_header_field(
      name  = if_http_header_fields=>content_type
      value = file_mime_type ).
  cached_response->set_status( code = 200 reason = 'OK' ).
  cached_response->server_cache_expire_rel(
      expires_rel = 180 ).

  DATA: guid TYPE guid_32.
  CALL FUNCTION 'GUID_CREATE' IMPORTING ev_guid_32 = guid.
  CONCATENATE runtime->application_url '/' guid
         INTO display_url.
  cl_http_server=>server_cache_upload(
         url      = display_url
```

```
        response = cached_response ).
    RETURN.
  ENDIF.
```

Listing 16.4 OnInputProcessing

To write the information into the ICM cache, it is necessary to create a complete HTTP response. Keep in mind that the browser will later send an HTTP request for this document, to which the ICM cache will return the cached HTTP response directly.

First, we create a new HTTP response object and add a new message. The message contains the actual buffers required to move the document from the ABAP VM into the kernel.

The next few lines were already discussed above. We set the content into the response and the content type. The `set_status()` call is required to indicate to the browser that for the cached request-response cycle everything went perfectly.

The next aspect is to set the time that the dynamic document will stay in the ICM cache. Keep in mind that this time should be long enough for the browser to load all URLs referenced in the HTML page. However, there is no need to leave the document in the ICM cache for a long time. Here a value of 3 minutes (180 seconds) is used. Any time interval between 1 and 5 minutes should be OK.

The more difficult problem is which URL to use. This URL serves as the "address" of the dynamic document on the server. The browser will later fetch the document from the server with this key.

The first idea was to use the uploaded filename as part of the URL. In this case, take care to replace the "`:`" and "`/`" characters in the URL to make it a new valid URL. However, such a static type of URL does not scale very well. What happens if different people are running the same application and uploading the same generic document, for example: "travel_expenses.xls"? Then, each new response will overwrite the previous copy in the cache. Therefore, the recommendation is to use some form of random number (GUID) in the URL that is generated.

We could place the generated URL anywhere in the "namespace" of valid URLs. However, we recommend placing the URL in the "namespace" of the current active BSP application. You also could copy the document extension (`.doc`, `.gif`, etc.) from the uploaded filename into the URL. However, this is not critical. It is more important that the MIME type is set correctly in the HTTP response.

The last step is to place the document into the ICM cache.

With the above coding, we successfully created a new HTTP response in the ICM cache that can be addressed under the URL stored in `display_url` (page attribute of type `STRING`). The last step is to change the rendered HTML coding so that it also displays the uploaded document. For this, we just use an `<iframe>`. The following HTML sequence is added in the layout, just before the end of the page.

```
      ... code previously displayed above ...
   <% IF display_type = 'html' AND
         display_url IS NOT INITIAL. %>
      <iframe src="<%=display_url%>" width="100%"
              height="500px">
      </iframe>
   <% ENDIF. %>
 </htmlb:page>
</htmlb:content>
```

Listing 16.5 Layout

This is just an `IF`-guard to check for the specific case of displaying the document inline, plus the `<iframe>` sequence to load the newly created URL.

The output is as expected. Both the data about the dynamic document and the document itself are displayed as shown in Figure 16.7.

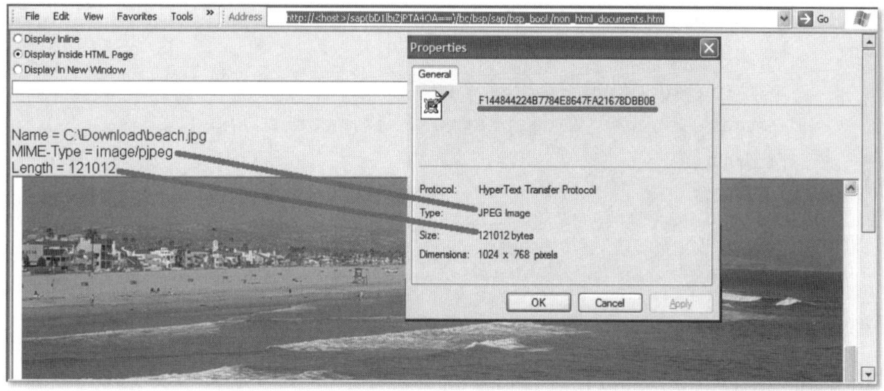

Figure 16.7 Document Display Inside Existing HTML Page

There is just one smaller problem with this approach that should not be forgotten. If the ICM cache is too small, or flushed by someone, we will get the dreaded broken image in the browser. But this is a small risk, considering the power of this technique.

16.3.4 Display Document in New Window

By now, most of the difficult work is complete. For the final leg of our explorations, we would like to place the dynamic document into a new window. The biggest problem is just how to trigger the opening of a new window.

It is not possible to open a new browser window from the server. The simplest technique is to open the new window directly in the browser with a small JavaScript sequence: `window.open(url)`.

The first step is to require the dynamic document stored as a URL on the server. All this coding is already in place. We just change the `IF`-guard to include this new case:

```
... code previously displayed above ...
IF ( display_type = 'html' OR display_type = 'window' )
   AND XSTRLEN( file_content ) > 0.
  ... code as previously displayed ...
ENDIF.
```

Listing 16.6 OnInputProcessing

Next, add the code in the layout to open the new window. This is quickly done with:

```
... code previously displayed above ...
<% IF display_type = 'window' AND
      display_url IS NOT INITIAL. %>
     <script language="Javascript">
       window.open("<%=display_url%>").focus();
     </script>
<% ENDIF. %>
 </htmlb:page>
</htmlb:content>
```

Listing 16.7 Layout

With the final results shown in Figure 16.8.

16.4 Data Manipulation

For binary documents, using `XSTRINGS` is always recommended. However, there are cases where it is worthwhile to have the data available as `STRING`, even if only for debugging! Another such case occurs when the data is actual text readable—as with XML data—and must be manipulated.

Figure 16.8 Document Display Inside New Window

One technique is to use the character interface of the request/response objects. For this, the `get_cdata()` and `set_cdata()` methods exist.

The alternative is to convert the `XSTRING` into a `STRING`. The simple sequence `string = xstring` does not work. A conversion can be done in ABAP using the following classes: `CL_ABAP_CONV_IN_CE` and `CL_ABAP_CONV_OUT_CE`.

Example coding for converting an `XSTRING` to a `STRING` is:

```
DATA: conv TYPE REF TO CL_ABAP_CONV_IN_CE.
conv = CL_ABAP_CONV_IN_CE=>CREATE( input = Xcontent ).
conv->READ( importing data = content len = len ).
```

Another alternative for converting `XSTRING` to `STRING` is use of the function modules contained in Function Group `SCMS_CONV`. There are also many function modules for converting from string types to internal tables or vise versa.

16.5 Microsoft Excel Download

If your users have a R/3 background, they might be slightly disappointed by the first reports and analytical applications that you build in BSP. Long-time SAP application users have grown accustomed to the impressive level of Microsoft Office integration that is delivered standard in SAP GUI transactions.

These users will especially miss the Microsoft Excel integration that is so commonly used, especially in the SAP ALV Grid. The ability to quickly download displayed data to Excel for some extensive analysis is a useful tool that your users will appreciate in their BSP applications.

In this section we will look at how to accomplish just this feat. We will start by studying how Excel reads its data files. We will then look at how to build a reusable component as a custom BSP extension element that will allow for simple inclusion of an Excel data download into just about any BSP application.

16.5.1 Excel Files

Before we get into the actual techniques for delivering Excel content from the BSP application through the browser and onto the client machine; we should first examine the way we want to format our data in ABAP so that it will be readable by Excel.

For this step we have several possible solutions. We could try to emulate the proprietary Office format. Even assuming you could find documentation on how Microsoft's internal format works, there is no guarantee of capability across the different releases of Office. In the end, this solution is needlessly complex.

A more viable option would be to use XML. While this seems like a logical choice because of XML's open nature, there are downsides. Not every version of Microsoft Office supports XML files. Also, due to the structure of the XML file needed to represent an Excel spreadsheet, the resulting XML file would be large and complex. This solution definitely adds to the amount of bandwidth needed to move the files to the client.

A third solution, and the one we will look at here in more detail, is the use of tab-delimited text files. Although this is not actually an open-standards-based approach, many applications have functionality to read tab-delimited text files due to their very simple structure. This simplicity also adds to the ease with which we can implement this solution within ABAP. This solution is also very commonly used in data downloads within the traditional SAP GUI R/3 environments. Finally, the size of the resulting dataset is usually quite reasonable, having very little overhead. There is one major drawback to this solution: we can only transfer the data itself, not any formatting information. If you need to retain any special formatting, such as fonts, macros, or calculations; you will want to look at the XML solution.

There are several different ways that you can convert your data from the internal ABAP formats into a tab-delimited string. The following is a simple code sample where we use control character definitions from the SAP class CL_ABAP_CHAR_UTILITIES.

```
DATA: l_string TYPE string.
LOOP AT itab INTO wa.
  CONCATENATE l_string wa-partner
     wa-adr_kind wa-addrnumber
```

```
      cl_abap_char_utilities=>cr_lf
      INTO l_string SEPARATED BY
           cl_abap_char_utilities=>horizontal_tab.
ENDLOOP.
```

This is obviously a simple example that requires specific knowledge of the data structure from which it originates. Later, we will see a code technique that works dynamically with internal tables by querying their structure definition through the RTTI[1].

16.5.2 Excel Unicode Text File

Once we have our data in a tab-delimited string, we need to decide what type of text format we want to use. Traditionally, ABAP programs would normally accept the use of regular text files. In the Internet environment, however, we should consider the use of Unicode tab-delimited text files.

There are two situations in which using a Unicode tab-delimited text file has definite advantages over the use of regular text files in avoiding data corruption. The first situation occurs when your SAP Web AS system is running as Unicode. If you download data from this Unicode system, you run a high risk that the data will not be read correctly by Excel unless you properly inform Excel that this file is Unicode.

The next situation can occur even in a non-Unicode Web AS system. If you are downloading Excel content to a client machine that has a different code page than the one your Web AS system is running on, data corruption will occur for any characters that are not common between the two code pages.

The image in Figure 16.9 demonstrates how data can be displayed correctly inline in the BSP application, but on the same computer it becomes corrupted once it is saved as a plain text file.

16.5.3 Unicode Formats and Endians with Excel

For general and detailed definitions of Unicode, Endians, and Byte Order Marks (BOMs), please see Section 15.4. For working with Unicode and Excel, the first thing we have to understand is what kind of Unicode file Excel wants. Excel expects a UTF-16 encoded file with a BOM of Little Endian, the native X86 Endian. Evidently all the Microsoft Office tools use UTF-16 when saving files in their primary format.

1 The SAP Runtime Type Information. This is a series of ABAP Classes that allow you to query the structure and type information for objects and object references.

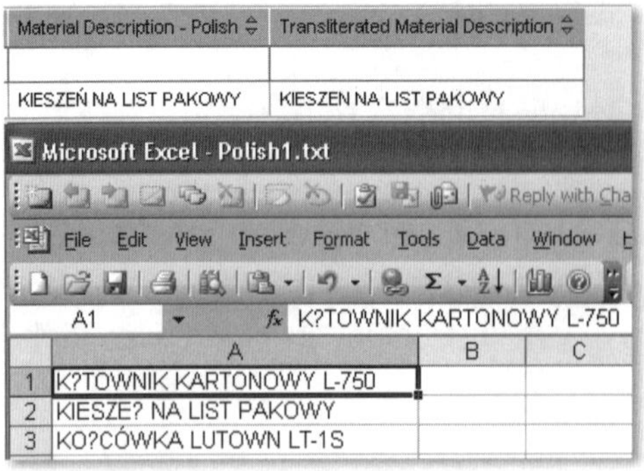

Figure 16.9 Plain Text File Data Corruption

If you want to verify this information, just open Excel and save a spreadsheet as Unicode text. This creates a tab-delimited text file in Unicode format. Then open the file in a Hex editor. You should see the UTF-16le, Little Endian, Byte Order Mark – FF FE – right at the beginning of the file.

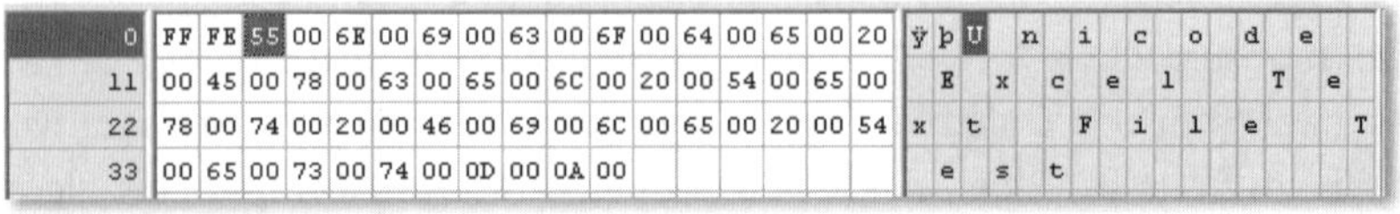

Figure 16.10 Unicode Text File Byte Order Mark as Seen from a Hex Editor

16.5.4 Conversion to Binary String

Earlier in this chapter, we assembled our ABAP data into a single string object. This string object will be encoded in whatever code page your Web AS system is currently running in. The next step to take will be to convert this string to a binary string. The conversion process gives us the opportunity to convert our character encoding from the internal Web AS code page to our needed UTF-16. Also by converting to a binary string, we will preserve the character encoding in our string. This allows us to have our string in UTF-16 even if our Web AS is not running the Unicode Kernel.

To accomplish this conversion, we will call the SAP-provided function module SCMS_STRING_TO_XSTRING.

```
DATA: l_xstring TYPE xstring.
CALL FUNCTION 'SCMS_STRING_TO_XSTRING'
  EXPORTING text     = l_string
            mimetype = app_type
  IMPORTING buffer   = l_xstring.
```

For this conversion to work, we must specify the character encoding that we want to use for the binary string. We do this through the mimetype parameter of the function call. The following is the value that we want to set for our conversion to UTF-16 Little Endian.

```
app_type = 'APPLICATION/MSEXCEL; charset=utf-16le'.
```

For reference, the SAP internal Code page numbers are 4102 for UTF-16be, 4103 for UTF-16le, and 4110 for UTF-8. These can be found in table TCP00A or by calling function module: SCP_CODEPAGE_BY_EXTERNAL_NAME.

16.5.5 Addition of the Byte Order Mark

That was actually quite easy. Now we have our output formatted as Unicode Text Tab Delimited – UTF-16, Little Endian; we just need to add the BOM to the beginning of the binary string.

```
CONCATENATE cl_abap_char_utilities=>byte_order_mark_little
            l_xstring INTO l_xstring IN BYTE MODE.
```

Once again, we have taken advantage of the functionality that SAP has provided in the form of the helper class for character manipulation: CL_ABAP_CHAR_UTILITIES. This class already has the BOMs for UTF-8, UTF-16be, and UTF-16le defined for you.

16.6 Pushing the Excel Content back through the browser

Now that you have your data reformatted in the way you want it and available as a binary string, you are ready to begin pushing this content back to your user though their browser.

16.6.1 Push Using the Current RESPONSE Object

There are two different options for doing this. The first one we will look at has the advantage of only requiring ABAP code in your event handler. However, in this approach we use the current response and navigation objects to deliver the content back to the user. While being the simpler of the two options to implement, this approach can complicate further event-processing that you want to take place within this same event.

The first thing we will want to do in the coding is to clear some header fields from the response object. These header fields can cause caching problems with some browsers when downloading files.

```
* some Browsers have caching problems when loading Excel
response->delete_header_field(
   name = if_http_header_fields=>cache_control ).
response->delete_header_field(
   name = if_http_header_fields=>expires ).
response->delete_header_field(
   name = if_http_header_fields=>pragma ).
```

The next section of code sets a header field in the `response` object that will inform the process that we are sending it a file. This should cause the browser to trigger a **SAVE/OPEN** Option. You can also see that we can use this header field to propose a filename for our content.

```
response->set_header_field(
    name = 'content-disposition'
    value = 'attachment; filename=excel_example.xls' ).
```

In the final section of code, we set our binary string as the main data of the `response` object, which also requires us to tell the `response` object how large the data object is. We then need to tell the `navigation` object that the response is complete so that further unnecessary processing can be avoided.

```
l_len = XSTRLEN( l_xstring ).
response->set_data( data = l_xstring
                    length = l_len ).
navigation->response_complete( ).
```

16.6.2 Push Using a Cached Response

This second approach is slightly more complicated to implement, but results in cleaner interaction with the BSP framework. In this approach, we will place our content into a cached response object. We will then place this cached object directly into the ICM and generate a URL that references this cached object. The URL will be placed within a hidden `IFrame` in our layout, thereby having the same effect for the user without the messy interaction with the main `response` and `navigation` objects.

Like our first example, nearly all the code takes place in an input `event handler`. As we saw in Section 16.3.3, we will create a new *cached* `response` object to work with instead of the main `response` object.

Next we will set our binary string content into this new cached `response` object.

```
cached_response->set_data( l_xstring ).
```

Since this is a new `response` object, we do not need to delete the header field as we did in the previous example. However, we do need to set header fields for the `content type` and the `content disposition`.

```
cached_response->set_header_field(
     name = if_http_header_fields=>content_type
     value = 'APPLICATION/XLS; charset=utf-16le' ).

cached_response->set_header_field(
     name  = 'Content-Disposition'
     value = 'attachment; filename=excel_example.xls' ).
```

Next, we want to set a good status code into the *cached* `response` object.

```
cached_response->set_status( code = 200 reason = 'OK' ).
```

We are going to be placing this cached `response` object directly into the ICM's server cache. We only need it to be there long enough to finish building the page and allow the `IFrame` object on the client to request this content. Therefore, we will set a reasonably short time, 60 seconds, to avoid consuming resources in the ICM Cache unnecessarily.

```
cached_response->server_cache_expire_rel(
     expires_rel = 60 ).
```

Before we insert this object into the server cache, we need to make sure that we have a completely Unique URL. The best way to do this is to simply generate a GUID and attach that to the end of our application URL.

```
DATA: guid TYPE guid_32.
DATA: url TYPE string.
CALL FUNCTION 'GUID_CREATE'
  IMPORTING ev_guid_32 = guid.
CONCATENATE runtime->application_url '/' guid INTO url.
```

Finally we will insert our cached `Response` into the server cache with the newly generated unique URL.

```
cl_http_server=>server_cache_upload(
      url      = url
      response = cached_response ).
```

Somehow you are going to want to impart persistence to this URL so that it is available in the processing of your layout. In this example, we are going to assume that we have a stateful application and that during the event processing we copied the generated URL for our cached `Response` into an attribute in the application class.

Therefore once we reach the processing of our layout, we can do a simple test to see if there is a value in this URL application-class attribute. If so, we will generate an IFrame to trigger the browser to fetch the cached content. We create an IFrame that is only 1 pixel by 1 pixel. That way we have an area that effectively does not take up any space in the rendered output.

```
<% IF application->display_url IS NOT INITIAL.
  MOVE application->display_url TO url_string. %>
  <iframe src="<%= application->display_url %>"
          width="1px" height="1px">
  </iframe>
<% ENDIF. %>
```

16.7 BSP Extension Element for Excel Download

So far, we have examined the logic necessary to convert an ABAP internal table to a Unicode tab-delimited text file ready for Excel consumption. We also have seen the coding necessary to pass this content back to the front-end client.

As you can see, a considerable amount of coding is involved in the overall process. It seems unwise to repeat this coding in each application that requires this functionality. Would it not be better if this functionality was available as a simple, reusable BSP extension element?

That is exactly what we are going to do next. We are going to use the techniques introduced in Chapter 11 to create this reusable element ourselves as a BSP extension element.

16.7.1 The Download Element User Interface

Our download element only needs a very simple user interface. This example is actually going to allow for the download of data in several different formats. Once we complete coding for downloading one data object type, it becomes quite simple to extend that to other useful data types. To start off with in addition to Microsoft Excel, we will also offer pure XML and HTML download options.

For our only UI element that the user will interact with, we will reuse the SAP provided `<phtmlb:popupMenu>`. This menu will give the user the opportunity to choose their download format.

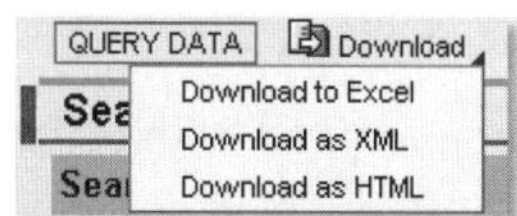

Figure 16.11 User Interface for the Download Extension

16.7.2 The Element Properties and Attributes

Following the instructions from Chapter 11, we will begin by creating a new element in our BSP extension. This element will be named `downloadTableExcel`. Our handler class for this element will be called `YCL_BSP_ELMNT_DWN_TBL_EXCEL`.

Next, we need to create the element's attributes. None of the elements are required, and all of them should be marked as supporting dynamic values. The `text` attribute should be marked as bindable.

Element Attribute	Description
`disabled`	The `disabled` attribute gets passed through to the inner `<phtmlb:popupMenu>`. This attribute allows you to disable the elements on the popup menu. For instance, you might use this if your table you are going to download is currently empty.
`display_url`	When this element generates the download content, it places it into the ICM cache. It then generates a temporary URL to this entry in the cache. Finally, it passes this URL back out of the event handler. The element then expects to receive this URL again on the Layout build (see Section 16.3.3). The BSP Element will then render this URL into a 1 pixel `IFrame`. All this allows for the download prompt to come up over the current page without disrupting the logic flow. All that the developers who are using this element need to know is that they must provide a variable that can be accessed both in the event handler and in the page or view.
`id`	Unique identification for an instance of this element. If the consumer does not specify an ID, the element will generate one later in processing.
`onDownload`	This attribute gives the calling program an option to specify its own event name for the `onDownload` event. This is helpful if you are going to place more than one instance of this element within one page. If the user does not specify a name for the event, it will later default a name of `DOWNLOAD`.
`text`	This attribute exists so the user can specify the text he or she wants to appear on the popup trigger. If nothing is specified, the element will default in the value `Download` later.

Table 16.1 Attributes of Element downloadTableExcel

16.7.3 Compile Time and Runtime Checks

Both a compile time and runtime syntax check can be programmed within the element. The methods for these checks should be inherited into our element handler class, YCL_BSP_ELMNT_DWN_TBL_EXCEL. If you want the compiler to call these methods, you must also select the **User Defined Validation** option in the element properties. You can implement these syntax checks by redefining the inherited methods.

This element is relatively simple. At compile time, the only check we need to perform is to make sure that the disabled flag has a valid Boolean flag.

```
validator->to_boolean( name = 'disabled' ).
valid = validator->m_all_values_valid.
```

Listing 16.8 Compile Time Syntax Check

The runtime check has a little more going on than the compile time-check did. First, the element needs to make sure that we are within an <htmlb:content> element and that this is DESIGN2003. The element needs DESIGN2003 because internally it is going to contain a PHTMLB element, which only supports this latest design. Next, it will generate an id if one was not supplied. Then it validates the text and disabled attributes.

```
data: content type ref to cl_htmlb_content.
content ?= me->get_class_named_parent(
   class_name = 'CL_HTMLB_CONTENT' ).
IF content->design <>
      cl_htmlb_content=>co_design_2003.
  me->raise_error( msg =
      'Supported for DESIGN2003 only.'(002) ).
ENDIF.
IF me->id IS INITIAL.
  content->m_button_id_counter =
      content->m_button_id_counter + 1.
  me->id = content->m_button_id_counter.
  CONDENSE me->id NO-GAPS.
  CONCATENATE 'z_download_' me->id INTO me->id.
ENDIF.
me->text = m_validator->bindable_to_string(
    name = 'text'   value = me->text
    binding_path = me->_text
    page_context = m_page_context ).
```

```
me->disabled = m_validator->to_boolean(
    name = 'Disabled' value = me->disabled ).
```

Listing 16.9 Runtime Syntax Check

16.7.4 Rendering Logic

Just as we did for our syntax checks, we have a method that we must redefine in order to program our rendering logic. This method is called `DO_AT_BEGINNING`.

This method is going to render several other SAP elements inside itself (`<phtmlb:popupTrigger>`, `<htmlb:image>`, `<htmlb:textView>`, and `<phtmlb:popupMenu>`). For all of these, it is going to use the `id` of itself for the inner element IDs. It will then tack on the `id_postfix` to create a unique id for each of the inner elements.

This method also provides the code that is necessary to redirect the `onSelect` event of the `<phtmlb:popupMenu>` into our event. We will have more code later to complete this event redirection. It then concatenates this class name (`me->m_class_name`) into the inner element's event handler. The BSP runtime then knows to send this event to our element handler class for processing.

Finally, the element has all the code it needs to render the standard HTML `IFrame` element. The code sample is abbreviated in text, but the complete source is available on the accompanying CD.

```
METHOD if_bsp_element~do_at_beginning .
  DATA: id_temp TYPE string.
  DATA: menu_id TYPE string.
  IF me->ondownload IS INITIAL.
     me->ondownload = 'DOWNLOAD'.
  ENDIF.
  DATA popup_trigger TYPE REF TO cl_phtmlb_popuptrigger.
  CONCATENATE me->id '__popupMenu' INTO menu_id.
  popup_trigger ?= cl_phtmlb_popuptrigger=>factory(
      id             = me->id
      id_postfix     = '__popupTrigger'
      isinteractive = 'true'
      popupmenuid    = menu_id ).
  WHILE m_page_context->element_process(
        element = popup_trigger ) = co_element_continue.

****Build the Download Image
    DATA: image TYPE REF TO cl_htmlb_image.
    ... Image Element Processing
```

```
****Build the Text Label
    DATA: label TYPE REF TO cl_htmlb_textview.
    ... Text Element Processing
  ENDWHILE. "End Popup Render

****Create the Popup Menu itself
  DATA: popupitems TYPE phtmlb_popupmenuitems.
  DATA popup_menu TYPE REF TO cl_phtmlb_popupmenu.
  FIELD-SYMBOLS <wa_menu> LIKE LINE OF popupitems.

****Excel Download Item
  APPEND INITIAL LINE TO popupitems ASSIGNING <wa_menu>.
  <wa_menu>-cancheck = ''.  <wa_menu>-checked = ''.
  IF me->disabled = 'TRUE'.
    <wa_menu>-enabled = ''.  ELSE. <wa_menu>-enabled = 'X'.
  ENDIF.
  <wa_menu>-hasseperator = ''.
  <wa_menu>-text = 'Download to Excel'(d02).
****XML Download Item
  ...
  <wa_menu>-text = 'Download as XML'(d03).
****HTML Download Item
  ...
  <wa_menu>-text = 'Download as HTML'(d04).
  popup_menu ?= cl_phtmlb_popupmenu=>factory( id = me->id
                 id_postfix = '__popupMenu'
                 firstlevelvisible = 'FALSE'
                 firstvisibleitemindex = '1'
                 maxvisibleitems = '7'
                 items = popupitems ).
  CONCATENATE me->ondownload '::' me->m_class_name
              '::DownloadChoosen'
         INTO popup_menu->onselect.
  WHILE m_page_context->element_process(
         element = popup_menu ) = co_element_continue.
  ENDWHILE.

****Get Link URL if it exists
  DATA html TYPE string.
  IF display_url IS NOT INITIAL.
    CONCATENATE `<iframe src="` display_url
```

```
        `" width="1px" height="1px"></iframe>` INTO html.
    me->print_string( html ).
  ENDIF.
  rc = co_element_done.
ENDMETHOD.
```

Listing 16.10 Rendering Logic

16.7.5 Trapping Events

Now we come to the coding that will allow for the trapping of incoming events to this element. We have four methods inherited from the interface IF_HTMLB_DATA. Once again, we will use the redefinition action to insert our own coding here.

This special logic is used to redirect the events of the <phtmlb:popupMenu> object into our own events in this element. This is quite useful because we can hide the fact that we have inner elements in this element. This also simplifies the event handling for the consumer of this new element. This technique was discussed in detail in Chapter 9.

```
METHOD if_htmlb_data~restore_from_request.
  IF me->if_htmlb_data~event_id IS INITIAL AND
     cl_htmlb_manager=>check_and_initialise_event(
        instance = me           request = request
        event_id_expected = id class_name = m_class_name
        ) IS NOT INITIAL.
    RETURN. " means an event found and restored
  ENDIF.
  me->id = id.
ENDMETHOD.
```

Listing 16.11 Restore from Request

```
METHOD if_htmlb_data~event_initialize .
  me->if_htmlb_data~event_id                = p_event_id.
  me->if_htmlb_data~event_type              = p_event_type.
  me->if_htmlb_data~event_class             = p_event_class.
  me->if_htmlb_data~event_name              = p_event_name.
  me->if_htmlb_data~event_server_name       =
      p_event_server_name.
  me->if_htmlb_data~event_defined           = p_event_defined.
  me->if_htmlb_data~event_intercept_depth =
      p_event_intercept_depth.
```

```
  me->if_htmlb_data~event_name = me->m_name.
  SPLIT me->if_htmlb_data~event_id AT '__'
    INTO me->if_htmlb_data~event_id
         me->if_htmlb_data~event_type.
* restore view state from the request
  me->if_htmlb_data~restore_from_request(
      request = p_request id = me->if_htmlb_data~event_id ).
ENDMETHOD.
```

Listing 16.12 Event Initialize

```
METHOD if_htmlb_data~event_set_parameters.
****Take parameters from the original event and map them
  IF p_param_count > 1.
    me->selected_string    = p_param_1.
    me->selected_id        = p_param_1.
    me->selected_text      = p_param_2.
  ENDIF.
ENDMETHOD.
```

Listing 16.13 Event-Set Parameters

```
****No coding necessary
```

Listing 16.14 Event Dispatch

16.7.6 Calling the Element from a Page Layout

Before we look at the code for the event handler, let us first examine the use of this element. The following is how it looks once inserted into the typical page or view:

```
<ybsp:downloadTableExcel id = "DOWNLOAD"
      disabled    = "<%= model->download_disabled %>"
      display_url = "<%= application->display_url %>" />
```

Listing 16.15 Page Layout

In this example, an ID is specified but not an event name because we only have one instance of this element in the application. The `disabled` flag comes from a model class. This example might actually test for an empty table and set this flag in the controller's `DO_REQUEST` method. Finally, the `display_url` variable comes from the stateful application class.

16.7.7 Event Handler

Now we are ready to look at the code in the controller's DO_HANDLE_EVENT method. You will see that the controller gets a pointer to both the application and model classes in this method so that critical data is easy to access.

The processing looks for the event_id and calls the event handler method for the element. Because the event handling is not overly complex, you can simply code the event handler logic into the same class that was used for the BSP element/element handler class. You will see in some of SAP's delivered elements that they create separate classes for this functionality.

In this instance, model->xref is the internal table that has the data that is to be downloaded. Only a reference to the table is passed into the event handler. Also we have used an <htmlb:tableView> iterator class to manipulate the structure of our internal table when we displayed it on the screen. If you would like to have this same manipulation done when you download the data, you can pass a reference to the iterator object as well.

```
DATA: model TYPE REF TO ycl_bsp_model_example.
DATA: appl TYPE REF TO ycl_bsp_appl_example.
appl ?= application.  model ?= appl->model.
DATA itab TYPE REF TO data.
GET REFERENCE OF model->xref INTO itab.
DATA iterator TYPE REF TO ycl_iterator_test.
CREATE OBJECT iterator.
appl->display_url =
      ycl_bsp_elmnt_dwn_tbl_excel=>handle_event(
        htmlb_event_ex = htmlb_event_ex
        runtime        = runtime
        iterator       = iterator
        itab           = itab ).
```

Listing 16.16 Do-Handle Event

Finally, we reach the event handler code of our element. In this example, the event handler is implemented as a static method of the main element class itself. This is done to simplify the understanding and maintenance of the code.

The main event handler is going to expect a few parameters. Naturally it wants a pointer to the data it is going to download (parameter itab). Next it wants a copy of the HTMLB_EVENT_EX structure so it can determine what <phtmlb:popupMenu> item was selected. Next it needs a reference to the runtime object so that it can use the application_name and application_url in its processing.

Finally it has an optional parameter, in case the consumer wants to specify the filename for the download. Otherwise the processing will generate a filename using the `application_name`. Another way to allow for the formatting of the table data before download, you can pass in a reference to an `<htmlb:tableView>` iterator or a column-definition table. All the method returns is the URL to the cached download content.

Parameter name	Direction	Type	Description
itab	Importing	Type Ref to DATA	Internal data table that will be downloaded
htmlb_event_ex	Importing	Type Ref to IF_HTMLB_DATA	HTMLB event data
runtime	Importing	Type Ref to IF_BSP_RUNTIME	The BSP runtime object
i_filename	Importing	Type STRING	Download file name
iterator	Importing	Type Ref to IF_HTMLB_TABLEVIEW_ITERATOR	Iterator for output formatting
col_def	Importing	Type TABLEVIEWCONTROLTAB	Table view column definitions
url	Returning	Type STRING	URL for the downloading of cached content

Table 16.2 Parameters for Main Event Handlers

In the coding you will see that processing branches the logic, depending upon what type of download the user requested. It then builds a filename.

```
METHOD handle_event .
  DATA: app_type TYPE string,    l_string TYPE string,
        l_xstring TYPE xstring, extension TYPE string.
  DATA: error TYPE REF TO cx_root.
  DATA: l_col_def TYPE tableviewcontroltab.
  IF col_def  IS INITIAL AND iterator IS NOT INITIAL.
    DATA: p_overwrites TYPE tableviewoverwritetab.
    iterator->get_column_definitions(
        EXPORTING  p_tableview_id        = 'DOWNLOAD'
        CHANGING   p_column_definitions = l_col_def
                      p_overwrites        = p_overwrites ).
  ELSEIF col_def IS NOT INITIAL.
    l_col_def = col_def.
  ENDIF.
  TRY.
```

```
DATA: ipopup TYPE REF TO cl_es_bsp_elmnt_dwn_tbl_excl.
ipopup ?= htmlb_event_ex.
IF ipopup->selected_id CS 'Item1'.
  app_type = 'APPLICATION/XLS; charset=utf-16le'.
  l_xstring =
  ycl_es_bsp_elmnt_dwn_tbl_excl=>process_xls_download(
           itab      = itab
           i_col_def = l_col_def ).
  extension = '.xls'.
ELSEIF ipopup->selected_id CS 'Item2'.
  ... xml processing
ELSEIF ipopup->selected_id cs 'Item3'.
  ... html processing
ENDIF.
DATA: value TYPE string.
IF i_filename IS NOT INITIAL.
    CONCATENATE 'attachment; filename='
      i_filename extension INTO value.
ELSE.
    CONCATENATE 'attachment; filename='
      runtime->application_name extension
      INTO value.
ENDIF.
```

The next small block of code below will handle any errors that we might encounter during the conversion of the content to Excel, XML, or HTML. Basically it catches all errors using the high-level exception handler class cx_root.

To support this error handling, this example creates a generic exception handler class called YCL_SERIALIZABLE_ERROR. This class includes the IF_SERIALIZABLE_OBJECT interface. That way, the element can take any error information and serialize it to XML. It then returns this erroneous XML to the user in the download instead of the content they expected. Not a great solution, but far better than just producing a short dump. This also allows the element to return error information to the user without having to disrupt the hosting layout's user interface.

```
method constructor .
  me->short_text = error->get_text( ).
  me->long_text  = error->get_longtext( ).
  call method error->get_source_position
    importing program_name = me->program
```

```
              include_name = me->include
              source_line  = me->source_line.
  me->kernel_errid = error->kernel_errid.
endmethod.
```

Listing 16.17 YCL_SERIALIZABLE_ERROR Constructor Coding

As we continue looking at the coding of the `event-handler` method, we can see how the error handling is resolved. We see how we finish the event handler by placing the content into the ICM cache with a generated unique URL and then passing this URL back to the calling program.

```
    CATCH cx_root INTO error.
      DATA: xml_err TYPE REF TO ycl_serializable_error.
      CREATE OBJECT xml_err EXPORTING error = error.
      DATA: g_ixml TYPE REF TO if_ixml,
            g_stream_factory
                   TYPE REF TO if_ixml_stream_factory,
            g_encoding TYPE REF TO if_ixml_encoding.
      CONSTANTS encoding TYPE string VALUE 'UTF-8'.
      DATA resstream TYPE REF TO if_ixml_ostream.
      g_ixml = cl_ixml=>create( ).
      g_stream_factory = g_ixml->create_stream_factory( ).
      g_encoding = g_ixml->create_encoding(
        character_set = encoding  byte_order = 0 ).
      resstream = g_stream_factory->create_ostream_xstring(
        l_xstring ).

      resstream->set_encoding( encoding = g_encoding ).
      CALL TRANSFORMATION id
        SOURCE error = xml_err result xml resstream.
      app_type = 'APPLICATION/XML; charset=UTF-8'.
      value = 'attachment; filename=Error.xml'.
    ENDTRY.

  DATA: cached_response TYPE REF TO if_http_response.
  CREATE OBJECT cached_response TYPE cl_http_response
         EXPORTING add_c_msg = 1.
  cached_response->set_data( l_xstring ).
  cached_response->set_header_field(
     name  = if_http_header_fields=>content_type
     value = app_type ).
```

```
  cached_response->set_header_field(
         name  = 'Content-Disposition'
         value = value ).
  cached_response->set_status( code = 200 reason = 'OK' ).
  cached_response->server_cache_expire_rel(
         expires_rel = 60 ).
  DATA: guid TYPE guid_32.
  CALL FUNCTION 'GUID_CREATE' IMPORTING ev_guid_32 = guid.
  CONCATENATE runtime->application_url '/' guid INTO url.
  cl_http_server=>server_cache_upload( url = url
        response = cached_response ).
ENDMETHOD.
```

Listing 16.18 Continuation of the Event Handler Method

16.7.8 Get Structure Definition

In order to support the methods that will convert our ABAP internal table to the different output types, the element handler has a static method that will determine the definition of the input internal table that is going to be downloaded. Much of the processing of this method was borrowed from the standard SAP coding of the `<htmlb:tableView>` class. After all, it has been said that good programmers write good code, but great programmers reuse the good programmers' good code.

This method has the following interface:

Parameter name	Direction	Type	Description
`itab`	Importing	Type Ref to DATA	Internal data table that will be downloaded
`struct`	Returning	Type EXTDFIEST	Data dictionary structure definition

Table 16.3 Interface of Static Element Handler Method

Basically this method is going to use the ABAP descriptor classes to determine the structure of the internal table that is being worked with. Due to the size of the code listing for this method and the fact that it is only marginally related to BSP; we have not included the source code in this text. It is however available, along with this entire solution, on the CD for this book.

16.7.9 Process Excel Download

This routine begins by concatenating the individual data elements of our downloaded internal table together, separated by `cl_abap_char_utilities=>horizontal_tab` and `cl_abap_char_utilities=>cr_lf`.

That means that this coding is responsible for the output format of all the possible intrinsic ABAP data types. Luckily, SAP has once again done most of the work for us. The routine just reuses the very useful `TO_STRING` method of the `IF_BSP_PAGE` object. The method then completes the conversion by transforming the string into UTF-16 as discussed earlier in this chapter.

This method does use functionality of the RTTS that was first introduced in Web AS 6.40 in order to dynamically build the new internal table that represents the modified structure of the iterator. There is a slightly more complex version of this method that does not use the RTTS and that is provided, along with all the source code for the book, on the accompanying CD.

```
DATA: r_string TYPE string.
DATA: lapp_type TYPE char30, str TYPE string.
DATA: l_col_def TYPE tableviewcontroltab.
l_col_def[] = i_col_def[].
****Set the application Type - character set for conversion
****Excel Requires UTF-16 with Little Endian
lapp_type = 'text/unicode; charset=utf-16le'.
FIELD-SYMBOLS: <tab> TYPE table, <wa> TYPE ANY,
    <wa2> TYPE ANY, <f> TYPE ANY.
****Get Reference to our Internal Table
ASSIGN itab->* TO <tab>.
****Read the Table Structure
DATA: struct  TYPE extdfiest.
DATA: struct2 TYPE extdfiest.
FIELD-SYMBOLS: <wa_struct> LIKE LINE OF struct.
FIELD-SYMBOLS <wa_desc> LIKE LINE OF struct.
CALL METHOD
   ycl_es_bsp_elmnt_dwn_tbl_excl=>get_table_structure
  EXPORTING itab   = itab
  RECEIVING struct = struct.
****Adjust the internal table and structure definitions
****for Iterators and Table View Column Definitions
IF l_col_def IS NOT INITIAL.
  FIELD-SYMBOLS: <wa_col> LIKE LINE OF l_col_def.
```

```
LOOP AT l_col_def ASSIGNING <wa_col>.
  READ TABLE struct ASSIGNING <wa_struct>
        WITH KEY fieldname = <wa_col>-columnname.
  IF sy-subrc = 0.
    IF <wa_col>-title IS NOT INITIAL.
      <wa_struct>-coltitle = <wa_col>-title.
    ENDIF.
    APPEND <wa_struct> TO struct2.
  ENDIF.
ENDLOOP.
struct[] = struct2[].
FREE struct2.
DATA: comp_tab TYPE
      cl_abap_structdescr=>component_table.
FIELD-SYMBOLS: <wa_comp> LIKE LINE OF comp_tab.
LOOP AT struct ASSIGNING <wa_struct>.
  APPEND INITIAL LINE TO comp_tab ASSIGNING <wa_comp>.
  IF <wa_struct>-rollname IS INITIAL.
    <wa_comp>-type ?=
     cl_abap_typedescr=>describe_by_name( 'STRINGVAR' ).
  ELSE.
    <wa_comp>-type ?=
     cl_abap_typedescr=>describe_by_name(
          <wa_struct>-rollname ).
  ENDIF.
  <wa_comp>-name  = <wa_struct>-fieldname.
ENDLOOP.
DATA: struct_type  TYPE REF TO cl_abap_structdescr,
      table_type   TYPE REF TO cl_abap_tabledescr.
struct_type = cl_abap_structdescr=>create( comp_tab ).
table_type = cl_abap_tabledescr=>create(
    p_line_type  = struct_type
    p_table_kind = cl_abap_tabledescr=>tablekind_std ).
DATA: dref TYPE REF TO data.
CREATE DATA dref TYPE HANDLE table_type.
FIELD-SYMBOLS <table> TYPE STANDARD TABLE.
ASSIGN dref->* TO <table>.
LOOP AT <tab> ASSIGNING <wa>.
  APPEND INITIAL LINE TO <table> ASSIGNING <wa2>.
  MOVE-CORRESPONDING <wa> TO <wa2>.
```

```
  ENDLOOP.
  UNASSIGN <tab>.
  ASSIGN dref->* TO <tab>.
ENDIF.
****Populate the Column Headers
LOOP AT struct ASSIGNING <wa_desc>.
  CONCATENATE r_string <wa_desc>-coltitle
              cl_abap_char_utilities=>horizontal_tab
              INTO r_string.
ENDLOOP.
CONCATENATE r_string cl_abap_char_utilities=>cr_lf
            INTO r_string.
DATA: output TYPE string, s(256) TYPE c.
DATA: l_page TYPE REF TO cl_bsp_page_base.
CREATE OBJECT l_page.
*****Loop through the Data Table
LOOP AT <tab> ASSIGNING <wa>.
****For each component (field) in the table -Output the data
  LOOP AT struct ASSIGNING <wa_desc>.
    ASSIGN COMPONENT sy-tabix OF STRUCTURE <wa> TO <f>.
    CHECK sy-subrc = 0.
    IF <wa_desc> IS ASSIGNED
       AND <wa_desc>-convexit IS NOT INITIAL.
****Process any output conversion routines
      CONCATENATE 'CONVERSION_EXIT_' <wa_desc>-convexit
                  '_OUTPUT' INTO str.
      CALL FUNCTION str
        EXPORTING input  = <f>
        IMPORTING output = s.
    ELSE.
****Use the BSP Page to_string Meth. to output any data type
      s = l_page->if_bsp_page~to_string( value = <f> ).
    ENDIF.
    CONCATENATE r_string s
                cl_abap_char_utilities=>horizontal_tab
                INTO r_string.
  ENDLOOP.
  CONCATENATE r_string cl_abap_char_utilities=>cr_lf
              INTO r_string.
ENDLOOP.
```

```
****Convert the string to Binary string (UTF-16le)
CALL FUNCTION 'SCMS_STRING_TO_XSTRING'
  EXPORTING text     = r_string
            mimetype = lapp_type
  IMPORTING buffer   = r_xstring.
****Add the UTF-16 Little Endian Byte Order Mark
CONCATENATE cl_abap_char_utilities=>byte_order_mark_little
            r_xstring INTO r_xstring IN BYTE MODE.
```

Listing 16.19 Process Excel Download

16.8 Alternatives to the MIME Repository

The SAP MIME Repository is really designed to hold development objects. Because of this, there is much overhead in its management of objects. The performance for uploading or reading many files or very large files is not optimal. Also the dependence upon the transport system for MIME objects, often removes flexibility that is needed when working with a large number of dynamic objects.

So what are some of the alternatives to using the MIME Repository? First you could simply store you binary content in a custom database table. This would remove the dependency upon the transport system and might improve performance. However this could require you to make extensive changes to your applications to read the content and present it to the users.

16.8.1 ICM File Handler

A better approach might be to take advantage of the ICM file handler functionality discussed in Section 16.2. By setting up a file handler to local disk storage, you now have an easy to manage and access approach that still is easy to reference from within BSP and takes advantage of the ICM caching functionality.

You could take this approach one step further and even create a BSP application for managing the objects within these file handler locations. This way users could maintain the objects, without needing Operating System access to the place they are stored.

Figure 16.12 demonstrates one such sample application. It allows you to choose the file handler you wish to manage. The drop down list of possible file handlers is read directly from the ICM configuration profile.

On the left hand side of the screen, we have the directory/file listing. This is our navigation area as well. On the right side, we display the currently selected object in an IFrame. The user has the ability to delete or update the current document.

Figure 16.12 Sample File Handler Maintenance Program

Although a simple example, this might serve as a starting point for something more specific. Perhaps you might decide to add SAP authorization checks on the file handler or directories within the file handler. The complete source code for the sample application is contained within the code samples on the enclosed CD.

16.8.2 SAP Content and Cache Server

A third approach might be to take advantage of the SAP Content and Cache Servers. The SAP Content and Cache Servers are an extension of the R/3 Document Management System. They allow for the easy distribution and access of documents across diverse geographies.

Let us consider for a moment a corporation that has operations in North America and Europe. Their centralized R/3 and Web AS systems reside in Europe. Therefore users in North America access BSP applications across the Wide Area Network from a data center in Europe.

This works fine for the BSP pages them selves, but for large MIME objects this is inefficient.

In this situation, both North America and Europe would have a Content and Cache Server. The index of all documents would still reside in the European R/3 system, as well as the BSP application itself. However the MIME objects could be cached and referenced from the North American Cache Server.

Two problems arise from this situation however. First, we do not want the application to have to be aware of the complexities of the underlying Cache Servers. You want the number and locations of the Cache servers to be dynamic.

The second problem involves the users passing around shortcuts to the document. Users will often cut and paste short cuts from such websites into Emails and other documents. If the URL to the document contains the direct address of the cache server for that user, this URL may break over time with the reorganization of cache servers. Also if the page was generated by a North American users but a European user accesses the URL, they will inefficiently directed to the North American cache Server.

To enhance this solution, you might consider creating your own ICF Service Handler. This way you could create URLs that are independent of Content/Cache server being used. The URLs instead would point to your custom Service Handler providing only the DMS document keys.

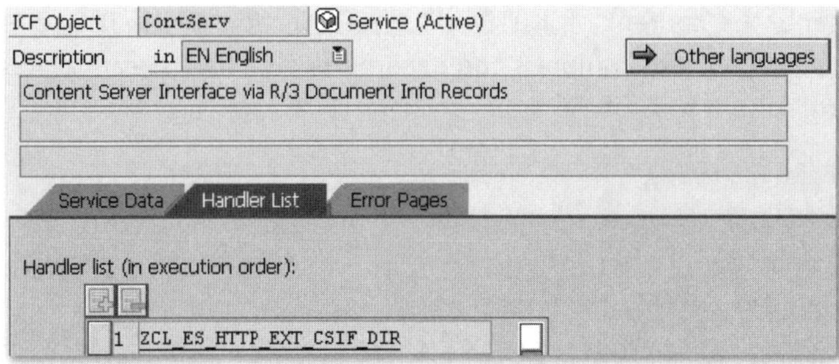

Figure 16.13 Custom ICF Service Handler for the SAP Content/Cache Server

This service handler could then lookup the DMS details about the document in question using a BAPI Call, `BAPI_DOCUMENT_GETDETAIL2`.

The service handler then uses the Client IP address, details from the DMS system, configuration about the Cache Servers stored in table `sdokstca`, and a call to the function module `SCMS_URL_GENERATE` to build a URL and to trigger a HTTP redirect to the best possible location to retrieve the file.

The complete source code to the described example, alone with all source code samples for this book, is available on the accompanying CD.

16.9 ZIP Tool

SAP has delivered GZip-based compression in the Web AS for some time now. GZip compression is used automatically by the ICM when acting as an HTTP server, if configured to do so.

In more recent support package levels for Web AS 620 and standard in Web AS 6.40, SAP provides a series of ABAP classes that allow for the compression and decompression of text and binary data steams. These classes are: CL_ABAP_GZIP, CL_ABAP_GZIP_BINARY_STEAM, CL_ABAP_GZIP_TEXT_STEAM, CL_ABAP_UNGZIP_BINARY_STEAM, and CL_ABAP_UNGZIP_TEXT_STEAM.

These classes allow you to compress and decompress one data stream, but you are still responsible for storing the results. This means that you can compress data and store it in a database table, but they do not have functionality for creating true stand-alone ZIP files that can be opened by PC based applications.

The following example works with a binary sting that is stored in a database table. This string represents the content of a BTF editor (see Section 12.1). The code example uses CL_ABAP_GZIP to compress and decompress the data stream as it is read from and written to the database table.

```
DATA: l_text TYPE xstring.
DATA: desc_text TYPE string.
SELECT SINGLE text FROM ybtf_text
         INTO l_text WHERE id = me->id.
CALL METHOD cl_abap_gzip=>decompress_binary
      EXPORTING gzip_in = l_text
      IMPORTING raw_out = desc_text.
```

Listing 16.20 Read and Decompress

```
DATA: btf_wa TYPE xstring.
CALL METHOD cl_abap_gzip=>compress_binary
      EXPORTING raw_in   = input_text
      IMPORTING gzip_out = btf_wa-text.
MOVE me->id    TO btf_wa-id.
MODIFY ybtf_text FROM btf_wa.
```

Listing 16.21 Write and Compress

The compression classes in ABAP are very useful for saving database size; however they lack the full functionality for integration with the client or other applications. For this we would want a class that could create a properly formatted ZIP file with multiple inner contents and CRC logic.

Web AS 6.40 SP13 delivers the class `CL_ABAP_ZIP` to do just that. You can add one or many text or binary objects to a compression steam that in turn can be downloaded to a file or send back through a BSP response stream.

In this next example, we will retrieve multiple documents from an SAP Content Server. We will ZIP all of these documents together and return them as a single ZIP file using the cached response technique that we looked at earlier in this chapter.

```
DATA: zip TYPE REF TO cl_abap_zip.
CREATE OBJECT zip.
DATA: absolute_uri(2000) TYPE c.
DATA: response_body TYPE TABLE OF x_table.
DATA: response_headers TYPE TABLE OF c_table.
DATA: content TYPE xstring.
LOOP AT  doc_details ASSIGNING <wa_doc>.
  CLEAR absolute_uri.
  CLEAR response_body.
  absolute_uri = <wa_dor>-url2.
  CALL FUNCTION 'HTTP2_GET'
    EXPORTING absolute_uri         = absolute_uri
    TABLES    response_entity_body = response_body
              response_headers     = response_headers
    EXCEPTIONS OTHERS               = 1.
  IF sy-subrc NE 0.
    message =
      'Unable to retrieve content for ZIP inclusion'(ez2).
    EXIT.
  ENDIF.
  CLEAR content.
  CALL FUNCTION 'SCMS_BINARY_TO_XSTRING'
    EXPORTING  input_length = '999999999'
    IMPORTING  buffer       = content
    TABLES     binary_tab   = response_body.
  zip->add( name = <wa_doc>-filename content = content ).
ENDLOOP.
DATA: zip_results TYPE xstring.
zip_results = zip->save( ).
****Create the cached response object
DATA: cached_response TYPE REF TO if_http_response.
CREATE OBJECT cached_response TYPE cl_http_response
```

```
       EXPORTING add_c_msg = 1.
cached_response->set_data( zip_results ).
cached_response->set_header_field(
       name  = if_http_header_fields=>content_type
       value = 'APPLICATION/ZIP' ).
****Set the filename into the response header
cached_response->set_header_field(
       name  = 'Content-Disposition'
       value = 'attachment; filename=download.zip' ).
cached_response->set_status( code = 200 reason = 'OK' ).
cached_response->server_cache_expire_rel(
       expires_rel = 60 ).
****Create a unique URL for the object
DATA: guid TYPE guid_32.
CALL FUNCTION 'GUID_CREATE'
  IMPORTING ev_guid_32 = guid.
CONCATENATE runtime->application_url '/' guid
       INTO dir_url.
cl_http_server=>server_cache_upload( url = dir_url
     response = cached_response ).
RETURN.
```

This example is slightly extreme, but it demonstrates retrieving the files for compression and download from an external content server. However, the ZIP approach works just as well with files that were stored in the MIME repository or files that we have stored on disk and read via an ICM handler.

17 Customization

Although SAP has spent considerable time and money designing professional themes for BSP applications, there may be valid business reasons for creating pages with your own unique look and feel. In this chapter, we will focus on the technologies and techniques that make this level of customization possible.

17.1 Customization Overview

At some point, you are likely to be asked to customize the look and feel of your BSP pages. For example, a corporate color scheme or special font must be applied to your application.

You could always just create your own CSS files to alter the look and feel of your application. This would mean either not using the BSP extension elements or trying to attach new style tags to the generated HTML using a mechanism like the `<bsp:findAndReplace>` element. Both of these approaches are less than optimal, so for the purposes of this text we will assume that you wish to continue to work within the standard extension framework.

If you are lucky enough to always run your BSP application within a recent version of the SAP Enterprise Portal, you should have no problem at all. As discussed in Section 9.1.5, BSP applications that use the BSP extension framework get their look and feel from a set of designs. However BSP applications also support portal integration. That means that they will automatically inherit the theme that the portal is currently running without any changes to the BSP application. This allows you to use all the theme editing capabilities within the Enterprise Portal. However, let us assume that you do not have the Enterprise Portal, or that you need your application to be available with or without the portal.

17.2 Export—Modify—Import

The first approach that we might take is to create our own design themes. If you are using DESIGN2003, the `<htmlb:content>` element allows you to specify one of several themes that SAP delivers. You can use BSP Application `SBSPEXT_HTMLB` to view samples of the different BSP extension elements under the various standard themes.

It is a fairly simple process to copy and then modify one of these delivered themes. SAP delivers a standard ABAP program, `BSP_UPDATE_MIMEREPOS`, to export and import objects from the MIME Repository. This program can work with a single MIME element, a single folder, or a folder and all of its sub-folders.

Let us say that we want to export the theme TRADESHOW as our staring point. We would just need to supply its MIME path (`/SAP/Public/BC/UR/Design2002/themes/sap_tradeshow`) to `BSP_UPDATE_MIMEREPOS`.

Update the MIME Repository based on frontend data

Resources
MIME Repository path: /SAP/BC/BSP/SAP/ybsp_book

Import/Export
○ Export to disk
◉ Import from disk ☐ Create with different LOIOs

Options
◉ Process whole structure
○ Process flat structure
○ Process individual file only

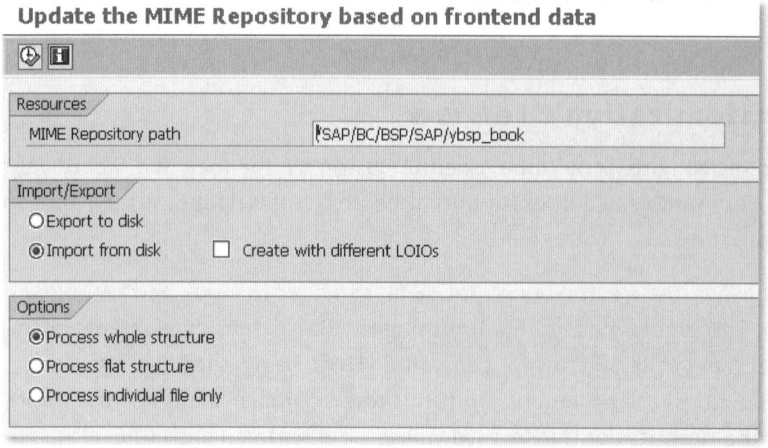

Figure 17.1 Theme Export Settings

You might be slightly confused by the use of the name DESIGN2002 within the path for the theme considering themes can only be used in DESIGN2003. As it turns out, the original project to create the Unified Renderer (the technology that packages all controls and all themes into a central technology that can be reused over all SAP platforms) was an off shoot from the DESIGN2002 project. Later the Unified Renderer, and its concept of themes, was ready to be integrated back into BSP. By this point however, DESIGN2002 had already shipped to customers and could not be changed. Therefore DESIGN2003 was born. Although within the terminology of BSP, we have the new DESIGN2003, the underlying code and paths could not change from their references to DESIGN2002.

You now have a copy of all the MIME objects that make up the TRADESHOW theme on your PC, and you are ready to edit in your favorite CSS or graphic editing tool.

After you make whatever changes you need, you use the same program to import the MIME objects back into SAP as a different theme. It is important to be careful not to overwrite SAP's delivered themes.

The path you then supply to `BSP_UPDATE_MIMEREPOS` will then be `/SAP/BC/BSP/SAP/ybsp_book`. Remember from reading Section 16.1 that a BSP application will automatically create a folder in the MIME Repository when it is created. Therefore we are using a MIME folder that to hold our new theme that corresponds to an existing BSP application.

We can now use our new theme in a BSP application by changing the `themeRoot` value of the `<htmlb:content>` element.

```
<htmlb:content design    = "DESIGN2003"
               themeRoot = "/SAP/BC/BSP/SAP/ybsp_book" >
```

There is a major disadvantage to using this approach, however. As SAP makes changes to the low-level rendering libraries, the developers often are forced to make changes to the structure and content of the underlying MIMEs. This means that it is very possible that every support package that you apply to your system will break your copied themes. In reality, you must re-copy the theme and re-apply your modifications after each support-package application.

17.3 NetWeaver Theme Editor

The idea of exporting and working with all the individual files is a little overwhelming. What we really need is a theme editor that understands the structure of the objects within SAP's themes and simplifies the process of updating them but without the reliance on the Enterprise Portal. Even if customers have the Enterprise Portal implemented, they may not have the version that has the theme editor (EP 6.0 running on at least Web AS 6.40 SP9).

To meet this need, SAP now has available a standalone version of the theme editor that runs within the NetWeaver Developer Studio. You can download the theme editor and the theme packages from SAP Developer Network (SDN). This is also where you must go to get support on the tool, because it is not officially supported through SAP's Online Support System (OSS).

This tool is heavily promoted as a solution for Web Dynpro. A standalone Web Dynpro application really has the same issue when it comes to themes that BSP has. Using the MIME import approach from the previous section, we can edit the themes in the standalone tool and then import them for use in BSP with `BSP_UPDATE_MIMEREPOS`.

As Figure 17.2 demonstrates, the theme editor is quite full featured. You have the listing of all the UI elements that are available for modification. Then you have your preview pane. Finally, you have a properties window with allowed values and color selectors built in.

The standalone theme editor does have the drawback of being very dependent upon matching the support package level of your Web AS. Just as when editing the raw MIMEs, you must make sure that the starting theme package and the release of the theme editor match exactly the release of the Web AS you are going to import the files into.

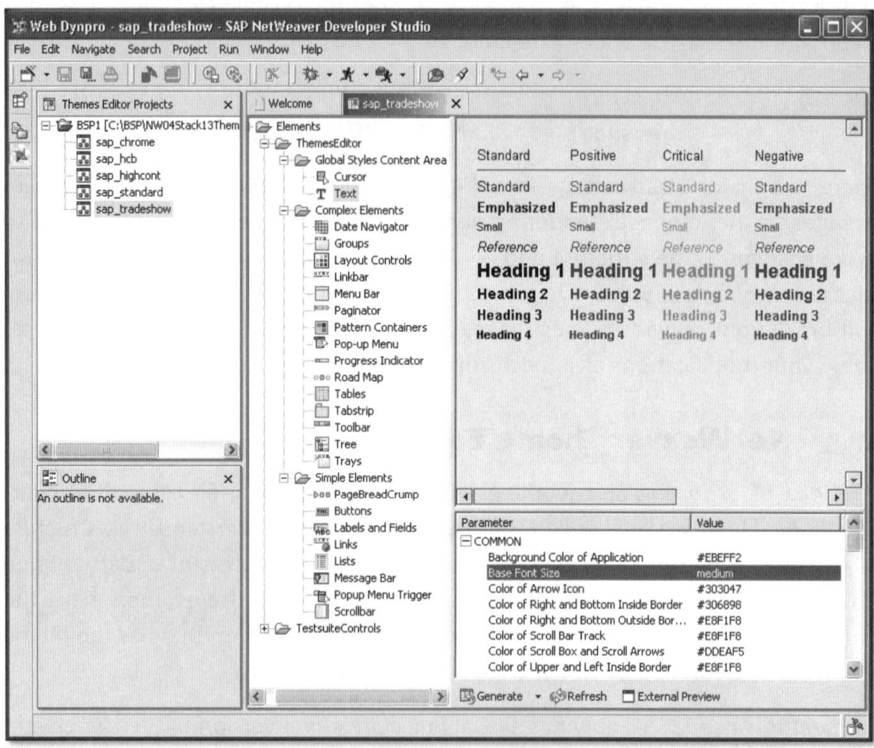

Figure 17.2 NetWeaver Standalone Theme Editor

17.4 ALFS—ABAP Look-and-Feel Service

So far, we have looked at two approaches for generating new themes for BSP applications. The first approach of directly modifying the underlying CSS files requires considerable effort. The second approach brings in the standalone theme editor to make the situation a bit easier. However if you only want to make a few simple adjustments, you might be overwhelmed by the sheer number of individual settings in this tool. In short, the power that it contains to tweak every detail of the theme might be overkill for some projects.

It might take many hours to change from any predefined SAP theme to a new corporate theme with either of these two previous approaches. In order to bridge that gap, SAP developed a quick-and-dirty *look-and-feel service* for the ABAP stack that allows us to have a new color scheme up and running in three minutes. The new scheme will probably not be a perfect match for anyone responsible for corporate branding. However, for a presentation or a project smaller than a complete re-branding, this tool fits the bill.

17.4.1 ALFS Tool Scope

The *quick-and-dirty* here refers in no way to the quality of the programming, or to the quality of the algorithm it uses. Some of the brightest minds at SAP worked diligently to put this solution together. Instead, the phrase reflects more on the scope of the solution and the constraints that are imposed by the implementation route that was chosen. This work was not done as part of any SAP development plan, but is more the result of *having some fun* over a series of lunch hours. As the tool was deemed to have value for a large group of people, the official decision was made to ship it.

Originally, this tool was developed on the Web AS, as SAP had many requirements from consultants who wanted to enhance their presentations at customers and did not have the space on their laptops to also run an Enterprise Portal installation. As they usually have already a mini-Web AS running, SAP decided to reuse this infrastructure.

Please note: This tool has a number of constraints. The use of the tool implies the acceptance of these limitations. Support for the tool will be provided via OSS on queue BC-BSP on a *best-effort* basis only. This means SAP will do everything possible to keep it running smoothly, but there are no guarantees that it will be supported indefinitely. Also, because ALFS is built upon the concept of themes, it will only work with BSP applications using DESIGN2003.

17.4.2 What is ALFS?

Figure 17.3 shows the same BSP application with different predefined themes. These themes were defined using ALFS to quickly show the effects of applying a new theme to a BSP application.

Figure 17.4 shows the complete theme editor. Effectively, you define five new colors from which the complete theme is then generated. If the corporate branding colors are already defined, then just plug them into the editor and press the preview button.

The editor generates new CSS files on the fly, as well as hundreds of new GIF images in exactly the right colors. Two interesting ideas flowed into this theme editor. The first is that a few basic colors are sufficient to specify the complete theme. The second is that it is possible, even with ABAP, to generate all the MIME objects on the fly as they are requested without a noticeable speed hit.

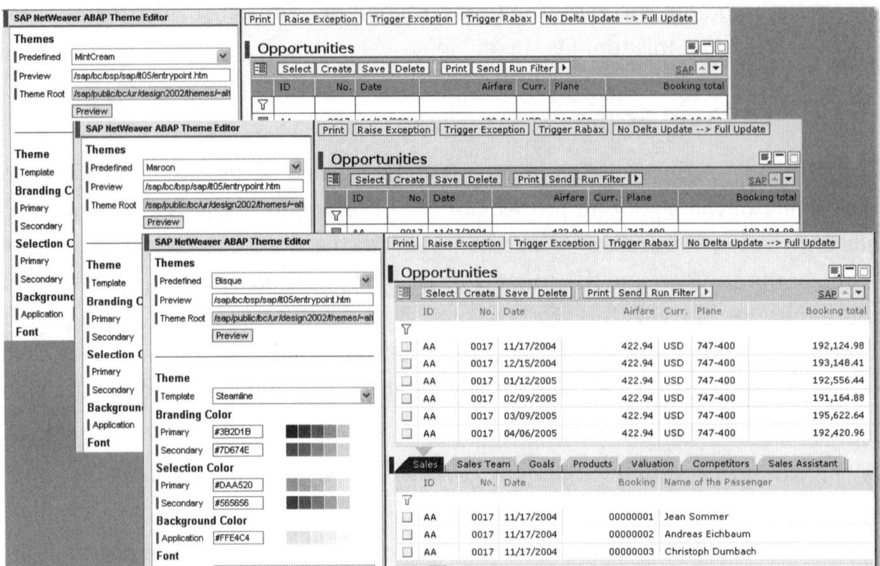

Figure 17.3 The Effects of ALFS on a BSP Application

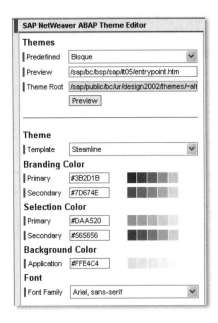

SAP NetWeaver ABAP Theme Editor

Themes

Predefined: Bisque

Preview: /sap/bc/bsp/sap/it05/entrypoint.htm

Theme Root: /sap/public/bc/ur/design2002/themes/~alt

Preview

Theme

Template: Steamline

Branding Color

Primary: #3B2D1B

Secondary: #7D674E

Selection Color

Primary: #DAA520

Secondary: #565656

Background Color

Application: #FFE4C4

Font

Font Family: Arial, sans-serif

Figure 17.4 The Complete ALFS Theme Editor

ALFS even parses and patches each GIF file that is used within the theme during the usual load process.

17.4.3 How Does Customization Normally Work?

The normal full process for customizing a theme is to use the tools provided by the Enterprise Portal. These tools provide the complete freedom to change all different aspects of the theme. This might be important for corporate branding purposes, but even getting an initial theme running is a lot of work. For example, the typical steps include all GIF images, over 300 per theme, being loaded into a bitmap editor individually to set their colors correctly. Even a first version can take hours to get up and running.

What the theme editor in the Enterprise Portal does is store all customer settings as metadata, rather than store them directly in the CSS files. Thereafter, in a generation step, the actual required CSS files are created. This is important for handling upgrades.

When SAP ships new rendering classes, the information required for the CSS files are also shipped only in metadata form. This is mixed with the old theme settings, and new CSS files then are generated at runtime.

Therefore the first requirement of ALFS was to have a solution that would *survive* a new service pack.

To work around this constraint, ALFS generates new themes on the fly. They are never stored in any database, but only cached on both the server and browser. After an upgrade, the BSP runtime will load the CSS files with a new version number. This bypasses the cache, causing the CSS files to be loaded and patched again. This implies that ALFS does *not* store any generated theme in the MIME Repository.

The goal of ALFS was never to replace the theme editor already available in the Enterprise Portal. This approach attempts only a quick approximation of the results, which should be sufficient for showing an application to a customer in nearly the correct color scheme. If fine-tuning of a theme is required, this must still be done with the usual theme editor.

17.4.4 A New Theme from Five Colors

The heart of ALFS is its simplicity. Instead of asking the user to configure and edit all colors, it only wants to have one color—for example, blue for SAP. Just give ALFS the base color, and it will do the rest.

In the end, it turns out that five colors are required and sufficient: one background color, two branding colors, and two selection colors.

What the BSP development team did was to manually analyze all style classes for all SAP base themes. From this, they grouped relevant classes together and determined heuristics of how the colors are used in the base themes. Specifically, they calculated the *distance* of a specific color from the base color of the theme. Then, given the five new colors, they apply the same distance to the base colors to have the data for the new theme. *Distance* is just a calculation of how much the color shifted in RGB space from the original source color.

The other important aspect is the template theme from which the new theme should be generated. SAP today ships five standard themes. Each theme is different in metrics such as padding, font sizes, and margins as well as different in the spectrum of colors used.

The distances between the different colors and the base color is an important aspect of the theme used as the template. For example, typically the high-contrast themes group colors more closely together at two extremes, achieving the required contrast on screen. Today, SAP sets as the default theme `Tradeshow`, and we recommend using this as the template in most cases.

17.4.5 Integration into Web AS

As we said earlier, the biggest constraint on the design for ALFS was that the new theme must be able to survive an upgrade. The first approach that was taken was to update all CSS and GIF files, and store them in the MIME Repository. However, this takes a very long time to generate, and had the side effect that ALFS had to patch resources that might not even be needed. The bigger problem was that it had no hooks to update the MIME Repository after a new service pack was applied.

The route that the BSP development team ended up taking was to write a new HTTP handler. This handler will intercept all requests to MIME objects. Once it detects that a customized object is required, the handler will load the MIME object, patch it, and then send it out to the browser. Typically, the time it takes to load a MIME object far exceeds the time required to quickly patch the colors in memory.

As a last step, the MIMEs are cached for seven days in both the server and browser caches. This works because the BSP runtime was changed in later service packs to load all MIMEs with a version number. Once a new service pack is installed; the version number changes and the MIMEs will be loaded anew. With the caching, the performance of this patch on-the-fly solution is blazing fast.

When using ALFS and this HTTP handler on lower service-pack levels, it is recommended to reduce the cache time back to one hour. This might negatively impact overall performance. Only with Web AS 6.20 SP54 and 6.40 SP13 will the caching automatically be updated to seven days.

The first problem the BSP development team had was where to store the new color information required. Initial approaches always placed this basic color data in the database. However with the browser caching seven days, once a color was changed the browser would not know, nor would it request, the update files until at the end of the seven days. After some deliberation, the BSP development team, taking into account that five colors is only 30 bytes, decided to add this information directly into the URL.

For example, for the `Bisque` theme shown in Figure 17.3, the theme root was set to:

```
/sap/public/bc/ur/design2002/themes/
~alfs~1000202FFE4C43B2D1B7D674EDAA520565656
```

Here, ALFS has encoded inside the URL the template to use (one byte), the font family to use (one byte with a lookup table) and then the 30 bytes for the five colors.

The big win in this approach was that any minor change in the theme resulted in a change of the generated URL. This effectively implied new objects that were not already in the cache. Thus, the complete theme again is loaded on the fly.

The other benefit was that it was now possible to have hundreds of themes active in parallel, without writing them into the MIME Repository. This was especially important when testing to find the right color combination. All the different tests with minor color changes have different URLs, thus keeping the cache content consistent for each test run and allowing you to quickly compare the different themes.

However, this solution does add about 50 bytes per roundtrip to the complete rendered overhead. The BSP development team did experiment with using a base64 encoding on the color values to reduce the overhead by about 20 bytes, but it was not worth the effort.

Looking at this solution in slightly more detail, we see that `DESIGN2003` MIME resources are loaded via the path `/sap/public/bc/ur/design2002/themes/sap_tradeshow/....` On this path there is already one HTTP handler installed. What was done was to write a new HTTP handler that is chained into this path. The new handler is called first. It looks at the incoming URL to search for its signature `~alfs~`. If the signature is found, the correct MIME is loaded, patched (with the color information from the URL), and the response is written (with caching). All other systems requesting the same resource will be served from the

ICM cache, thus making the patch work a one-off process. Should the URL not contain the correct signature, the handler will just signal that it did not handle the incoming HTTP request, and the usual MIME repository handler will then be scheduled.

17.4.6 The Source Code: Making It Work

By now, you should be really excited about ALFS and ready to dig in and try it out. ALFS is officially shipped with Web AS 6.20 SP54, 6.40 SP13, and 7.00 SP03.

However, if you are not at those service-package levels yet, you are not out of luck. OSS Note 850851, "ALFS: ABAP (Quick and Dirty) Look and Feel Service," has the complete source code. A ZIP file with the source code is attached to the note. This can be manually installed on any Web AS system.

No Note assisted corrections are provided for this solution, so manual application of the code will be required.

To install the code, create a new class and add the interface `IF_HTTP_EXTENSION`. Paste the following code into the `HANDLE_REQUEST` method:

```
METHOD if_http_extension~handle_request.
  TRY.
    server->transactional = if_http_server=>co_enabled.
    if_http_extension~flow_rc =
       if_http_extension=>co_flow_ok_others_mand.
    IF server->request->get_header_field(
       if_http_header_fields_sap=>path_info ) CS '~alfs~'.
       lcl_alfs=>handle_request( server ).
       if_http_extension~flow_rc =
          if_http_extension=>co_flow_ok.
    ENDIF.
  CATCH cx_root.
  ENDTRY.
ENDMETHOD.
```

All that this code does is quickly check for the ALFS signature. Once it is found, all further processing is done in local classes. Observe the setting of the `flow_rc` variable to signal whether the HTTP request has been handled or not.

In the next step, edit both the definition and implementation sections of this class. Paste the complete source from the OSS note into the corresponding sections. Save and activate the class. Keep in mind that the supplied code is slightly different between Web AS 6.20 and 6.40.

As the final step, start transaction SICF. Find the node /sap/public/bc/ur and edit it. Add the new handler class to the list of handler classes.

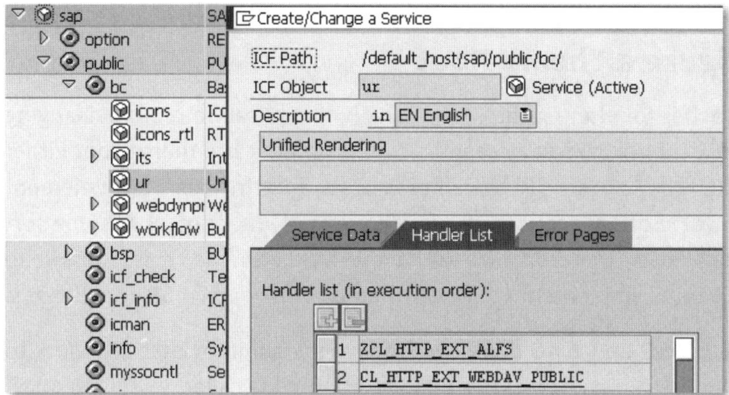

Figure 17.5 Editing the Service Node to Add the New Handler Class

If you are manually applying this change to a Web AS 6.20, the ICF node is deactivated after the change and must be activated again.

17.4.7 ALFS Theme Editor in Detail

Now that you have ALFS installed in your system, you are ready to start using it. The editor can be started with the URL:

```
/sap/public/bc/ur/design2002/themes/~alfs~editor
```

Now you just decide which template theme to start from, pick one font, and set the required five colors. Press the **Preview** button to see the new theme in action.

The most important output is the theme root that is displayed. This string can later be integrated in a number of ways into one BSP application.

The simplest way, at least for testing, is to use the sap-themeRoot URL parameter. It is very important, though, to note that the string must be URL-encoded ("/" → "%2f").

```
http://<host>:<port>/sap/bc/bsp/sap/it05/entrypoint.htm?sap-
themeRoot=%2fsap%2fpublic%2fbc%2fur%2fdesign2002%2fthemes%2f
~alfs~1000202FFE4C43B2D1B7D674EDAA520565656
```

The alternative technique would be to set the theme root directly on the <htmlb:content> tag. This has the benefit that it is always formatted correctly as far as URL encoding is concerned and does not require external configuration data, which is more difficult to manage.

```
<htmlb:content design="DESIGN2003"
        themeRoot="/sap/public/bc/ur/design2002/themes/~alfs
~1000202FFE4C43B2D1B7D674EDAA520565656">
```

17.5 Configure a Theme Root

All three approaches for altering the theme of a BSP application require changing the theme-root attribute. We have seen that you can alter the theme root either through the `sap-themeRoot` URL parameter or as an attribute of the element `<htmlb:content>`. Both of these methods require applying changes of some sort to each BSP application that you wish to have the new theme. This is less than optimal if you want to implement your new theme across many BSP applications.

In Web AS 6.20 SP50 and 6.40 SP12, SAP delivers a solution that attempts to solve this problem. They have created a configuration table called `BSPTHEMEROOT`. If no theme root is supplied by the URL parameter or in the `<htmlb:content>` element, the BSP runtime will check this configuration table before applying the standard theme.

Since there is no standard table maintenance for `BSPTHEMEROOT` delivered, you will have to use transaction SE16 to maintain it or create your own maintenance view.

The following are the fields in `BSPTHEMEROOT` and the effects that they have on processing.

- `SORT_KEY`: In this field you must supply an unique key. Entries are processed in order by sorting on this field.
- `URL`: This is a string that will be matched against the URL to determine what theme to use. You can wildcard this match with the character `*`. Through the use of aliases that can be setup in transaction SICF, it is possible to have more than one theme for the same application. The matching process is always case insensitve.
- `THEMEROOT`: The new theme to use. You can supply one of the SAP predefined themes by name; for example `sap_tradeshow`. You can also specify a URL to the themeRoot on your local Web AS or on a remote one.

17.6 Theme Root White List

Regardless of the method used to set the theme root, the fact that the theme root supports remote URLs poses a potential security risk. Imagine if someone was able to supply a bogus theme root to your application. This would not be very difficult to accomplish especially considering that the theme root can be set via a

URL parameter. In this situation a malicious theme root URL on a remote server could be designed to open your application to a Cross Site Scripting attack.

To protect their customers, SAP has developed a white list solution in the HTTP framework as of Web AS 6.20 SP54, 6.40 SP14 and 7.00 SP3. This white list gives the customer the capability to create patterns that will be checked against external URLs before been used in generated HTML code.

Similar to the `BSPTHEMEROOT` table, the white list is delivered as a configuration table, `HTTP_WHITELIST`, which has no table maintenance. So, once again, you can either use SE16 to maintain it or create your own maintenance view.

SAP delivers the white-list table empty. If there are no entries in the white- list table, all checking is disabled. Therefore, it would be advisable to at least setup an entry that checks that the request is coming from any server within your corporate domain.

For the purpose of the processing of the white list, we will break a typical URL request into the following parts:

```
protocol://host.domain.extension:port/url
```

The following are the fields in `HTTP_WHITELIST` and the effects that they have on processing.

- `ENTRY_TYPE`: This field lets you identify what type of URL matching you want to check against. For instance you might mark an entry as BSP Theme Matching.
- `HOST`: Value to be checked against the host+domain+extension portion of the URL as described above. If this entry is left blank then no check is performed. The entry can be wildcarded with the * character.
- `PROTOCOL`: Protocol, generally HTTP or HTTPS, to be verified. Leave this field empty if you do not want to check against the protocol.
- `PORT`: Port number in digits only that you want to check. Once again simply leave this field blank if you do not want to check against the port. Keep in mind that even if a port is not specified in a URL, it still has one. For HTTP the standard defined port is 80, for HTTPS it is 443.
- `URL`: This is the check against the remainder of the entire URL specification after the protocol+host+domain+extension+port. The wildcard * is accepted here as well.

It is important to distinguish between leaving an entry blank and using the wildcard. In the case of protocol if you left the entry blank, all protocols would pass the check. Therefore the protocol might be HTTP, HTTPS, or FILE. That last protocol in the list might be a bit suspicious. Therefore in this case, to be safe it would be better to use the wildcard with an entry `HTTP*`. That way we allow both HTTP and HTTPS.

17.7 Error Pages

So far, all of our customization options are centered on changing the look and feel of BSP applications via the use of themes. There are two other types of BSP pages that have special opportunities for customization. The first of these two types is BSP Error Pages.

17.7.1 Historical BSP Error Pages

SAP introduced the concept of BSP error pages so that, inside each application, you could designate one or more pages or views to act as error pages. These pages were marked with a special icon in the Workbench object viewer. On the rest of your pages or views, you could then designate which error page would be responsible for it. This relationship can be seen in Figure 17.6

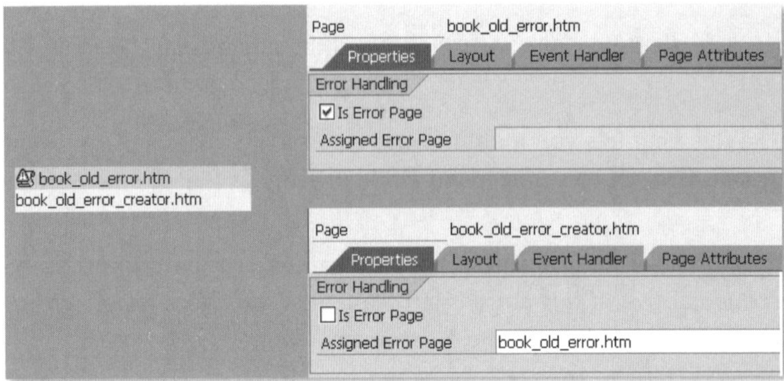

Figure 17.6 Classic Error Pages

The BSP runtime places a `TRY/CATCH` check around every call to a page, view or controller. If an exception occurs within the processing of the inner object, the BSP runtime will catch it and then pass control to the configured error page.

The main problem with this approach is that the error page itself is another BSP page. Therefore, this error page has been started within the error environment of the original page. The error page has no knowledge of what may or may not already have been written out by the original page into the HTTP response object.

Also, the BSP element stack could be in a questionable state. If the original page has already created an `<htmlb:content>` element, the error page can not create another element because you can only have one instance on the stack. On the other hand, the original page may have produced an error before reaching or while processing the `<htmlb:content>` element. Now the error page is responsible for creating an `<htmlb:content>` element itself. In the worst-case situation, the error page itself might produce an error while processing the output from the original error.

Because of these complexities, SAP has discontinued support for the BSP error page as of Web AS 6.20 SP48 and 6.40 SP11. As of these releases, any configuration for the error-page options will simply be ignored by the BSP runtime.

17.7.2 Error Pages—New Approach

Although SAP has stopped support for the old BSP error pages solution, the company has not left customers without a method for creating custom error pages. As of the same support package levels that disable the old approach, SAP also delivers a new method for producing custom error pages.

Now when an exception occurs, control exits the BSP framework completely, allowing the exception to pass all the way up to the ICF (Internet Communication Framework). Inside the ICF there is the BSP class that integrates into ICF, CL_HTTP_EXT_BSP, which is now responsible for catching exceptions from BSP applications and producing a generic error page. The rendering routine in this class that is mostly likely used to produce this generic error page is REPORT_ERROR_HTML.

In order to test this new exception-handling technique, we will create a BSP page that purposely has a runtime error. We will simply use the programmer's worst enemy—divide by zero!

```
<htmlb:content design="design2003" >
  <htmlb:page title=" " >
    <htmlb:form>
      <% data: results type i.
           results = 1 / 0. %>
      ...
    </htmlb:form>
  </htmlb:page>
</htmlb:content>
```

The amount and type of information on this generic error page is quite impressive. It contains most all the information anyone could want to begin diagnosing a problem. SAP understands that many customers are going to want to customize this error page, so they deliver a table where you can configure an alternative class and method to be called in the error condition.

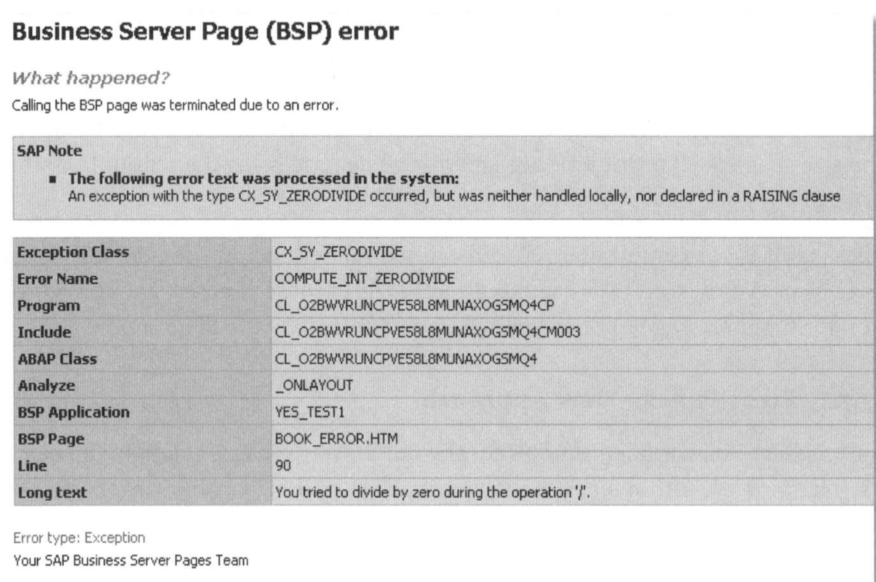

Business Server Page (BSP) error

What happened?

Calling the BSP page was terminated due to an error.

SAP Note

- **The following error text was processed in the system:**
An exception with the type CX_SY_ZERODIVIDE occurred, but was neither handled locally, nor declared in a RAISING clause

Exception Class	CX_SY_ZERODIVIDE
Error Name	COMPUTE_INT_ZERODIVIDE
Program	CL_O2BWVRUNCPVE58L8MUNAXOGSMQ4CP
Include	CL_O2BWVRUNCPVE58L8MUNAXOGSMQ4CM003
ABAP Class	CL_O2BWVRUNCPVE58L8MUNAXOGSMQ4
Analyze	_ONLAYOUT
BSP Application	YES_TEST1
BSP Page	BOOK_ERROR.HTM
Line	90
Long text	You tried to divide by zero during the operation '/'.

Error type: Exception

Your SAP Business Server Pages Team

Figure 17.7 Generic Error Page Produced by REPORT_ERROR_HTML

This way each customer can create their own `REPORT_ERROR` method. The only requirement is that the signature (`exception type ref to cx_root` and `server type ref to if_http_server`) of the customer method matches that of `REPORT_ERROR` from `CL_HTTP_EXT_BSP`. Also, the method must be defined as `STATIC` and `PUBLIC`.

The configuration table, `BSPERRHANDLER`, is maintained in transaction SE16. During maintenance, we can use wildcards (*) in the URL to set custom error handlers for entire sets of BSP applications. Creating aliases in transaction SICF even allows us to have multiple error pages for the same application.

Figure 17.8 shows the entry for setting up a custom error handler for a single BSP application.

Table BSPERRHANDLER Insert

Reset

MANDT	088
SORT KEY	0001
URL	*/YES_TEST1/*
ERR CLASS	YCL_BSP_EXCEPTIONS
ERR METHOD	REPORT_ERROR_HTML

Figure 17.8 BSPERRHANDLER Table Maintenance

In Figure 17.9, we see the results from a sample handler class, `CL_BSP_ERRHANDLER_SAMPLE`, which SAP delivers. It creates an error page with a very different look and feel than the standard one.

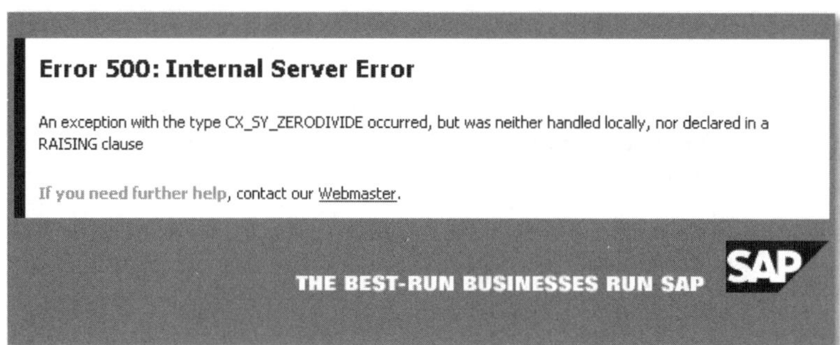

Figure 17.9 CL_BSP_ERRHANDLER_SAMPLE Output

You could copy the sample class and use it as your starting point. However, the generic output from `CL_HTTP_EXT_BSP` actually has a lot more detail and is already nicely formatted. If all you want to do is add some company specific contact information, you might consider copying the `REPORT_ERROR_HTML` method from this class as your starting point instead.

Long text	You tried to divide by zero during the operation '/'.

Error type: Exception
Your SAP Business Server Pages Team
If you feel you need additional support for this problem, please call 001-800-555-5555

Figure 17.10 Slightly Modified Output from the CL_HTTP_EXT_BSP Class

Keep in mind that as you implement the coding of these error pages that you are not inside the BSP framework. That means that you cannot rely on the BSP Extensions. You have to build your own style sheets and raw HTML directly into the response object. This is just one more reason why you might want to start with `CL_HTTP_EXT_BSP`.

To achieve our modification of adding the support phone number in Figure 17.10, we only had to add the following to the coding of our error method.

```
concatenate `<tr>` &
            `<td>` &
              `<p class="note">` "#EC NOTEXT
                'Business Server Page (BSP) Fehler'(011)
                ' '
```

```
                    strexception
                  `</p>` &
                  `<p>` "#EC NOTEXT
                    'Ihr SAP Business Server Pages Team'(012)
                  `</p>` &
                  `<p>`
                    'If you feel you need additional support _
            for this problem, please call 001-800-555-5555'(c01)
                  `</p>` &
                 `</td>` &
                `</tr>` &
               `</table>` &
              `</body>` &
             `</html>` "#EC NOTEXT
   into html.
   server->response->append_cdata( html ).
```

17.8 Logon Application

The other special type of page that can be customized is on the opposite end of the spectrum from error pages. This is the use of a web based logon page, instead of the default browser popup for name and password. Such a web based logon page enables supporting of additional features such as a password change sequence, and also enables the support of displaying more information (from SM02, typically maintenance information, etc).

Starting in Web AS 6.40, SAP delivers a new, highly customizable logon page. You will find this referred to in the documentation as the System Logon. This should not be confused with the 6.20 BSP application `SYSTEM` and its `logon.htm` page. The customization of this new logon page begins within transaction SICF.

In 6.20, BSP applications could choose to use the `SYSTEM` logon application. The use of this older logon method should be replaced with the System Logon on Web AS 6.40 and higher. The new System Logon has significant enhancements and is not tied to the BSP framework. As an example, both Web Dynpro ABAP and the integrated ITS use the new System Logon.

If you go into maintenance mode on an individual service and then navigate to the **Error Pages** tab, you should see several options for **Logon Errors**. In Web AS 6.20, you could use the **Redirect to URL** approach and send the user to a BSP application called `SYSTEM`. This approach was nice and somewhat customizable, but has no where near the functional of the new System Logon approach.

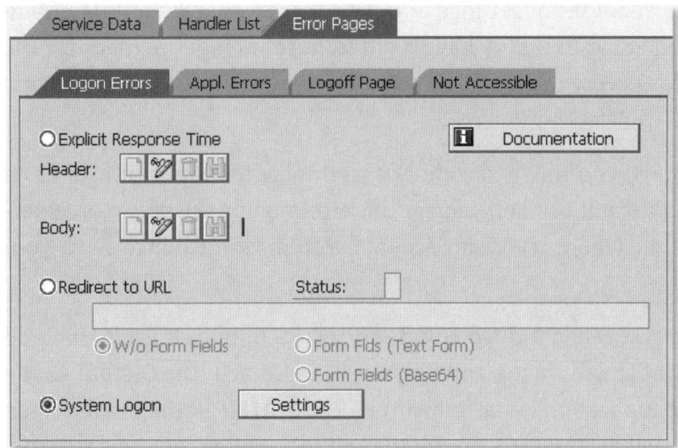

Figure 17.11 Service Node Maintenance

In order to use the new functionality, you must choose **System Logon** option. You then can hit the **Settings** button to begin the customization fun.

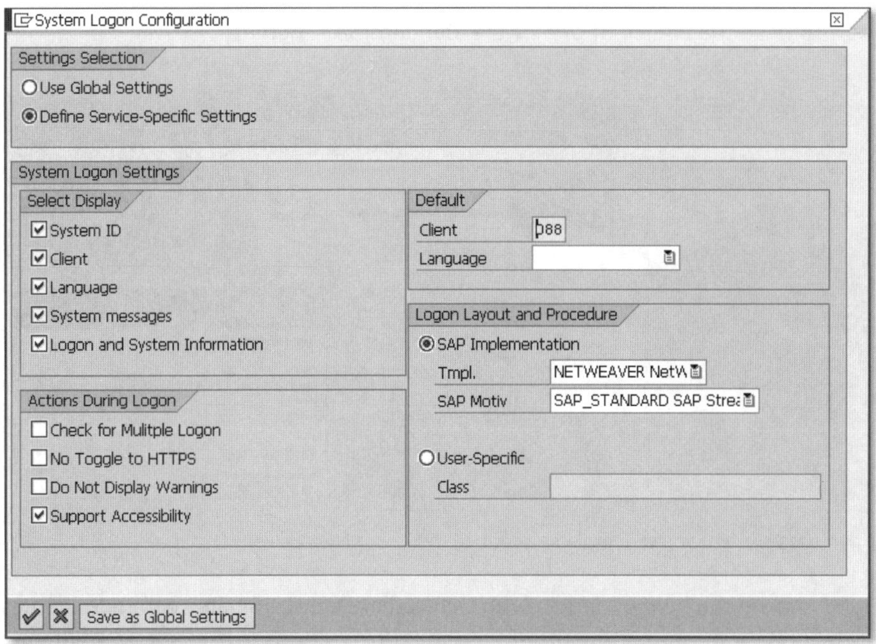

Figure 17.12 System Logon Configuration

Figure 17.12 demonstrates the many customization options that are possible with a simple dialog. Right away, you might notice that for each service node you have the ability to reuse a global set of settings or define service-specific settings. With the use of aliases, you could in theory have a different set of logon screens for the same application. This is very useful if you need to support separate internal and external views of an application.

With the many options, you might decide not to display the input of client and language and instead default to fixed values. This also might be useful in an externally facing application where the term "client" would be meaningless to your users.

One option you should note is the **No Toggle to HTTPS** option. It is advisable to use HTTPS to encrypt the user name and password. By default, the System Logon does not care if your application is started with HTTPS or HTTP. If the logon screen is configured, it will switch to HTTPS during the redirect. Following the successful logon, the application will be started with the originally requested protocol. Therefore it is not advisable to check the option **No Toggle to HTTPS**.

Now we come to the section where we can adjust the look and feel of the system logon page. In the **Logon Layout and Procedure** section of the customization, you will see that we have the choice of three different templates. To add to this we also have the choice of one of the standard SAP themes.

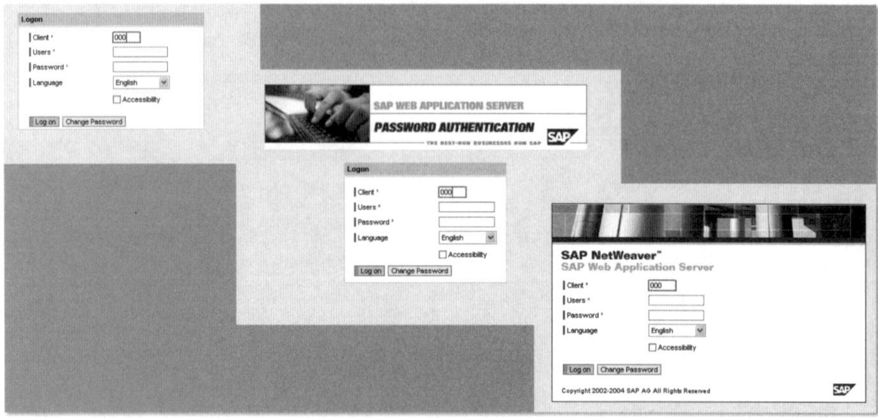

Figure 17.13 System Logon Templates: Normal, IDES, and NetWeaver

But if you are the type of person who thinks that three templates with five themes each, along with numerous other configuration options just is not enough customization, then you will still be quite happy with the System Logon. The very last option in the dialog is **User-Specific Class**. That is right: You have the ability to create your own logon class inheriting from the SAP class `CL_ICF_SYSTEM_LOGIN`. Actually, each of the three templates are all separate classes and available as starting points: CL_ICF_BASIC_LOGIN, CL_ICF_IDES_LOGIN, and CL_ICF_NW04_LOGIN. SAP also sends along an example customized logon class, CL_ICF_EXAMPLE01_LOGIN.

You will find that the coding in these classes is very similar to the ABAP programming for BSP extension-element handler classes. Using inheritance, you have the freedom to redefine most any of the rendering methods and either make small changes or go crazy and create an all-new interface.

In the following example we have redefined the method RENDER. We are going to replace the copyright section with our own little text. A comment must be made about the way the coding works in general within the System Logon. The System Logon application was designed and implemented to work directly against the Unified Rendering library; thus the use of UR in the class names such as clur_* and ifur_*.

Although you have to use these classes within a custom System Logon rendering class, they are not technically released for customer use. This means there is not any documentation on their use. You will probably notice that their structure is very close to that of the underlying classes of the HTMLB libraries. Therefore, the only other concern to deal with is the fact that SAP does not guarantee that it will not change the interfaces to these classes in the future. However the risk of massive changes to these classes in the future is very slight and should not necessarily deter you from creating a custom System Logon rendering class.

```
lr_gridlayoutcell = clur_d2_factory=>gridlayoutcell(
    halign        = ifur_d2=>cellhalign_left
    valign        = ifur_d2=>cellvalign_bottom
    paddingtop    = '10px'
    paddingbottom = '10px'
    paddingleft   = '15px' ).
  lr_gridlayoutrow->cells_add( lr_gridlayoutcell ).
  lr_textview = clur_d2_factory=>textview(
    text     = 'BSP Book Example System Logon'
    tooltip  = 'BSP Book Example System Logon'
    design   = ifur_d2=>textviewdesign_header1
    wrapping = abap_false ).
  lr_gridlayoutcell->content = lr_textview.
```

These changes produce the new logon screen seen in Figure 17.14.

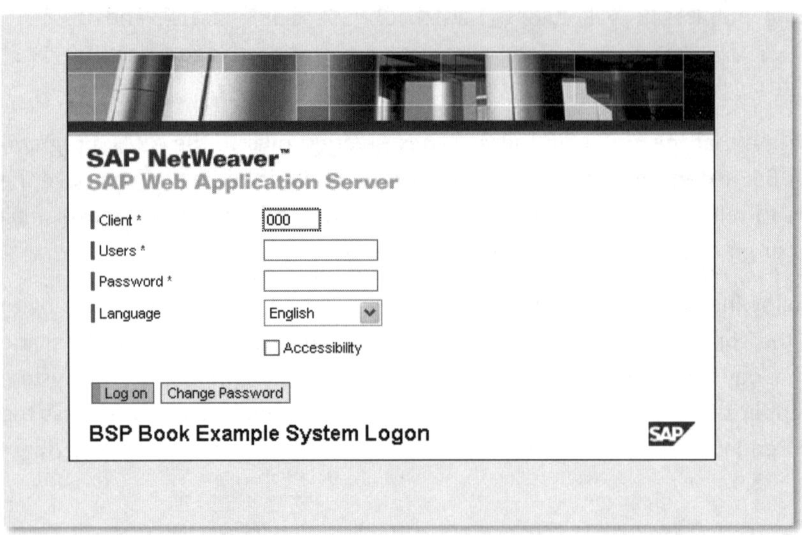

Figure 17.14 Customized System Logon Class

18 Skilled in the Art

Until now, we have been studying a great deal of foundation technology. Now it is time to learn how we can put this technology to good use in the form of some real-life BSP example applications.

Now that you have spent some time learning the advanced technologies within BSP, such as Model View Controller and Pattern Engines, you will begin to see how you can apply these technologies to meet unique and difficult programming tasks.

In this chapter, we will challenge ourselves to *think outside of the box* and begin to apply many of the technologies and techniques introduced in previous chapters.

18.1 Field History

In Section 9.6, we discussed the fact that the implementation of `<htmlb:form>` combined with the dynamic nature of element ids causes the browser's field history or auto-complete functionality to be disabled in BSP.

Although the technical reasons this functionality is missing make perfectly good sense, that does not change the fact that users really miss it. The question becomes: Why not create our own server side field history?

We have a UI element that would fit nicely. The `<phtmlb:comboBox>` has an attribute called `behavior`. If this attribute is set to `FREETEXT`, you essentially get an input field that allows free-text input. But you also get a drop-down list box attached to this input field. We can use the drop-down list box to store the field history. Users can then browse back through the last 20 or so entries they have made on this field using the drop-down list box and selectively reuse one of the old values.

This means that when a user manually types in a new value, we will need to trap that value and store it somewhere, as well as update that value into the history drop-down list box.

18.1.1 Working with <phtmlb:comboBox>

Before jumping into the coding solution for this example, it is important to note a small problem with the `<phtmlb:comboBox>` when using `behavior = FREETEXT` and Model View Binding. Apparently, the raw HTML generated by the `<phtmlb:comboBox>` in `FREETEXT` mode creates two separate elements. By default, model-binding logic can only restore values from one HTML form field.

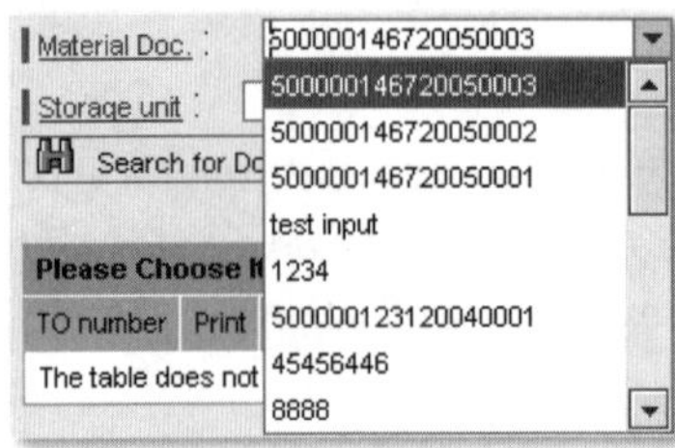

Figure 18.1 Custom Field History Using a <phtmlb:comboBox>

One quick call to the friendly SAP BSP support desk, and we have a simple solution: You just need to implement a small bit of JavaScript that will sync the values between these two elements before input. This script does interact with the underlying rendered HTML and therefore might be broken by a future support package. This should be considered a possible sample solution to the problem that might require some adjustment based upon your particular support package level.

In the following example, please note that the element ids are hard-coded. They correspond to the `<phtmlb:comboBox>` ID of `DDLB`. Also you must take into account the controller id, which is `s2`.

```
<phtmlb:comboBox id      = "DDLB"
      selection          = "//model/matdoc_sel.material_doc"
      table              = "//model/matdoc_hist"
      behavior           = "FREETEXT"
      onSelect           = "show_DDLB"
      onClientSelect     = "setMyNewKey();"
      nameOfKeyColumn    = "key"
      nameOfValueColumn  = "value"
      width              = "150" />

<script defer language="JavaScript">
function setMyNewKey(){
  var sList=sapUrMapi_ItemListBox_getList(
      "s2_DDLB-lb",document);
  var sListArray=sList.split("||");
  var sListTable=new Object;
  for(var i=0;i<sListArray.lenght;i++){
    var sListItem=sListArray[i].split("|");
    if(typeof sListItem[1]!="undefined")
    sListTable[sListItem[1]]=sListItem[0];
    }
```

```
var value=sapUrMapi_ComboBox_getSelectedValue("s2_DDLB");
document.getElementById('s2_DDLBKey').value=value;
for(var key in sListTable){
  if(value==sListTable[key]){
     var o=sapUrMapi_ComboBox_getObject("s2_DDLB");
     o.txt.setAttribute("k",key);
     o.txt.setAttribute("ks",key);
     document.getElementById('s2_DDLBKey').value=
           key;break;
     }
  }
}
</script>
```

18.1.2 Processing the Field History

As you can see from the `<phtmlb:comboBox>` code sample in the previous section, we are going to have an internal table in our model class to house the history values. This table, `matdoc_hist`, just needs to be defined as the typical drop-down list box key/value pair. You might consider using the table type `SHSVALTAB` or `TIHTTPNVP` for its definition.

In order to keep the data in this history table persistent, we will create a database table. This table will be designed to be generic enough to hold input history for almost any type of field. We want to store input history specific to a user and a particular field. We also want to store the timestamp for the last time that value was used. This gives us something to use when determining which value should come off the list once it is full. It also allows us to sort our history according to most recently used values.

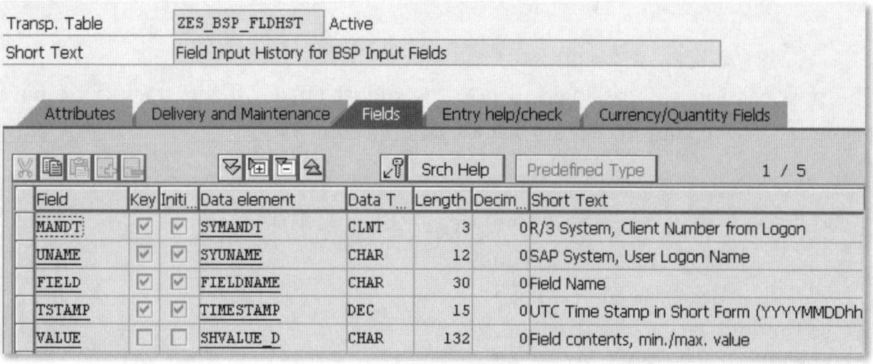

Transp. Table: ZES_BSP_FLDHST Active
Short Text: Field Input History for BSP Input Fields

Attributes | Delivery and Maintenance | Fields | Entry help/check | Currency/Quantity Fields

Srch Help | Predefined Type | 1 / 5

Field	Key	Initi...	Data element	Data T...	Length	Decim...	Short Text
MANDT	☑	☑	SYMANDT	CLNT	3	0	R/3 System, Client Number from Logon
UNAME	☑	☑	SYUNAME	CHAR	12	0	SAP System, User Logon Name
FIELD	☑	☑	FIELDNAME	CHAR	30	0	Field Name
TSTAMP	☑	☑	TIMESTAMP	DEC	15	0	UTC Time Stamp in Short Form (YYYYMMDDhh
VALUE	☐	☐	SHVALUE_D	CHAR	132	0	Field contents, min./max. value

Figure 18.2 Field Input History Database Table Definition

Now we need a generic routine that will sync the values between this database table and our internal table for a given field. For easy reusability, we will create this as a static method of a utility class.

This method will have two importing and one changing parameters. The changing parameter C_HIST is for the history table itself. It is defined as SHSVALTAB. The first importing parameter is NEW_VALUE type CSEQUENCE. This is where the new input value is passed in. Declaring this parameter as CSEQUENCE gives us the freedom to supply this value via any text-type field, character, or string. The final importing parameter is FIELD. This is how we specify the field name under which we want to store this history. By using a consistent fieldname here, we can share input help across multiple input fields in the user interface.

```
METHOD update_bsp_field_hist.
*Importing   NEW_VALUE   TYPE CSEQUENCE
*Importing   FIELD       TYPE FIELDNAME     Field Name
*Changing    I_HIST      TYPE SHSVALTAB
CHECK new_value IS NOT INITIAL.
```

In this first section of code, we will remove the new value from the history table if it is already in there. This allows us to re-insert it later with a new timestamp. This way it moves to the top of the stack.

```
  READ TABLE c_hist TRANSPORTING NO FIELDS
        WITH KEY key = new_value.
  IF sy-subrc = 0.
    DATA: l_value TYPE shvalue_d.
    l_value = new_value.
    DELETE FROM zes_bsp_fldhst
     WHERE uname = sy-uname
       AND field = field
       AND value = l_value.
  ENDIF.
```

The next section has the logic to pop the oldest entry off the stack if we have exceeded our maximum history size of 20 entries.

```
  DATA: icount TYPE i.
  SELECT COUNT( * ) FROM zes_bsp_fldhst INTO icount
         WHERE uname = sy-uname
           AND field = field.
  IF icount >= 20.
    DATA: old_tstamp TYPE timestamp.
```

```
    SELECT MIN( tstamp ) FROM zes_bsp_fldhst INTO old_tstamp
         WHERE uname = sy-uname
           AND field = field.
    DELETE FROM zes_bsp_fldhst
     WHERE uname  = sy-uname
       AND field  = field
       AND tstamp = old_tstamp.
  ENDIF.
```

This final section of code will record the new value into the history database table. It will then rebuild the history internal table.

```
  DATA: inew  TYPE zes_bsp_fldhst.
  inew-uname = sy-uname.
  inew-field = field.
  inew-value = new_value.
  GET TIME STAMP FIELD inew-tstamp.
  INSERT zes_bsp_fldhst FROM inew.
  CLEAR i_hist.
  DATA: ihist TYPE TABLE OF zes_bsp_fldhst.
  FIELD-SYMBOLS: <wa_string> LIKE LINE OF ihist,
                 <wa_hist>   LIKE LINE OF i_hist.
  SELECT * FROM zes_bsp_fldhst INTO table ihist
   WHERE uname = sy-uname
     AND field = field
     ORDER BY tstamp DESCENDING.
  LOOP AT ihist ASSIGNING <wa_string>.
    APPEND INITIAL LINE TO i_hist ASSIGNING <wa_hist>.
    <wa_hist>-key   = <wa_string>-value.
    <wa_hist>-value = <wa_string>-value.
  ENDLOOP.
ENDMETHOD.
```

All that is left now is to put the pieces together and make sure that we process the field history on an input event for our `<phtmlb:comboBox>`. For this, we will use the `DO_HANDLE_DATA` method of our controller class.

We will directly query the `<phtmlb:comboBox>` and use the current value to update the field history.

```
  DATA: combobox TYPE REF TO cl_phtmlb_combobox.
  combobox ?= cl_htmlb_manager=>get_data(
              request = request
```

```
            name     = 'phtmlb:comboBox'
            id       = 's2_DDLB' ).
IF combobox IS NOT INITIAL.
 CALL METHOD ycl_abap_utilities=>update_bsp_field_hist
   EXPORTING new_value = combobox->value
             field     = 'MATDOC'
   CHANGING  i_hist    = model->matdoc_hist.
ENDIF.
```

18.2 Server-Side Printing

It is generally accepted that printing from the browsers leaves something to be desired. Printing usually brings about alignment problems, such as text running off the side of the page, or loss of background graphics. Consider also that a good user interface often hides many elements or only allows for a small number of records in a table to be displayed at a time, thereby making a good printout from the browser nearly impossible.

There are many possible solutions. You might decide to open a separate page with dedicated rendering better suited to a print layout. You could also consider third-party solutions that will re-render the output to PDF.

But why not instead leverage the server side print infrastructure that is already in place in any ABAP based SAP solution? The purpose of this example was to come up with a reusable approach that would allow you to take an internal table that was being used as the source of an `<htmlb:tableView>` and output it using ALV Grid. That way, we could take advantage of all the rich printing and formatting that ABAP programmers had come to rely on in classical dynpro development.

This example is implemented as a static class method that will process an internal table and, using the ALV Grid List output mode, force the results to the print spooler. We have used the new Web AS 6.40 ALV object model. However, since the ALV classes are mostly wrappers around the ALV control or reuse function modules, it should be easy to back port this solution to Web AS 6.20.

Naturally, though, we did not want just to output the entire internal table. You often have extra fields used in internal processing that you do not display in the output. We also may have changed the column headers. To support these situations, the static method will also apply a table-view iterator or column-definition table to the data before processing it in the ALV Grid.

As if this was not enough, you probably will soon realize that you need a reusable printer dialog. You need a way for users to choose which printer they want and set other printer settings such as **Print Immediately** or **Delete after Output**. Luckily it is not too difficult to take what we know about custom BSP extensions (Chapter 11) and dialog windows (Chapter 14) and build a new BSP extension element that will provide the UI elements for querying the printer, number of copies, etc. during server-side printing.

18.2.1 PRINT Method Interface

We will start with the coding for the static method that performs the output. First we need to have a look at the interface of this method.

```
CLASS-METHODS print
  IMPORTING
    itab          TYPE REF TO data
    iterator      TYPE REF TO
                       if_htmlb_tableview_iterator OPTIONAL
    col_def       TYPE tableviewcontroltab OPTIONAL
    print_options TYPE sfpprip
    messages      TYPE REF TO cl_bsp_messages.
```

We have five importing parameters. The first is a reference to the data table we want to process. By declaring this as a `TYPE REF TO DATA`, we can receive and process an internal table of any flat structure. Next, we have two optional parameters: the iterator and the column-definition table. Neither are critical to the overall process, but if we want control over what columns are output or what column headers are used we will want to use one of them. The column definitions table has priority over the iterator.

Next, we have a structure in which we will pass in our printer parameters. This example used type `SFPPRIP` because that is what the printer dialog expects. The printer dialog was originally designed for the output of Adobe Print Forms, so this is the structure for Adobe Forms.

If you are not on Web AS 6.40, you might not have this structure. Most of the fields are the same as the SmartForms or List processing options structure, but the names might be different. Later, you will see that we map these values to the list options. If you are not on 6.40, or if you are not going to use the example printer dialog, you might want to go ahead and defining a different importing structure.

Finally, we have a reference to the messages object so that any processing errors can be passed back out to the calling routine. Using the `CL_BSP_MESSAGES` object is not required; you could just as easily pass an error string in and out of the method.

18.2.2 PRINT Method Coding

We start our processing by getting a usable handle to our internal table reference. You then can see some variables we will use later: a reference to the ALV Grid class and the variables for list-print output. If you did not want to pass in SFPPRIP, you might want to just fill a structure of type PRI_PARAMS and pass it in instead.

```
METHOD print.
  FIELD-SYMBOLS: <tab> TYPE table.
  ASSIGN itab->* TO <tab>.
  DATA: table   TYPE REF TO cl_salv_table.
  DATA: print_parameters TYPE pri_params,
        valid_flag(1) TYPE c.
```

Next, we need to map the input print options structure into the one needed for list processing. You never want to attempt to fill PRI_PARAMS yourself. You should always use the function module GET_PRINT_PARAMETERS.

```
  CALL FUNCTION 'GET_PRINT_PARAMETERS'
  ...
    IMPORTING out_parameters = print_parameters
  ...
```

Even though we are inside BSP processing, we can still force list output directly to the print spool with the printer options our user selected. To do this, we just need a call to NEW-PAGE.

```
  NEW-PAGE PRINT ON PARAMETERS print_parameters
                 NO DIALOG.
```

Next, we will create our instance of ALV and get a pointer to the columns object. You will see that while the processing is very different from that used by the pre-6.40 ALV Grid, it has been streamlined.

```
  DATA: salv_msg TYPE REF TO cx_salv_msg.
  DATA: error_string TYPE string.
  TRY.
      cl_salv_table=>factory(
        EXPORTING list_display = abap_true
        IMPORTING r_salv_table = table
        CHANGING  t_table      = <tab> ).
  CATCH cx_salv_msg INTO salv_msg.
      messages->add_message_from_exception(
          condition = 'print'
```

```
        exception = salv_msg ).
    RETURN.
ENDTRY.
DATA: columns TYPE REF TO cl_salv_columns_table.
columns = table->get_columns( ).
columns->set_optimize( abap_true ).
```

If the caller of this method has supplied an iterator or table-column definition, we need to apply it here by altering the columns object of ALV. For pre-6.40 this would be the same as generating a field catalog and manipulating it.

```
DATA: l_col_def TYPE tableviewcontroltab.
DATA: iterator_error TYPE REF TO
      cx_sy_dyn_call_illegal_method.

IF col_def IS INITIAL AND iterator IS NOT INITIAL.
  DATA: p_overwrites TYPE tableviewoverwritetab.
  TRY.
      iterator->get_column_definitions(
          EXPORTING p_tableview_id = 'itab'
          CHANGING  p_column_definitions = l_col_def
                    p_overwrites         = p_overwrites ).
  CATCH cx_sy_dyn_call_illegal_method INTO iterator_error.
     messages->add_message_from_exception(
          condition = 'print'
          exception = iterator_error ).
     RETURN.
  ENDTRY.
ELSEIF col_def  IS NOT INITIAL.
  l_col_def = col_def.
ENDIF.
IF l_col_def IS NOT INITIAL.
  DATA: scrtext_l TYPE scrtext_l,
        scrtext_m TYPE scrtext_m,
        scrtext_s TYPE scrtext_s,
        tooltip   TYPE lvc_tip.
  DATA: col TYPE salv_t_column_ref.
  FIELD-SYMBOLS: <wa_col> LIKE LINE OF col,
                 <wa_col_def> LIKE LINE OF l_col_def.
  col = columns->get( ).
  LOOP AT col ASSIGNING <wa_col>.
    READ TABLE l_col_def ASSIGNING <wa_col_def>
```

```
          WITH KEY columnname = <wa_col>-columnname.
      IF sy-subrc = 0.
        <wa_col>-r_column->set_visible( abap_true ).
        IF <wa_col_def>-title IS NOT INITIAL.
          scrtext_l = <wa_col_def>-title.
          ...
          <wa_col>-r_column->set_short_text( scrtext_s ).
        ENDIF.
      ELSE.
        <wa_col>-r_column->set_visible( abap_false ).
      ENDIF.
    ENDLOOP.
  ENDIF.
```

Finally, we close out the processing by forcing the ALV to produce its output and then closing the list processing.

```
  table->display( ).
  NEW-PAGE PRINT OFF.
  messages->add_message2(
            condition   = 'print'
            message     = 'Print Output is complete'(i01)
            messagetype = 'I' ).
ENDMETHOD.
```

18.2.3 Printer Dialog

The coding supplied here is not so much a complete solution as a starting point. You have the structure and rendering of the UI element in order to save time in case you want to implement something similar. You could just render these elements in line in an existing application. In that case you could just about use all the coding as is.

You might want instead to open this dialog in another window. For this, you might use the modal window using the floating IFrame solution from Section 14.2. This keeps the browser from treating the area as another window, so that instead it can share the model class that contains the results directly via a stateful application. For this reason you will find a small block of JavaScript code toward the end of the element processing.

```
  DATA: javascript_close TYPE string.
  CONCATENATE me->id '_Close' INTO javascript_close.
  DATA: closedialog TYPE REF TO
```

```
      ycl_bsp_elmnt_close_dialog.
closedialog ?= ycl_bsp_elmnt_close_dialog=>factory(
            clientevent = javascript_close ).
WHILE m_page_context->element_process(
      element = closedialog ) = co_element_continue.
ENDWHILE.
CONCATENATE javascript_close '();' INTO javascript_close.
DATA: button TYPE REF TO cl_htmlb_button.
button ?= cl_htmlb_button=>factory(
       id = me->id
       id_postfix = '__PrintBtn'
       onclientclick = javascript_close
       text = 'Print'(p01) ).
```

Listing 18.1 Printer Dialog—Close Hook

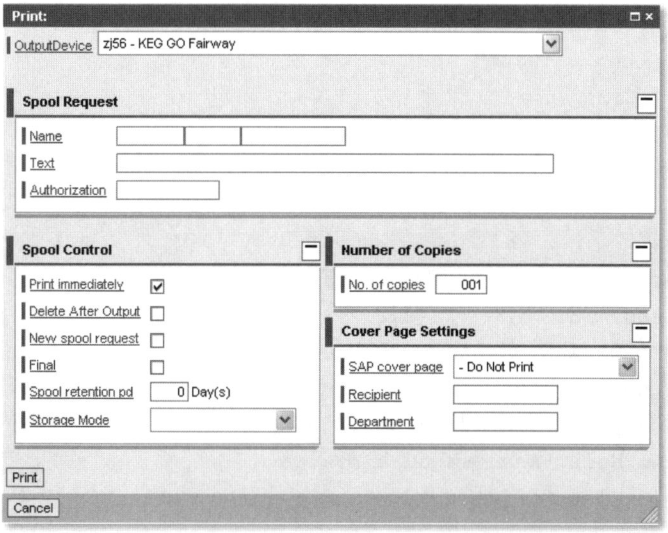

Figure 18.3 Printer Dialog User Interface

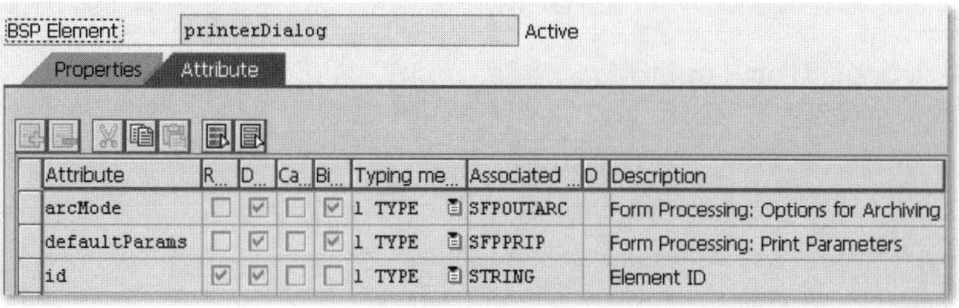

Attribute	R...	D...	Ca...	Bi...	Typing me...	Associated ...	D	Description
arcMode	☐	☑	☐	☑	1 TYPE	SFPOUTARC		Form Processing: Options for Archiving
defaultParams	☐	☑	☐	☑	1 TYPE	SFPPRIP		Form Processing: Print Parameters
id	☑	☑	☐	☐	1 TYPE	STRING		Element ID

Figure 18.4 Printer Dialog Element Attributes

Most likely you can ignore this section of code that hooks the JavaScript function into the close button, since it is specific to the dialog window processing. Or perhaps this is where you can put your own logic to close your processing area.

```
IF _defaultparams IS NOT INITIAL.
  CONCATENATE _defaultparams `.DEST` INTO binding.
  CLEAR text.
ELSE.
  text = ycl_abap_utilities=>read_field_desc(
        defaultparams-dest ).
  CLEAR binding.
ENDIF.
CLEAR f1label.
f1label ?= ycl_bsp_elmnt_f1_help_lbl=>factory(
        id = me->id
        id_postfix = '_DestLbl'
        for = 'defaultparams.dest'
        text = text
        _for = binding ).
WHILE m_page_context->element_process( element = f1label )
        = co_element_continue.
ENDWHILE.
CLEAR ddlb_values.
SELECT padest pamsg FROM tsp03 INTO TABLE ddlb_values.
LOOP AT ddlb_values ASSIGNING <wa_ddlb>.
   CALL FUNCTION 'CONVERSION_EXIT_SPDEV_OUTPUT'
      EXPORTING input  = <wa_ddlb>-key
      IMPORTING output = <wa_ddlb>-key.
   CONCATENATE <wa_ddlb>-key <wa_ddlb>-value
   INTO <wa_ddlb>-value SEPARATED BY ` - `.
ENDLOOP.
SORT ddlb_values BY value.
GET REFERENCE OF ddlb_values INTO itab.
CLEAR ddlb.
ddlb ?= cl_htmlb_dropdownlistbox=>factory(
        id = me->id
        id_postfix = '_DestDDLB'
        _selection  = binding
        selection = defaultparams-dest
        nameofkeycolumn = 'KEY'
        nameofvaluecolumn = 'VALUE'
```

```
        table = itab ).
WHILE m_page_context->element_process( element = ddlb )
        = co_element_continue.
ENDWHILE.
```

Listing 18.2 Printer Dialog—Rendering Example

You might also notice that we use the context-help label from Section 14.1. You probably are beginning to see how these solutions can layer one on top of the other to provide even more value.

If you do not want to implement this custom extension as well, just adjust the calls to `ycl_bsp_elmnt_fl_help_lbl` with `cl_htmlb_label`. We also have a routine called `ycl_abap_utilities=>read_field_desc`. We use this routine in case you did not take advantage of data binding. This static method will look up the language-dependent descriptions from the data dictionary. It is not terribly impressive, but it is a nice little space saver.

```
METHOD read_field_desc .
*Importing  FIELD  TYPE ANY
*Returning  VALUE( DESC )  TYPE SCRTEXT_M  Medium lbl
  DATA: el_desc TYPE REF TO cl_abap_elemdescr,
        isddic  TYPE abap_bool,
        field_d TYPE dfies.
  TRY.
   el_desc ?= cl_abap_typedescr=>describe_by_data( field ).
   isddic = el_desc->is_ddic_type( ).
   CHECK isddic = abap_true.
   field_d = el_desc->get_ddic_field( ).
   desc = field_d-scrtext_m.
  CATCH cx_root.
  ENDTRY.
ENDMETHOD.
```

18.3 Select-Options/Parameters

If you are a long-time ABAP programmer but have never done much programming outside this area, you might not realize just what a luxury `Select-Options` and `Parameters` provide.

Without hardly any effort on the programmer's part, they are able to generate powerful UI elements for performing data selection. That single element allows for multiple ranges of input criteria, wild card values, negative and positive selections, greater than/less than evaluations, etc.

As you might imagine, recreating or adapting this solution to BSP was a bit of a challenge. The goal was to create a solution that was flexible and easy to integrate into existing BSP applications, yet still produced ABAP `RANGES` for back-end data selection.

While this solution needed to keep back-end compatibility to ABAP `RANGES`, it also needed to change the UI to adapt to the Web environment. We kept many of the icons used in the SAP GUI. On the other hand, the SAP GUI approach uses many dialog windows to manipulate the `Select-Options`. Although dialog windows can technically be used within BSP, they complicate the programming task considerably. Instead, this solution takes the route of rendering additional fields inline when needed.

18.3.1 UI Design

As you can see from Figure 18.5, there are three different display levels to each `Select-Option`. The Date `Select-Option` shows the default fully collapsed element. We have the selection options icon—the red, yellow and blue *flower*—which expands the display to the second level.

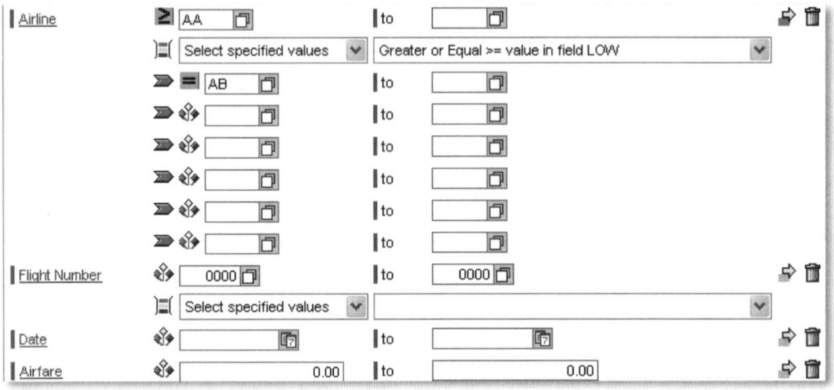

Figure 18.5 Select-Options UI Example

This level, as shown in the Flight Number selection, renders additional fields to choose positive or negative selection options. These options are sensitive to the value already placed in the `Select-Option`. Therefore, if your value contains a wildcard character, you will see the extra **Contains Pattern/Not Contains Pattern** criteria.

The fully expanded level, shown in the field Airline, provides an area to input multiple ranges. The UI will always generate five empty input areas. If you fill those up, you can press on any of the red arrows to generate another set of five empty inputs. The yellow arrow on the far right side collapses and expands the additional selections area.

Finally, all elements have a trash-can icon in order to quickly clear out all input values and criteria.

18.3.2 Solution Structure

In order to study the architecture for this solution, we will begin at the end. We start by looking at the coding that must be placed in the view in order to house the `Select-Option` area.

```
<bsp:call url      = "selop.do"
          comp_id = "SOC" >
   <bsp:parameter name  = "MODEL"
                  value = "<%= model %>" />
</bsp:call>
```

You might have expected to see a BSP extension element used here. However we can see from the UI that we will need a lot of event handling for the elements inside the `Select-Option` area. Rather than put the burden on the calling program to even to have to dispatch these events, would it not be better to completely encapsulate them as well?

Therefore, we take the approach that we studied in Section 13.6. Similar to the pattern engine that was built in that section, we will place the entire UI rendering and event handling within a reusable controller class. An application merely has to define a controller object and then hook it into this reusable controller class in order to have access to the 1,000 or so lines of ABAP code that control the UI rendering and event handling.

The controller class is fixed in its coding and interface. It was never intended to be inherited or redefined; in fact, we have marked it as `FINAL` to protect it from any such attempts. However, we still need a flexible way of defining our `Select-Options`. For this we have created a model class that is intentionally designed to be inheritable.

We are able to create a generic model class that has all the basic methods necessary for initializing, building and retrieving a set of `Select-Options`. It is this generic class that the controller will reference and work with. We then have the freedom to inherit this model and provide more specific implementations of the generic methods through redefinition.

The model will have two ways of building the `Select-Options`. First there is a method that can be redefined and allows for a completely customized list of

Select-Options. The other choice is to supply the name of a data-dictionary structure. The model will then use this structure as the definition of the listing of Select-Options; pulling details for each field from the data dictionary.

18.3.3 Select-Option Controller Class Attributes

Our controller class begins with three public attributes that can be set via the <bsp:parameter> call in our view. These three attributes function as the settings that will choose the path that the controller will take.

```
model         TYPE REF TO  ycl_bsp_m_selop_param
model_class   TYPE         seoclsname
dd_structure TYPE          tabname16
```

We have two options for supplying the model to be used. First the view could pass in an already created instance of a model class. This model object needs to be of our generic Select-Options model type or it needs to inherit from that type.

The other option is to request that the controller class creates the model instance for you. To do this, you specify the name of the model class in the attribute MODEL_CLASS. The controller will then place this instance into the attribute MODEL. The same rules apply in that the model class name specified must be the generic Select-Options model or it must inherit from it.

18.3.4 Select-Option Controller Class Coding

Once again, all the source code for all solutions can be found on the book CD. There is far too much coding in the controller class to list it all within this text.

The vast majority of the coding is UI rendering logic like that we have already seen many times within this book. We will use certain internal tables from the model class that define the Select-Options and their listings of values to loop through and generate UI elements. We will use the technique of dynamic model binding introduced in Section 13.4. The following is a small excerpt of the UI coding.

```
LOOP AT model->fields ASSIGNING <wa_fields>
     WHERE group = <wa_group>-group.
   tabix = sy-tabix.
   CONDENSE tabix.
   CLEAR label.
   CLEAR binding_master.
   READ TABLE model->values ASSIGNING <wa_values>
         WITH KEY id = <wa_fields>-id.
```

```
   IF sy-subrc NE 0.
    ...
   ENDIF.
   CONCATENATE '//model/values[' tabix '].'
               INTO binding_master.
   ...
   CONCATENATE binding_master 'LOW' INTO binding_string.
   CLEAR input.
   input ?= ycl_bsp_elmnt_input_help_v2=>factory(
            id          = <wa_fields>-id
            id_postfix = '_InputLow'
            dataref     = <wa_fields>-dataref
           _value       = binding_string ).
   WHILE page_context->element_process( element = input )
       = if_bsp_element=>co_element_continue.
   ENDWHILE.
```

Once again, we continue to reuse custom elements that were created earlier, such as the Help Values element from Section 14.3, providing more and more value with each layer.

The only other code section of particular importance within the controller class comes at the very beginning of the processing in DO_REQUEST. This is the section that initializes the model object and hooks into the initialization of the Select-Options.

```
IF model IS initial.
   IF model_class IS INITIAL.
      model_class = 'YCL_BSP_M_SELOP_PARAM'.
   ENDIF.
   model ?= create_model( model_id   = 'SO'
                          class_name = model_class ).
   model->initialize_selection_screen( ).
   IF dd_structure IS NOT INITIAL.
      model->initialize_fields_from_dd( dd_structure ).
   ENDIF.
ELSE.
   IF get_model( 'SO' ) IS INITIAL.
      set_model( model_id = 'SO' model_instance = model ).
   ENDIF.
ENDIF.
```

You can see the multiple options within the initialization of our controller. If the model instance is not supplied, we must create it. The consumer of the controller might have specified a model class. If not, we will simply use the default one.

Once the model is created, we will call the base method to initialize it, `initialize_selection_screen`. If this was an inherited model class, the `initialize_selection_screen` method may have been redefined to supply a custom set of `Select-Options`. On the other hand, perhaps the consumer is going to supply the definition of the `Select-Options` via a data dictionary structure. In that case, they will have passed the name of that structure in through the attribute `DD_STRUCTURE`, and we will now process it using the method `initialize_fields_from_dd`.

The other option is that the caller of this controller already would have created an instance of the model object. This allows complete control to initialize the model class with whatever custom methods are necessary. The controller now is only responsible for making sure the model instance is properly registered to the controller in the MVC framework so that the data binding will work correctly.

18.3.5 Select-Option Model Class Attributes

The heart of the `Select-Option` definition is really spread across three different internal tables all exposed as public attributes of the model class.

Structure: ZES_BSP_SEL_GROUPS Active
Short Text: BSP Select Options/Parameters Groups

Attributes | Components | Entry help/check | Currency/quantity fields

Predefined Type

Compone...	RT...	Co...	Data Type	Length	Decim...	Short Text
GROUP	☐		CHAR	20	0	Group
TITLE	☐		STRING	0	0	Title
TOOLTIP	☐		STRING	0	0	Quick Info
WIDTH	☐		STRING	0	0	Width

Figure 18.6 Select-Options Groups

The first internal table is the listing of groups. We have the ability to define multiple groups of `Select-Options`. Each group will be rendered out into its own `<htmlb:tray>`.

The next internal table, `FIELDS`, has the definition of each `Select-Option`. This is where you can set the type of `Select-Option`: drop-down list box, checkbox, date, basic help, and BAPI help.

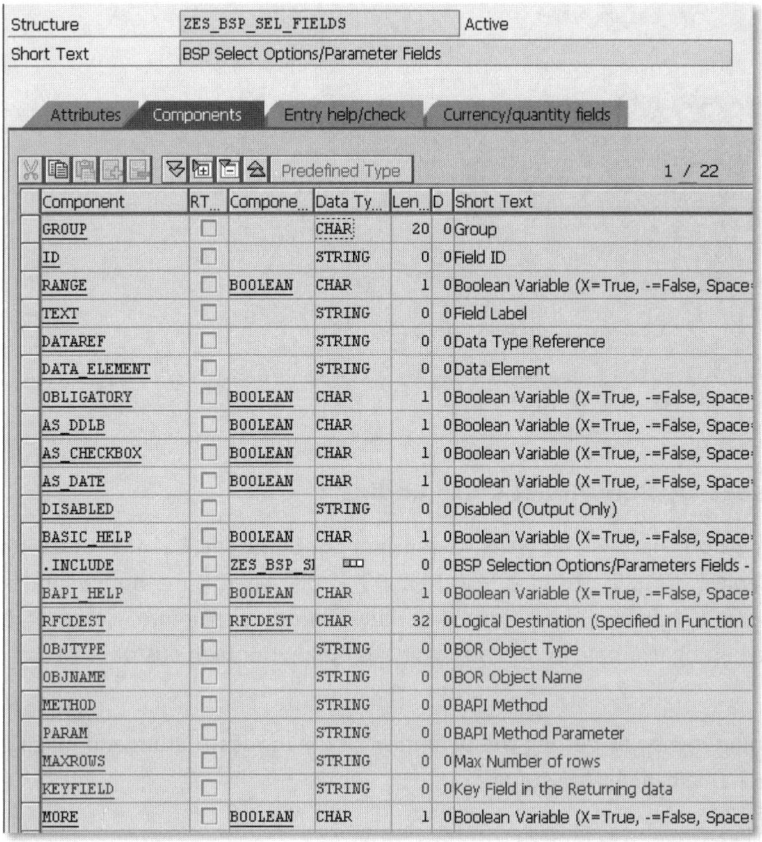

Structure: ZES_BSP_SEL_FIELDS — Active
Short Text: BSP Select Options/Parameter Fields

Attributes | Components | Entry help/check | Currency/quantity fields

Predefined Type — 1 / 22

Component	RT...	Compone...	Data Ty...	Len...	D	Short Text
GROUP	☐		CHAR	20	0	Group
ID	☐		STRING	0	0	Field ID
RANGE	☐	BOOLEAN	CHAR	1	0	Boolean Variable (X=True, -=False, Space
TEXT	☐		STRING	0	0	Field Label
DATAREF	☐		STRING	0	0	Data Type Reference
DATA_ELEMENT	☐		STRING	0	0	Data Element
OBLIGATORY	☐	BOOLEAN	CHAR	1	0	Boolean Variable (X=True, -=False, Space
AS_DDLB	☐	BOOLEAN	CHAR	1	0	Boolean Variable (X=True, -=False, Space
AS_CHECKBOX	☐	BOOLEAN	CHAR	1	0	Boolean Variable (X=True, -=False, Space
AS_DATE	☐	BOOLEAN	CHAR	1	0	Boolean Variable (X=True, -=False, Space
DISABLED	☐		STRING	0	0	Disabled (Output Only)
BASIC_HELP	☐	BOOLEAN	CHAR	1	0	Boolean Variable (X=True, -=False, Space
.INCLUDE	☐	ZES_BSP_SI		0	0	BSP Selection Options/Parameters Fields -
BAPI_HELP	☐	BOOLEAN	CHAR	1	0	Boolean Variable (X=True, -=False, Space
RFCDEST	☐	RFCDEST	CHAR	32	0	Logical Destination (Specified in Function
OBJTYPE	☐		STRING	0	0	BOR Object Type
OBJNAME	☐		STRING	0	0	BOR Object Name
METHOD	☐		STRING	0	0	BAPI Method
PARAM	☐		STRING	0	0	BAPI Method Parameter
MAXROWS	☐		STRING	0	0	Max Number of rows
KEYFIELD	☐		STRING	0	0	Key Field in the Returning data
MORE	☐	BOOLEAN	CHAR	1	0	Boolean Variable (X=True, -=False, Space

Figure 18.7 Select-Options Fields

You choose whether this element is rendered as a `Select-Option` or a `Parameter` based upon the value of the field `RANGE`. Finally, the `DATAREF` field must contain a valid reference to a data-dictionary element. We will use this reference for data binding and to create the dynamic element within the ABAP `RANGE`.

The final internal table, `VALUES`, will contain the input values for each `Select-Option`. This is the internal table that we will actually bind to. Notice, however, that the `LOW` and `HIGH` fields must be defined generically, as simple strings. Because this internal table must be a public attribute in order to bind to it, we needed to keep its definition static. Later, you will see how we will use custom Getter and Setter methods to keep referencing the specific data type as defined in the internal table `FIELDS` for our data binding.

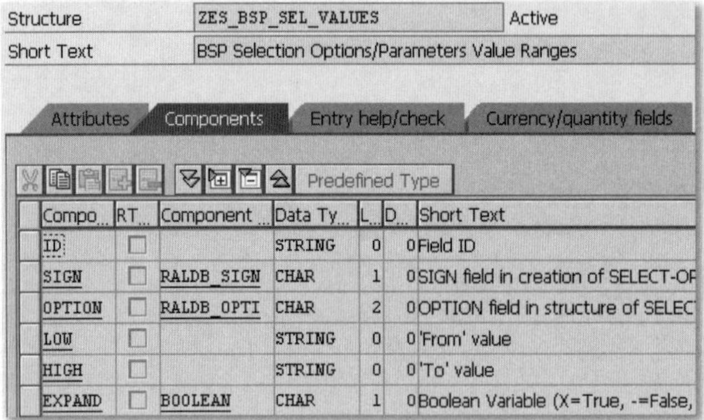

Structure	ZES_BSP_SEL_VALUES	Active
Short Text	BSP Selection Options/Parameters Value Ranges	

Attributes | Components | Entry help/check | Currency/quantity fields

Predefined Type

Compo...	RT...	Component ...	Data Ty...	L...	D...	Short Text
ID	☐		STRING	0	0	Field ID
SIGN	☐	RALDB_SIGN	CHAR	1	0	SIGN field in creation of SELECT-OP
OPTION	☐	RALDB_OPTI	CHAR	2	0	OPTION field in structure of SELEC
LOW	☐		STRING	0	0	'From' value
HIGH	☐		STRING	0	0	'To' value
EXPAND	☐	BOOLEAN	CHAR	1	0	Boolean Variable (X=True, -=False,

Figure 18.8 Select-Options Values

18.3.6 Select-Option Model Class Coding

The main method that we will want to consider for filling the `Select-Options` definition table `FIELDS` is `INITIALIZE_FIELDS_FROM_DD`. This method will populate the `Select-Options` definitions via a data-dictionary structure. However, it also offers a coding example in case you want to build your own custom `Select-Options`.

Our processing begins by getting the definition of the input structure and making sure that it is a data-dictionary type.

```
METHOD initialize_fields_from_dd .
*ImportingI_STRUCTTYPE TABNAME16
  CLEAR: fields, groups, values.
  DATA: descriptor TYPE REF TO cl_abap_structdescr.
  descriptor ?= cl_abap_structdescr=>describe_by_name(
        i_struct ).
  DATA: flddescr TYPE ddfields.
  flddescr = descriptor->get_ddic_field_list( ).
  IF flddescr IS INITIAL. RETURN. ENDIF.
  FIELD-SYMBOLS: <wa_def>   LIKE LINE OF flddescr,
                 <wa_field> LIKE LINE OF me->fields,
                 <wa_group> LIKE LINE OF me->groups.
```

Next, we have some processing to get the description of the structure to use in the title and tooltip of the group.

```
  DATA: rel_name TYPE string.
  DATA: str_desc TYPE string.
  DATA: l_dd071  TYPE dd071.
```

```
rel_name = descriptor->get_relative_name( ).
SELECT SINGLE ddtext FROM dd02t INTO str_desc
        WHERE tabname    = rel_name
          AND ddlanguage = sy-langu
          AND as4local   = 'A'.

IF str_desc IS INITIAL.
  str_desc = rel_name.
ENDIF.
APPEND INITIAL LINE TO me->groups ASSIGNING <wa_group>.
<wa_group>-group = '1000'.
<wa_group>-title = str_desc.
CONCATENATE rel_name str_desc INTO <wa_group>-tooltip
            SEPARATED BY ` - `.
<wa_group>-width = '100%'.
```

We are going to look at each field contained in the structure and create an entry in `Select-Options` internal table.

```
LOOP AT flddescr ASSIGNING <wa_def>
  WHERE fieldname  NE 'MANDT'.
  APPEND INITIAL LINE TO me->fields ASSIGNING <wa_field>.
  <wa_field>-group        = '1000'.
  <wa_field>-id           = <wa_def>-fieldname.
  <wa_field>-text         = <wa_def>-scrtext_m.
  <wa_field>-data_element = <wa_def>-rollname.
  <wa_field>-range        = abap_true.
  CONCATENATE <wa_def>-tabname <wa_def>-fieldname INTO
      <wa_field>-dataref SEPARATED BY '-'.
```

Depending upon the metadata about the field that was retrieved from the Runtime Type Identification (RTTI), we will decide what kind of `Select-Option` we want. If the field is a `DATE` data type, we will naturally use the date selection. If the field has simple domain values, we will use the drop-down list box. Otherwise, if the field has F4 help attached to it we will use the basic help rendering. This will produce a field with the pop up help selection described in Section 14.3.

```
  IF <wa_def>-inttype = 'D'.
    <wa_field>-as_date = abap_true.
  ELSEIF <wa_def>-valexi = abap_true.
    SELECT SINGLE * FROM dd071 INTO l_dd071
     WHERE domname = <wa_def>-domname.
     IF l_dd071-domvalue_h IS INITIAL.
```

```
        <wa_field>-as_ddlb = abap_true.
       ELSE.
        <wa_field>-basic_help = abap_false.
       ENDIF.
    ELSEIF <wa_def>-f4availabl = abap_false.
      CLEAR <wa_field>-basic_help.
    ELSE.
      <wa_field>-basic_help = abap_true.
    ENDIF.
  ENDLOOP.
ENDMETHOD.
```

After we have created our Select-Options, the next thing we need to be concerned with is the data binding for their values. We saw earlier how we are using simple string fields for the LOW and HIGH values of the Select-Options. However for binding to work correctly, we really need to reflect the true data type of the underlying field.

By writing our own methods we can control the binding processing and make sure that the proper conversion exits are being fired. For a detailed discussion on custom GETTER/SETTERS, please see Section 13.3.

We will look at the custom SETTER method to get an idea of the processing required. This routine will be fired when data binding brings data in from the browser. It will be responsible for properly restoring it back into the corresponding ABAP data field.

We begin processing by using the model attribute path to get a grip on the corresponding ABAP data field.

```
METHOD set_t_values.
*Importing   ATTRIBUTE_PATH      TYPE STRING  Attribute Path
*Importing   INDEX               TYPE I       Table Index
*Importing   COMPONENT           TYPE STRING  Table Column
*Importing   VALUE( VALUE )      TYPE STRING  Value Assigned

DATA: l_attr_ref  TYPE REF TO data,
      l_field_ref TYPE REF TO data.
...

CALL METHOD if_bsp_model_util~disassemble_path
    EXPORTING  path      = attribute_path
    IMPORTING  name      = l_name.
  FIELD-SYMBOLS: <l_attribute> TYPE ANY.
```

```
ASSIGN me->(l_name) TO <l_attribute>.
GET REFERENCE OF <l_attribute> INTO l_attr_ref.
l_field_ref = if_bsp_model_util~get_attribute_as_ref(
        attribute_ref = l_attr_ref
        index         = index
        component     = component ).
ASSIGN l_field_ref->* TO <l_comp>.
```

We next need to split up the attribute path so that we can get the binding field name we are dealing with. We only need special logic for the binding of the LOW and HIGH fields.

```
FIELD-SYMBOLS: <o_data> TYPE ANY,
               <n_data> TYPE ANY,
               <l_comp> TYPE ANY.
DATA: junk TYPE string,
      rest TYPE string,
      t_index(10) TYPE c.
SPLIT attribute_path AT '[' INTO junk rest.
SPLIT rest           AT ']' INTO t_index junk.
DATA: field TYPE REF TO data.
DATA: t_string TYPE string.
IF junk CS '.sign' OR junk CS '.option'.
  <l_comp> = value.
  RETURN.
ELSE.
```

If we are processing LOW or HIGH fields, we will now dynamically create a field with the data type matching the underlying data base element for that Select-Option.

```
  FIELD-SYMBOLS: <wa_values> LIKE LINE OF me->values,
                 <wa_fields> LIKE LINE OF me->fields.
  READ TABLE me->values INDEX t_index
       ASSIGNING <wa_values>.
  IF sy-subrc = 0.
    READ TABLE me->fields ASSIGNING <wa_fields>
          WITH KEY id = <wa_values>-id.
    IF sy-subrc = 0.
      TRANSLATE <wa_fields>-dataref TO UPPER CASE.
      IF <wa_fields>-dataref IS INITIAL.
        RETURN.
      ENDIF.
```

```
        TRY.
          CREATE DATA field TYPE (<wa_fields>-dataref).
        CATCH cx_sy_create_data_error.
          EXIT.
        ENDTRY.
        ASSIGN field->* TO <n_data>.
        MOVE <l_comp> TO <n_data>.
      ENDIF.
    ENDIF.
```

Now that we have a reference to a field with our specific data type, we can use that to process the input value.

```
TRY.
   if_bsp_model_util~convert_from_string(
           data_ref            = field
           value               = value
           attribute_path      = attribute_path
           use_bsp_exceptions = abap_true
           no_conversion_exit = 0 ).
      ... Exceptions
ENDTRY.
IF <n_data> IS INITIAL.
   CLEAR <l_comp>.
ELSE.
   MOVE <n_data> TO <l_comp>.
ENDIF.
```

The last problem we will want to look at is how to return an ABAP RANGE table out of the model class. We have two methods for this. The first, GET_GENERIC_RANGE_TABLE, returns a fixed table of type RSELOPTION. This table type uses generic CHARACTER 45 fields for the LOW and HIGH values. This method is very easy to implement and works fine, especially if you need to pass the range back across an RFC connection.

However, if you want to generate a RANGE that accurately represents the underlying data type, you will need the slightly more complex rendering logic of GET_SPECIFIC_RANGE_TABLE. For this second method, we use functionality of the Runtime Type Services (RTTS) that is only available in Web AS 6.40 and higher.

We will start our processing by dynamically creating a field with the data definition of the value in question.

```
METHOD get_specific_range_table.
*Importing   I_ID                TYPE STRING
*Exporting   VALUE( RANGE )      TYPE REF TO DATA
*Exporting   DATAREF             TYPE STRING
FIELD-SYMBOLS: <wa_values> LIKE LINE OF me->values,
               <wa_fields> LIKE LINE OF me->fields.
READ TABLE me->values WITH KEY id = i_id
     TRANSPORTING NO FIELDS.
IF sy-subrc NE 0.
   RETURN.
ELSE.
   READ TABLE me->fields ASSIGNING <wa_fields>
         WITH KEY id = i_id.
   IF sy-subrc NE 0.
      RETURN.
   ELSE.
      DATA: field TYPE REF TO DATA.
      IF <wa_fields>-dataref IS INITIAL.
        RETURN.
      ENDIF.
      TRANSLATE <wa_fields>-dataref TO UPPER CASE.
      dataref = <wa_fields>-dataref.
      TRY.
         CREATE DATA field TYPE (<wa_fields>-dataref).
      CATCH cx_sy_create_data_error.
         EXIT.
      ENDTRY.
    ENDIF.
ENDIF.
```

We will use the RTTI to generate a starting point structure like RSDSSELOPT. We will then replace the data type for the LOW and HIGH fields with one generated by our new data field.

```
 DATA: g_range_type TYPE REF TO cl_abap_structdescr,
       comp_tab TYPE cl_abap_structdescr=>component_table,
       rtti     TYPE REF TO cl_abap_elemdescr.
  g_range_type ?=
       cl_abap_typedescr=>describe_by_name( 'RSDSSELOPT' ).
  FIELD-SYMBOLS: <wa_comp> LIKE LINE OF comp_tab.
  comp_tab = g_range_type->get_components( ).
```

```
rtti ?= cl_abap_typedescr=>describe_by_data_ref( field ).
LOOP AT comp_tab ASSIGNING <wa_comp>.
  IF <wa_comp>-name = 'LOW' OR <wa_comp>-name = 'HIGH'.
    <wa_comp>-type ?= rtti.
  ENDIF.
ENDLOOP.
```

Now we can use the RTTS to create a new internal table with the override structure.

```
DATA: range_type       TYPE REF TO cl_abap_structdescr,
      range_tabletype TYPE REF TO cl_abap_tabledescr.
range_type = cl_abap_structdescr=>create( comp_tab ).
range_tabletype = cl_abap_tabledescr=>create(
    p_line_type  = range_type
    p_table_kind = cl_abap_tabledescr=>tablekind_std ).
FIELD-SYMBOLS <table> TYPE STANDARD TABLE.
CREATE DATA range TYPE HANDLE range_tabletype.
ASSIGN range->* TO <table>.
```

Finally, we assign the values from our generic `Select-Options` value internal table to the more specific `RANGE` table.

```
FIELD-SYMBOLS: <wa_value> LIKE LINE OF me->values,
               <wa_range> TYPE ANY,
               <field>    TYPE ANY.
LOOP AT me->values ASSIGNING <wa_value> WHERE id = i_id.
  APPEND INITIAL LINE TO <table> ASSIGNING <wa_range>.
  ASSIGN COMPONENT 1 OF STRUCTURE <wa_range> TO <field>.
  <field> = <wa_value>-sign.
  ...
ENDLOOP.
```

18.3.7 Recreating Transaction SE16

To demonstrate the power and flexibility of these new `Select-Options`, let us try and use them in an extremely dynamic application. What better solution than trying to recreate SE16 (the generic table query transaction) as a BSP application.

When you use SE16 inside the SAP GUI, the system is actually dynamically generating and storing entire programs. That means that if you run SE16 for `SFLIGHT` and for `SBOOK`, there are two different programs behind the scenes.

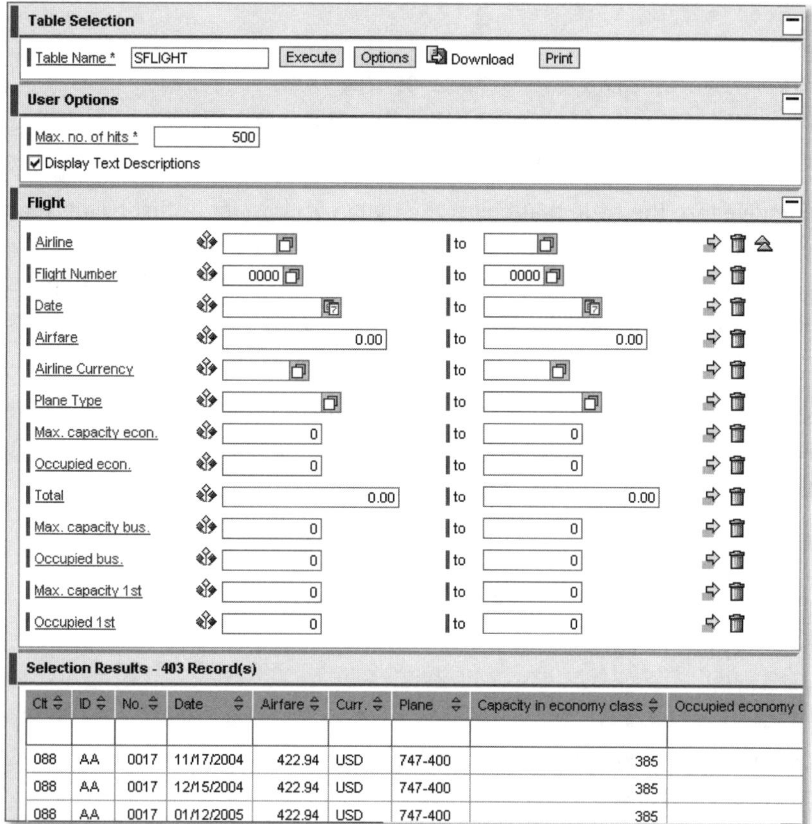

Figure 18.9 Select-Options Example—SE16 Recreated in BSP

Instead we will use the dynamic power of BSP to generate the UI at runtime depending upon what table the user selects.

Using the `INITIALIZE_FIELDS_FROM_DD` method, we are able to regenerate our `Select-Options` easily as users choose a new table to query. We will output our data using an `<htmlb:tableView>`. So that the structure of the table is adjustable, we will simply define an attribute as `TYPE REF TO DATA`.

This does mean that we are going to need a single dynamic routine that will redefine the output data table and generate a SQL command that uses our `Select-Option RANGES`. For this, we will dynamically generate a class at runtime.

We will start our processing by dynamically redefining our output data table.

```
DATA itab1  TYPE TABLE OF string.
DATA prog  TYPE string.
DATA class TYPE string.
```

```
  DATA code_string TYPE string.
  CLEAR me->itab.
  CREATE DATA me->itab TYPE TABLE OF (me->ddstructure).
  FIELD-SYMBOLS: <wa_fields> LIKE LINE OF me->fields,
                 <wa_values> LIKE LINE OF me->values.
```

Before we dive into the code that builds the dynamic class, let us first have a look at the resulting code that will be executed. It really only needs to define the ranges and then perform a SQL statement. We could code the SQL statement dynamically without the need for the generated class, however the key here is the variable number of ranges that need to be defined for the where condition.

In this example generated code we are reading from SFLIGHT with a single where condition of airline carrier id (CARRID) is equal to AA and Flight Number (CONNID) is equal to 0017.

```
PROGRAM.
CLASS main DEFINITION.
  PUBLIC SECTION.
    CLASS-METHODS meth
    IMPORTING
      itab TYPE REF TO data
      values TYPE zes_bsp_sel_values_tbl
      fields TYPE zes_bsp_sel_fields_tbl.
ENDCLASS.                       "main DEFINITION
CLASS main IMPLEMENTATION.
  METHOD meth.
    FIELD-SYMBOLS <table> TYPE ANY TABLE.
    ASSIGN itab->* TO <table>.
    FIELD-SYMBOLS: <wa_value> LIKE LINE OF values.
    FIELD-SYMBOLS: <wa_field> LIKE LINE OF fields.
    DATA carrid TYPE RANGE OF sflight-carrid.
    FIELD-SYMBOLS <wa_carrid> LIKE LINE OF carrid.
    READ TABLE fields ASSIGNING <wa_field>
         WITH KEY id = 'CARRID'.
    LOOP AT values ASSIGNING <wa_value>
         WHERE id = <wa_field>-id.
      APPEND INITIAL LINE TO carrid ASSIGNING <wa_carrid>.
      MOVE-CORRESPONDING <wa_value> TO <wa_carrid>.
    ENDLOOP.
    DATA connid TYPE RANGE OF sflight-connid.
    FIELD-SYMBOLS <wa_connid> LIKE LINE OF connid.
```

```
    READ TABLE fields ASSIGNING <wa_field>
         WITH KEY id = 'CONNID'.
    LOOP AT values ASSIGNING <wa_value>
         WHERE id = <wa_field>-id.
      APPEND INITIAL LINE TO connid ASSIGNING <wa_connid>.
      MOVE-CORRESPONDING <wa_value> TO <wa_connid>.
    ENDLOOP.
    SELECT * FROM sflight INTO TABLE <table>
        UP TO 500  ROWS
     WHERE carrid IN carrid
       AND connid IN connid.
  ENDMETHOD.                    "meth
ENDCLASS.                     "main IMPLEMENTATION
```

Next we will study the code for creating our dynamic class by inserting the source code into an internal table. As you can see we are going to pass our model `Select-Options` `VALUES` and `FIELDS` internal table into our dynamic class.

```
  APPEND `PROGRAM.`                     TO itab1.
  APPEND `CLASS main DEFINITION.`       TO itab1.
  APPEND `  PUBLIC SECTION.`            TO itab1.
  APPEND `    CLASS-METHODS meth `      TO itab1.
  APPEND `    IMPORTING `               TO itab1.
  APPEND `      itab TYPE REF TO DATA ` TO itab1.
  APPEND `      values TYPE ZES_BSP_SEL_VALUES_TBL `
      TO itab1.
  APPEND `      fields TYPE ZES_BSP_SEL_FIELDS_TBL.`
      TO itab1.
  APPEND `ENDCLASS.`                    TO itab1.
  APPEND `CLASS main IMPLEMENTATION.`   TO itab1.
  APPEND `  METHOD meth.`               TO itab1.
  APPEND `    FIELD-SYMBOLS <table> TYPE ANY TABLE.`
      TO itab1.
  APPEND `    ASSIGN itab->* TO <table>.` TO itab1.
  APPEND `   FIELD-SYMBOLS: <wa_value> LIKE LINE OF values.`
      TO itab1.
  APPEND `   FIELD-SYMBOLS: <wa_field> LIKE LINE OF fields.`
      TO itab1.
```

We now will loop through our listing of `Select-Options` with input values in our model. For each record, we find we will generate corresponding data definition entries and population logic in our dynamic class.

```
LOOP AT me->fields ASSIGNING <wa_fields>.
    READ TABLE me->values TRANSPORTING NO FIELDS
          WITH KEY id = <wa_fields>-id.
    CHECK sy-subrc = 0.
    CONCATENATE `data ` <wa_fields>-id ` TYPE RANGE OF `
                <wa_fields>-dataref `.` INTO code_string.
    APPEND code_string TO itab1.
    CONCATENATE `FIELD-SYMBOLS <wa_` <wa_fields>-id `>`
                ` LIKE LINE OF ` <wa_fields>-id `.`
       INTO code_string.
    APPEND code_string TO itab1.
    CONCATENATE `READ TABLE fields ASSIGNING <wa_field> `
       `WITH KEY id = '`
       <wa_fields>-id `'.` INTO code_string.
    APPEND code_string TO itab1.
    APPEND `LOOP AT values ASSIGNING <wa_value> `
           `WHERE id = <wa_field>-id.` TO itab1.
    CONCATENATE `APPEND INITIAL LINE TO `
                <wa_fields>-id ` ASSIGNING <wa_`
                <wa_fields>-id `>.` INTO code_string.
    APPEND code_string TO itab1.
    CONCATENATE `MOVE-CORRESPONDING <wa_value> TO <wa_`
                <wa_fields>-id `>.` INTO code_string.
    APPEND code_string TO itab1.
    APPEND `ENDLOOP.` TO itab1.
  ENDLOOP.
```

Using the same process we will dynamically generate our SQL statement.

```
DATA: s_max_records TYPE string.
MOVE me->max_records TO s_max_records.
CONCATENATE `SELECT * FROM ` me->ddstructure
            ` INTO TABLE <table> `
            ` UP TO ` s_max_records ` ROWS `
            INTO code_string.
APPEND code_string TO itab1.
DATA: first_pass TYPE boolean VALUE abap_true.
LOOP AT me->fields ASSIGNING <wa_fields>.
  READ TABLE me->values TRANSPORTING NO FIELDS
        WITH KEY id = <wa_fields>-id.
  CHECK sy-subrc = 0.
```

```
    IF first_pass = abap_true.
      first_pass = abap_false.
      MOVE ` WHERE ` TO code_string.
    ELSE.
      MOVE ` AND ` to code_string.
    ENDIF.
    CONCATENATE code_string <wa_fields>-id
                ` IN ` <wa_fields>-id INTO code_string.
    APPEND code_string TO itab1.
  ENDLOOP.
  MOVE `.` TO code_string.
  APPEND code_string TO itab1.
  APPEND `  ENDMETHOD.`                   TO itab1.
  APPEND `ENDCLASS.`                      TO itab1.
```

We finish our processing by generating our dynamic class. We then can prepare the model internal tables for passing to the dynamic-class method. Finally, we are able to call our dynamic-model method.

```
GENERATE SUBROUTINE POOL itab1 NAME prog.
CONCATENATE `\PROGRAM=` prog `\CLASS=MAIN` INTO class.
DATA: ptab TYPE abap_parmbind_tab,
      ptab_line TYPE abap_parmbind.
ptab_line-name = 'ITAB'.
ptab_line-kind = cl_abap_objectdescr=>exporting.
GET REFERENCE OF itab INTO ptab_line-value.
INSERT ptab_line INTO TABLE ptab.
...
CALL METHOD (class)=>meth
  PARAMETER-TABLE ptab.
```

19 Breaking Out of the Mold

Eventually, all programmers encounter development requirements that will push them to break the rules. In this chapter, we will focus on solutions that—while useful—certainly push the boundaries of traditional BSP development.

19.1 Interactive Excel

Downloading data to Excel is a critical functionality, but relatively well known. Eventually everyone gets a business requirement for greater interactivity. Users who are accustomed to full interactive Excel in their applications will expect it in BSP applications as well.

Perhaps you have to integrate existing Excel spreadsheets into your application. You might have extensive macros or complex formatting. Therefore recreating this functionality in some other tool is often just not reasonable.

Luckily there is a solution provided by Microsoft that integrates quite well into BSP. It is called *Office Web Components* (OWC). This is basically an ActiveX interface to the Microsoft Office Suite. If you have Office XP or higher installed, then you should have the necessary control. However, a read-only version of the control can also be downloaded from Microsoft's website.

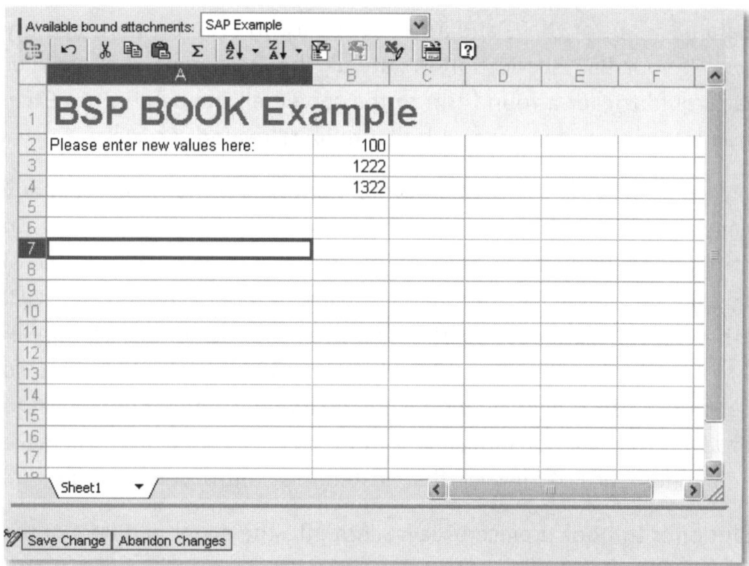

Figure 19.1 OWC Inside a BSP Application

Calling this ActiveX control from BSP is really very simple, even though there is no SAP standard function for this solution. We will simply use the open power of BSP that allows us to include any standard HTML content. The following is all the code that it takes to instantiate the OWC control in a BSP application.

```
<OBJECT id=myexcel
        style='LEFT:0px; WIDTH:593px;TOP:0px;HEIGHT:377px'
        height=377 width=593
        classid='clsid:0002E551-0000-0000-C000-000000000046'
        name=myexcel VIEWASTEXT>
     <PARAM NAME='DataType' VALUE='XMLDATA'>
     <PARAM NAME='XMLData' VALUE='<%= model->my_out_xml %>'>
</OBJECT>
```

In this example, you can see that there are some simple parameters for setting the position and size of the control. There are many more parameters that affect the use of this control. However, this text will concentrate instead on getting data in and out of this control. If you wish to further explore other options on this control, they are well documented in Microsoft's online repository.

We are going to use the XML capabilities of Excel to pass data in and out of the control. If you have an existing template or spreadsheet that you want to start with, you can simply save it as XML to get a starting XML stream. The data in this stream is what we use to pass into the OWC control in the example (`model->my_out_xml`).

Getting the data back out of OWC and into our application can be another story altogether. Even if your BSP application is stateful, the Excel control is not. For any event that would trigger a round trip to the server, all the data in the Excel control must be retrieved and re-sent with that request/response cycle.

The only way to pull the current state of the Office control is with JavaScript. Many other examples have some sort of trigger, such as a button, that allows the data in the Excel control to update the back-end system. However, to emulate the kind of functionality your users might be used to from working with standard SAP GUI transactions, this control might need to be embedded inside rather complex applications. Add to this the architecture of the delivered BSP extensions, where so many of the elements can trigger server events. It simply is not very practical to have to hook a JavaScript function into each of those objects. That would also make reusability and maintenance of the view that hosted this control very difficult.

The better solution is to hook a piece of JavaScript into the event handlers of the Office control itself. This will allow you to trap the `SheetChange` event which gives you access to the office control content after every cell change.

Then, you can use JavaScript to copy this content into a hidden input field. You can even go as far as to make this hidden input field an <htmlb:inputField> with model binding. That way your Excel content is copied directly back into our model class at any server event.

The following small amount of code accomplishes what has just been described. Notice that in this example we have JavaScript code that will run within the browser. This example also follows the Model View Controller principle. Therefore, if this JavaScript code is going to work correctly, you must remember to concatenate the controller's component ID onto the front of the fieldname of our hidden Input Field.

```
<htmlb:inputField id      = "sendinfo_bnd"
                  visible = " "
                  value   = "//model/sendinfo_bnd" />
<script language='javascript' for='myexcel'
        event='SheetChange(Sh, Target)'>
    document.update.<%= controller->component_id
    %>_sendinfo_bnd.value =
    document.update.myexcel.XMLData;
</script>
```

19.2 RSS Feeds

RSS is an acronym that can stand for really simple syndication, RDF site summary, or rich-site summary. Whatever term one uses, RSS—an XML format for syndicating Web content—is undeniably important to the modern Internet. So much information is available on the Internet that the most important tools are those that help people shift through the madness to find gems. RSS is an important technology that fills just such a role.

RSS, at its heart, is built on top of established technologies such as HTTP and XML. Luckily, these technologies are readily available within the ABAP/BSP world as well. We will take a look at two different approaches for working with RSS within BSP. First we will look at how to create a BSP page that consumes an external RSS feed and presents its content to the user. In the second example, we will use BSP to host an RSS feed.

19.2.1 Consuming an RSS Feed

Whenever one thinks of HTTP in the context of BSP, one pictures the browser starting the HTTP request, and that the server returns an HTTP response. However, in the Web AS it is also possible to play the role of a browser and to effectively make outgoing HTTP calls. For a detailed example of this process, have a look at program RSHTTP01.

It is precisely this role of HTTP client that our system will be using to call to an external system and ask for its RSS XML. We will use this example program to open a connection to the SAP Developer Network (SDN) website and request the RSS feed for all recent BSP Weblogs.

19.2.2 HTTP Client

For this example, we decided to use the minimum number of lines of code. No error handling is done. If the exceptions are not mapped onto sy-subrc during the method calls, they will just be raised and the BSP program will be terminated. This is acceptable for our example.

```
DATA: url         TYPE STRING,
      http_client TYPE REF TO IF_HTTP_CLIENT,
      rc          TYPE I,
      content     TYPE STRING.
url = 'http://weblogs.sdn.sap.com/pub/q/weblog_rss_topic?
       x-topic=24&x-ver=1.0'.
cl_http_client=>create_by_url(
                EXPORTING url    = url
                IMPORTING client = http_client ).
http_client->send( ).
http_client->receive( ).
http_client->response->get_status( IMPORTING code = rc ).
content = http_client->response->get_cdata( ).
http_client->close( ).
```

These few lines are sufficient to pull the RSS data from SDN. The first line creates a new client using a complete URL that already contains the protocol to use ("http:"), plus destination system and port (implicitly port 80) and the requested URL. Once we have the HTTP client instance, we send the request and receive the answer. It is very important to include the close method call, to ensure that the resources held by the HTTP client are released.

When using the HTTP client, there are a number of interesting additional aspects to consider:

- Setting headers such as Accept-Encoding and User-Agent in the request.
- Setting the HTTP protocol and version to use and the method GET or POST.

- Setting up of authentication information for the remote site, possibly also proxy authentication information. Proxy setup can be maintained from transaction SICF.
- Looking at the `rc` (return code) and taking additional action. Interesting values would be `rc=200` (OK), `rc=302` (Redirect), `rc=401` (Authentication Required) and `rc=500` (Server Error).

19.2.3 XML

Once the RSS data has been retrieved, the next step is to parse this into an XML document. One could consider using normal string operations to extract the interesting data, but it does not have the same elegance. Instead, we will take full advantage of the power of the ABAP XML API.

```
TYPE-POOLS: ixml.
DATA: ixml          TYPE REF TO if_ixml,
      streamFactory TYPE REF TO if_ixml_stream_factory,
      istream       TYPE REF TO if_ixml_istream,
      parser        TYPE REF TO if_ixml_parser,
      document      TYPE REF TO if_ixml_document.
IF content CS '<!DOCTYPE' AND content CS ']>'.
  DATA dummy type string.
  SPLIT content AT '<!DOCTYPE' INTO dummy content.
  SPLIT content AT ']>'        INTO dummy content.
ENDIF.
ixml     = cl_ixml=>create( ).
streamFactory = ixml->create_stream_factory( ).
istream  = streamFactory->create_istream_cstring(
      content ).
document = ixml->create_document( ).
parser   = ixml->create_parser(
     stream_factory = streamFactory
     istream         = iStream
     document        = document ).
parser->set_normalizing( ).
parser->set_validating(
      mode = if_ixml_parser=>co_no_validation ).
parser->parse( ).
```

The only unusual code from above is the handling of the `DOCTYPE`. The content returned from SDN is formatted in such a way that the ABAP XML parser has problems with it. Therefore, a small modification was made to eliminate the section.

Later for the display of the Weblogs, we would like to extract relevant <item> sequences from the RSS feed into an internal table. Let us define the table to use.

```
TYPES: BEGIN OF t_blog,
          title       TYPE string,
          link        TYPE string,
          description TYPE string,
          creator     TYPE string,
          date        TYPE string,
       END OF t_blog,
       t_blogs TYPE TABLE OF t_blog.
DATA:          blogs type t_blogs.
FIELD-SYMBOLS: <blog> type t_blog.
```

With this, everything is in place to iterate over the XML document, gather all <item> nodes, and extract the relevant bits and pieces.

```
DATA:  collection      TYPE REF TO if_ixml_node_collection,
       node            TYPE REF TO if_ixml_node,
       element         TYPE REF TO if_ixml_element,
       index           TYPE i.
collection = document->get_elements_by_tag_name(
       name = 'item' ).
WHILE index < collection->get_length( ).
  APPEND INITIAL LINE TO blogs ASSIGNING <blog>.
  node     = collection->get_item( index ).
  element ?= node->query_interface( ixml_iid_element ).
  index    = index + 1.
  node = element->find_from_name( name = 'title' ).
  <blog>-title = node->get_value( ).
  .... repeat above two line sequence for all info
       required ....
ENDWHILE.
```

The main part of the code just loops over the collection of <item> nodes. For each node, we look under it five times to find sub-nodes with specific names. We are interested in the title, link, description, creator and date sub-nodes. All the data is accumulated into an internal table.

19.2.4 BSP Output

The final part of the puzzle is to display the output. One technique could be to use an <htmlb:tableView>. Another could be to transform the table into raw

HTML. However, let us have some fun and use a <phtmlb:formattedText> element.

The <phtmlb:formattedText> element accepts as input an XML string that contains markup sequences, similar to those of HTML. As a first step, just loop over the internal table with acquired data and generate the XML string.

```
DATA: formattedText TYPE string.
formattedText = '<ROOT><H1>BSP Weblogs</H1>'.
LOOP AT blogs ASSIGNING <blog>.
  CONCATENATE formattedText
  '<P>' '<LINK href="' <blog>-link '"><B>'
  <blog>-title '</B></LINK>'
  ` by <I>` <blog>-creator `</I> on ` <blog>-date `  --  `
  <blog>-description '</P>' INTO formattedText.
ENDLOOP.
CONCATENATE formattedText '</ROOT>' INTO formattedText.
```

Notice the use of `` sequences in the CONCATENATE command to preserve trailing spaces in the strings. The <ROOT> elements are required to make this a valid XML document.

The display of results is now very easy.

```
<%@page language="abap"%>
<%@extension name="htmlb"  prefix="htmlb"%>
<%@extension name="phtmlb" prefix="phtmlb"%>
<htmlb:content design="design2003">
  <htmlb:page>
    <htmlb:form>
     <phtmlb:formattedText text = "<%=formattedText%>" />
    </htmlb:form>
  </htmlb:page>
</htmlb:content>
```

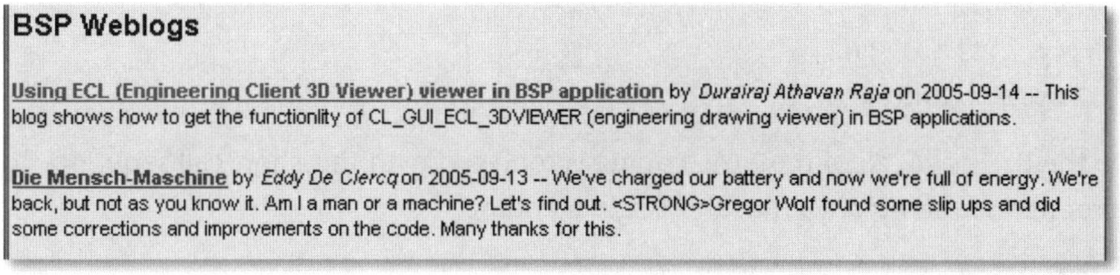

BSP Weblogs

Using ECL (Engineering Client 3D Viewer) viewer in BSP application by *Durairaj Athavan Raja* on 2005-09-14 -- This blog shows how to get the functionlity of CL_GUI_ECL_3DVIEWER (engineering drawing viewer) in BSP applications.

Die Mensch-Maschine by *Eddy De Clercq* on 2005-09-13 -- We've charged our battery and now we're full of energy. We're back, but not as you know it. Am I a man or a machine? Let's find out. <STRONG>Gregor Wolf found some slip ups and did some corrections and improvements on the code. Many thanks for this.

Figure 19.2 RSS Consumption – Final Output

19.2.5 XSLT

Looking at the final program, it is clear that the XML code required to parse the RSS data feed and extract the relevant data, is nearly 70 % of the entire application. XML definitely has a highly granular API!

However, we have XML as input (the RSS data), and we want XML as output, the formatted text. For this, the perfect tool of choice is Extensible Stylesheet Language Transformations (XSLT).

All it takes is these few lines of magic to replace all of the XML parsing and iterator code.

```
<xsl:transform version="1.0"
     xmlns:xsl="http://www.w3.org/1999/XSL/Transform"
     xmlns:rss="http://purl.org/rss/1.0/"
     xmlns:dc="http://purl.org/dc/elements/1.1/"
     exclude-result-prefixes="rss dc">
  <xsl:output method="html"/>
  <xsl:template match="/">
   <ROOT>
    <H1>BSP Weblogs</H1>
     <xsl:for-each select="*/rss:item">
      <P>
       <LINK href="https://weblogs.sdn.sap.com{rss:link}">
        <B> <xsl:value-of select="rss:title"
            disable-output-escaping="yes"/> </B>
       </LINK>
       by <I> <xsl:value-of select="dc:creator"/> </I>
       on <xsl:value-of select="substring(dc:date,1,10)"/>
       -- <xsl:value-of select="rss:description"
       disable-output-escaping="yes"/>
      </P>
     </xsl:for-each>
   </ROOT>
  </xsl:template>
  </xsl:transform>
```

In the BSP page, all of the XML coding is replaced with this short call sequence to produce the same output as the original coding.

```
DATA: formattedText TYPE string.
CALL TRANSFORMATION Y_BSP_BOOK_SDN_RSS_TO_FTEXT
```

```
  SOURCE XML content
  RESULT XML formattedText.
```

19.2.6 Creating an RSS Feed

You will probably be happy to note that creating an RSS feed from BSP is considerably simpler than consuming one. We quite often assume that a BSP "page" is delivering content as HTML Text. However there are actually many formats that can be delivered by BSP. By simply setting the MIME type on the Page or **View Properties** tab, we can force our content to be interpreted as XML.

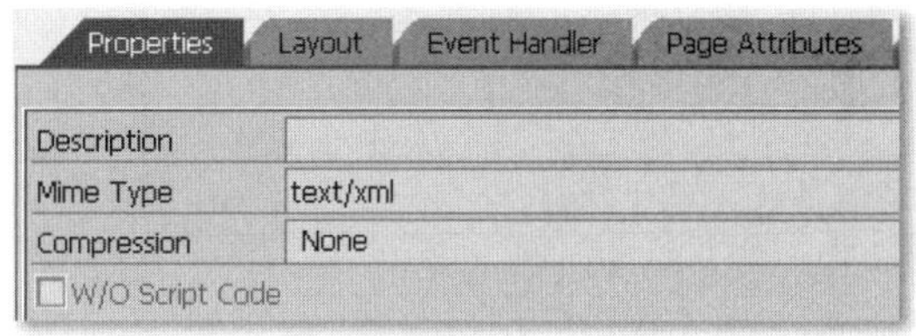

Figure 19.3 BSP Page Set to the XML MIME Type

We can then build the content of the XML document in the **Page Layout** just like we would on an HTML page.

```
<?xml version="1.0"?>
<rdf:RDF xmlns="http://purl.org/rss/1.0/"
   xmlns:rdf="http://www.w3.org/1999/02/22-rdf-syntax-ns#" >
      <channel rdf:about="<%= url %>">
...
</rdf:RDF>
```

By studying the documented XML format for RSS, you can easily build your own feeds. You still have the ability to loop through and cut in dynamic ABAP elements.

You can image the possibilities that exposing your system via RSS brings. Users can now subscribe to the data events and alerts that interest them and are critical to their jobs. You might, for instance, create an RSS feed for all new purchase requisitions over a certain monetary value. Using a commercial RSS Reader, users can monitor and receive alerts when new data is ready for review.

Another example, for which the sample source code is available on the book CD, would be to expose ABAP short dumps via a RSS feed. System administrators could subscribe to such a feed and receive notification within seconds of the dump occurring. You could even take this example further and link into transaction ST22 to display the details, using the ITS or by building a custom BSP application to display the dump.

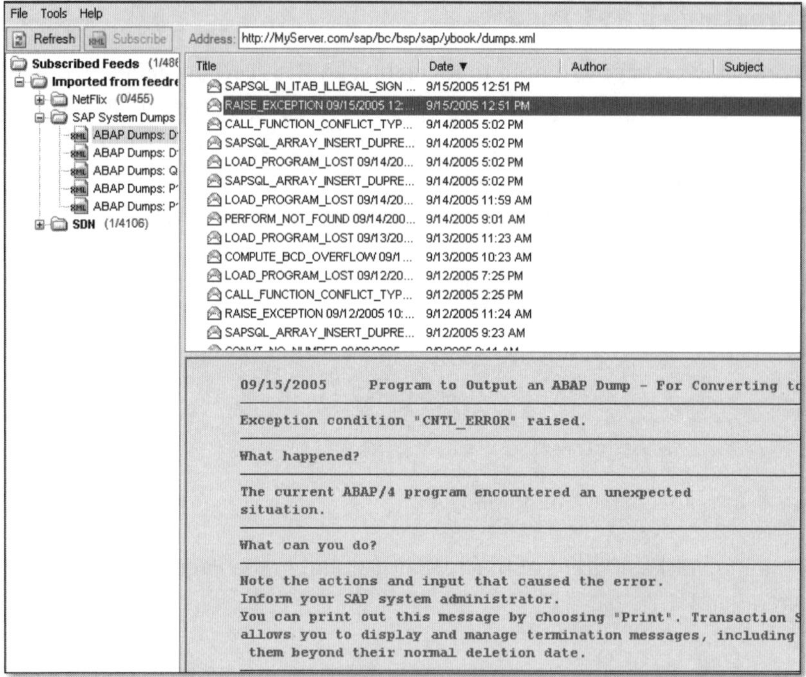

Figure 19.4 RSS Feed for ABAP Short Dumps

19.3 Mini-Portal

This section of the book is not intended to discourage you from using or exploring the SAP Enterprise Portal. It is an excellent tool that just about any SAP customer could benefit from using. However, there are situations where you need some of the functionality of a common portal framework, such as personalization and navigation, but your company is not in a position to implement the full Enterprise Portal.

In this situation, you may very well look to BSP to fill that gap. We are going to look at two such mini-portals. As you will see, the power, flexibility and openness of BSP is more than enough to build such a tool.

19.3.1 Mini-Portal Example 1—Common Page Header

In the first example we have a relatively simple common header implemented as custom BSP Extension Element. This element provides a common branding and personalization interface with a minimal impact to the application that hosts it.

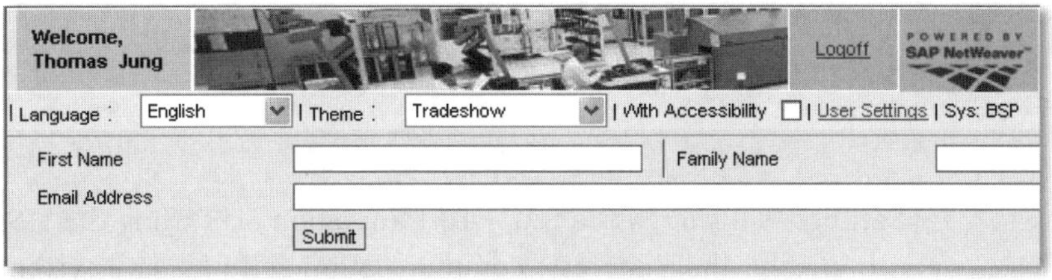

Figure 19.5 Mini-Portal Example 1—Common Header

It can be inserted within its own HTML frame in an application. It then only requires the following small amount of coding.

```
<%@page language="abap" %>
<%@extension name="htmlb" prefix="htmlb" %>
<%@extension name="YBOOK" prefix="YBOOK" %>
<htmlb:content design          = "design2003"
               labelDesignBar = "light" >
  <htmlb:document>
    <htmlb:documentHead>
    </htmlb:documentHead>
    <htmlb:documentBody>
      <htmlb:form action = "Index_Frames.htm"
                  target = "_parent" >
        <YBOOK:pageHeaderDesign2003 NumberOfParents = "2"
               CustomLogo = "logo_netweaver.gif"
                  RFCDest = "REMOTE_SYS" />
      </htmlb:form>
    </htmlb:documentBody>
  </htmlb:document>
</htmlb:content>
```

In this interface, we provide the means to set basic personalization across all BSP applications. The user can switch his or her logon language and DESIGN2003 theme, and activate the accessibility features. These settings are changed by reloading the current application and passing the new values via their URL parameters.

```
IF htmlb_event->server_event EQ 'HandleLangSubmit'.
   CONCATENATE url '?sap-language=' s_spras
          INTO url.
   currenttime = sy-uzeit.
   CALL METHOD cl_http_server=>append_field_url
     EXPORTING name  = 'sap-unique'
```

```
                 value = currenttime
      CHANGING url   = url.
   navigation->exit( url ).
ENDIF.
```

The link to User Settings will launch the SAP GUI transaction SU3 using the ITS. This allows users to change their address, communication settings, and system defaults such as decimal notation and date format.

Finally, this header also provides information about what system you are connected to. In the **Sys** area, we display the system ID that you are currently connected to. If the user clicks on this area, he or she will receive a popup window that contains more details that might be useful when troubleshooting.

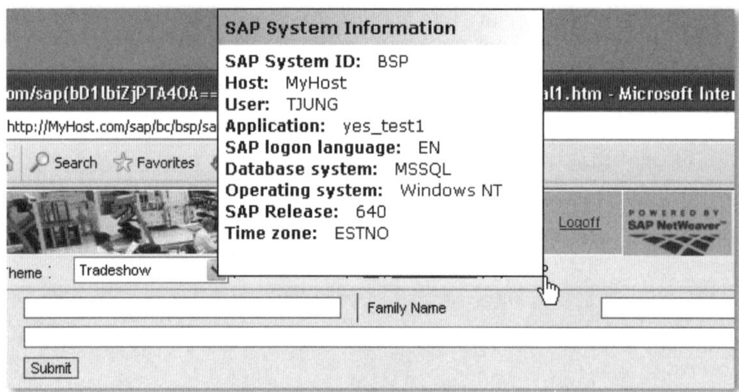

Figure 19.6 Mini-Portal Example 1—Common Header—System Information

19.3.2 Mini-Portal Example 2—Portal with Navigation

Our first example provides a nice common header for each application. However this is not a high-level framework. It also does nothing to support navigation between different applications. It has the disadvantage of needing to be inserted, although with very little effort, into each application.

A more encompassing approach would be to build a framework page in BSP that can host inner pages inside of HTML IFrames. Figure 19.7 demonstrates just such a framework.

However this example goes just a little bit further. It actually uses the flexibility of BSP to share very similar stylesheets and JavaScript with the Enterprise Portal. Therefore, the look and feel of the page along with the two-tier navigation bar really comes right from the Enterprise Portal. The framework, navigation area, and even the elements you see on the home page all are built in BSP.

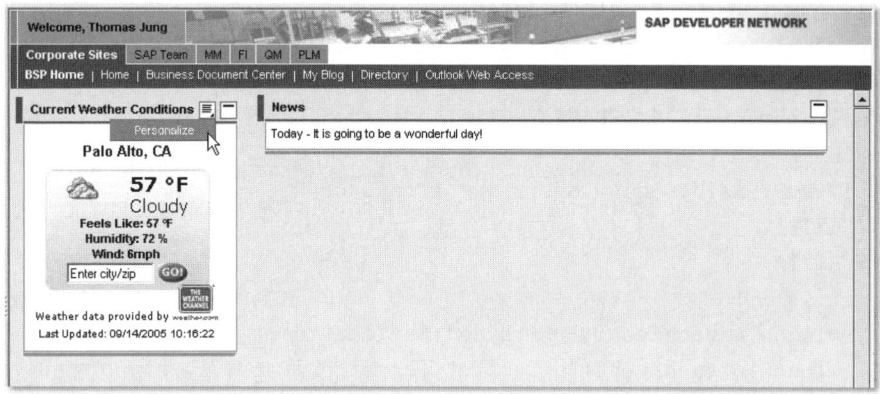

Figure 19.7 Mini-Portal Example 2—Portal with Navigation

Further taking advantage of the SAP Unified Framework for rendering; the news and weather areas, built using <htmlb:tray>, look just like normal EP IViews. We are even able to support personalization through the standard BSP elements.

Looking at the coding of the framework page we can see that mostly we are just interacting with the JavaScript functions necessary to build the UI for the navigation menu.

```
gNavTree = new NavNode("Top", "Top", 0, 0, 0, 0,
  new NavNode("#", "<OTR>Corporate Sites</OTR>", 0, 0, 0, 0,
    new NavNode("portal_home.htm", "BSP <OTR>Home</OTR>",
                 0, 0, 0, 0),
    new NavNode("http://www.sap.com/", "<OTR>Home</OTR>",
                 0, 0, 0, 0),
...
  new NavNode("#", "SAP Team", 0, 0, 0, 0,
    new NavNode("http://help.sap.com", "<OTR>Help</OTR>",
                 0, 0, 0, 0),
...
    new NavNode("/sap/bc/bsp/sap/Y_DOC_SEARCH/main.do?
sap-themeRoot=<%= themeRoot%>&themeRoot=<%= themeRoot%>",
"<OTR>Document Search</OTR>", 0, 0, 0, 0)
  )
);
```

The inner content itself is then hosted within an IFrame. JavaScript functions are fired on the window-resize event to make sure that the inner content continues to fill the content IFrame area.

```
<IFRAME frameBorder="0" id="iViewFrameId" name="iViewFrameId"
src="content_sap.html?themeRoot=<%= themeRoot%>&applUrl=
<%= applUrl%>&s=<%= script%>" style="WIDTH:100%;"
fullPage="true"></IFRAME>
<SCRIPT>
  iViewFrameId.window.onerror = stopError
</SCRIPT>
<SCRIPT>
  if(isIE){
   window.attachEvent("onresize",SetTLNSize);
   window.attachEvent("onresize",adjustFullPageIViews);
   window.attachEvent("onload",adjustFullPageIViews);
  } else{
   window.addEventListener("resize",SetTLNSize,false);
   window.addEventListener("resize",adjustFullPageIViews,
false);
   window.addEventListener("load",adjustFullPageIViews,
false); }
 </SCRIPT>
```

The navigation menu sets the URL for the inner content via a call to the BSP Page CONTENT_SAP.HTML. This is the BSP Page that is hosted within the framework page's IFrame. It in turn hosts the actual content URL within its own inner IFrame.

```
<% data applUrl type string.
   applUrl = request->get_form_field( 'applUrl' ).
  IF applUrl IS initial.
    applUrl = 'portal_home.htm'.
  ELSE.
    themeRoot = cl_http_utility=>escape_url(
      unescaped = themeRoot ).
  ENDIF.
  CONCATENATE applUrl '?sap-themeRoot=' themeRoot
    INTO applUrl.
  DATA accessibility TYPE string.
  accessibility = runtime->WITH_ACCESSIBILITY( ).
  IF accessibility IS NOT initial.
     CONCATENATE applUrl '&sap-accessibility=X'
        INTO applUrl.
  ENDIF.
  DATA is_rtl TYPE string.
    is_rtl = runtime->with_right_to_left( ).
```

```
  IF is_rtl IS NOT initial.
    CONCATENATE applUrl '&sap-rtl=X' INTO applUrl.
  ENDIF. %>
<IFRAME frameBorder="0" id="iViewFrameContentId"
name="iViewFrameContentId" src="<%= applUrl%>"
style="WIDTH:100%;height:100%"></IFRAME>
```

Listing 19.1 CONTENT_SAP.HTML

This structure of IFrames allows for the ability to host external content inside our BSP mini-portal as well. Figure 19.8 shows three such examples. We have another BSP Application, a page from the Internet, and Microsoft Outlook Web Access for reading email all hosted within our BSP mini-portal. None of these other applications were designed for or modified in any way in order to be hosted.

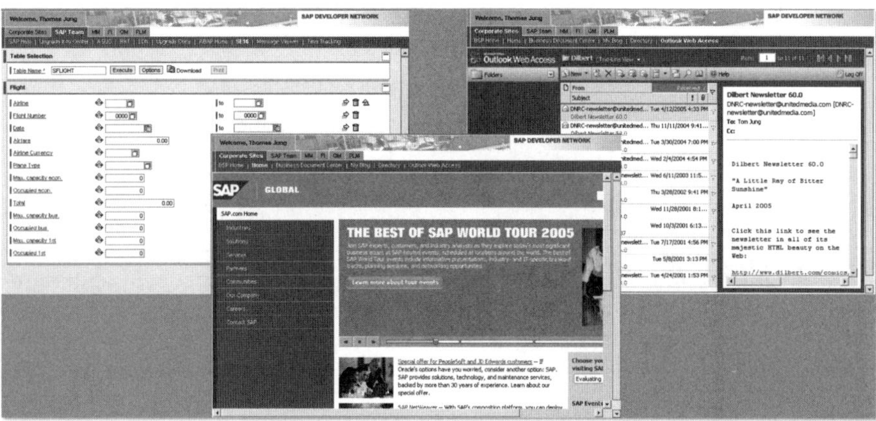

Figure 19.8 Mini-Portal Example 2—Hosting External Content

But hosting full applications within the content area of our mini-portal page is not really enough. We want to be able to arrange multiple smaller elements, commonly referred to as IViews within the SAP Enterprise Portal, together in one area. We may even want to support personalization for the layout of these IViews.

This can be done as well using BSP and IFrames. Our sample start page had two areas: one that displayed the current weather and one for news. The weather section of this page is actually a separate BSP application hosted in place using an IFrame. We lay out the individual elements within the BSP page using a `<phtmlb:matrix>`.

```
<%@page language="abap" %>
<%@extension name="htmlb" prefix="htmlb" %>
```

```
<%@extension name="phtmlb" prefix="phtmlb" %>
<htmlb:content design="design2003" >
  <htmlb:page title="Main Home Page " >
    <htmlb:form>
      <phtmlb:matrix cellWidths = "30%,70%"
                     height     = "100%" >
        <phtmlb:matrixCell vAlign="TOP" />
        <IFRAME frameBorder="0" id="iViewWeatherFrame"
                name="iViewWeatherFrame"
                src="../zes_weather/weather.do"
                style="WIDTH:100%;HEIGHT:250px" ></IFRAME>
        <phtmlb:matrixCell vAlign="TOP" />
        <htmlb:tray id    = "News"
                    width = "100%"
                    title = "News" >
          <htmlb:trayBody>
            <htmlb:textView wrapping="TRUE" >
              Today - It is going to be a wonderful day!
            </htmlb:textView>
          </htmlb:trayBody>
        </htmlb:tray>
      </phtmlb:matrix>
    </htmlb:form>
  </htmlb:page>
</htmlb:content>
```

19.3.3 Portal within the SAP GUI

Although many companies look to a portal as an option to replace the SAP GUI on user's desktops; there still remains considerable demand to have users work directly within the SAP GUI fat-client environment. This is not meant to be a discussion on the pros and cons of using the SAP GUI client; instead, we want to look at how you might embed your BSP mini-portal within the SAP GUI start transaction.

Unfortunately, SAP does not offer an exit mechanism to insert custom content within this area of the main start transaction. In order to insert our page, we will need to make a small modification to the delivered SAP program. Remember that SAP does not recommend or support modifications to its code. If you implement these modifications, you are on your own.

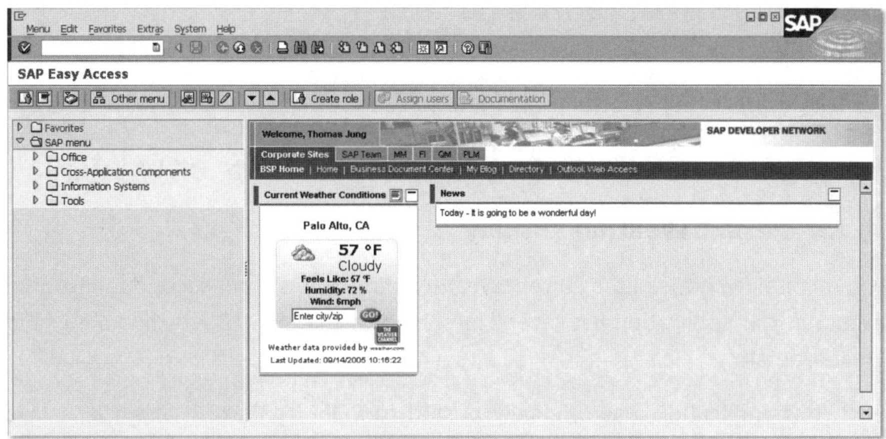

Figure 19.9 Mini-Portal Example 2—Running Within the SAP GUI Start Transaction

The main-menu application is SAPLSMTR_NAVIGATION. The first modification will be in the form control_createimagecontrol in include LSMTR_NAVIGATIONF17. We will replace the current call to WB_BITMAP_SHOW, which displays the static image, with the code to host our BSP mini-portal application within an HTML control.

```
*{    REPLACE
*\  call function 'WB_BITMAP_SHOW'
...
CREATE OBJECT html_control
    EXPORTING  parent = image_cont
   EXCEPTIONS  others = 1.
  html_control->enable_sapsso( enabled = 'x' ).
  DATA: zz_url TYPE string.
  DATA: zz_url2(255) TYPE c.
    CALL METHOD cl_bsp_runtime=>construct_bsp_url
      EXPORTING  in_application = 'Z_PORTAL'
                 in_page        = 'default_SAP.htm'
      IMPORTING  out_abs_url    = zz_url.
  MOVE zz_url TO zz_url2.
  CALL METHOD html_control->show_url
    EXPORTING  url    = zz_url2
    EXCEPTIONS others = 1.
*}    REPLACE
```

The only other small modification that must be made is to declare the definition of our html_control instance in the top Include, LSMTR_NAVIGATIONTOP.

```
DATA: image_control TYPE REF TO  cl_gui_picture,
*{   INSERT
      html_control TYPE REF TO cl_gui_html_viewer,
*}   INSERT
      custom_container TYPE REF TO  cl_gui_custom_container.
```

19.3.4 Current Weather Display

You might have noticed the current weather window from our second mini-portal example. This application has several interesting aspects and is worth looking at in greater detail.

First, this application was originally posted to SDN by Prakash Singh as a Java application. Right from the start, we can see that converting this application from Java to ABAP/BSP is a relatively simple process. Looking at the complete source code for each solution, one might even make the case that the implementation within ABAP/BSP is simpler.

The other interesting aspect is the technology that sits behind this technology. In both the Java and BSP versions, an HTTP client call is made to *Weather.com*, in much the same way as was done in the RSS consumer example earlier this chapter. If you have any problems making the HTTP client connection to *Weather.com* because of the handling of the default port, please read OSS Note 858970.

Weather.com then returns an XML stream as the body of the response. Using an XSLT script, the XML from *Weather.com* is transformed into HTTP. Even the exact same XSLT script can be used from both Java and ABAP!

```
METHOD call_webservice.
  DATA:  url        TYPE string.
  DATA:  t_url      TYPE string.
  DATA:  client     TYPE REF TO if_http_client.
  DATA:  x_xml      TYPE xstring.
  CONCATENATE `http://xoap.weather.com/weather/local/`
              i_key `?cc=*&prod=xoap&par=`
              zcl_es_shared_mem_weather_com=>partner_num

              `&key=`
              zcl_es_shared_mem_weather_com=>license_key
              `&unit=` i_unit INTO url.
  CONDENSE url NO-GAPS.

  CALL METHOD cl_http_client=>create_by_url
    EXPORTING  url    = url
```

```
    IMPORTING  client = client
    EXCEPTIONS others = 1.
  client->send( ).
  CALL METHOD client->receive
    EXCEPTIONS others  = 4.
  e_xml = client->response->get_data( ).
  DATA: xslt_err TYPE REF TO cx_xslt_exception,
          s TYPE string.
  TRY.
      CALL TRANSFORMATION zes_weather
           SOURCE xml e_xml
           RESULT xml e_html.
    CATCH cx_xslt_exception INTO xslt_err.
      IF NOT xslt_err IS INITIAL.
        s = xslt_err->get_text( ).
      ENDIF.
  ENDTRY.
ENDMETHOD.
```

The rendering of the output from the XML to HTML transformation is quite simple.

```
<htmlb:tray id     = "WeatherTray"
          onEdit = "Personalize"
          width  = "100%"
          title  = "<OTR>Current Weather Conditions</OTR>" >
   <phtmlb:matrix cellWidths = "100%"
                 width      = "100%" >
    <phtmlb:matrixCell hAlign="CENTER" />
      <%= controller->model->html %>
    <phtmlb:matrixCell hAlign = "CENTER"
                       row    = "+1" />
      <htmlb:textView design="LABELSMALL" >
        <OTR>Last Updated: </OTR>
             <%= controller->model->s_time %>
      </htmlb:textView>
   </phtmlb:matrix>
</htmlb:tray>
```

At this point we will diverge from the original Java example and include some additional features. First it would be nice to allow the user to set some customizing settings, such as location for which to display weather and whether to display temperature in Celsius or Fahrenheit. This is especially useful when running inside a portal where users expect a certain measure of personalization.

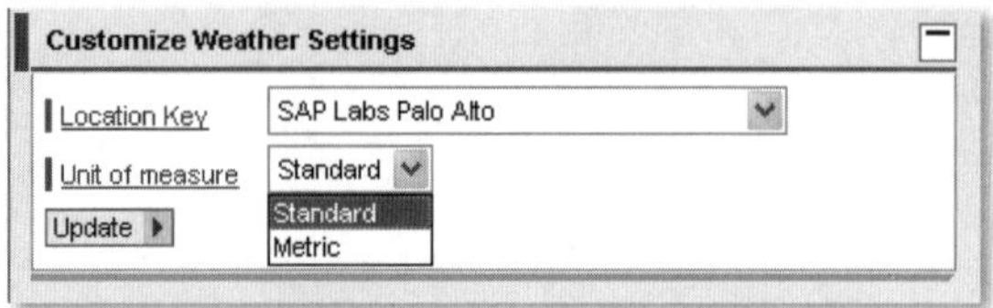

Figure 19.10 Weather Example—Personalization

We already activated the personalization event in the surrounding `<htmlb:tray>` when we first rendered it.

```
<htmlb:tray id    = "WeatherTray"
            onEdit = "Personalize"
            width  = "100%"
            title  = "<OTR>Current Weather Conditions</OTR>" >
```

When the `onEdit` event is triggered, we will just navigate to a different controller.

```
IF  htmlb_event_ex IS NOT INITIAL
  AND htmlb_event_ex->event_name = phtmlb_events=>popupmenu
  AND htmlb_event_ex->event_type =
        phtmlb_events=>popupmenu_select.
    navigation->goto_page( 'customizing.do' ).
ENDIF.
```

We are going to store the user's personalization in a simple browser cookie. Therefore, as we load the customizing controller we need to read any previous settings from that cookie before we display the view.

```
*****Restore Default Settings from the Browser Cookie
  CALL METHOD i_runtime->server->request->get_cookie
    EXPORTING name  = 'WeatherSettings'
    IMPORTING value = l_settings.
```

Likewise, when the user wishes to return from the customizing screen, we need to record his or her new settings back into the browser cookie.

```
IF  htmlb_event_ex IS NOT INITIAL
AND htmlb_event_ex->event_name = htmlb_events=>button
AND htmlb_event_ex->event_type = htmlb_events=>button_click.
  DATA: l_settings TYPE string.
  CONCATENATE me->unit me->key INTO l_settings.
```

```
  CALL METHOD i_runtime->server->response->set_cookie
    EXPORTING name  = 'WeatherSettings'
              path  = '/'
              value = l_settings.
    navigation->goto_page( 'weather.do' ).
ENDIF.
```

Our second major change has to do with the HTTP call to *Weather.com*. We really do not want to have to make the call, request the XML and then convert it every time any user accesses this page. There should be a mechanism to cache the returned data.

You could take several approaches to this caching. You might decide to write the information into the database or store it as a server cookie. However, for maximum performance, this example will take advantage of the new Web AS 6.40 shared-memory classes. Shared-memory classes allow for copy-free reading of memory in a cross-process pool. That means that all users can read from the single shared-memory area allowing for caching across user sessions.

In our processing, we will need to attach to our shared-memory class and then attempt to read from it.

```
DATA: area TYPE REF TO zcl_es_area_weather_com.
TRY.
    area = zcl_es_area_weather_com=>attach_for_read( ).
CATCH cx_shm_no_active_version.
    WAIT UP TO 1 SECONDS.
    area = zcl_es_area_weather_com=>attach_for_read( ).
ENDTRY.
FIELD-SYMBOLS: <wa_cache> LIKE LINE OF area->root->icache.
DATA: l_cache LIKE LINE OF area->root->icache.
READ TABLE area->root->icache ASSIGNING <wa_cache>
      WITH KEY w_key = i_key   unit = i_unit.
```

If we found a record, we need to make sure it is not too old. If the record is older than 15 minutes, we want to ignore it and request new information from *Weather.com*.

```
e_html      = <wa_cache>-html.
e_timestamp = <wa_cache>-tstamp.
DATA: l_tstmp TYPE timestamp.
GET TIME STAMP FIELD l_tstmp.
DATA: l_secs TYPE tzntstmpl.
```

```
l_secs = cl_abap_tstmp=>subtract(
         tstmp1 = l_tstmp
         tstmp2 = <wa_cache>-tstamp ).
```

If we were able to find a valid record, then we have our HTML output, and we can proceed with processing. Otherwise, we need to request the data from *Weather.com*, convert it from XML to HTML and then store it away in our shared-memory class.

```
METHOD update_cache.
  DATA: area TYPE REF TO zcl_es_area_weather_com,
        root TYPE REF TO zcl_es_shared_mem_weather_com.
****get a pointer to the Shared Area
  TRY.
      area = zcl_es_area_weather_com=>attach_for_update( ).
  CATCH cx_shm_no_active_version.
      WAIT UP TO 1 SECONDS.
      area = zcl_es_area_weather_com=>attach_for_update( ).
  ENDTRY.
****Get a pointer to the Root
  root ?= area->get_root( ).
  IF root IS INITIAL.
****Create an instance of our root
    CREATE OBJECT root AREA HANDLE area.
  ENDIF.
****Delete any old records
  DELETE root->icache WHERE w_key = i_key
                        AND unit  = i_unit.
****Create new records
  FIELD-SYMBOLS: <wa_cache> LIKE LINE OF root->icache.
  APPEND INITIAL LINE TO root->icache ASSIGNING <wa_cache>.
  <wa_cache>-w_key = i_key.
  <wa_cache>-unit  = i_unit.
  <wa_cache>-html  = i_html.
  <wa_cache>-xml   = i_xml.
  GET TIME STAMP FIELD <wa_cache>-tstamp.
  r_timestamp = <wa_cache>-tstamp.
****Set the root back into the Area
  area->set_root(  root ).
****Commit and detatch
  area->detach_commit( ).
ENDMETHOD.
```

20 Closing

We have taken a journey through the world of BSP development. We have shared tips and tricks and insider information for those who may have always wanted to know what made BSP tick.

As you set out on your own to put what you have learned to good use, you are not alone. Remember all the code samples and examples from this book are available on the CD for this book. BSP also has a strong presence on the SAP Developer's Network. This book would not likely exist without the start that it got within SDN.

Whenever you have a question about BSP or anything you read about in this book, a great place to go would be SDN. You can find unique code samples, over 200 weblogs, and a BSP forum with over 2,000 questions and 12,000 individual postings. Chances are very good that you will find someone on the BSP forum just about any day of the year that can help you out. Whether your answer comes from Raja, Craig, Maximilian, Rainer, Thomas R., Eddy or any of the other frequent contributors, you can be sure you are in good hands.

A Appendix—BSP Utility Classes

There are many classes that can play important roles during BSP development. Unfortunately, many of these are not documented to their fullest potential. In this appendix, we list many of the more useful classes and briefly describe their uses.

This appendix offers a collection of many of the useful classes related to BSP development. It should not be treated as a replacement for online help. It is merely a starting point for further research.

IF_BSP_RUNTIME

This class represents the BSP runtime itself, so naturally there are many useful methods in it. Most are instance methods, but it is not too difficult to get a reference to the runtime object from MVC, Pages, or BSP Extensions.

`CONSTRUCT_BSP_URL`: This is a static method for building the full URL given the BSP application name (and other optional parameters).

`GET_OTR_TEXT`: Have you ever wanted to read a particular OTR text programmatically? This is the method for doing that. Give it the alias and it will return the text string back to you. Details on OTR can be found in Chapter 15.

`WITH_ACCESSIBILITY` and `SET_ACCESSIBILITY`: These methods allow you read the status of or set the accessibility flag. This attribute can also be set via URL parameter: `sap-accessibility`. The accessibility flag only expresses the wish for accessibility support. The application itself must contain the additional rendering logic to handle this case. If the HTMLB libraries are used, accessibility is handled correctly for the relevant rendered HTML.

`WITH_RIGHT_TO_LEFT`: This is similar to the `WITH_ACCESSIBILITY` method, except that it returns the current status of the right-to-left status. This flag (RTL) is the special setting for languages that read from right to left (such as Hebrew and Arabic). This flag only has meaning for the HTMLB rendering library. If you have hand-coded HTML on the page, you have to test this flag and add your own additional support.

`GET_URL`: This method returns the URL for the current page.

`GET_DOMAIN_RELAX_SCRIPT`: Have you ever had to include the domain-relaxation script in your page? This is the method that will write that script into the page for you. Most often you see it included directly in a page or View just like the following:

```
<%= runtime->GET_DOMAIN_RELAX_SCRIPT( ) %>
```

GET_URL_SAME_SESSION, GET_URL_STATELESS, and GET_URL_NEW_SESSION: These methods generate URLs for BSP applications that either will run in the same session as the current application, either statelessly or statefully but in a new session. The difference between these three methods only makes sense when the session id is transported via URL. This is true if the application is called with the parameter sap-syscmd=nocookie, or if it is called from the portal.

CL_BSP_UTILITY

All the methods in this class are public and static and obviously designed to be reusable utilities.

CREATE_REWRITE_URL: This method will recreate the input URL adding in a list of URI parameters. Most developers will probably find CL_BSP_RUNTIME, method CONSTRUCT_BSP_URL more useful.

DOWNLOAD: This method has all the coding you need to download a binary string or content from an internal table into a HTTP response object. We have seen this same coding used in examples to download Excel files. By using this method, you could avoid having to set all the response header fields yourself. The following simple little example from an OnInitialization event of the BSP page shows the downloading of records from SFLIGHT as Unicode tab-delimited.

```
DATA: flights TYPE flighttab,
      flight LIKE LINE OF flights,
      output TYPE string,
      app_type TYPE string,
      l_xstring TYPE xstring.
CONSTANTS:
 crlf TYPE string VALUE
         cl_abap_char_utilities=>cr_lf,
     tab TYPE string VALUE
         cl_abap_char_utilities=>horizontal_tab.
SELECT * FROM sflight INTO TABLE flights UP TO 20 ROWS.
LOOP AT flights INTO flight.
  ...
 CONCATENATE output flight-carrid tab ...
  crlf INTO output.
ENDLOOP.
```

```
app_type = 'APPLICATION/MSEXCEL;charset=utf-16le'.
CALL FUNCTION 'SCMS_STRING_TO_XSTRING'
  EXPORTING    text = output
           mimetype = 'APPLICATION/MSEXCEL;charset=utf-16le'
  IMPORTING  buffer   = l_xstring.
* Add the Byte Order Mark - UTF-16 Little Endian
CONCATENATE cl_abap_char_utilities=>byte_order_mark_little
            l_xstring INTO l_xstring IN BYTE MODE.
CALL METHOD cl_bsp_utility=>download
  EXPORTING      object_s = l_xstring
            content_type = app_type
     content_disposition = 'attachment;filename=webforms.xls'
                response = response
              navigation = navigation.
```

CHANGE_URL: This method merges a full and a relative URL.

```
original URL = '/a/b/c.htm'
relative URL = '../d/e.htm'
results      = '/a/d/e.htm'
```

INSTANTIATE_DATA and INSTANTIATE_SIMPLE_DATA: These methods are used to take a HTTP form field and create an ABAP data object to hold the corresponding data. These methods are better left to their higher- level consumers (CL_BSP_MODEL, CL_HTMLB_EVENT_TABLEVIEW, and CL_HTMLB_MANAGER). But if you want a nice example of how they work, have a look at CL_HTMLB_MANAGER, method GET_SIMPLE_DATA.

SERIALIZE_DATA: This method is the opposite of the two we just looked at. It takes an ABAP data object and writes it into a HTML form field. Its best example can be found in CL_BSP_NAVIGATION, method SET_PARAMETER.

MAKE_STRING: This method takes any of ABAP's various data types and turns it into an output string. It has very similar functionality to the page->to_string( ) method. The main difference is that MAKE_STRING throws exceptions instead of issuing page messages (if_bsp_page~messages->add_message).

GET_TAGLIBS: This method will scan BSP source code and report back on BSP Extension Libraries being used. This method is probably nothing more than a curiosity to the average BSP developer. This would probably only be useful if you are interested in dynamically generating BSP pages via CL_BSP_API_GENERATE.

DATE_TO_STRING_HTTP: This method will take an ABAP timestamp and convert it to the HTTP header format. The use of this method comes right from the method SET_BROWSER_CACHE.

```
DATA: ts TYPE timestamp,
      tz TYPE timezone VALUE 'UTC' .
GET TIME STAMP FIELD ts.
ts = cl_abap_tstmp=>add( tstmp = ts secs = max_age ).
CONVERT TIME STAMP ts TIME ZONE tz
   INTO DATE l_date TIME l_uzeit.
time_rel(8) = l_date.
time_rel+8(6) = l_uzeit.
exp_value = cl_bsp_utility=>date_to_string_http( time_rel ).
```

CREATE_PUBLIC_URL: Give this method a BSP application and page name, and it will create a full URL for it. This method also adds the current language as a URI parameter.

SET_BROWSER_CACHE: This method allows you to set the expiration for the browser cache. You can see an example in CL_BSP_CONTEXT, method SET_CACHING.

UPLOAD: This method is the opposite of the earlier DOWNLOAD method. In this case, however, you could always use the <htmlb:fileUpload> and the CL_HTMLB_MANAGER=>GET_DATA to read the content. However this method would be useful if you were not using the HTMLB libraries.

ENCODE_STRING: This very helpful utility allows you to encode a string for use (RAW, URL, HTML, WML, or JavaScript) inside other elements. In the following example, we take an OTR string that happened to contain an apostrophe (test encoding: it's a nice day) and encoded it for safe use in JavaScript.

```
<script>
  <% data: otr_string type string.
     otr_string = page->OTR_TRIM( '$TMP/mytext' ). %>
  alert("<%= cl_bsp_utility=>encode_string( in = otr_string
          encoding = if_bsp_writer=>co_javascript ).%>");
</script>
```

CL_HTTP_UTILITY

CL_HTTP_UTILITY is another helpful utility class to use with all public static methods. As we go through it, you will see that many of the methods are very similar to those in CL_BSP_UTITLITY. It is heavily focused on encoding, decoding, and escaping strings. If you look at the coding, most of these methods are just wrappers for kernel calls (for faster performance).

DECODE_BASE64 and ENCODE_BASE64: As their names imply, these two methods decode/encode a string to Base64. There is an example of SAP's use of both methods in the class CL_BSP_VHELP_CONTROLLER.

ESCAPE_HTML, ESCAPE_URL, and ESCAPE_WML: These methods provide the same functionality as CL_BSP_UTILITY=>ENCODE_STRING. In fact if you look at the coding of ENCODE_STRING, it just has calls to these methods. However you might prefer the ENCODE_STRING method because it is more concise and also has the JavaScript encoding, which we do not have in this class.

UNESCAPE_URL: It is logical that if you have methods to escape a sequence, you also should have a method to undo that escaping. That is the role this method plays.

STRING_TO_FIELDS and FIELDS_TO_STRING: These methods are used to put field information into the URL. If you want to decode a BSP URL, you can always use the ABAP Program BSP_DECODE_URL. It is the perfect example of how to use these methods.

REWRITE_URL: This method is used to take input form fields and write them into the URL. This method, combined with FIELDS_TO_STRING, is what SAP uses to encode fields like client, logon language, etc. and put them into the URL.

CL_HTMLB_MANAGER

This is a very important class when working with events in BSP extension libraries. See Chapters 9 and 11 for more details on the use of this class.

CL_HTTP_SERVER

For the most part, we are only interested in the static methods within this class. This class represents the HTTP server itself. You will find this object as one of many public attributes in a controller class. These static methods have many uses. Once again we can find many redundant functions between this class and the ones we have already seen.

APPEND_FIELD_URL: This is a very helpful method that allows you to set or change any of SAP's special URL attributes, such as sap-language, sap-theme, etc. These attributes are listed in Section 4.4.

```
CALL METHOD cl_http_server=>append_field_url
     EXPORTING name  = 'sap-language'
               value = s_spras
```

```
        CHANGING url    = url.
navigation->exit( url ).
```

GET_LOCATION and GET_LOCATION_EXCEPTION: These two methods return information, such as host name and port, for a given protocol.

GET_LOCATION_EXCEPTION will make a lookup in the HTTPURLLOC table to see how URLs should be generated in cases where external proxies are in use. For a detailed description of this relatively new development, see SAP Note 871004, "Use of HTTPURLLOC Table for Generating SE80 URLs". GET_LOCATION is the recommended method to use. It will first look up exception information, and, if none is available, return the current system information for URL generation.

Note We recommend that you never explicitly supply a protocol as in parameter, but to rather accept the returned protocol. This also allows the code to work correctly in cases where only HTTPS is configured, or in scenarios where HTTPS in used from the browser to the proxy and HTTP is used from the proxy to the server (and an HTTPS URL is then required for the browser).

CREATE_ABS_URL and CREATE_REL_URL: These two methods are useful when assembling absolute or relative URLs. Perhaps you only know the path you want to link to, but you need an absolute URL. That is where CREATE_ABS_URL comes in. It accepts PROTOCOL, HOST, PORT, PATH, and QUERYSTRING as input parameters. These are all optional parameters, so the method can fill in the protocol, host, and port for you.

CL_BSP_SERVICES

This class has many static public methods. Most of the methods here provide data dictionary services, such as labels and help values. These methods are especially useful, though, because they work off a direct data reference.

GET_FIELD_LABEL and GET_QUICKINFO: These methods read the label or quick info for a given data reference from the data dictionary. The quick info will return the 60-character short text description of a field. The GET_FIELD_LABEL will analyze the size to give either the small, medium, or large label from the data dictionary.

```
DATA: mandt1 TYPE symandt.
DATA: label1 TYPE string.
DATA: data_ref TYPE REF TO data.
GET REFERENCE OF mandt1 INTO data_ref.
CALL METHOD cl_bsp_services=>get_field_label
```

```
  EXPORTING data_object_ref = data_ref
  RECEIVING label           = label1.
WRITE:/ label1.
```

GET_SIMPLE_HELPVALUES and GET_SIMPLE_HELPVALUES2: These methods are similar to the first two in that they import a data-object reference. However, these methods return a set of help values. These methods are great for returning a small set of configuration codes for a data dictionary field. The main difference between the two is that HELVALUES2 returns the key, value, and maximum value. HELPVALUES only returns the key and value. In the example below, we dynamically get field values for a field (described via just the field name).

```
DATA: DATA_REF TYPE string.
data_ref = 'SYMANDT'.
DATA: field TYPE REF TO data.
DATA: help1 TYPE SHSVALTAB.
CREATE DATA field TYPE (me->data_ref).
CALL METHOD cl_bsp_services=>if_bsp_services~get_simple_helpvalues
   EXPORTING data_object_ref = field
   CHANGING  helpvalue_tab   = help1.
```

GET_HISTORY_ID and GET_LOCAL_HISTORY_ID: Both of these methods are used to generate history ids. They fetch the ABAP parameter id that is attached to a field in the data dictionary. It is then formatted as such: sap.mat for field MATNR.

GET_DAY_COLLECTION and GET_MONTH_COLLECTION: These are nice little utility methods for returning the abbreviations and names of the days of the week and months respectively.

GET_TABL_INFO: This method, given a data reference to an internal table, will return the structural information about it. The functions of this method are also provided by the Runtime Type Services (RTTS) classes.

CL_BSP_APPLICATION

If you declare an application class for your BSP application, you are going to want to implement the IF_BSP_APPLICATION interface and thereby inherit the functionality of the CL_BSP_APPLICATION class. Most of the methods are very straightforward and allow your BSP application to query information about itself at runtime.

GET_APPLICATION_NAME, GET_APPLICATION_NAMESPACE, GET_APPLICATION_START_PAGE, GET_APPLICATION_THEME and GET_APPLICATION_URL: These methods allow you to read application settings at runtime.

GET_REQUEST, GET_RESPONSE and GET_RUNTIME: These methods give you pointers to the corresponding objects (Request – IF_HTTP_REQUEST, Response – IF_HTTP_RESPONSE, and the BSP runtime – IF_BSP_RUNTIME).

GET_TIMEOUT and SET_TIMEOUT: For stateful applications, this allows you to read or set the timeout measured in seconds.

IS_STATEFUL and SET_STATEFUL: These methods will query whether your application is running statefully or dynamically switch its stateful status.

IF_HTTP_REQUEST

This is the class that represents the request data object coming from the HTTP client. Most of the important methods in this class are going to involve reading from this request object.

IF_HTTP_RESPONSE

The counterpart to the HTTP request object, this class represents the HTTP response object. Most often we work with the response object when we want to set certain header fields (most common when downloading data; see CL_BSP_UTILITY=>DOWNLOAD). Note that both the RESPONSE and REQUEST objects have methods for manipulating cookies at the client side.

IF_BSP_NAVIGATION

Just like its name suggests, this class represents the navigation object. It is concerned with navigation from page to page and application to application. Most of the methods are self-explanatory. You have methods such as EXIT, GOTO_PAGE, NEXT_PAGE, SET_PARAMETER, and RESPONSE_COMPLETE.

CL_BSP_PAGE

This class represents the page object itself. As you look through the methods in this class, most of which are inherited from IF_BSP_PAGE, you will see that many of them are duplicates of those within CL_BSP_APPLICATION.

GET_APPLICATION_NAME, GET_APPLICATION_NAMESPACE, GET_APPLICATION_START_PAGE, GET_APPLICATION_THEME and GET_APPLICATION_URL: These methods allow you to read application settings at runtime.

GET_REQUEST, GET_RESPONSE and GET_RUNTIME: These methods give you pointers to the corresponding objects (Request – IF_HTTP_REQUEST, Response – IF_HTTP_RESPONSE, and the BSP runtime – IF_BSP_RUNTIME).

OTR_TRIM: This is another method that will read OTR texts. It is similar to CL_BSP_RUNTIME=>GET_OTR_TEXT.

GET_PAGE_NAME and GET_PAGE_URL: These methods read the name or URL of a page at runtime.

TO_STRING: This nice little method will take a field of any data type and write it out as a string. This is especially useful for outputting dates, times, currency amounts, etc.

CL_BCS

Although not unique to BSP, sending emails is a normal requested activity that many BSP developers encounter. The Business Communication Service (BCS) classes provide a simple method for sending emails from ABAP.

CL_BSP_SERVER_SIDE_COOKIE

This is the class that provides the interface to the server-side cookie mechanism with BSP. Section 13.5 contains an example of the use of this class to store a model-class state from a stateless application.

IF_MR_API

Sometime people would like to access data from or write data to the MIME Repository. For this there is an excellent API called IF_MR_API that can be instantiated via the class CL_MIME_REPOSITORY_API. This avoids having to interact directly with LOIOs.

CL_HTTP_EXT_BASE_HANDLER

This class provides an excellent starting point for creating your own HTTP handler classes. For more details, see Chapter 3.

IF_HTTP_HEADER_FIELDS and IF_HTTP_FORM_FIELDS

IF_HTTP_HEADER_FIELDS/IF_HTTP_HEADER_FIELDS_SAP and IF_HTTP_FORM_FIELDS/IF_HTTP_FORM_FIELDS_SAP contain constant strings of all header/form fields that you regularly use. The use of constants from this interface prevents typing mistakes like "Content_Disposition" (that should have been spelled with a hyphen). Typical examples:

```
request->get_header_field( if_http_header_fields=>host ).
response->set_header_field(
      name  = if_http_header_fields=>content_type
      value = 'text/html' ).
```

B The Authors

Brian McKellar is Development Architect for BSP and Web Dynpro ABAP at SAP in Walldorf. The past five years he has worked on the development of first BSP, and slowly moved over to Web Dynpro. He knows the complete BSP runtime better than the back of his hand, having worked on the development of large parts of it. Also, from handling problem tickets of years, there is not a problem within the BSP field which he has not seen at least once. Brian is also very active in SDN, and regularly contributes with technical weblogs on BSP.

Thomas Jung is an applications developer for the Kimball Electronics Group. He has been involved in SAP implementations at Kimball as an ABAP Developer since 1996. He has done some work in the Microsoft world with VB and .NET Development, but his first love remains as always: ABAP.

For the past several years, Tom has been involved in the use of BSP Development at Kimball and more recently the introduction of ABAP Web Services for critical interfaces. Tom also holds the Chair position for the Web Technologies Special Interest Group within ASUG (Americas' SAP Users' Group). In 2004 and 2005, Tom won the award for overall top contributor to SDN.

This book was born of the Business Server Pages (BSP) community on the SAP Developer Network (SDN). SDN is where ABAP, Java, .NET, and other cutting-edge technologies converge, forming the premier technical resource and collaboration channel for SAP developers, consultants, integrators, and business analysts. Authors Thomas Jung and Brian McKellar, both longtime SDN members and contributors, met on SDN. As virtual collaborators (Thomas and Brian have never met, or even spoken to one another), the two authors used content and ideas originally published in their respective SDN blogs as the foundation of this excellent book. *Advanced BSP Programming* is a testimony to the strength and innovative spirit of the SDN community. Be a part of it at *http://sdn.sap.com*.

Index

B

C

U

V

W

X

Z

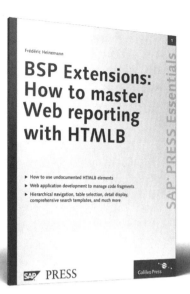

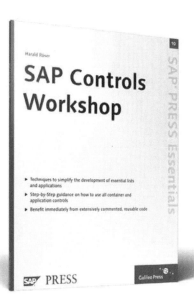

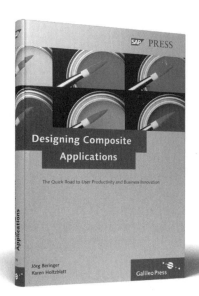

ISBN 1-59229-030-2

All-new edition–Thoroughly revised and significantly extended

Detailed descriptions of all ABAP language elements through Release 6.40

Includes SAP Web AS 6.20 test version on 3 CDs

1216 pp., 2. edition 2005, with 3 CDs, US$ 149,95
ISBN 1-59229-039-6

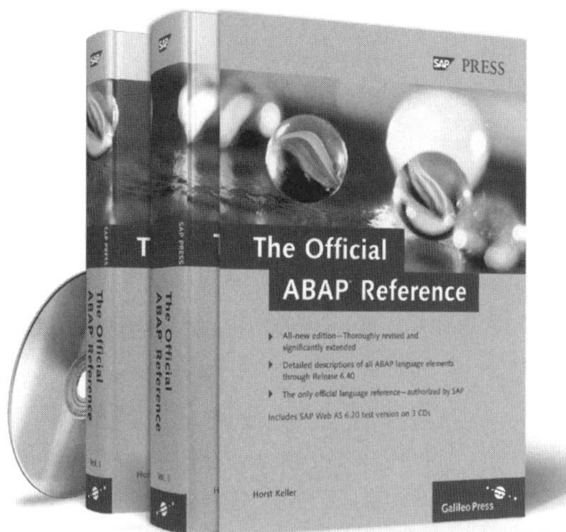

The Official ABAP Reference

www.sap-press.com

H. Keller

The Official ABAP Reference

Thoroughly revised and significantly extended, this all-new edition of our acclaimed reference, contains complete descriptions of all commands in ABAP and ABAP Objects, Release 6.40.

Not only will you find explanations and examples of all commands, you'll also be able to hit the ground running with key insights and complete reviews of all relevant usage contexts. Fully updated for the current Release 6.40, many topics in this new book have been revised completely. Plus, we've added full coverage of ABAP and XML, which are now described in detail for the very first time. The book comes complete with a test version of the latest Mini-SAP System 6.20!
>> www.sap-press.de/946